GLOBAL OUTLOOK ON EDUCATION

Editors

Dr. Shobana Nelasco
Dr. Peter Stewart
Dr. Tola Olujuvan

KANISHKA PUBLISHERS, DISTRIBUTORS
NEW DELHI-110 002

KANISHKA PUBLISHERS, DISTRIBUTORS
4697/5-21A, Ansari Road, Daryaganj
New Delhi-110 002
Phones : 2327 0497, 2328 8285
Fax : 011-2328 8285
E-mail : kanishka_publishing@yahoo.co.in

First Published 2009

ISBN 978-81-8457-125-7

PRINTED IN INDIA

Published by Madan Sachdeva for Kanishka Publishers, Distributors, 4697/5-21A, Ansari Road, Daryaganj, New Delhi-110 002. Typeset by Sunshine Graphics, Delhi, and Printed at Rajdhani Printers, Delhi.

Contents

1. Educational Issues on Global Platform 1
SHOBANA NELASCO, INDIA
PETER STEWART, SOUTH AFRICA
TOLA OLUJUVAN, NIGERIA

2. Role of Parents in the Successful Implementation of Universal Basic Education (UBE) in Ogun State, Nigeria 5
DR. ADENUGA, R. ALABA, NIGERIA,
ADENUGA, F. TITILOLA, NIGERIA
DR. ADEYEMI, NIGERIA

3. Professionalization of Teaching in Nigeria: Issues and Challenges 22
ADEOLA KIADESE, NIGERIA
KEMI ADEKOLA, NIGERIA

4. Effects of Metacognitive Regulation on English Vocabulary Knowledge 35
AHMAD AZMAN MOKHTAR, MALAYSIA
RAFIZAH MOHD. RAWIAN, MALAYSIA

5. Communication in Innovation Paradise: The Importance of Language Proficiency for Phuket ICT Innovation Paradise 59
ANDREAS BECKER, THAILAND

6. Education Reform and the Changing Role of Secondary School Administrators in the Public-Private-Partnership Model in Nigeria 72
DR. ANNE FABIYI, NIGERIA
DR. SIMEON A. OLADIPO, NIGERIA

7. Managing Student's Unrest in Institutions of Higher Education in Nigeria — 85
DR. AUSTIN NJIRIBEAKO NOSIKE, SPAIN,
NKASIOBI S. OGUZOR, NIGERIA
PROF. M.O.N. OBAGAH, NIGERIA

8. Is Education to Fill the Pail or Light the Fire? – A Study on Higher Education in Ethiopia — 94
DR. R. DAYANANDAN, ETHIOPIA

9. The Ethics of Care and Education: Cultivating a Culture of Care in PAREF Schools — 108
EMYLOU C. VISAYA, PHILIPPINES

10. Developing an Indigenous Science Curriculum for Kindergarten in the Philippines — 119
GREG TABIOS PAWILEN, PHILIPPINES
DR. MANABU SUMIDA, JAPAN

11. Engineering Education System in Europe and the Next Future: Spanish G9 Group of Universities — 141
JAVIER BILBAO, SPAIN
EUGENIO BRAVO, SPAIN
OLATZ GARCÍA, SPAIN
CONCEPCIÓN VARELA, SPAIN
MIGUEL RODRÍGUEZ, SPAIN
PURIFICACIÓN GONZÁLEZ, SPAIN
M.E. URANGA, SPAIN

12. Emergence of Research and Entrepreneurial Activities of Universities in Korea — 158
KI-SEOK KWON, U.K.

13. Strategies in Reading Instruction — 192
DR. MARLOW EDIGER, USA

14. Professionalization in Physical Education — 198
OGUNLEYE, S.B., NIGERIA

15. Integration of Vocational Agriculture Education for Effective Citizenship Development in Nigeria — 206
ONANUGA, P. ABAYOMI, NIGERIA

16. Cultivating the Culture of Reading for Effective Communication and Sustainable Development in Nigerian Schools — 216
B. OLUWAKEMI ADEKOLA, NIGERIA

17. Marketing Practices in Thai Higher Education Competing in Recessive Environments for Domestic and International Students — 225
DR. PAUL TJ JAMES, THAILAND

18. Manpower Development and Lecturer's Productivity in Tertiary Institutions in Nigeria — 237
PROF. V.F. PERETOMODE, NIGERIA
DR. R.A. CHUKWUMA, NIGERIA

19. Building School Capacity in Indonesia — 250
DR. RAIHANI, INDONESIA

20. Hermeneutics and Disciplinary Perspectives of Education: The Education-Socio-Cultural Perspectives in Relation to Research Trend in Indian Academia — 271
RAJARSHI ROY, INDIA

21. Education for Development in Mauritius: Achievements and Challenges Ahead — 304
SAREETAH DEVI MOTEE, MAURITIUS
DR. HEMANT B. CHITTOO, MAURITIUS
B. NOWBUTSING, MAURITIUS
M.P. ODIT, MAURITIUS

22. A Comparative Study of Indian and Britain Educational System — 311
DR. SHOBANA NELASCO, INDIA
MALAYA KUMAR NAYAK, LONDON

23. Examination Malpractices: Implication for Educational Quality in Nigeria — 325
DR. TOLA OLUJUWON, NIGERIA

24. Education System and Labour Market in Vietnam: Economy and Education in Transition — 338
DR. ULAS BASAR GEZGIN, VIETNAM

Contributors — 347
Index — 357

1
Educational Issues on Global Platform

Shobana Nelasco, India
Peter Stewart, South Africa
Tola Olujuwan, Nigeria

"Education for all" is one of the Millennium Development Goals, and education and literacy attainments comprise one of the three important components which determine the Human Development Index (HDI), which is a strong indicator of the quality of life of people. *Yet "education for all" remains elusive for the developing countries, despite education being at the top of the development agenda and appropriate and critical education are still more distant.*

This edited work seeks to examine some of the issues and context of education, principally in countries of the South. It does so by presenting studies from Africa and South and East Asia, and individual contributions from Europe and the United States, thus presenting a suggestive global sample. This work reflects different issues in different areas: The articles on Africa reflect issues such as lack of IT resources, conflict in education, and the need for and processes of institution building. The chapters from authors situated in Asia and Europe generally take IT resources and successful informational capitalism as a given, and some chapters explore how education can assist economic growth through the private sector or government.

This mainstream perspective takes education to be Human Resources Development (HRD) at the service of the many private and multinational industries looking for suitable and plentiful human resources.

Further, this dominant analysis sees the rise of a global economy based on IT as changing the nature of knowledge but also restructuring higher education, research and learning in the tide of a 'knowledge economy'. In this view, today's world is a fast moving place where decisions are made with an ever-increasing speed, and the success of an organization rests on its ability to correctly make these decisions. This shift in paradigms has made knowledge the key resource as organizations shift their focus from natural resources to intellectual assets, heralding the use of a concept called Knowledge Management (KM).

From this mindset, the main educational issue is to be effectively competitive, and to find a niche in the knowledge economy and to instill a culture of constant change to this market's opportunities and risks.

However, there are cross-cutting issues, which reflect universals such as the growth of inequality amidst the new wealth, the widespread marginalization of women, the power of the private sector, and issues of language in education that derive both from colonial times and from current foreign cultural dominance in business and technology. There are also common changes in higher education, as it becomes mass-based, underfunded and more accountable. An increasing number of institutions of higher learning are being established with new missions and innovative configurations of training, serving populations that previously had little access to higher education. Apart from accommodating a larger number of students, higher education institutions are required to improve their administrative efficiency and accountability in response to the demands of different stakeholders such as government, business, industry, and labour organizations, as well as students and parents.

There are therefore some major challenges to which the governments must address. One is that of inclusive education. The gross enrolment rate has to be raised both at primary and secondary levels. Strategies of economic growth can be made inclusive with the help of prime mover education. The policy of inclusive education has to mainstream and take care of the neglected communities of the societies such as Scheduled Caste/Scheduled Tribe (SC/ST) groups, minority students and the exploited women community. Adult education also is very important. Value-oriented education is the universal need of the day in all school and higher education. Healthy competition among the educators should be promoted to enhance the quality of education. To absorb the unutilized, misutilized and underutilized human resourses, we need brain as well as brawn to drive the economy to a higher level of achievement. It calls for a sound education system and effective delivery mechanisms.

There are also issues of the negative effects of the new competitive culture. In India, for example, some institutions have become insiders in the new competitive setup, whereas most have not. Only well reputed, premium educational institutes are imparting the required education to top ranked students, based on "need of the day" and industrial requirements and they place their wards in employment easily and with lucrative salary packages. At the same time, thousands of educational institutes in India are struggling to place their wards for employment.

The quality of education is sometimes completely undermined by cutthroat competition. This occurs as there is increasing privatization of educational institutions. International bodies such as the IMF, World Bank, WTO and GATS are pressurizing the developing countries to shift education from the realm of public good to private good and open it to the for-profit business of private local and international universities and multinational corporations. This is being done mainly to enable the educational institutions of the developing countries to achieve efficiency, standards, and international acceptability and produce advanced level research in science and technology.

In recent years, various members of WTO have been campaigning to include education in the remit of GATS, defining education in terms of 'educational services' and treating it as if it was no different from other commercial services.

While this competitive educational economy brings some benefits, it also brings a range of new problems, which may combine with unresolved issues of the past to from an educational environment of mushrooming malpractice and dubious quality.

So in addition to studying how we can adapt our education to the new economy, there is a need to study the negative side of education attempting to be globalised and competitive. Further, there is a need to re-instill a critical consciousness in the debate on education, so that we can go beyond conformist adaptation to the current economy, and consider the aims of education in a more rounded and empowering way. Perhaps education should start by addressing and enhancing what Amartya Sen has described as 'the human capability ... of people to lead the lives they have reason to value and to enhance the real choices that they have' (Sen 1999: 293). Could this be more basic than training our students for competition?

What is clear is that these issues need debate, and this debate must be about educational values, social and national needs, and the opportunities and problems arising from the current neoliberal global economy?

This edited collection must be seen as contributing to a wide debate through putting together a wide variety of voices on many of the issues raised in this introductory chapter.

2

Role of Parents in the Successful Implementation of Universal Basic Education (UBE) in Ogun State, Nigeria

Dr. Adenuga, R. Alaba, Nigeria
Adenuga, F. Titilola, Nigeria
Dr. Adeyemi, Nigeria

Introduction

The provision of education in Nigeria is a huge government venture that has witnessed many reformatory approaches. Hence, government's adoption of education as an instrument per excellence as it affects national development. The Nigerian government has come to realize the benefits of education to its citizens in terms of its relevance to the needs of the individual as well as in terms of the kind of society desired in relation to the environment and the realities of the modern world and rapid social changes (Adeyemi, 2005). It is only natural then, that government should clarify the philosophy and objectives that underline its current massive interest in education, and spell out in clear, unequivocal terms, the policies that guide government educational efforts. This has been reflected in the National Policy on Education (FRN, 2004).

Philosophy of Nigerian Education

The National Policy on Education (FRN, 2004) has been seen as governments' way of achieving that part of its national objectives that can be achieved using education as an instrument. No policy be it on education, population, transportation, agriculture, health, industry etc. can be formulated, without first identifying the overall philosophy and objectives of the nation.

The five (5) national objectives of Nigeria, as stated in the constitution and in the National Policy on Education, are the building of;

- a free and democratic society;

- a just and egalitarian society;
- a united, strong and self-reliant nation;
- a great and dynamic economy; and
- a land of bright and full opportunities for all citizens.

Nigeria's philosophy of education, therefore, is based on the integration of the individual into a sound and effective citizenry and equal educational opportunities for all citizens of the nation at the primary, secondary and tertiary levels, both inside and outside the formal school system. As a result of these, the quality of instruction at all levels has to be oriented towards inculcating the following values:

- respect for the worth and dignity of the individuals;
- faith in man's ability to make rational decisions;
- moral and spiritual values in inter-personal and human relations;
- shared responsibility for the common good of society;
- respect for the dignity of labour; and
- promotion of the emotional, physical and psychological health of all children.

For the philosophy to be in harmony with Nigeria's national objectives, it has to be geared towards self-realization, better human relationship, individual and national efficiency, effective citizenship, national consciousness, national unity, as well as towards social, cultural, economic, political, scientific and technological progress. The national aims and objectives to which the philosophy is linked are therefore:

- the inculcation of national consciousness and national unity;
- the inculcation of the right type of values and attitudes for the survival of the individual and the Nigerian society;
- the training of the mind in the understanding of the world around; and
- the acquisition of appropriate skills, abilities and competence both mental and physical as equipment for individual to live in and contribute to the development of his society (FRN, 2004; Adeyemi, 2005).

A New Facilitative Education Culture for UBE

It must be noted that universal access to education has been the prime target for Nigeria, since the middle of the 1970s when the

Universal Primary Education (UPE) scheme took off, predictably, pupils' enrolment rapidly increased from 6.2 million in the 1975/76 session to 14.8 million in 1992. As usual, the burst of educational activities brought in its wake a plethora of changes, some positive, some negative. The overwhelming unanticipated results of this sudden educational expansion brought about a profound shortage of learning facilities including space, a severe dearth of teacher and funds to implement the scheme. These problems still persist in our schools today especially, at the primary school level (FGN, 1993 and NPEC/World Bank, 1997). The Nigerian Government therefore, working in partnership with world development agencies, other stakeholders in the education industry especially parents has been trying to take a right step in the right direction for the development of new efforts to activate an education boom through the provision of basic education under the UBE scheme.

The following suggestions embodied the new education culture (UBE Scheme) in consonance with the current problems highlighted earlier:

- We need to realize that education goes beyond literacy and numeracy. It embraces all kinds of basic knowledge and skills necessary for an individual to lead a useful and contented life. We must therefore, encourage children to develop a scientific outlook and rudimentary understanding of the natural and social environment.
- Our basic education must adopt a two-fold approach. We need to educate young children on the one hand, and promote adult literacy and continuing education, on the other hand, to help develop their basic skills in child parenting, family management and civic participation.
- Our new education culture must embody effective planning using appropriate data banks in all spheres of education.
- Guidance service must be emphasized to deal with current behavioural problems, which have plagued the education industry at all levels in Nigeria.
- Educational experts should sensitize the government to become more aware of their services and contributions through regular publications of research findings in their areas of specialization (Denga, 1999; FGN, 1999; FRN, 2004; Adeyemi, 2005).

The Advent and Historical Background of UBE in Nigeria

The Universal Basic Education scheme is an educational programme put in place by the Nigerian government to provide the foundation for sustainable life-long learning. It is therefore aimed at eradicating illiteracy, ignorance and poverty as well as to stimulate and accelerate national development, political consciousness and national integration. Before the advent of the new initiative UBE which was majorly triggered by the world conference on education for all which was held in Jomtien, Thailand 5th-9th March 1990 organized by the World Bank, UNDP, UNESCO and UNICEF, there were attempts in 1950s and 1970s aimed towards the provision of basic learning.

These attempts at providing basic education in Nigeria can be summarized as follows:

- the defunct Western Region free Primary Education programme of 1955;
- the defunct Eastern Region Education of 1957; and
- the Federal Government National Universal Primary Education of 1976.

It should be noted that the new initiative UBE programme was launched on 30 September, 1999 in Sokoto, Sokoto State by president Olusegun Obasanjo. UBE is seen as Nigeria's way of fulfilling its commitments to the provision of basic education to its teeming population as a member of the global community. For example, Nigeria is a signatory to the 1990 Jomtien Declaration of Education for All by the year 2000 and also a member of the Group of E-9 nations committed to the total eradication of illiteracy (www.nigeriafirst.org). Obanya (2000), Olubor and Unyimadu (2001), The Universal Basic Education Commission (2002) asserts that other covenants and protocols to which Nigeria is a signatory include:

- the OAU Decade of Education in Africa (1997-2006), on Inter-African cooperation calling for a massive reduction of illiteracy within the shortest possible time span;
- the Ouagadougou (1992) pan-African declaration on the education of girls and women;
- the Amman re-affirmation (1995) calling for the forceful pursuit of the Jomtien recommendations on basic education for all;
- the Durban (1998) statement of commitment to the promotion

of education for all with a strong emphasis on the vigorous pursuit of basic education; and

- Darker World Education Forum (2000), which set "an agenda for education in the 21st century."

Important indicators of educational progress, shows that Nigeria was lagging behind expectation, at the time the programme was launched in 1999 (Nwagwu, 2002). And as pointed out in the background to this study, the nations literacy level was estimated to be 52 per cent. Many children of school age were outside the four walls of the classroom (www.UBEnigeria.org,2002). It was further cited that for instance, in 1996, figure available indicated that out of the 21 million children of school age, only 14.1 million children were enrolled in schools, the completion rate was 0.4 per cent, while transition to Junior Secondary School was only 43.5 per cent. It was also observed that matters were worse when gender and geographical correlates were taken into consideration.

There were substantial shortcomings in Nigerians institutional and personnel capacities for the delivery of a sound basic education for all citizens at the time of take-off of the programme. Available instructional facilities, teaching and learning materials as well as qualified teachers were grossly inadequate (Dike, 2002). There were also widespread disparities both in quality of and access to basic education across the nation. It was observed that the problem highlighted above appear worse at the primary, adult and non-formal education levels where a solid foundation ought to have been laid for higher forms of education (www.UBEnigeria.org,2003).

For the nation to achieve the desired 100 per cent literacy rate and make basic education available to all its citizens within the shortest possible time, it has to take quick and urgent steps to universalize basic education. The Universal Basic Education Programme in Nigeria is therefore, a response to section 19 of the 1989 constitution and section 18(1) of the 1999 constitution, which reads:

> *Government shall direct its policy towards ensuring that there are equal and adequate educational opportunities at all level.*

Such educational scheme as the UBE is therefore, expected to encourage attempts at increasing literacy rate and productive work force in all areas of the economy. These are the reasons why at the launch of the UBE, president Olusegun Obasanjo asserts that the UBE cannot afford to fail this time around.

Goals and Objectives of the UBE

Obanya (2000), Babalola, (2000) and Adeyemi (2005) states that the UBE has its objectives defined as follow:

- developing in its entire citizenry, a strong consciousness for education and a strong commitment to its various promotion;
- the drastic reduction of the incidences of dropouts from formal school system (through improved relevance, quality and efficiency);
- catering for young persons, who for one reason or another, have had to interrupt their schooling, through appropriate forms of complementary approaches to the provision and promotion of Basic Education; and
- ensuring the acquisition of appropriate level of literacy, numeracy, manipulative, communicative and life-long learning.

In a bid to achieving these goals and objectives, efforts have been directed towards addressing factors that are inhibiting the development of basic education in Nigeria, especially, in the area of facilities provision. The Universal Basic Education Commission in 2002 notes that appropriate approaches were being developed for public enlightenment and social mobilization; data collection and analysis, planning, monitoring and evaluation; teachers recruitment, education, training, retraining and motivation; infrastructural facilities, enriched curricula, textbooks and instructional materials, funding and management of the entire process.

Components of the Scheme

There are three components of the UBE scheme, namely:

(i) formal basic education encompassing the first nine years of schooling (primary and junior secondary education) for all children;

(ii) nomadic education for school age children for pastoral nomads and migrant fishermen; and

(iii) literacy and non-formal education for out-of school children, youth and adults.

Some other Basic Information on UBE

The following basic information are provided on UBE by the Universal Basic Commission (2005).

Highlight of the Compulsory Universal Basic Education Act

- Makes 9-year basic education universal, free and compulsory in public primary and junior secondary schools.
- Recognizes and preserves the exclusive constitutional responsibility of states and local governments in Nigeria to provide basic education.
- UBE to be implemented by SUBEBs and LGEAs at the states and local government levels respectively.
- The federal government's role is an intervention to ensure uniform, equitable and qualitative provision of basic education throughout the country.
- Prescribes punishments for parents and guardians who keep their wards away from school.
- Makes it incumbent on governments to provide adequate basic education opportunities for all school-age children.
- Outlaws fees in public primary and junior secondary schools and prescribes punishment for contravention of this provision.
- Provides for free tuition, books, instructional materials, classrooms, furniture and lunch.

Funding UBE

- Federal Intervention in UBE will be funded through:
  - *(i)* Not less than 2 per cent of the Consolidated Revenue Fund (CRF) of the Federal Government.
  - *(ii)* Funds/contributions in form of Federal Government Guaranteed credits.
  - *(iii)* Local/international donor grants.
  - *(iv)* The federal intervention fund to states will be used for the purpose of broadening access, improving quality and ensuring equity in basic education, but not for teachers' emoluments and overhead costs. The components are as follows:
  - *(a)* Substantial part of the CRF will be disbursed to states as matching grants.
  - *(b)* Part of it will be disbursed to states for special intervention support:
    - ❖ Initiatives by states to correct educational imbalance up to 2010.

  - ❖ Efforts by states to provide special education for the physically and mentally challenged.
  - ❖ Efforts by states to implement school feeding programmes.

- Disbursement of funds to states will be through SUBEBs.
- Disbursement of grants to states will be dependent on the provision of 50 per cent counterpart funds by states.
- UBEC may withhold further disbursement to a state if it is not satisfied that funds earlier disbursed had been judiciously utilized.
- To access the fund, states shall.
- Present acceptable annual implementation plans based on EFA/MDGS and those projects and programmes that address their peculiar educational problems.
- Show evidence of State UBE law or a strong commitment to enacting it.
- Show evidence of lodgment of the State's 50 per cent counterpart fund in a separate SUBEB account for specific UBE programme.
- Set up an appropriate mechanism that ensures transparency for the procurement of goods and services.
- Monitoring of fund utilization will be multi-sectoral involving the Universal Basic Education Commission, Federal Ministry of Education, National Assembly, Budget Office of the Federation, Budget Monitoring (Presidency), Accountant General of the Federal and Auditor General of the Federal.

Method of Work

- Effective consultations to create synergies and consensus building through meetings, panel discussions, dialogues, conversations, briefings, visits, conferences, seminars, ceremonies, courtesies, shows, features, fieldworks etc.
- Out-sourcing through consultants, specialists and experts.
- Procurement of materials, technology and services through various shopping mechanisms in compliance with the requirements of the Federal Government.

UBE Vision Statement

At the end of nine years of continuous education, every child that passes through the system should acquire appropriate levels of literacy, numeracy, communication, manipulative and life-skills and be employable, useful to himself and the society at large by possessing relevant ethical, moral and civic values.

UBE Mission Statement

To serve as a prime energizer of a national movement for the actualization of the nation's Universal Basic Education (UBE) vision, working in concert with all stakeholders, thus mobilizing the nation's creative energies to ensure that ***"education for all"*** becomes the ***"responsibility of all"***.

The Governing Board

The UBE Act 2004, Part II Section 7 establishes the Universal Basic Education Commission (UBEC) and its Governing Board, which has the following as members:

(i) a part-time chairman who is a seasoned educationist;

(ii) one representative each not below the rank of a director from:

- the Federal Ministry of Education; and
- the Federal Ministry of Finance.

(iii) one member representing each of the six geo-political zones of the country;

(iv) one representative each from:

- the Nigeria Union of Teachers;
- the National Parents/Teachers Association of Nigeria; and
- Women groups or societies.

(v) two other members appointed on personal merit to represent a variety of interests;

(vi) one representative each not below the rank of a director from:

- National Teachers Institute;
- National Commission for Colleges of Education;
- National Commission for Mass Literacy Adult and Non-formal Education;
- Nigerian Education Research and Development Council; and
- National Commission for Nomadic Education.

(vii) the Executive Secretary of the Commission, who is the secretary and Member;

(viii) two Deputy Executive Secretaries (Technical and Services) who shall assist the Executive Secretary.

Zonal Offices

There are 17 UBEC zonal offices and one sub-zonal office to ensure proper and effective monitoring of the UBE programme in the states, FCT and local governments. The Zonal Offices are located in Ibadan, Ado-Ekiti, Lagos, Benin, Uyo, Port Harcourt, Owerri, Enugu, Makurdi, Ilorin, Jos, Bauchi, Yola, Maiduguri, Kano, Sokoto and Kaduna. Each of the zones monitors the implementation of the UBE programme in two contiguous (or three as in the case of Enugu and Sokoto) states. The Abuja sub-zonal office monitors the implementation of the

Table–1
Zonal Offices of Universal Basic Education Commission

Sl. No.	*Zonal Office*	*States Covered*
1.	Ado-Ekiti	Ekiti and Ondo
2.	Ibadan	Oyo and Osun
3.	Lagos	Lagos and Ogun
4.	Owerri	Abia and Imo
5.	Enugu	Enugu, Anambra and Ebonyi
6.	Benin	Edo and Delta
7.	Uyo	Akwa-Ibom and Cross River
8.	Port-Harcourt	Rivers and Bayelsa
9.	Ilorin	Kwara and Niger
10.	Makurdi	Benue and Kogi
11.	Jos	Plateau and Nasarawa
12.	Bauchi	Bauchi and Gombe
13.	Yola	Adamawa and Taraba
14.	Maiduguri	Borno and Yobe
15.	Sokoto	Sokoto, Zamfara and Kebbi
16.	Kano	Kano and Jigawa
17.	Kaduna	Kaduna and Katsina
18.	Abuja (sub-zone)	FCT

Source: Universal Basic Education Commission (2005) *Basic Education Manual and Adeyemi (2005) Impact Assessment of Universal Basic Education Facilities on Primary School Performance in Ogun State.*

programme in the FCT. The zonal offices are headed by UBE Zonal Coordinators and are directly supervised by the Monitoring and Evaluation Department.

UBE Facilities Provision and Programme Support Strategies

A 15-year deadline has been set for the achievement of the objectives of the UBE scheme. Thus, in the past five years, a massive programme support in the area of funding and provision of school facilities have been embarked upon by the Nigerian Government, these include:

- Rehabilitation of schools and the construction of new schools and classroom blocks.
- Special programmes targeted at girls and hard-to-reach groups such as children of fishermen and nomadic communities.
- Reduction of high pupil -teacher ratio.
- Formation of partnerships with local governments and communities on education.

The building programme of the UBE programme involves three components:

(a) The provision of additional classrooms/offices/stores/toilets/special rooms to existing schools that are short of such facilities.

(b) The renovation of existing structures in bad condition. This involves a number of minor works on floors, walls, openings and most importantly, the repairs of old/poor furniture.

(c) It also involves the construction of new schools for which a new layout plan has been made. An alternative design is also included in this plan for urban schools that are tight on the availability of land. The designs in both cases have been made fairly flexible to fit into different sites while growing by simple linear additions of classrooms.

The construction and supply of furniture for classrooms, office and special rooms, that is, laboratories, workshops and libraries.

Other strategies include:

- Expansion of early childhood care education.
- Improvement of teacher training.
- Provision of teaching-learning materials.
- Provision of other forms of teacher support programme.

A Sequential Implementation Plan

The federal government of Nigeria provided a sequential implementation plan. Its pointed out that strategic planning is needed to ensure the unqualified success of the UBE programme. One sure way of ensuring this is a process of sequential implementation that starts by focusing on the primary one cohort of 2000/2001 and progressively ensuring qualitative education for them over a nine-year basic (formal) education cycle (i.e., 2000-2001 to 2008/2009). According to Obanya (2000), the progressive and cumulative nature of this approach will be as follows:

- UBE year I........primary 1 class of 2000/2001.
- UBE year II.......primary 1 and 2 classes of 2001/2002.
- UBE year III......primary 1, 2, and 3 classes of 2002/2003.
- UBE year IV......primary 1, 2, 3, and 4 classes of 2003/2004.
- UBE year V.......primary 1-5 classes of 2004/2005.
- UBE year VI......primary 1-6 classes of 2005/2006.
- UBE year VII......primary 1-6/JSS I classes of 2006/2007.
- UBE year VIII....primary 1-6/JSS I-II classes of 2007/2008.
- UBE year IX......primary 1-6/JSS I-III classes of 2008/2009.

During the 9-year "gestation period" states and local governments will progressively improve the conditions of teaching and learning in schools through:

- teacher quality improvement;
- up-dating of infrastructural facilities; and
- enhanced availability of instructional material.

The first six years of the nine-year "gestation period" will be devoted to revitalizing junior secondary education through improved access, relevance, and efficiency. With the ultimate goal of eventually ensuring universal access to junior secondary education, the sequential, improved access will be undertaken in the following manner:

2000-2001...........55%
2001-2002...........65%
2002-2003...........75%
2003-2004...........85%
2004-2005...........90%
2005-2006.........100%

This process of 10 per cent expanded access per year, from 2000/2001 to 2005-06 will ensure 100 per cent transition rate from primary to junior secondary education of the first year primary cohort of 2000-01. It also allows a 9-year period of sequential, cumulative action leading to a full fledge UBE programme in 2008-09.

There will be an analytical evaluation of the Nation's gains from the mass literacy and nomadic education programmes. This will lead to highlighting areas needing serious attention in the years to come. A sequential implementation plan will also be worked out and vigorously pursued to ensure an early, complete mainstreaming of non-formal and adult literacy programmes into UBE.

It should be noted, that government alone cannot ensure the full implementation of the UBE programme. Hence, collaboration is expected from local communities, local councils, states as well as parents, teachers, Non-Governmental Organizations (NGOs) and Community Based Organizations (CBOs). The programme has so far focused on and made progress in the development of infrastructure, the supply of teachers, and the improvement of curricula. It was identified that main key strategy in implementing the UBE successfully, include a teacher training programme for curriculum defined; a building programme designed for the new curriculum; a curriculum, the heart of which is science and technology an equipment programme including laboratories, books, workshops, teaching aids, a guidance and counselling programme; a management and administrative programme in schools; State and Federal Ministries of Education; and a deployment programme for distributing the graduates of the junior secondary to senior secondary schools, trade centers and apprenticeship and employment (www.nigeriafirst.org2003).

In the implementation strategies of the UBE programme, the rehabilitation and provision of new and additional facilities in form of block of classrooms, furniture, teachers were adequately emphasized as these have been identified as problems facing the successive implementation of basic education in Nigeria. Scholars like Ayeni and Atanda (2001) notes that the national attempt at implementing the UPE scheme was not a success. They pointed out that a year after the commencement of the scheme, some problems such as shortage of classrooms, school equipment, crises of over-demand and under-supply of teachers surfaced. These problems, were also observed by Nwagwu (2002), Dike (2000), Obanya (2002) and Adeyemi (2005) in their various studies.

Opportunities for Strategic Partnership in Facilities Provision for UBE – ROLE OF PARENTS

The implementation of the UBE programme has been following a collaborative approach. Thus the Federal, State and Local Governments on the one hand and the International Development Partners such as the World Bank, Commonwealth of Learning, UNESCO, UNICEF, DFID, JICA, USAID, etc. NGOs, CBOs and the civil society on the other hand, are complementing one another's efforts in the prosecution of the UBE programme. In this implementation strategy, the role of parents has also been adequately recognized in the Universal Basic Education Acts (2005) earlier stated in this paper. There private investment in education cannot be underestimated as parents are partakers in the funding and general management of the school system especially at the primary and junior secondary level of education. These levels form the formal aspect/arm of the Universal Basic Education in Nigeria. The Parents-Teachers Association as a body is expected to collaborate with other partners to make the programme functional and achieved the goals from which it is created. Specifically, the Federal Government as the initiator of the programme deals on policy articulation, quality control, evaluation and research. It also supports states, local governments and communities with funds to construct and renovate classrooms, train and re-train teachers and procure instructional materials. The day-to-day operation of the programme is done at the state, local government and community levels.

International Development Partners have been involved in such areas as capacity building and the strengthening of personnel and institutions executing different aspects of the programme. For example, the World Bank and DFID through the Primary Education Project (PEP) II are assisting 16 States in the implementation of UBE. On the same project, the World Bank, UNESCO and USAID are assisting with funds to collect and process a backlog of basic education data. The Japanese Government DFID have also provided different forms of technical assistance.

Opportunities for strategic partnership and especially the role of parents still exist in so many other areas including provision of mid-day meals, provision of additional infrastructure and facilities, staff training and research. These areas of strategic partnership of parents in the successful implementation of the Universal Basic Education also include the following:

- Massive provision and improvement of existing learning facilities including instructional materials of good quality. Massive provision as well as improvement of existing instructional and supervisory/inspectorate personnel in correct mix and of high quality.
- Aggressive social mobilization and advocacy for effective participation and to engender support for UBE programmes so as to ensure ethnic ownership by Nigerian people.
- Effective management of zonal offices.
- Create effective linkages and harmonious working relationships with implementing, collaborating and supporting agencies.
- Develop and apply comprehensive monitoring and evaluation mechanisms to ensure the attainment of minimum standard and eventually high quality teaching and learning in schools.
- Parents through the PTA could ensure quality using the following way:
  - establish shortages in facilities and teachers;
  - establish enrolment, retention including benchmarks for annual projections for next 5 and 10 years;
  - plan to provide support to states to establish targets and how to achieve them; and
  - provide support/funds to states and other providers for:

    (a) renovation
    (b) construction
    (c) furnishing
    (d) training and retraining of teachers and allied staff
    (e) exercise books
    (f) pencils, pens, erasers, and sharpeners
    (g) basic textbooks: English, Maths, Primary/ Integrated Science, and Social Studies
    (h) first aid kits
    (i) school feeding
    (j) academic support (library etc.)
    (k) students' support (guidance and counselling, sports, health etc.)
    (l) innovative activities, etc.

Parents could also ensure access and equity, through the following that are necessary:

(i) Mobilization and advocacy for enrolment, retention and completion of learners in the compulsory 9-year basic education programme.
(ii) Focus on the girl-child.
(iii) Focus on the boy-child.
(iv) Focus on the special need groups.
(v) Focus on the street children.
(vi) Focus on Quranic integration within UBEP.
(vii) Focus on other cross-country issues such as HIV/AIDs, etc.

- Ensure effective management of UBEC that is transparent, proactive and goal-oriented etc.
- Conduct research to address problems of implementing the compulsory 9-year basic education programme and publish their findings.
- Parents can equally adopt the Try-out solutions/ recommendations in the areas of:

  (i) capacity building
  (ii) teaching and learning
  (iii) the curriculum
  (iv) school management
  (v) community support
  (vi) policy

Conclusion

The Universal Basic Education with the motto: "*Education for All*" is the "*Business of All*" is an educational programme that is expected not only to bring about functionality in Nigerian Education but also for the growth and development of the nation in general. To this extent therefore, all stakeholders must contribute to its successful implementation not only in Ogun State but in the country as a whole. Both governmental and non-governmental organizations are expected to collaborate, parents through the Parents-Teachers Association and other relevant agency should strengthen their contributions both as private/individual and social investments. With this joint approach to making success out of the UBE, Nigeria will definitely be on the part to eradicating the various indices of underdevelopment identify earlier in this paper and thereby achieved its development in the various sectors of the nations life.

Parents must see it as a social duty to ensure Nigeria of a tomorrow using education as a tool.

REFERENCES

Adeyemi, 'Muyiwa B. (2005). Impact Assessment of Universal Basic Education (UBE) Facilities on Primary School Performance in Ogun State. *Unpublished Ph.D.Thesis.*

Babalola, S.K. (2000). *Blue Print for the Management of the UBE at the Secondary School Level.* Paper presented at the National workshop of effective school management and challenges of conducting school examination in Nigeria organized by All Nigerian Conference of Secondary School principals (ANCOPSS).

Denga, D.I. (1999). *The Eve of the 21st Century: Threshold Education Strategies for Entry and Sustainable Development.* Calabar: Rapid Educational Publishers Ltd.

Dike, Victor (2000). The Universal Basic Education Programme Educating the Educators in *Nigeria Online* Posting – http://www.nigeriaworld.com, July 14.

Dike, Victor (2002). The State of Education in Nigeria and the health of the nation. *The Guardian Online*, www.afbis.com

Federal Government of Nigeria (1999). UBE: Strategies for Effective Implementation *Nigerian Tribune* Friday, December 3, pp. 26 and 27.

Federal Government of Nigeria/UNICEF (1993). *Situation and Policy Analysis.*

Federal Republic of Nigeria (2004). *National Policy on Education.* Lagos; Federal Ministry of Information.

National Primary Education Commission/World Bank (1997). *Nigerian Primary Education Project (CR 2191 UNI);* National Report, Kaduna; NPEC.

Nwagwu, N.A. (2002). *From UPE to UBE: Some Basic Planning Considerations for Effectiveness.* Lead paper presented at a conference organized by the National Institute of Educational Planning and Administration, Ondo May 30-31.

Obanya, P. (2000). *Challenges of Universal Primary Education.* Keynote Address Presented at NIEPA National Conference on Planning and Administration for a Successful Implementation of UBE programme in Nigeria, May 29-31.

Obanya, P. (2002). *Revitalizing Education in Africa.* Stirling-Horden Publishers, Nigeria.

Olubor, R.O. and Unyimadu, S. (2001). Management Demand of Universal Basic Education Programme in Nwagwu, N.A., Ehiametalor, E.T., Ogunu, M.A. and Nwadiani, Mon (Eds.) *Current Issues in Educational Management in Nigeria.* A Publication of the Nigerian Association for Educational Administration and Planning Amik press, Benink.

Universal Basic Education Commission (2002). *Nigeria-Universal Basic Education Project*, Abuja.

www.nigeriafirst.org(2004)

www.UBE-nigeria.org (2002)

3

Professionalization of Teaching in Nigeria: Issues and Challenges

Adeola Kiadese, Nigeria
Kemi Adekola, Nigeria

Introduction

A teacher can be defined as the person who manages the teaching learning activities in a school system. In order to do that well, the professional teacher is one who has a clear understanding of the social, political, physical and intellectual aspects of the world around him, who helps the learners to develop skills, knowledge, understanding, good work and study habits, appreciation of art and their own innate and creative potentials, who understands child growth and development and learning principles related to such growth and development, who frees the learners to recognize, express, actualize and experience his own uniqueness, who creates effective relationship and understanding between himself and the pupils and among himself, the pupils, the parents and other teachers.

The activities involved in the process of teaching by a professional teacher include the following:

- Explaining, informing and demonstrating certain ideas to pupils.
- Initiating directing and organizing learning activities.
- Promoting and encouraging individual and/or group learning activities among the pupils.
- Providing some security, comfort or convenience for pupils during teaching-learning activities.
- Clarifying the issues problems or points to pupils.
- Developing desirable attitudes, values and skills in the pupils.
- Diagnosing learning situations, conditions and problems.

- Preparing suitable educational materials according to the objectives of the learning, the class, the age, or the maturity of the learners.
- Evaluating the learning and teaching progress and outcomes.
- Recording and reporting progress at work.
- Relating teaching-learning activities to the needs and problems of the community or society.
- Participating in educative co-curricular and extra-curricular activities.
- And participating in all activities related to his professional growth and development.

In realization of the role of the teachers in the society, the National Policy on Education (NPE, 2004) stated that: Teacher Education will continue to be given a major emphasis in all out educational planning because no nation can rise above the quality of its teachers. The policy went further to state the purpose of teacher education in Nigeria as follows:

- To produce highly motivated, conscientious and efficient classroom teachers for all levels of our educational system;
- Encourage further the spirit of enquiry and creativity in teachers;
- Help teachers to fit into social life of the community and the society at large and enhance their commitment to national goals;
- Provide teachers with the intellectual and professional background adequate for their assignment and make them adaptable to changing situations; and
- Enhance teachers' commitment to the teaching profession.

In the context of the present day Nigeria, can it be said that our teachers are highly motivated, conscientious and efficient classroom teachers? Reviewing the literature, one finds that the average Nigerian teacher is no more committed to his job (Oyekan, 2000). The reasons for this state of affairs are many, namely, those of the poor image of teachers in society, the low status accorded to teachers compared to other professionals, e.g., doctors, lawyers, architects, etc., and the inability to make teaching really professionals as in other disciplines, and the fact that teaching has become, invariably, a haven for "all-comers" without the necessary demands which other professionals require and maintain.

In this chapter, the issues concerning professionalization of teaching are examined and our discussion is guided against the back-drop of the following questions raised and answered:

(a) What is a profession?
(b) What are the traits of "professionalism?"
(c) Is there any need for the professionalization of teaching in Nigeria?
(d) What is the current status of teaching in Nigeria?
(e) What problems have hindered teaching from attaining full professional status in Nigeria?
(f) What can be done to make teaching attain full professional status in Nigeria?

What is a Profession?

According to Oyekan (2000) a profession is an occupation whose basic responsibility, public status and expertise are continually strengthened by specialized education and training within a specific period of time. It is a body of experts that provides a special service and exemplary leadership for harmonious survival of their community based on their accumulated knowledge, skills and wisdom. Afe (1995) provides two criteria by which the professional is judged.

1. The job of the professional is technical-based on systematic knowledge or ,doctrine acquired only through long prescribed training.
2. The professional man adheres to a set of professional norms.

However, a profession can be defined as an occupation that claims exclusive technical competence and also adheres to the service ideal and avowed ethics of professional conduct. Professionalism of teaching has been an age old controversy. In Nigeria, it has been a topic of concern among educators, teachers, administrators, organization and the public at large. The question of whether teaching is an occupation, a vocation, a calling, semi-profession or a profession has further complicated the situation of the extent that members of the public have accorded low status and recognition to teachers and no one is proud to identify or introduce himself as a teacher in the manner and way a lawyer of medical doctor would proudly and gladly do. The situation was worsened by the lingering social, economic and political crisis in Nigeria. Hence, the teachers were compelled to demand for:

- Better condition of service.
- Special Teachers' Salary Structure. This recently forced the Nigerian Union of Teachers to three days strike which was observed on June 11th to 13th 2008.
- Sufficient funds for sound educational infrastructures and regular sponsorship of in-service training programmes.
- Prompt payment of gratuities and pension on retirement.
- Establishment of Teachers' Registration Council of Nigeria to regulate teaching force, register and discipline teachers.
- Setting up of National Commissions for Primary and Secondary Education to control and support the primary and secondary school.
- Adequate public recognition for the teachers that adequate public recognition for the teachers that nurture all the productive citizens of the society.

Traits of Professionalism

According to Afe (1995), the following are the traits of profess-ionalism:

- Performing essentials social services.
- A body of specialized knowledge.
- A high degree of autonomy.
- A code of ethics.
- Organization into professional groups.
- Exalting service above personal gains.
- Recognition by the public.
- Setting its own standards.

Performing an Essential Social Service

A traits of a profession is that it performs essential social service. Teaching meets this criterion. The service which education performs is essential to the individual child who cannot be fully socialized into our modern society if he does not receive a long full time formal education. To the society, education fulfils a very vital function. Apart from providing a base for the needed socialization of the individual in the society, it prepares individuals for various occupational roles. The manpower needs of the society as well as the various educational, cultural, economic and technological aspirations of the country can only remain a dream without effective education.

A Body of Specialized Knowledge

There are some differences of opinion as to whether teaching meets this requirement. In teaching the intellectual foundations include both the subject matter knowledge and knowledge of educational theory, which are essential to the preparation of competent teachers. What is not appreciated is the fact that education differs from other professions in having the subject matter component, but in many ways the theoretical knowledge needed by the teacher is the same as that needed by the doctor. Both education and medicine are secondary disciplines which are informed by a number of primary disciplines. In the case of medicine these primary disciplines include anatomy, physiology and biology, and in the case of education they include philosophy, sociology and psychology. From this, it could be said that education meets this particular criterion.

A High Degree of Autonomy

The autonomy to practice the profession relates to two main factors which are inter-dependent. First, there is the autonomy of the individual professional to perceive his role and responsibilities the way he feels bests in the interest of the profession. This means that the professional is autonomous in his relationship with his client. This freedom however, must be such that respects not only the interest of the client, but also recognizes the ethics of the profession, the second factor is that which centres on the autonomy of the profession as a whole. These two factors of autonomy are mutually dependent on each other. Interference with the individual professional, for instance, definitely detracts from the freedom of the entire profession.

Professional autonomy is not easy to achieve because of a number of conflicting factors that relate to employment and code of ethical behaviour. A profession as a whole is autonomous if it has the freedom to control its functions. That is, a profession must be self-regulating and self-governing.

A Code of Ethics

In order to regulate the conduct of its accredited practitioners, professions usually have well defined code of ethics. This constitutes the main yard-stick for measuring the practitioners' standards of behaviour required in the profession. In addition code stipulates the appropriate relationship between practitioner and client which will protect the client and between the practitioner themselves for their mutual protection.

Organization into Professional Group

Every profession institutes and operates a professional association or organization to which it ascribes certain functions and powers such as the advancement of the professional competence and maintenance of prescribed standards. Every professional associations has a self-concept that transcends that of a mere trade union. It provides the essential framework for regulating the practice of the profession by its members. A profession provides in-service training for professional growth. Providing in-service courses for its practitioners is an important criterion of a good profession. This is so because a profession is founded upon a body of knowledge and skill which are constantly changing.

Exalting Service above Personal Gains

Members of the profession are expected to regard their services to the public as altruistic, with public interest put over and above financial and other gains.

Recognition by the Public

Recognition by the public is closely linked to the nature of the service which the profession renders. It must be such that is very essential to humanity. Further still, the practitioners or the profession must have a high self-esteem, coupled with this is the question of self-satisfaction demonstrated by members of the profession. It can also be asserted that recognition by the public is often related to historical precedence and level of evolution of the profession.

Setting its Own Standards

Any profession demands a minimum duration of intense exposure to theoretical and practical knowledge so as to ensure an adequate understanding of the various ramifications of that profession. Standards are set and it is only when the new entrant satisfies the stipulated requirements that he or she can be registered as a number of the profession. The medical and legal professions for example have laid down standards which new entrants must meet before they are admitted into the professions.

Current Status of Teaching as a Profession in Nigeria

The characteristics of a profession have been briefly discussed. It is against these that we examine the teaching profession in Nigeria. Nigeria's hurry towards the building up of the much needed manpower to run the civil service, the teaching services, the ever growing industries and other civil service, and other establishments, has put a heavy demand on educational services. According to the National Policy on Education (2004), no education system can rise above the quality of its teachers. Consequently, the implementation of the various policies of the different governments of the federation, depends on the efficiency of the teaching profession to produce the trained personnel, i.e., teachers who can help translate the policies into reality. Thus, the demand for a technologically developing state, the policy of providing free medical services to all citizens, all depend on the efficiency of educational institutions which are expected to supply the manpower needed to implement the policies. The recognition of this fact has made the various government in the past to launch schemes for the speeding up of, the process of mass literacy, and second, that of advanced education. As a result, Nigeria has witnessed a number of educational reforms during the past four decades. Examples abound: The Western Region Government launched the free primary education scheme in 1954, then the Eastern Region government took steps that considerably encouraged universal primary education in the later 1950s. Later, the Federal Military Government launched the Universal Primary Education Scheme in 1974, while the elected governments in Bendel, Ondo, Oyo, Ogun and Lagos States during the Second Republic, simultaneously launched the free secondary education scheme in 1980. And most recently the launching of Universal Basic Education (UBE) in September 1999 by the Federal Government of Nigeria.

Laudable as each of these schemes are, the launching of each is invariably accompanied by concomitant problems, which tend to militate against the maintenance of the high standard of teaching. Each time any of the schemes is launched, the number of teachers is always inadequate in quality and quantity. A case in point was the Universal Primary Education (UPE) take off in 1976. There were no preparations in terms of buildings, facilities, books, teachers for effective takeoff. Consequently, panic measures had to be taken, such as the mass construction of real and imaginary classrooms and crash programmes for teacher training e.g., the training of UBE teachers. The situation was similar in secondary schools. The solutions are usually found in the recruitment of untrained hands, the merging of several classes into one or two, the employment of retired people as teachers, and, in the urban areas, the running of morning and afternoon shifts. Needless to say that, even with the best on intentions on the part of the teachers, these strategies have hardly promoted or maintained a high standard of scholarship.

The presence in the classroom of any army of untrained teachers definitely cannot promote the quality of teaching or enhance the status of the profession. One of the characteristics of a profession is the need for a long period of education and training. Examining the teaching climate in Nigeria against the background of this characteristics, it is obvious that the presence of non-professionals on the scene make teaching more of an occupation than a profession. Of all professionals in Nigeria today, teaching appears to be the most infested by untrained hands.

As regards the criterion that any professions must have an optimal base of knowledge, teaching profession in Nigeria seems to fulfill this requirement. It has been pointed out by Afe (1995) and Oyekan (2000) that teaching demands a core of specialized knowledge and a relatively high level of intelligence. To operate as a teacher one needs a knowledge of psychology, sociology, administration, philosophy, group dynamics and many others. These disciplines service education during professional preparation of teachers. Thus, it could be said that there is a well established, specialized knowledge, skills and attitudes utilized by those in the business of teaching. In this aspect teaching in Nigeria or elsewhere is a profession.

If we examine teaching as a profession against the characteristics of control of entry, conditions of service, maintenance of standards and autonomy, we run into problems about teaching a profession in Nigeria. Again, one of the hallmarks of a profession is that it should be organized in such a way that the members would have a sense of belonging to a particular body, which stipulates codes of conduct, regulates conditions for entry into the profession, plans for the welfare of members, organizes fora for the exchange of ideas and disciplines the erring members. Today in Nigeria, the Nigerian Union of Teachers (NUT) which is charged with all these responsibilities, functions more as a trade union than a truly professional regulating body. It seems only interested in pressing for higher wages and better conditions of service. What it ought to do is to champion the need for changes in the syllabus, the necessity for having equipment in the classrooms, the need for some educational reforms, the need for the provision of library and equipments for all schools and many more other professional functions.

There is the issue of discrepancies among the standards of teachers produced in Nigeria. At each level, standards usually vary considerably, especially at the primary level. At the level, teachers whose standards are even lower than the secondary certificate, and who are untrained for teaching, work side by side others who are secondary certificate holders and who are formally trained. At the secondary level, there are holders of the Bachelor's and Master's degree in education on the one hand and ordinary level (O/L) certificate holders on the other hand. Situations such as these cannot promote the cohesion which an organization needs to function as a true profession.

Lastly, the teacher registration council recently established by the Federal Government with the mandate to register qualified teachers and regulate teaching profession in Nigeria is yet to come out with the full registered of qualified teachers in Nigeria, hence meaningful result has not been achieved in this direction.

Problems Hindering Professionalization of Teaching in Nigeria

The problem that hinder the professionalization of teaching in Nigeria can be identified as these: Firstly, the social status of entrants and practitioners into the profession constitutes a problem. Secondly, there is the problem of the inability of its practitioners, through their associations or umbrella union to control or legalize entry and lay standards for regulating the conduct as well as the discipline of members. Thirdly, the non-existence of a body of professional associations where necessary disciplinary steps in respect of erring registered members are decided is a serious factor in the consideration of this matter. Fourthly, the none recognition or otherwise of the need to take appropriate measures to satisfactorily reward members who have distinguished themselves in the profession has also served as a negative incentive for the professionalization of teaching in Nigeria. As a matter of fact, the combination of these factors has, in no small way, hindered the growth and recognition of teaching in a bid to become truly and justifiably a profession or a vocation.

The Future of Teaching as a Profession in Nigeria

Afe (1995) identified five stages for the development of professionalism. The stages are *(a)* the emergence of a full time occupation; *(b)* establishment of a training school; *(c)* a professional association; *(d)* political agitation directed towards the projection of the association *(e)* adoption of a formal Code of Conduct or Ethics.

Oyekan (2005) is of the view that against the suggested developmental progression, all these five stages have been reached, but the degree of effectiveness is still very questionable. Starting from the time when formal education or Western type of education was trained and in most cases were wives of missionaries.

Teachers categories produced performed other functions as community leader, interpreters, dispensers and counselors. With time, a distinct group emerged which was enlarged with the increases in the population of school children and widening curricula of the schools. With this development, it can be said that the teaching profession in Nigeria has successfully passed through the first stage of development.

As for the second stage, which is the establishment of a training school, the teaching profession in Nigeria can also be considered as having attained this stage. The earliest teacher-training institutions among which were St. Andrew's Oyo and Awka Training College among others had fully developed programmes which required three years of pre-training teaching as pupil-teacher, while the training programme took a total of nine year followed by one of practical teaching (Afe, 1995). Such a programme would easily pass the criterion of a long period of specialized training.

At present in Nigeria, there are 76 Colleges of Education, 32 faculties of education and 2 universities of education. With this development, it is easy to see that, for teaching profession in Nigeria, training schools for teachers abound thereby meeting the relevant requirement.

The establishment of a professional association has also been met with the formation of the Nigerian Union of Teacher (NUT), which started in 1931, with the basic aims of studying, promoting and improving conditions affecting the teaching profession, creating a better understanding among teachers, and serving as an organ through which teachers' opinions on matters affecting the teaching profession could be channeled to the government (Fafunwa, 1974). Since its founding, other professional associations in Education have sprung up including associations of psychologist, administrators as well as subject groupings, for example, the Nigeria English Studies Association, the Scheme Teachers Association of Nigeria (STAN) etc. Consequently, the third stage necessary for professionalization has been attained.

The next stage, which is marked by political agitation directed towards the projection of the association by law, has also been attained to a large extent. The National Policy on Education has stated inter-alia.

Teaching like other professions, will be legally and publicly recognized as a profession. Nigeria is already a signatory to the International Labour Organization/UNESCO's 1996 recommendation on the state of teachers.

Government has set-up a Teacher's Council among whose functions will be accreditation, certification, registration, discipline and regulation, governing the profession of teaching. When this is done, it would promote the standard of teaching and enhance the prestige of the profession. Although NUT has successfully prosecuted issues such as salary increases, maternity leave for women members, the issues pertaining to those who can teach in the nation's school have not been fully addressed. Therefore, it cannot be said, with any degree of certainty, that the stage of political agitation towards the protection of the association has been fully attained.

The next stage of development is that of adopting a formal code of conduct of ethics. This has also not been fully attained. From the foregoing, we may ask: What are the prospects of teaching developing into a full profession in Nigeria?

(i) Raise the standard of the profession;
(ii) Enhance the status of the teachers in public estimate;
(iii) Facilitate teachers' performance and achievement as they render speedy and efficient services;
(iv) Protect the interest and performance of the students;
(v) Nurture a healthy and productive citizenry for sustainable national development;
(vi) Improve the quality of schooling and educational system;
(vii) Exclude quacks or unqualified teachers from teaching or educational practice;
(viii) Attract better conditions of service for practicing teachers;
(ix) Ensure the prescription and strict enforcement of professional code of ethics that encourages good conduct and practice;
(x) Provide opportunities for obtaining professional development at regularly organized seminars workshops and conferences;

(xi) Plant hopes in the heart of distressed schools; parents and the public for quality instruction and productive citizenry.

Recommendations

The following recommendations are made towards this end:

1. There is the need for educational planners and policy formulators to ensure that accurate statistics are compiled prior to the adoption and execution of any new policy. It is only in this way that the incidence of having much larger numbers of pupils than anticipated turning up for a course can be minimized.
2. A strong demand for meaningful commencement of work by the recently established Teachers' Registration Council of Nigeria.
3. Registration of professionally trained teachers with a special license for intelligent professional practice. It could be formally withdrawn from indiscipline and corrupt teachers after an organized fair hearing and trail.
4. A unified salary structure such as Teachers Salary Structure (TSS) specially designed for teachers to enhance their remuneration and welfare package above other workers being the brainpower of any prosperous society.
5. The Federal government of Nigeria should as a matter of urgency establish SIX UNIVERSITY OF EDUCATION in the six geo-political zones of Nigeria where there should be extension of the period of professional training for the teachers to a minimum of 5 years. It is expected to ensure sufficient theoretical, practical and industrial training backgrounds for career teachers. Acquisition of adequate amounts of specialized knowledge, skills and experiences would strengthen their professional practice and vision for effective citizenship.
6. A review of teaching practice exercise duration from a minimum of 12 weeks to 1 year like other professions such as law, medicine, engineering, pharmacy and accountancy to ensure a broad spectrum of professional development and orientation to school setting.
7. The Nigerian professional teaching organizations must strive for more efficiency and excellence in their services, by producing and promoting publications. Publications by the

Nigerian English Studies Association, the Science Teachers Association in Nigeria, among others, are grossly irregular mainly because of serious lack of funds. Some other subjects organizations simply do not have journals. This is an area where the Nigerian Union of Teachers should address. It needs to cast off some of its trade union garment and consciously assume some professional appearance by promoting the establishment and regular publication of journals for subject organizations.

REFERENCES

Adewuyi, J.O., Abodurin, G.O. and Ogunwuyi, A.O., (2000). *Teacher Education.* Ibadan: Afolabi Press Ltd.

Afe, J.O. (1995). *Teacher Education in Nigeria.* Benin City: Nigerian Educational Research Association.

Castle, E.B. (1975). *Principles of Education for Teachers in Africa.* Nairobi: Oxford University Press.

Cohen, L. and Marion, L. (1997). *A Guide to Teaching Practice.* Akure: Fagbamigbe Publishers.

Durojaiye, M.O.A. (1981). *A New Introduction to Educational Psychology.* Ibadan: Evans Brothers Ltd.

Fafunwa, A.B. (1974). *History of Education in Nigeria.* London: George Allen and Urwin.

Farrant, J.S. (1976). *Principles and Practice of Education in Nigeria.* London: Longman Group.

Federal Republic of Nigeria. (2004). National Policy on Education. Abuja: Nigerian Educational Research and Educational Council.

Legatt, T. (1970). Teaching as a Profession in Jackson J.A. (ed.). *Professional and Professionalization.* Cambridge: University Press.

Onwueegbu (1970). *Discover Teaching.* Enugu: Fourth Dimension.

Oyekan, O.O. (2000). *Foundations of Teachers Education.* Ondo: Ebunola Printers.

Tella, O. Ajayi, T. and Olowoye, B. (1990). *Becoming a Teacher (An Introduction to Teacher Education).* Abeokuta: Gbemi Sodipo Press Ltd.

4

Effects of Metacognitive Regulation on English Vocabulary Knowledge

Ahmad Azman Mokhtar, Malaysia
Rafizah Mohd. Rawian, Malaysia

Introduction

The issue of ease and difficulty in vocabulary learning is important to language teachers who have to make various decisions about ways of enriching language learners' vocabulary. Though some teachers think vocabulary learning is easy, language learners always have a serious problem remembering the large amounts of vocabulary necessary to achieve fluency. "Vocabulary is by far the most sizeable and unmanageable component in the learning of any language, whether a foreign or one's mother tongue" because of "tens of thousands of different meanings," according to Hague (1987, p. 219).

To overcome this problem, second language (L2) learners have to use certain vocabulary learning strategies. 'Vocabulary learning strategies' refers to a wide spectrum of strategies used as part of an on-going process of vocabulary learning (Schmitt & Schmitt, 1995). According to Schmitt (2000), there are five major groups of vocabulary learning strategies: Determination, social, memory, cognitive, and metacognitive strategies.

Literature Review

Metacognitive strategies involve decisions about planning, monitoring, or/and evaluating the best ways to study a new word. They include for example, using English-language media such as songs, movies, and newscasts, using spaced word practice such as expansion of rehearsal, testing oneself with word tests, skipping or passing new word, continuing to study a word over time. Cook (2001) suggests 6 language-learning metacognitive strategies that good language learners use, that should be known by vocabulary learners. These are: (1) find a learning style that suits you, (2) involve yourself in the language learning process, (3) develop an awareness of language both as system and as communication, (4) pay constant attention to expanding your language knowledge, (5) develop a second language as a separate system, and (6) take into account the demands that L2 learning imposes. In addition, Eyraud *et al.*, (2000) puts forward, "most vocabulary growth takes place through incidental learning, that is, through exposure to comprehensible language in reading, listening, discussions, bulletin board displays, videos, and so forth" (p. 2).

Productive word knowledge is usually defined as what one needs to know about a word in order to use it in speaking or writing. Receptive word knowledge, on the other hand, is the word knowledge needed to understand a word while reading or listening.

A commonly held notion is that productive word knowledge is "more elusive, more difficult to learn, and possibly more fragile" (Waring, 1997). Another typical assumption is that receptive word knowledge always precedes productive word knowledge, and that accordingly a word is either receptively or receptively and productively known. However, there is agreement in the literature that this picture is rather too simplistic: The boundaries between receptive and productive word knowledge are not fixed, and each of the different types of word knowledge is arguably known to different receptive and productive degrees. This led many researchers to invoke the notion of a bi-polar continuum of word knowledge ranging from receptive to productive word knowledge.

Carson (1995) uses the terms active and passive to refer to productive and receptive vocabularies. Passive vocabulary, according to Corson, includes the active vocabulary and three other kinds of vocabulary words that are only partly known, low-frequency words not readily available for use and words that are avoided in active use. These three kinds of vocabulary overlap to some degree. Corson's description of active and passive vocabulary is strongly based on the idea of use and not solely on degrees of knowledge. Some passive vocabulary may be very well known but never use and therefore never active. Some people may be able to curse and swear but never do. From Corson's viewpoint, the terms active and passive are more suitable than receptive and productive. He occasionally uses the term unmotivated to refer to some of the passive vocabulary.

Aim of the Study

The aim of the study is to examine the effects of the students' metacognitive regulation on the acquisition of vocabulary knowledge. In particular, the study addresses the following research questions:

1. Do the students prefer metacognitive regulation as their vocabulary learning strategy?
2. What are the students' levels of the passive, controlled active, free active vocabulary knowledge?
3. What are the correlations between the students' metacognitive regulation and their passive, controlled active, free active vocabulary knowledge?

Sample

There were 5413 diploma students and according to Wunsch (1986), for a group of 5413 students, at least a sample of 346 was needed to make an estimation with a sampling error of ± 5 per cent at 95 per cent confidence level. Nevertheless, 360 students were chosen. The sample size for this study was determined using the formula for estimating sample size and the table for sample size (Wunsch, 1986).

(i) Formula for Estimating Sample Size

$$n = \frac{t^2pq}{d^2}$$

n = sample size

t = risk taking ($t = 1.96$)

p = estimated proportion per cent of males and females

q = $1 - p$

d = acceptable margin of error ($\pm$ % = 0.05)

$$n = \frac{t^2pq}{d^2}$$

t = 1.96

p = (% of male –37.6%/0.376) (% of female –62.4%/0.624)

q = $1 - 0.376 = 0.624$

d = 0.05

$$n = \frac{(1.96)^2\,(0.376)\,(0.624)}{(0.05)^2}$$

$$n = \frac{(3.84)(0.24)}{0.0025}$$

$$n = \frac{0.9216}{0.0025}$$

$$n = 368.6$$

$$n = 369$$

Since the estimated sample size (369) was more than five per cent (5%) of the population, a correction formula was used to adjust the sample size.

(ii) Formula to Adjust Sample Size

$$n_1 = \frac{n}{1 + \frac{n}{N}}$$

n_1 = adjusted sample size

n = sample size before the adjustment

N = population

$$n_1 = \frac{n}{1 + \frac{n}{N}}$$

n_1 = adjusted sample size

n = 369

N = 5413

$$n_1 = \frac{369}{1 + \frac{369}{5413}}$$

$$= \frac{369}{1 + 0.068}$$

$$= \frac{369}{1.068}$$

$$= 345.5$$

$$n_1 = 346$$

According to Wunsch (1986), for a group of 5413 students, at least a sample of 346 was needed to make an estimation with a sampling error of ± 5 per cent at 95 per cent confidence level.

Methodology

An English vocabulary learning questionnaire, translated into Malay, was used to elicit students' self-reported vocabulary learning strategies. The questionnaire had two sections. Section 1, Personal Data and Section 2, Vocabulary Learning Strategies, contained 78 vocabulary learning behaviors divided into seven major parts namely metacognitive regulation, guessing strategies, dictionary strategies, note-taking strategies, memory strategies (rehearsal), memory strategies (encoding) and activation strategies. Respondents were asked to rate each statement on a 4-point scale, ranging from Extremely Untrue of Me (1) to Extremely True of Me (4).

The Vocabulary Levels Test which consisted of three different vocabulary tests was used to measure the three dimensions of the students' English vocabulary knowledge. The three different vocabulary tests were:

1. The Passive Vocabulary Test for passive vocabulary size (Nation, 1990);
2. The Controlled Active Vocabulary Test for controlled active vocabulary size (Laufer & Nation, 1995); and
3. The Free Active Vocabulary Test for lexical richness in free written expression (Laufer & Nation, 1995).

The Passive Vocabulary Test measures passive vocabulary knowledge and is originally based on words from five word-frequency levels namely the first 2,000 words, 3,000 words, 5,000 words, the University word level (beyond 5,000 words) and 10,000 words. However, in this study only the first four levels were used. The levels were initially defined by reference to the word-frequency data in Thorndike and Lorge's list (1944), with cross-checking against the General Service List (West, 1953) for the 2000-word level and Kucera and Francis (1967). Words for the University Word Level, on the other hand, were taken from a specialized list compiled by Campion and Elley (1971), which is based on a frequency count of words in university textbooks. Since Campion and Elley excluded from their list words that occurred in the first 5,000 of Thorndike and Lorge's list, Nation located the University Word Level after the 5,000-word level in the test.

Each level is intended to relate to specific vocabulary learning objectives. According to Nation (1990), the 2,000-and 3,000-word levels contain the high-frequency words that all learners need to know in order to function effectively in English. For instance, it is difficult for learners to read unsimplified texts unless they know these words. The 5,000-word level represents the upper limit of general high-frequency vocabulary that is worth spending time on in class. Finally, words at the University level should help students in reading their textbooks and other academic reading material.

As for the format, the test involves word-definition matching although, in a reversal of the standard practice, the test-takers are required to match the words to the definitions. That is, the definitions are the test items rather than the words. Each frequency level of the test comprises 6 sections and each section includes 6 words and 3 definitions. In other words, there are 36 words and 18 definitions at each level. Although there are only 18 words at each level, Nation (1990) argues that 36 words are tested because the test-takers need to check every word against the definitions in order to make the correct matches. Words in each level of the test are representative of all the words at that level. In fact, the test was designed to be sensitive to any vocabulary knowledge held by the learner. Therefore, each word in the test was distinctly different within each set of words being tested.

The words for each level were also selected on a random basis but with proper nouns and compound nouns excluded so that the results of the test give a reasonable indication of what proportion of the total number of words at each frequency level the learner has some knowledge of. In addition, all the words in each group belong to the same word class in order to avoid giving any grammatical clue as to the correct definition. On the other hand, apart from the correct matches, care is taken not to group together words definitions that are related in meaning. The test is intended as a broad measure of word knowledge, without the test-takers to distinguish between semantically related words.

The test has 72 items (18 in each level). It tests the target words out of context because context might provide clues to their meanings. The researcher is only interested in the number of words the students could understand without any clues, rather than their guessing ability. The answers are scored as correct or incorrect. Each correct answer is given one point. Since the test has 72 items, the maximum score is therefore 72. "A weak score at any level is defined as knowing fewer than 15 out of 18 items, or less than 83 per cent" according to Nation's experience using the test (Nation, 1990, p. 140).

The Controlled Active Vocabulary Test is modeled on the Passive Vocabulary Test, in the sense that it uses the same frequency bands and the same items. It elicits target items from four frequency levels in short sentences with the items' first few letters provided in order to eliminate other possibilities. The test-takers provide the missing word in each sentence. The test has 72 items 18 in each level.

The scoring is in terms of correct (1 point) or incorrect/blank (0 point). An item is considered correct when it is semantically correct- the appropriate word is used to express the intended meaning. If used in the wrong grammatical form, it is not marked as incorrect. A word with a spelling error which does not distort the word is not marked as incorrect either. Most of the incorrect answers are non-words or existing words which are incorrect in the provided context. As in the test of passive vocabulary size, the maximum score is 72. "A weak score at any level is defined as knowing fewer than 15 out of 18 items, or less than 83 per cent", according to Nation's experience using the test (Nation, 1990, p. 140).

To obtain the passive and controlled active vocabulary size, a calculation is done as follows:

> The first 1000 level and the second are assumed to have the same score, the 4th 1000 level score is taken as an average of the 3rd and 5th levels. The sum of the scores at all the levels is multiplied by 5000 (as the test without the 10th level represents a size of 5000 word families) and divided by 108 (18 items per level for 6 levels—1, 2, 3, 4, 5, UWL). Even though learners were tested on 72 items (4 levels + UWL), two missing levels, 1 and 4 are 'filled in'. The UWL is not a separate frequency level, but consists mainly of words at 4th and 5th level. Therefore it is added to the 5000 sample.
>
> *(Laufer, 1998)*

When testing vocabulary, it is important to distinguish between how well a word is known and how well a word is used. One way to do this is by using the Lexical Frequency Profile (LFP). The LFP measures the amount of vocabulary from different frequency levels used by learners in their composition writing. The measure is normally applied using a computer programme called VocabProfile which compares words in a text with word lists that accompany the programme. A learner's lexical frequency profile is the percentage of word types at the high-frequency level (2000 word family), the

University Word List level (Xue & Nation, 1984), and not in those levels, totaling 100 per cent. The LFP does not show how well particular words are known but indicates what use learners are making of words at a particular frequency level. This is useful for diagnostic purposes to see if the vocabulary shown to be known on texts like the Vocabulary Levels Test is actually being used in meaning-focused performance.

In the Free Active Vocabulary Test the learners were required to write a composition of about 300-400 words entitled "University education should be made free for all Malaysians. Do you agree?" The compositions then were analyzed using the VocabProfile programme. This measure showed the percentage of words in the writing samples that come from different vocabulary frequency levels. For instance, a composition consisting of 200 word families contains 150 belonging to the first 1,000 most frequent words, 20 belonging to the second, 20 from the University Word List and 10 not in any list and if these figures are converted into percentages out of the total of 200–word types, the LFP of the composition is therefore 75 per cent-10 per cent-10 per cent-5 per cent. Laufer (1994) found that simply taking the percentage of words that were not within the first 2000 words gave a clearer indication of progress in vocabulary use over one or two semesters of university study than the full profile did. The 'beyond 2000' percentage is in fact an alternative way of calculating lexical sophistication. Since the profile always adds up to 100 per cent, more words beyond the 2000-word level inevitably means a smaller proportion of the high-frequency words.

The entire calculation was done by the VocabProfile programme which matched vocabulary frequency lists with a text that was typed into the computer. For the LFP analysis to be performed, the compositions were typed into the computer with the following modifications:

1. Spelling errors that did not distort the words were corrected in order to make the word recognizable by computer.
2. Proper nouns were omitted- they were not considered as belonging to the lexis of a given language.
3. Words that were semantically incorrect such as wrong meaning and wrong collocation were omitted as well since they could not be regarded as known by the learners.

Because LFP is defined in terms of word frequency and not specific vocabulary items taught in a given course, it can be used to compare learner groups from different educational contexts. The LFP is also topic-independent. It is stable for compositions on different topics written by the same students, as long as these are of a general nature and do not involve infrequently-used jargon words (Laufer & Nation, 1995).

Findings

Research Question # 1

Table 1 presented the descriptive statistics of the seven categories of the vocabulary learning strategies and their sub-strategies. The first category was metacognitive regulation which basically meant learning through the natural exposure. The metacognitive regulation had two sub-strategies namely selective attention such as having a sense of which word meanings could be guessed and which could not and making notes of words which seem important and self-initiation for instance deciding to read other English reading materials besides textbooks to expand one's vocabulary knowledge. Semester 1 students seemed to prefer the metacognitive regulation the most (M = 2.85, SD = 0.32) compared to Semester 2 (M = 2.74, SD = 0.32) and Semester 3 (M = 2.83, SD = 0.34). As for the selective attention and self-initiation, they ranked the selective attention higher than self-initiation. Semester 1 students ranked the selective attention the highest (M = 2.90, SD = 0.34) and Semester 2 students the lowest (M = 2.87, SD = 0.37).

Table-1

How Semester 1, 2, and 3 Students Learn Vocabulary

VOCABULARY LEARNING QUESTIONNAIRE

	Semester 1		*Semester 2*		*Semester 3*	
Categories and Strategies	*M*	*SD*	*M*	*SD*	*M*	*SD*
Metacognitive regulation	2.85	0.32	2.74	0.32	2.83	0.34
Selective attention	2.90	0.34	2.87	0.37	2.89	0.36
Self-initiation	2.78	0.45	2.58	0.49	2.74	0.49
Guessing strategies	2.92	0.30	2.97	0.37	3.01	0.31
Using backward knowledge	2.99	0.29	3.05	0.42	3.09	0.33
Using linguistic cues	2.76	0.43	2.81	0.47	2.84	0.43
Dictionary strategies	3.00	0.29	2.93	0.31	2.94	0.30
Dictionary strategies for comprehension	3.29	0.40	3.21	0.42	3.28	0.44
Extended dictionary strategies	2.80	0.38	2.76	0.38	2.75	0.35

Contd...

Categories and Strategies	Semester 1 M	Semester 1 SD	Semester 2 M	Semester 2 SD	Semester 3 M	Semester 3 SD
Looking-up strategies	3.07	0.41	2.98	0.42	2.94	0.37
Note-Taking strategies	2.63	0.34	2.58	0.38	2.52	0.35
Meaning-oriented note-taking	2.60	0.38	2.55	0.47	2.50	0.38
Usage-oriented note-taking	2.67	0.44	2.61	0.41	2.54	0.43
Rehearsal strategies	2.58	0.26	2.52	0.38	2.48	0.29
Using word lists	2.42	0.32	2.36	0.39	2.31	0.32
Oral repetition	2.90	0.44	2.82	0.43	2.85	0.38
Visual repetition	2.69	0.38	2.62	0.46	2.57	0.48
Encoding strategies	2.61	0.22	2.70	0.22	2.64	0.27
Association/ Elaboration	2.61	0.32	2.71	0.35	2.64	0.32
Imagery	2.49	0.35	2.60	0.37	2.49	0.40
Visual encoding	2.54	0.39	2.61	0.35	2.54	0.44
Auditory encoding	2.59	0.53	2.64	0.47	2.64	0.49
Using word-structure	2.69	0.36	2.80	0.36	2.77	0.39
Semantic encoding	2.37	0.40	2.54	0.41	2.48	0.41
Contextual encoding	2.92	0.36	2.96	0.39	2.91	0.40
Activation strategies	2.77	0.41	2.77	0.35	2.81	0.42

***Research Question* # 2**

Passive Vocabulary Test which has four word-frequency levels namely the first 2000 words, 3000 words, University Word List (UWL), and 5000 words was used to evaluate the students' receptive vocabulary knowledge. Each level was intended to relate to specific vocabulary learning objectives. According to Nation (1990), the 2,000- and 3,000-word levels contain the high-frequency words that all learners need to know in order to function effectively in English. For instance, it is difficult for learners to read unsimplified texts unless they know these words. The 5,000-word level represents the upper limit of general high-frequency vocabulary that is worth spending time on in class. Finally, words at the UWL level should help students in reading their textbooks and other academic reading material. A weak score at any level is defined as knowing fewer than 15 out of 18 items, or less than 83 per cent according to Nation's (1990, p. 140) experience using the test.

First of all, at the 2000 word level, 95.2 per cent ($n = 120$) Semester 1 students, 91.2 per cent ($n = 93$) Semester 2 students and 84 per cent ($n = 111$) Semester 3 students were in the weak group. For the 3000 word level, 96 per cent ($n = 121$) Semester 1 students, 90.2 per cent

($n = 92$) Semester 2 and 77.2 per cent ($n = 102$) Semester 3 students were categorized as weak. Then, 99.2 per cent ($n = 125$) Semester 1, 97.1 per cent ($n = 99$) Semester 2 and 91.7 per cent ($n = 121$) students were in the weak group for the UWL. Finally, none of the Semester 1 students managed to pass the test at the 5000 word level; only 1 per cent ($n = 1$) Semester 2 and 4.6 per cent ($n = 6$) Semester 3 students passed (Table 2).

The Controlled Active Vocabulary Test was modeled on the Passive Vocabulary Test. It elicited target items from four frequency levels in short sentences with the items' first few letters provided in order to eliminate other possibilities. The test-takers provided the missing word in each sentence. A weak score at any level is defined as knowing fewer than 15 out of 18 items, or less than 83 per cent according to Nation's (1990, p. 140) experience using the test.

At the 2000 word level, 76.9 per cent ($n = 97$) of Semester 1 students were categorized as weak as compared to 60.8 per cent ($n = 62$) for Semester 2 and 53.1 per cent ($n = 70$) Semester 3. As for the 3000-word level, only 1.6 per cent ($n = 2$) of Semester 1 students were not in the weak category. However, Semester 2 and 3 students comprised 6.8 per cent ($n = 7$) and 12.9 per cent ($n = 17$) respectively. Moving to the University Word List (UWL), 95.2 per cent ($n = 120$) of Semester 1, 85.3 per cent ($n = 87$) Semester 2, and 87.1 per cent ($n = 115$) Semester 3 students failed to get the minimum scores of 15 correct answers out of 18 which made them eligible to be put in the good group. Finally, results in the 5000 word level indicated that more students failed the test-Semester 1 students 93.6 per cent ($n = 118$), Semester 2, 85.3 per cent ($n = 87$) and Semester 3, 87.1 per cent ($n = 115$) (Table 3).

Lexical Frequency Profile (LFP) which measures the amount of vocabulary from different frequency levels used by learners in their composition writing was utilized to diagnose how well a word is used. A learner's lexical frequency profile is the percentage of word types at the high-frequency (2000 word family) level, the University Word List (Xue and Nation, 1964) level, and not in those levels or off-list words-less frequent words, totaling 100 per cent. This is useful for diagnostic purposes to see if the vocabulary shown to be known on texts like the Vocabulary Levels Test is actually being used in meaning-focused performance. Laufer (1994, 1995) found that simply taking the percentage of words that were not within the first 2000

Table–2
Frequencies and Percentages of Passive Vocabulary Test Scores for Four Different Word Levels

	PASSIVE VOCABULARY TEST																							
	2000-Word Level						*3000-Word Level*						*University Word List*						*5000-Word Level*					
Sco-	*Semester1*		*Semester2*		*Semester3*		*Semester1*		*Semester2*		*Semester3*		*Semester1*		*Semester2*		*Semester3*		*Semester1*		*Semester2*		*Semester3*	
res	Freq.	%	Freq.	%	Freq.	%	Freq.	%	Freq.	%	Freq.	%	Freq.	%	Freq.	%	Freq.	%	Freq.	%	Freq.	%	Freq.	%
1.									1	1.0			1	0.8					1	0.8				
2.	2	1.6			1	0.8	2	1.6	1	1.0	1	0.8	1	0.8					1	0.8			1	0.8
3.	3	2.4					4	3.2	2	2.0			1	0.8	3	2.9	2	1.5	1	0.8	4	3.9		
4.	2	1.6	3	2.9	3	2.3	6	4.8	3	2.9	3	2.3	7	5.6	1	1.0	1	0.8	14	11.1	8	7.8	1	0.8
5.	8	6.3	3	2.9	2	1.5	8	6.3	2	2.0	3	2.3	10	7.9	5	4.9	3	2.3	13	10.3	18	17.6	4	3.0
6.	14	11.1	7	6.9	4	3.0	11	8.7	13	12.7	5	3.8	8	6.3	4	3.9	4	3.0	11	8.7	9	8.8	9	6.8
7.	11	8.7	13	12.7	9	6.8	12	9.5	9	8.8	10	7.6	11	8.7	9	8.8	7	5.3	25	19.8	16	15.6	14	10.6
8.	24	19.0	16	15.7	11	8.3	25	19.8	10	9.8	10	7.6	24	19.0	20	19.6	9	6.8	27	21.5	18	17.7	18	13.6
9.	23	18.3	16	15.6	7	5.3	27	21.5	14	13.7	9	6.8	21	16.7	14	13.7	12	9.1	10	7.9	8	7.8	26	19.7
10.	8	6.3	10	9.8	12	9.1	11	8.7	17	16.7	2	1.5	8	6.3	13	12.8	24	18.2	7	5.6	9	8.8	24	18.2
11.	10	7.9	9	8.8	23	17.4	5	4.0	5	4.9	19	14.4	11	8.7	14	13.7	21	15.9	5	4.0	5	4.9	7	5.3
12.	8	6.3	6	5.9	24	18.2	4	3.2	8	7.8	22	16.7	13	10.3	10	9.8	22	16.7	5	4.0	1	1.0	12	9.1
13.	4	3.2	3	2.9	5	3.8	4	3.2	5	4.9	6	4.5	6	4.8	1	1.0	8	6.1	4	3.2	4	3.9	5	3.8
14.	3	2.4	7	6.9	10	7.6	2	1.6	2	2.0	12	9.1	3	2.4	5	4.9	8	6.1	2	1.6	1	1.0	5	3.8
15.	3	2.4	4	3.9	8	6.1	2	1.6	1	1.0	10	7.6	1	0.8	3	2.9	5	3.8			1	1.0	3	2.3
16.	3	2.4	3	2.9	8	6.1	1	0.8	5	4.9	12	9.1					4	3.0					1	0.8
17.			2	2.0	5	3.8	2	1.6	4	3.9	7	5.3					2	1.5					2	1.5
18.											1	0.8												
Total	126	100	102	100	132	100	126	100	102	100	132	100	126	100	102	100	132	100	126	100	102	100	132	100

Table–3

Frequencies and Percentages of Controlled Active Vocabulary Test Scores for Four Different Word Levels

	CONTROLLED ACTIVE VOCABULARY TEST																							
	2000-Word Level						*3000-Word Level*						*University Word List*						*5000-Word Level*					
Sco-	*Semester1*		*Semester2*		*Semester3*		*Semester1*		*Semester2*		*Semester3*		*Semester1*		*Semester2*		*Semester3*		*Semester1*		*Semester2*		*Semester3*	
res	*Freq.*	%	*Freq.*	%	*Freq.*	%	*Freq.*	%	*Freq.*	%	*Freq.*	%	*Freq.*	%	*Freq.*	%	*Freq.*	%	*Freq.*	%	*Freq.*	%	*Freq.*	%
1.							2	1.6					2	1.6					1	0.8				
2.							1	0.8	1	1.0					1	1.0			4	3.2	1	1.0	1	0.8
3.	1	0.8					3	2.4	1	1.0	1	0.8	6	4.8	1	1.0	1	0.8	6	4.8	1	1.0	2	1.5
4.	1	0.8			1	0.8	4	3.2	1	1.0	4	3.0	8	6.3	2	2.0	1	0.8	5	4.0				
5.	2	1.6					13	10.3	3	2.9	4	3.0	17	13.5	4	3.9	11	8.3	10	7.9	3	2.9	8	6.1
6.	3	2.4	1	1.0	1	0.8	15	11.9	4	3.9	6	4.5	12	9.5	4	3.9	7	5.3	3	2.4	5	4.9	7	5.3
7.	7	5.6	2	2.0	5	3.8	15	11.9	4	3.9	9	6.8	14	11.1	11	10.8	5	3.8	10	7.9	6	5.9	6	4.5
8.	8	6.3	1	1.0	4	3.0	26	20.6	9	8.8	8	6.1	20	15.8	4	3.9	4	3.0	26	20.7	4	3.9	5	3.8
9.	4	3.2	2	2.0	2	1.5	10	7.9	14	13.7	9	6.8	9	7.1	14	13.7	6	4.5	19	15.1	7	6.9	11	8.3
10.	14	11.1	3	2.9	7	5.3	16	12.7	24	23.5	13	9.8	10	7.9	17	16.6	13	9.8	14	11.1	8	7.8	10	7.6
11.	9	7.1	5	4.9	9	6.8	3	2.4	5	4.9	18	13.6	6	4.8	7	6.9	18	13.6	7	5.6	19	18.6	15	11.4
12.	17	13.4	16	15.7	11	8.3	9	7.1	14	13.7	18	13.6	6	4.8	9	8.8	13	9.8	8	6.3	11	10.8	18	13.6
13.	13	10.3	12	11.8	10	7.6	3	2.4	13	12.7	15	11.4	5	4.0	9	8.8	14	10.6	3	2.4	13	12.7	21	15.9
14.	18	14.3	20	19.6	20	15.2	4	3.2	2	2.0	10	7.6	5	4.0	4	3.9	22	16.7	2	1.6	9	8.8	11	8.3
15.	15	11.9	12	11.8	23	17.4	2	1.6	3	2.9	8	6.1	4	3.2	8	7.8	9	6.8	4	3.2	5	4.9	8	6.1
16.	7	5.6	8	7.8	19	14.4			3	2.9	6	4.5	2	1.6	5	4.9	4	3.0	1	0.8	4	3.9	6	4.5
17.	5	4.0	16	15.7	11	8.3			1	1.0	3	2.3			2	2.0	3	2.3	2	1.6	4	3.9	3	2.3
18.	2	1.6	4	3.9	9	6.8											1	0.8	1	0.8	2	2.0		
Total	126	100	102	100	132	100	126	100	102	100	132	100	126	100	102	100	132	100	126	100	102	100	132	100

Table-4
Frequencies and Percentages of Free Active Vocabulary Test Scores for Four Different Word Levels
FREE ACTIVE VOCABULARY TEST

1st. 1000 Words							*2nd. 2000 Words*							
Score	*Sem. 1*		*Sem. 2*		*Sem. 3*		*Score*	*Sem. 1*		*Sem. 2*		*Sem. 3*		*Score*
(%)	*Freq.*	*%*	*Freq.*	*%*	*Freq.*	*%*	*(%)*	*Freq.*	*%*	*Freq.*	*%*	*Freq.*	*%*	*(%)*
80-81	1	0.8	2	1.9	1	0.8	0.5-1.09	1	0.8					0.5-1.09
82-83	5	3.9	3	2.9	4	3.1	1.1-1.59							1.1-1.59
84-85	7	5.6	22	21.6	17	12.9	1.6-2.09	1	0.8	1	0.9	1	0.8	1.6-2.09
86-87	31	24.6	17	16.7	38	%	2.1-2.59	5	4.0	2	2.0	1	0.8	2.1-2.59
88-89	34	27.2	27	26.5	38	28.8	2.6-3.09	8	6.4	6	5.9	5	3.8	2.6-3.09
90-91	33	26.4	24	23.5	29	21.9	3.1-3.59	7	5.6	5	4.9	10	7.6	3.1-3.59
92-93	9	7.2	5	4.9	5	3.8	3.6-4.09	9	7.2	8	7.8	9	6.8	3.6-4.09
94-95	6	4.8	2	1.9			4.1-4.59	14	11.2	6	5.9	10	7.6	4.1-4.59
							4.6-5.09	16	12.8	18	17.6	13	9.9	4.6-5.09
							5.1-5.59	12	9.6	12	11.8	17	12.9	5.1-5.59
							5.6-6.09	16	12.8	12	11.8	15	11.4	5.6-6.09
							6.1-6.59	7	5.6	7	6.9	16	12.1	6.1-6.59
							6.6-7.09	12	9.6	6	5.9	12	9.1	6.6-7.09
							7.1-7.59	6	4.8	8	7.8	7	5.3	7.1-7.59
							7.6-8.09	4	3.2	2	1.9	7	5.3	7.6-8.09
							8.1-8.59	3	2.4	4	3.9	7	5.3	8.1-8.59
							8.6-9.09	2	1.6	3	2.9	1	0.8	8.6-9.09
							9.1-9.59	2	1.6	1	0.9			9.1-9.59
							9.6-10.09	1	0.8			1	0.8	9.6-10.09
							10.1-10.59							10.1-10.59
							10.6-11.09							10.6-11.09
							11.1-11.59							11.1-11.59
							11.6-12.09							11.6-12.09
							12.1-12.59			1	0.9			12.1-12.59
Total	126	100	102	100	132	100	Total	126	100	102	100	132	100	Total

Table-4
Frequencies and Percentages of Free Active Vocabulary Test Scores for Four Different Word Levels
FREE ACTIVE VOCABULARY TEST

University Word List							*Off-list Words*					
Sem. 1		*Sem.2*		*Sem.3*		*Score*	*Sem. 1*		*Sem. 2*		*Sem. 3*	
Freq.	*%*	*Freq.*	*%*	*Freq.*	*%*	*(%)*	*Freq.*	*%*	*Freq.*	*%*	*Freq.*	*%*
5	3.9	1	0.9	2	1.5	0.5-1.09	25	19.8	14	13.7	22	16.7
7	5.6	1	0.9	5	3.8	1.1-1.59	18	14.1	12	11.8	21	15.9
9	7.1	9	8.8	3	2.3	1.6-2.09	24	19.1	17	16.7	30	22.7
16	12.7	6	5.9	13	9.8	2.1-2.59	20	15.9	21	20.7	20	15.1
17	13.5	12	11.8	16	12.1	2.6-3.09	15	11.9	14	13.8	12	9.1
14	11.1	20	19.6	17	12.9	3.1-3.59	7	5.6	9	8.8	11	8.3
18	14.3	15	14.8	11	8.3	3.6-4.09	14	11.2	6	5.9	9	6.8
11	8.7	9	8.9	17	12.9	4.1-4.59	1	0.8	5	4.9	3	2.3
11	8.7	7	6.9	20	15.1	4.6-5.09	1	0.8	1	0.9	2	1.5
7	5.5	6	5.9	11	8.3	5.1-5.59	1	0.8	1	0.9	1	0.8
6	4.8	7	6.9	7	5.3	5.6-6.09					1	0.8
3	2.4	4	3.9	2	1.5	6.1-6.59						
		1	0.9	4	3.0	6.6-7.09			2	1.9		
		4	3.9	2	1.5	7.1-7.59						
2	1.6			2	1.5	7.6-8.09						
						8.1-8.59						
						8.6-9.09						
						9.1-9.59						
						9.6-10.09						
						10.1-10.59						
						10.6-11.09						
						11.1-11.59						
						11.6-12.09						
						12.1-12.59						
126	100	102	100	132	100	Total	126	100	102	100	132	100

words gave a clearer indication of progress in vocabulary use over one or two semesters of university study than the full profile did. The 'beyond 2000' percentage is in fact an alternative way of calculating lexical sophistication. Since the profile always adds up to 100 per cent, more words beyond the 2000-word level inevitably means a smaller proportion of the high-frequency words.

For a minimum score of 81.03 per cent and a maximum of 94.85 per cent, 38 per cent ($n = 48$) compositions written by Semester 1 students contained more than 90 per cent the 1st 1000 words compared to Semester 2 students which represented 30.3 per cent ($n = 31$) and 25.7 per cent ($n = 34$) for Semester 3. As for the 2nd 1000 words, with a minimum score of 0.52 per cent and 12.14 per cent maximum, 29.6 per cent ($n = 37$) of Semester 1 students' compositions have between 6.0 per cent to 12.5 per cent of the 2nd 1000 words, 31.1 per cent ($n = 32$) of Semester 2 and 38.7 per cent ($n = 51$) of Semester 3 students' respectively. Moreover, with a minimum score of 0.53 per cent and maximum 9.59 per cent, 4.1 per cent to 8.0 per cent of the words in 31.7 per cent ($n = 40$) of the compositions written by Semester 1 students were controlled by the University Word List (UWL). As for the Semester 2 students' compositions, 37.3 per cent ($n = 38$) contained between 4.1 per cent to 8.0 per cent of the UWL but 49.1 per cent ($n = 65$) for Semester 3 students. Moving to the last level- the off-list words, 13.6 per cent ($n = 17$) Semester 1 students' compositions contained between 3.6 per cent to 6.09 per cent of the off-list words. However, 14.5 per cent ($n = 15$) of Semester 2 and 12.2 per cent ($n = 16$) Semester 3 compositions were covered with 3.6 per cent to 7.09 per cent of the off-list words. The minimum score for the off-list words was 0.00 per cent and the maximum was 6.88 per cent (Table 4).

Research Question # 3

According to Table 5, the metacognitive regulation was positively correlated with the passive vocabulary knowledge and it was significant at the 0.01 level (2-tailed) ($r = 0.15$, $p = 0.004$). The two metacognitive regulation variables, the selective attention ($r = 0.13$, $p = 0.017$) and self-initiation ($r = 0.11$, $p = 0.029$) were also positively correlated with the passive vocabulary knowledge and were significant but at the 0.05 level (2-tailed). The positive relationships suggested that the students' high preference of the selective attention and self-initiation could be associated with a high level of passive vocabulary knowledge.

Table-5
Correlation between Vocabulary Learning Strategies and Passive Vocabulary Test

Vocabulary Learning Strategies	*PVT*	*Vocabulary Learning Strategies*	*PVT*
Metacognitive Regulation	0.15**	**Memory Strategies-Rehearsal**	-0.19**
Selective attention	0.13*	Word list	-0.18**
Self-initiation	0.11*	Oral repetition	0.08
Guessing Strategies	0.19**	Visual repetition	-0.24**
Use backward knowledge	0.17**	**Memory Strategies-Encoding**	0.08
Use linguistic cues	0.17**	Association	0.14**
Dictionary Strategies	-0.01	Imagery	-0.07
For comprehension	-0.03	Visual encoding	-0.005
Extended	-0.003	Auditory encoding	-0.01
Looking-up	0.003	Word structure	0.10*
Note-Taking Strategies	-0.11*	Semantic encoding	0.001
Meaning-oriented	-0.15**	Contextual encoding	0.16**
Usage-oriented	-0.04	**Activation Strategies**	0.14**

*** Correlation is significant at the 0.01 level (2-tailed), PVT = Passive Vocabulary Test*
** Correlation is significant at the 0.05 level (2-tailed).*

Based on Table 6, the metacognitive regulation correlated positively with the controlled active vocabulary knowledge and it was significant at the 0.01 level (2-tailed) ($r = 0.18$, $p = 0.001$). The two metacognitive regulation variables, the selective attention ($r = 0.15$, $p = 0.01$) and self-initiation ($r = 0.14$, $p = 0.01$) were also positively correlated with the controlled active vocabulary knowledge and were significant at the 0.01 level (2-tailed). The positive relationships suggested that the students' high preference of the selective attention and self-initiation could be associated with a high level of the controlled active vocabulary knowledge.

Analyzing the correlation between the students' vocabulary learning strategies and their free active vocabulary knowledge was done at the basic 2000 and beyond 2000 word levels (Table 7).

All the positive and negative correlations between the seven vocabulary learning strategies and the basic 2000 and beyond 2000 word level of the free active vocabulary knowledge were negligible because they were not significant except the correlation between the

Table-6
Correlation between Vocabulary Learning Strategies and Controlled Active Vocabulary Test

Vocabulary Learning Strategies	*CAVT*	*Vocabulary Learning Strategies*	*CAVT*
Metacognitive Regulation	0.18**	**Memory Strategies-Rehearsal**	-0.16**
Selective attention	0.15**	Word list	-0.15**
Self-initiation	0.14**	Oral repetition	0.15**
Guessing Strategies	0.24**	Visual repetition	-0.25
Use backward knowledge	0.23**	**Memory Strategies-Encoding**	0.10
Use linguistic cues	0.17**	Association	0.17**
Dictionary Strategies	-0.03	Imagery	-0.08
For comprehension	-0.08	Visual encoding	-0.04
Extended	-0.01	Auditory encoding	0.03
Looking-up	0.01	Word structure	0.14**
Note-Taking Strategies	-0.05	Semantic encoding	0.06
Meaning-oriented	-0.09	Contextual encoding	0.16**
Usage-oriented	-0.01	**Activation Strategies**	0.13*

** Correlation is significant at the 0.01 level (2-tailed), CAVT= Controlled Active.
* Correlation is significant at the 0.05 level (2-tailed).

contextual encoding-one of the variables of the memory strategies-encoding- and the free active vocabulary knowledge. The contextual encoding had a significant negative correlation at the 0.05 level (2-tailed) with the basic 2000 word level of the free active vocabulary knowledge ($r = -0.11, p = 0.04$). Such a correlation suggested that a high preference of using the contextual encoding to learn the meanings of English words would produce a low level of the free active vocabulary knowledge at the basic 2000-word level.

At the beyond 2000-word level, on the other hand, a significant positive correlation existed ($r = 0.11, p = 0.04$) between the contextual encoding and the free active vocabulary knowledge. Such existence indicated that the students' high preference of using contextual encoding could be associated with a high level of the free active vocabulary knowledge at the beyond 2000-word level.

Table–7
Correlations between Vocabulary Learning Strategies and Free Active Vocabulary Test

Vocabulary Learning Strategies	*FAVT* Basic 2000	*FAVT* Beyond 2000	*Vocabulary Learning Strategies*	*FAVT* Basic 2000	*FAVT* Beyond 2000
Metacognitive Regulation	**0.02**	**-0.03**	**Memory Strategies-Rehearsal**	-0.05	0.03
Selective attention	-0.04	0.03	Word list	-0.05	0.03
Self-initiation	0.06	-0.07	Oral repetition	-0.07	0.07
Guessing Strategies	**-0.06**	**0.07**	Visual repetition	-0.002	-0.01
Use backward knowledge	-0.08	0.09	**Memory Strategies-Encoding**	-0.08	0.10
Use linguistic cues	-0.01	0.01	Association	-0.05	0.05
Dictionary Strategies	**0.08**	**-0.09**	Imagery	-0.04	0.06
For comprehension	0.05	-0.05	Visual encoding	0.02	0.01
Extended	0.06	-0.07	Auditory encoding	-0.01	0.02
Looking-up	0.07	-0.08	Word structure	-0.09	0.10
Note-Taking Strategies	**0.02**	**-0.04**	Semantic encoding	-0.07	0.08
Meaning-oriented	-0.01	-0.02	Contextual encoding	-0.11*	0.11*
Usage-oriented	0.03	-0.05	**Activation Strategies**	-0.09	0.07

** *Correlation is significant at the 0.01 level (2-tailed) FAVT= Free Active Vocabulary Test.*

* *Correlation is significant at the 0.05 level (2-tailed).*

Discussion

The students also learned the meanings of English words through metacognitive regulation. The metacognitive regulation, which had two variables, focused on the natural exposure in learning English words. The ANOVA analysis produced a significant result where Semester 1 students used the metacognitive regulation the most. Furthermore, it seemed that the students were more inclined to choose the selective attention than self-initiation in learning English words in the natural setting. Such a finding about how the students approach learning L2 vocabulary supported Sanaoui's (1995) which distinguish between unstructured and structured students. Unstructured learners depend more on class materials, take less initiative and do less regular review. Structured learners are better organized and systematically carry out independent study, self-initiated activities, regularly record new words in notebooks and review them, and seek out opportunities to use previously met lexis. The students therefore should develop a wide variety of strategies that could appropriately be applied and combined to meet the requirements of specific tasks.

For the passive vocabulary knowledge, at the 2000-word level, 120 Semester 1 students, 93 Semester 2, and 111 Semester 3 were in the weak group. For the 3000-word level, 121 Semester 1 students, 92 Semester 2, and 102 Semester 3 students were categorized as weak. Then, 125 Semester 1, 99 Semester 2, and 121 students were in the weak group for the UWL. Finally, none of the Semester 1 students managed to pass the test at the 5000-Word Level. Only one Semester 2 and six Semester 3 students were not in the weak category. "A weak score at any level is defined as knowing fewer than 15 out of 18 items, or less than 83 per cent" according to Nation's (1990, p. 140) experience using the test.

As for the controlled active vocabulary knowledge, at the 2000-word level, 97 Semester 1 students were categorized as weak as compared to 62 for Semester 2 and 70 Semester 3. At the 3000 word level, only two Semester 1 students were not in the weak category. However, Semester 2 and 3 students comprised seven and 17 respectively. Moving to the University Word List (UWL), 120 Semester 1, 87 Semester 2, and 115 Semester 3 students failed to get the minimum scores of 15 correct answers out of 18 which made them eligible to be put in the good group. Finally, results in the 5000-word level indicated that more students fail the test- Semester 1 students, 118, Semester 2, 87, and Semester 3, 115. Similar to the Passive Vocabulary Test, "a weak score at any level is defined as knowing fewer than 15 out of 18 items, or less than 83 per cent" according to Nation's (1990, p. 140) experience using the test.

Lexical Frequency Profile (LFP) which measures the amount of vocabulary from different frequency levels used by learners in their composition writing was utilized to diagnose how well a word is used- free active vocabulary knowledge. This is useful for diagnostic purposes to see if the vocabulary shown to be known on texts like the Vocabulary Levels Test is actually being used in meaning-focused performance. Laufer (1995) found that simply taking the percentage of words that were not within the first 2000 words gave a clearer indication of progress in vocabulary use over one or two semesters of university study than the full profile did. The 'beyond 2000' percentage is in fact an alternative way of calculating lexical sophistication. Since the profile always adds up to 100 per cent, more words beyond the 2000-word level inevitably means a smaller proportion of the high-frequency words. With a minimum score of 0.53 per cent and maximum 9.59 per cent, 4.1 per cent to 8.0 per cent of the words in 40 of the compositions written by Semester 1 students were controlled by the University Word List (UWL). As for the Semester 2 students' compositions, 38 contained between 4.1 per cent to 8.0 per cent of the UWL but 65 for Semester 3 students. Moving to the last level-the off-list words, 17 Semester 1 students' compositions contained between 3.6 per cent to 6.09 per cent of the off-list words. However, 15 of Semester 2 and 16 Semester 3 compositions were covered with 3.6 per cent to 7.09 per cent of the off-list words. The minimum score for the off-list words was 0.00 per cent and the maximum was 6.88 per cent.

Since the results clearly showed that majority of the students failed to achieved the passing level of 83 per cent for the Passive Vocabulary Test and Controlled Active Vocabulary Test and the percentages of the beyond 2000-word level of the free active vocabulary knowledge assessed by the Lexical Frequency Profile were very low, a conclusion could be made that the students have poor breath of vocabulary knowledge. They might have problems to understand English reading materials and to use English productively. This conclusion was made based on research for example done by Laufer (1989) and Hirsh and Nation (1992). Research by Laufer (1989) suggests that 95 per cent coverage is sufficient to allow reasonable comprehension of a text. Moreover, a study done by Hirsh and Nation (1992) which analysed novels written for teenage or younger readers shows that under favourable conditions, a vocabulary size of 2,000 to 3,000 words provides a very good basis for language use.

Third, the metacognitive regulation was positively and significantly correlated with the passive and controlled active vocabulary knowledge. The two metacognitive regulation variables, the selective attention and self-initiation also produced the same results. The significant positive correlations suggested that the students' high preference of metacognitive regulation could be associated with high levels of passive and controlled active vocabulary knowledge. Being metacognitively alert has a few advantages. First, Eyraud *et al.,* (2000) put forward, "most vocabulary growth takes place through incidental learning, that is, through exposure to comprehensible language in reading, listening, discussions, bulletin board displays, videos, and so forth" (p. 2). Thus, being aware of metacognitive and cognitive strategies is one key to the students becoming more independent and responsible for their own learning; therefore, they should be encouraged to individualize their strategy use, which may vary based on ethnic or educational background and learning style (Yamato, 2000). Second, metacognitive strategies involve regulating, directing, monitoring and evaluating one's language learning. Effective students apply metacognitive knowledge and strategies by planning their approach to the task, monitoring their comprehension and production for overall meaningfulness (Chamot & O'Malley, 1994) and using strategies flexibly (Gu & Johnson, 1996). For example, the students need to develop an awareness of when to infer vocabulary meaning, use a dictionary, or ignore lexis (Hulstijn, 1993). This means that the students will need to practice making deliberate decisions about which tasks and vocabulary learning goals are best served by using one strategy or combining several.

On the other hand, a negative correlation existed between the metacognitive regulation and free active vocabulary knowledge. Such a phenomenon again indicated the students' metacognitive regulation did not give any positive impacts to their depth of vocabulary knowledge; they were unable to use the language. There are a few possible reasons why the depth of vocabulary knowledge did not improve.

Prior to developing metacognitive competence, the students need to become familiar with a variety of cognitive strategies, which entail manipulating material or applying techniques (Chamot & O'Malley, 1994). While beginning and lower proficiency students often rely on the repetition of word form and meaning to acquire new lexis, more proficient students report more frequent and elaborate strategy use (Gu & Johnson, 1996), use a greater variety of strategies and apply them to tasks for which they are well suited (Chamot & O'Malley, 1994). In a study of self-reported strategies by non-English major Chinese university students, Gu and Johnson (1996) found a positive correlation between both proficiency and vocabulary size and such strategies as guessing from context and using dictionaries. They also found that the overuse of visual repetition (repeatedly writing words) as a means of memorizing new vocabulary correlated negatively with proficiency and vocabulary size. Unlike the more successful strategy of memorization and repetition of L1 and L2 word pairs, visual repetition makes no meaning connection. However, students who overuse or do not expand their strategy repertoire beyond memorizing L1 and L2 word pairs may be doing so as a part of a low effort strategy (Prince, 1996).

BIBLIOGRAPHY

Campion, M.E. & Elley, W.B. (1971). *An Academic Vocabulary List.* Wellington: New Zealand Council for Educational Research.

Carson, D. (1995). The semantisation of vocabulary in foreign language learning. *System,* 15, 55-67.

Chamot, A. & O'Malley, M. (1994). *The CALLA Handbook: Implementing the Cognitive Academic Language Learning Approach.* Reading, MA: Addison Wesley.

Eyraud, K., Giles, G., Koenig, S., & Stoller, F.L. (2000). The Word Wall Approach: Promoting L2 Vocabulary Learning. *English Teaching Forum,* 38, 2-11.

Gu, Y. & Johnson, R.K. (1996). Vocabulary learning strategies and language learning outcome. *Language Learning,* 46(4), 643-679.

Hague, S.A. (1987). Vocabulary instruction: What L2 can learn from L1. *Foreign Language Annals,* 20(3), 217-225.

Hirsh, D. & Nation, P. (1992). What vocabulary is needed to read unsimplified texts for pleasure. *Reading in a Foreign Language,* 8, 689-696.

Hulstijn, J. H. (1993). When do foreign-language readers look up the meaning of unfamiliar words? The influence of task and learner variables. *The Modern Language Journal, 77,* 139-147.

Kucera, H. & Francis, W.M. (1967). *A Computational Analysis of Present Day American English.* Providence, RI: Brown University Press.

Laufer, B. (1989). What percentage of text-lexis is essential for comprehension? In C. Lauren & L. Nordman (Eds.), *Special Language: From Human Thinking to Thinking Machines* (pp. 316-323). Clevedon, UK: Multilingual Matters.

Laufer, B. (1994). The lexical profile of second language writing: Does it change over time. *RELC Journal,* 25, 21-33.

Laufer, B. (1998). The Development of Passive and Active Vocabulary in a Second Language: Same or Different. *Applied Linguistics,* 19/2, 255-271.

Laufer, B. & Nation, P. (1995). Vocabulary size and use: Lexical richness in L2 written production. *Applied Linguistics,* 16, 307-322.

Nation, I.S.P. (1990). *Teaching and Learning Vocabulary.* Heinle & Heinle, Boston, MA.

Prince, P. (1996). Second language vocabulary learning: The role of context versus translations as a function of proficiency. *The Modern Language*

Journal, 80, 478-493.

Sanaoui, R. (1995). Adults learners' approaches to learning vocabulary in second languages. *Modern Language Journal*, 79, 15-28.

Schmitt, N. (2000). *Vocabulary in Language Teaching*. Cambridge: Cambridge University Press.

Schmitt, N. & Schmitt, D. (1995). Vocabulary notebook: Theoretical underpinnings and practical suggestions. *ELT Journal*. 49, 133-143.

Thorndike, E.L. & Lorge, I. (1944). *The Teacher's Word Book of 30,000 Words*. New York: Teachers College, Columbia University.

Waring, R. (1997). A study of receptive and productive learning from word cards. Retrieved May 11, 2003 from http://www.1harenet.ne.jp/~waring/paper/papers.html.

West, M. (1953). *A General Service List of English Words*. London: Longman, Green & Co.

Wunsch, D.R. (1986). Action research in business education. *Business Education Forum*. XXXX(5), 31-33.

Xue, G. & Nation, I.S.P. (1984). A university word list. *Language Leaning and Communication*, 3, 215-229.

Yamato, R. (2000). Awareness and real use of reading strategies. *JALT* Journal, 22, 140-164.

5

Communication in Innovation Paradise: The Importance of Language Proficiency for Phuket ICT Innovation Paradise

Andreas Becker, Thailand

Phuket–Innovations Made in Thailand

Thousands of developers and their families will approach Phuket in the next years to settle down and work here. Most of them won't be able to speak any words in Thai. Nor would they be able to communicate or even read one of those lots contracts and papers they would need to sign.

To prepare Phuket for 2010 and as world centre of Innovations it needs more. Especially English and Multilingual Proficiency will be one of the key "players" for employment and success.

While Europeans already learn more than one language starting from Kindergarten/Elementary School, most Americans still suffer from monolinguals. Even their mother-tongue is English; they are often lost in multilingual settings.

Thailand is another example of a "one way road" in Language Education, as most Thai People won't be able to communicate successfully with foreigners after leaving school.

To catch up with the global society it needs more then speaking about 10,000 words in English. New learning methods i.e., like Suggestopedia (Super Learning – Loszanov) could help.

Multilingual cultural settings like the future of Innovation Paradise Phuket will bring also Thailand a big push in better Multilingual Proficiency. They simply have to change the current system of repeating words without understanding them or writing them by ear.

This paper will discuss essential needs of a 2010 Society living in ICT Innovation Paradise. It will lively demonstrate some examples of do's and don'ts and of course visions for a world-centre of ICT Innovation in Thailand.

> **Those who know nothing of foreign languages know nothing of their own.**
>
> **(J.W. v. Goethe)**

It will name the needs and problems of developers communicating with their teams in a global virtual and local surrounding. The aspects concerning governmental and other institutions or companies foreigners will have to deal with. The needs of the multilingual families approaching Phuket from all around the world should be faced rather than ignored.

Let's start to make Phuket - Thailand a No.1 Innovation Paradise not only for ICT but also for Multilingual Proficiency and new modern, efficient iLearn Methods and Centres.

Definition

"*Language proficiency or linguistic proficiency* is the ability of an individual to speak or perform in an acquired language." (div., 2008)

Stand up!
"Good morning teacher!"
"Good morning how are you?"
"I'm fine, thank you and you?"
"I am fine too! Sit down please."

A Dialog you can hear daily all over Thailand from kindergarten, schools up to universities and real live settings. Have you ever tried to answer differently, to change the well formed order of those words?

I did it when it was my first day teaching in a Thai School. I asked them: "Would you like to sit down?" and nobody moved. I wondered and with the help of a student who remind me of the right terminology I was able to place the students on their chairs and start my lesson.

This example should only illustrate the big problem when you are only repeating a language instead of learning it.

Small Children learn thru imitating their parents and surrounding. Maria Montessori an Italian Pedagogue promoted multilingual and multicultural big classes in starting 20th century. Her ideas are still very common as the prepared surrounding will normalise the kids and motivate them to teach themselves multiple languages and subjects individually in their own pace.

Especially here in Thailand we have still mono cultural and monolingual classrooms dominating the landscape. It is difficult and mostly even impossible for other nationalities and cultures to participate officially in a Thai school, if you are not born in Thailand as a "farang" child.

> **Bulgarian: (Čovekăt e tolkova păti čovek, kolkoto ezika znae)**
> ***the more languages you know, the more you are a person.***

> **Chinese: (Shû bù jìn yán yán bù jìn yì)** ***Writing cannot express all words, words cannot encompass all ideas.***
> **—Confucius**

> **Italian:** ***A dictionary can embrace only a small part of the vast tapestry of a language.***
> **—Giacomo Leopardi**

This result in a monolingual surrounding with no need communicate and start thinking in other languages. Instead of using the free self motivating power of a multilingual surrounding like described by Maria Montessori English Programmes implemented in more and more schools should compensate this deficit. Many non educational qualified native speakers with about 80–200h English learning experience get English Certificates and standing in front of Thai Students even they won't be able to teach in a regular school in their home country.

How could they improve English Proficiency? How could they even understand a curriculum or lesson plan if they have one?

To improve English proficiency it needs much more then native speakers and some repeating sentences, it needs an openhearted multicultural and multilingual surrounding.

Babylon – Mono Meets Multi

"Hi Multi how many languages can you speak now?"

"Скільки мов ти знаєш - стільки разів ти людина"

Mono could not understand so he was trying to talk in sign language and started counting his fingers in the hope Multi would understand.

> **Ukrainian: (Skil□ky mov ty znaješ- stil□ky raziv ty ljudyna)**
> ***How many languages you know - that many times you are a person.***
> **Павло Тичина (Pavlo Tychvna)**

"Човекът е толкова пъти човек, колкото езика знае"

"Hi Multi, I don't understand! Can you please write it down for me?"

"□□□□ □□□□"

"Come on, what did you say? Please help me to find it in my dictionary!"

"Un vocabolario può contenere solo una piccola parte del patrimonio di una lingua."

"Multi, please, how can I understand you?"

"Deter viktig hvilke ord du bruker, men viktigere hvilket språk du bruker.

Du kan bytte ut ordene og si nesten det samme, men bytter du ut språket, hjelper det ikke om ordene er like."

"Sorry but I don't get it!"

"Wer fremde Sprachen nicht kennt, weiß nichts von seiner eigenen."

> **Norwegian:** ***Your choice of words is important, but more important is your choice of language.***
> ***You can replace the words, saying roughly the same, but if you replace the language, it won't help you that the words are the same.***
> **–Joachim Aremk**

> **German:** *Those who know no foreign language knows nothing of their mother tongue.*
> **– Johann Wolfgang von Goethe**

"What did you say - OK!", Mono resigns frustrated not being capable to understand even one word what was multi talking about.

Phuket – ICT Innovation Paradise Thailand

On 23rd May 2008 SIPA, CAT, TOT joined forces to make "Phuket ICT Innovation Paradise." The world's ICT Hub based in the heart of South East Asia.

International ICT Companies are coming to invest in Phuket with its already existing international community and good infrastructure. People and Families from all around the world will join and form the new Phuket International Live Style – the HKT – the Hong Kong of Thailand.

> **Un homme qui parle trois langues est trilingue.**
> **Un homme qui parle deux langues est bilingue.**
> **Un homme qui ne parle qu'une langue est anglais.**
> **(Claude Gagnière)**

They won't come only from a native English spoken country. They will increase the need of multilingualism and multiculturalism at Phuket. Repeating sentences and words learned long time ago without knowing their real meaning won't help any longer.

English will stay as the "world language" the "lingua franca" and everyone needs to be able to speak and write it. Technical Vocabulary will be needed as well as a fluent English administration in speaking and writing.

> ***A man who speaks three languages is trilingual.***
> ***A man who speaks two languages is bilingual.***
> ***A man who speaks only one language is English.***
> ***- Claude Gagnière***

Contracts, Official Papers, Visa, Licenses, and Company Papers need to be translated into proper understandable English to attract foreign investors.

Especially in the ICT Field where English is essential to collaborate with developers all around the world, the proficiency needs to be improved a lot.

To accomplish all this better and more effective, more professional and more reliable methods in English Learning will be needed. These methods have to reach adults as well as students in our schools and it should be possible to achieve big changes nearly in no time as the time won't stop running until Thailand is on a certain English level. Changes must be made now!

Looking Over the Rim

USA is a big nation with many English spoken people. Unfortunately only a small percentage is capable to communicate in a second language beside English. Claude Ganiere brought it to a point in his quote. The USA itself criticises often its own English proficiency and developed various programs to improve it - No child left behind.

On the other hand and compared to Thailand native English speakers don't have to fear getting lost, as in every country they will find someone being able to communicate in English. But teaching English as a second language without ever been taught in another language isn't the best foundation for training others.

Many American citizens—especially those who have neither lived nor traveled extensively in other countries—lack knowledge of the realities in other parts of the world and therefore have fewer opportunities to compare and contrast or even consider perspectives of others (Brown & Kysilka, 2002).

Looking to Germany we realize that students start learning foreign languages from Kindergarten up to university level. Some even start with a third language in 5th, 7th or 9th Grade. During one year they learn about the same amount of words what a student is facing in Thailand during 6 years. For countries like Germany but even more for smaller European countries it is essential to know another language.

Some countries even are bilingual like Belgium or even Quatrilingual like Suisse-German, French, Italian, and Roman. Europe has been a melting Pot of many languages ever since. Depending on which country conquered which parts words and idioms from this time are still in use. Therefore "Butterbrot" has the same meaning in Russian like in German and "portemonaie" (Geldbeutel) in German has its Origin in France. People are used to use other languages besides their own. In France this led to a ban of English words in the 80's which still holds on and is causing meanwhile problems for French people travelling abroad communicating i.e., in English.

In Taiwan the The General English Proficiency Test (GEPT), a criterion-referenced test has been developed in 2002. There are four levels of the test currently being administered: Elementary, intermediate, high-intermediate, and advanced (GEPT). The Taiwan Ministry of Education promotes the idea of life-long learning and to further encourage the study of English.

Teaching English in Thailand in November, 2008

Do you want to teach in Thailand??

Experience Thai culture and way of life.

Degree?? **No degree????**
Experienced teacher????

We offer a four month contract starting in November, 2008.

We offer competitive salary, free accommodation, free orientation, training, curriculum and free work permit.

If you are interested please do send a resume, copy of.

Degrees and diplomas as well as a copy of photo page of your Passport. Please also apply for a criminal clearance certificate from your country.

We look forward to hearing from you!!!

Weena

MediaKids Job Description / Expectation 2/2008.

...

Erforderliche Qualifikation/ Ausbildung:

Nicht Spezifiziert (not specified)

Berufserfahrung (in Jahren): **No experience.**

...

In Thailand foreign teachers are very welcome (Thailand). They have to pass an esl, efl, toefl, toeic ... examine before being allowed to teach Thai students. The predicate "native speaker" is another guarantee for jobs in Thailand but not necessarily the best foundation for improving and teaching English proficiency in Thailand (Thailand). In most cases Teaching English or ICT in Thailand is big business for some companies and fun for people with no teaching qualifications at all like the following add from Mediakids Academy Bangkok shows. They even specify the applicants' qualifications as (it has been advertised on a German website, (Kids, 2008):

Fortunately this will now be changed as since February, 2008 everyone who wants to teach in Thailand would need a proper teacher qualification–if this gets enforced (New Teaching Qualification Requirements)!

"2002 CIO Magazine rates Thailand as a "rookie" in its buyer's guide to offshore outsourcing. Geopolitical risk rated low, infrastruction/communications: Fair. Solid infrastructure. English Proficiency Poor, but notes that in Thailand there is a "decent supply of customer-service-oriented, low-cost tech talent along with government support make Thailand attractive. (Runckel, 2004)."

ICT – Language is English

Information and Communication Technology (ICT) plays a vital role in supporting the development of a country. The advancement of network technology provides new opportunities to interact with people from the other side of the world.

Talking about ICT proficiency without talking about English proficiency too would be absurd. Nearly all aspects in ICT are managed in English Language. In ICT English is the "lingua franca". Programming, templating, database design is mainly based on English words and syntax. International collaborative works weren't possible without a communication language on a certain level of proficiency. This must be and is English followed by German. German language communities are the second largest active software developer communities after the English one. Especially many Open Source Projects have their roots in German spoken countries.

Meeting West in Paradise

Developers coming to Innovation Paradise will be able to communicate in English language. On the other hand they won't be able to communicate or even understand Thai at all. Besides being a number one holiday destination, you can't compare holiday makers with foreigners living and working here long-term.

Until now it is still a very difficult procedure to receive and manage all the necessary paperwork as most of it hasn't been translated into English language. As a foreigner you often sign papers and documents without actually knowing what you are signing. All these processes have to change to attract foreign people to invest with their business in Phuket and to make it a world hub of software technology.

Foreign Investors and employers should feel comfortable to stay here without facing language barriers.

While more and more foreign investors and companies will approach Innovation Paradise there will be a need on qualified workers with a certain high standard in English proficiency. Since the 90's Thailand has promoted their ICT infrastructure and build up software parks. Unfortunately the English standards seem to be kept on the same level ever since. Therefore programmes need to be established to improve people's communicational English language abilities.

Most companies coming or already operating on Phuket Island deal with customers abroad. Therefore they need qualified Thai personal which will be capable in communicating fluently in the customers' language or in English.

Usually the process in learning a language takes very long and won't be suitable for the situation now in Phuket. New accelerated language teaching methods need to be implemented to train Thai staff in English. Besides training language capabilities also cultural aspects have to be emphasised.

Some Real Life Examples

Situation: Internet or Power Blackout

When this happens you usually call you Service Provide i.e., TOT to figure out how long this failure might last until you can continue work. Friendly people will pick up your call and often get passed over to someone else who might understand your English much better. Some even seem to be afraid talking to a foreigner.

It might be common strategy and of course meant very friendly in Thailand to let customers know from hotline staff that a technician will check the internet tomorrow if it isn't working. On the other hand a software developer who depends on a good, fast and of course working adsl connection to his customer abroad won't be amused about this answer too much. In most of these cases the problem could be solved easily by informing a technician who checks and fixes the problem from his Desktop Computer, but missing English and multicultural proficiency causes perhaps fear at the hotline staff desk.

They seem using a well prepared standard answering form – the technician will check tomorrow – if a farang calls. It is quite similar to the inherited "Good Morning Teacher!" If you need to call quite often because the problem hasn't been fixed you will realize that there is always a technician checking tomorrow even it is already tomorrow.

You can't say that there isn't enough problem solution awareness as if you go to talk to the hotline in person they will usually bring you immediately to someone who can understand English and very often even to the technician himself who solves the problem in some minutes. They are missing communicational skills to communicate with a variety of answers in English.

Situation: Programming

Global collaborating in setting up websites i.e., for the worldwide number 1 open source content management system TYPO3 or any other software isn't possible if developers aren't able to understand each other. To discuss programming issues in a video or phone conference we need the same terminology on both ends of the line so that people will be able to transform i.e., the spoken words into working variables.

As a single developer, running a project completely by himself, there could not be a better place then Thailand. The developers are excellent educated and are committed to what they are doing. On the other hand in global team settings the missing English proficiency can cause bigger delays and even problems. When variables get written down by ear instead and often spelled differently in one programme or template. This part of software architecture would simply not work at all. Writing down everything or using always a dictionary would be consuming too much time.

To compensate this problem we created even an easy "letter/number" variable system instead of real names, i.e., <div id="a12">

instead of <div id ="topHeaderPicture">. This works quite well and reduced errors to an absolute minimum.

Situation: Support Forum, Mailing Lists

To develop software, especially Open Source software involves you in a global communication process thru forums and mailing lists. That is subscribed to the TYPO3 English and the TYPO3 German mailing list and am receiving about 50-100 English and about 100-150 German threads a day. I am not able to read them all of course but I will read those of interest for our recent developments. It takes only some minutes to "scan" the threads with my eyes. It's possible as I understand German as well as English. Someone who won't be capable understanding the languages would face bigger problems in finding a solution for his problems. The TYPO3 community is one of the biggest and most active in the world and you have usually very short response times, often directly with the developer of an extension himself. But you need to communicate at least in English.

Programmes are needed to enable Thai developers to follow up these technical conversations in English. Time is money and especially adults won't like to go to school again for years, new approaches will be needed to achieve international standards. One of these accelerated methods I had the chance to practice by myself, is Suggestopedia – or so called Super Learning.

Super-Learning—Suggestopedia

Wake Up and Speak Another Language!

Since 1966 Dr. Lozanov developed his new learning which enables people to learn about 1200 foreign words a day (Lozanov, 1978)!

The genuine method has been also officially tested and highly evaluated from one international expert group of UNESCO that recommended the method to be applied all over the world in 1978 (The Journal of the Society for Accelerative Learning and Teaching, Fall 1978). To know about this valuable number more we should have a look to Dowroong Wittaya School, a well known private catholic school with English Programme. A Dowroong student in Elementary Class 1-6 is learning in his complete 6 years Primary School period about 6,000–7,000 English words (counted the different words in the used English books). This is far not enough to compete with international standards. Imagine how the proficiency could be improved if those students who have at least 3 times English a week, would use Lozanov's method and only about 100 words a day.

They could speak and communicate fluently even during their first year of English – for sure!

Learning languages when you are able to communicate in a language with many already known words is so much easier than trying to inherit a language thru sole repetitions of what an English teacher has told you even he is native. This really doesn't matter.

With Suggestopedia Language Lessons students will be enabled in very short time to participate in other cultural and lingual surroundings.

Dr. Charles Schmid, in San Francisco, has reported students being presented with 400 foreign words in a day and being able to use them in conversation within three days (Chapter 9, Page 232, 2008) (div., 2008).

How Does it Work?

Lozanov Students are working in Groups actually in two different Levels. One Goal is to learn a foreign language together but the other is to interact as a "new" individual. Everyone receives a new identity at the beginning of the course. The acquisition of the language is being supported by therapeutic role-playing grounds. It lifts up inhibitions and enables a barrier free communication without any borders.

The teaching process is enhanced by games. Rhythmical and interactive games are preferred, i.e., throwing a ball while being asked something or clapping hands.

The word suggestopaedia is a mixture of suggestion and pedagogic. What would you motivate more to learn a language? Would it be a teacher standing in his sleeping robe in front of you or a vital nice dressed teacher who is wandering up and down in the classroom or even the punk who is joking and talking very fast or the one talking slowly with a low voice? His movements, the kind of hos voice everything he is doing and presenting and how he is doing it will influence you. These are suggestions which can be used in an educational context to increase the students' motivation in specific situations. We know from the theme centred interaction TZI that individuals influence themselves when they meet. Suggestopedia uses these phenomena to set student in a well prepared learn surrounding where the teacher is the most important factor at all. How does he present himself, the learning materials and last but not least the lesson itself.

Learning Materials are designed to activate all our senses. Fantasy travels, relaxation Exercises and learn concerts are presenting the content in a very relaxed situation with slow quiet music in the background.

The daily lessons are structured to a "suggestopaedical circle."

Centering (Arrival and Concentration Relaxation).

Introduction to the Learning Content.

Active Learn Concert (classical music in the background. Lively presentation of the content in a real context where students can read the text in parallel in their bilingual textbooks).

Passive Learn Concert (quiet slow classical music, starting with a relaxation and breathing exercise followed by a relaxed but concentrated presentation of the key contents i.e., vocabulary).

Practice of the learning content using games i.e., memory to memorize vocabulary.

Role plays to practice the vocabulary in real settings.

Integration (Repetition and summary of the learning content key aspects.)

After their three weeks UNESCOs observers came to the conclusion that the students have been acquired an important part of the materials and that the acquired material is immediately available and used in communication.

"In any case, after three weeks, the majority of students are able to express themselves on a given topic, within a large range of vocabulary, with for some of them a genuine possibility of flexibility of the expression." (F. Winnykamen, Universite R. Descartes)

Conclusion

Learning with accelerating learning techniques like suggestopedia, super learning, edu kinaesthetic, TZI, NLP, mind mapping techniques enable us to reach goals much faster than in traditional classroom settings. The most important factor is still the teacher itself who needs to be empowered to use these powerful tools. Education of the teachers and language trainers has to start in universities at first place. Companies need to implement special inhouse language trainings to increase communicational English skills among their employees.

The Thai School system should face the big chance of a multilingual and multicaltural classroom and open up their schools for foreign students. This will help to increae language abilities of Thai students and future generations with nearly no external effort and costs. In the same way foreign children will be able to participate in Thai culture.

Besides emporwering Thailand with ICT tools and skills, there must be a movement towards a better multilingual and multicultural awareness. Thailand, especially Phuket, will need highly qualified teachers – real teachers – to improve overall communicational skills with foreigners in the next decade.

BIBLIOGRAPHY

Brown, S.C., & Kysilka, M.L. (2002). Applying multicultural and global concepts in the classroom and beyond. In Allyn, & Bacon. Boston, MA.

Chapter 9, Page 232. (2008, 08 16). Retrieved 08 16, 2008, from The Learning Web: http://www.thelearningweb.net/chapter09/page323.html

div. (2008, 08 16). *Language Proficiency.* Retrieved 08 16, 2008, from Wikipedia: http://en.wikipedia.org/wiki/Language_proficiency

(Fall 1978, Volume 3 Number 3). *The Journal of the Society for Accelerative Learning and Teaching,* p. 211.

GEPT. (n.d.). *General English Proficiency Test.* Retrieved from GEPT: http://www.lttc.ntu.edu.tw/E_LTTC/gept_eng_main.htm

Kids, M. (2008, 08 16). *Learn 4 Good Jobs.* Retrieved 08 16, 2008, from Media Kids: http://www.learn4good.com/jobs/language/german/search/job/53579/

Lozanov, D. (1978). *Suggestology and Outlines od Suggestopedy.* New York: Gordon and Breach.

New Teaching Qualification Requirements. (n.d.). Retrieved from http://www.associatedcontent.com/article/610131/new_teaching_qualification_requirements.html?

Runckel, C.W. (2004), Thailand's Road to a Better Software Industry. Retrieved 08-16, 2008, from Business in Asia: http://www.business-in-asia.com/telecom_software_electronic.html?

6

Education Reform and the Changing Role of Secondary School Administrators in the Public-Private-Partnership Model in Nigeria

Dr. Anne Fabiyi, Nigeria
Dr. Simeon A. Oladipo, Nigeria

Introduction and Background

Education is believed to be the core instrument for human development Fagbamiye, (1986); Obemeata, (1995); and Adepoju, (2003). Being educated is seen as the key to guaranteed success in life for an individual and the surest means of social upward mobility in the community and society. Similarly, nations of the world are categorized into developed, developing and underdeveloped mostly on the basis of the amount of education of the citizenry Oyebade, Oladipo and Adetoro (2007). It is in full realization of the pivotal role education can plays in developing and empowering the citizen to master their natural and social environments and to compete successfully in a globalized economy that "the Federal Government,... adopted education, as an instrument par excellence for effecting national development" (Nation Policy on Education, 2004:4) and defines its national policy on education as "Government's way of realizing that part of its national goals that can be achieved using education as a tool (NPE2004:6).

The agreement among nations and their citizens that education is the key to solving individual and national problems justifies the equalization of education opportunities. In Nigeria and indeed most developing nations, the issue of access to education has become highly contentious, emotive and explosive. The Federal Government of Nigeria responded to the agitation for equality and access to education in Nigeria when it stated that.... Government shall direct its policy toward ensuring that there are equal and adequate opportunities at all levels... (Federal Republic of Nigeria, 1999

Constitution). In order to ensure compliance to the above statement, the National Policy on Education (FRN 2004) gave private individuals and organization the authority to operate schools when it stated that:

> *Education is an expensive social service and requires adequate financial provision from all tiers of government for a successful implementation of the education programmes....In this connection, government welcomes and encourages the participation of local communities, individuals and other organization.(p. 61)*

Judging from the foregoing. It is established that the funding of education in Nigeria involves three distinct groups: The government, the private sector and the beneficiaries. This calls for adequate striking of an effective balance among the three stakeholders in order to ensure success in providing quantitative and qualitative education.

The Federal Government of Nigeria solely manages the 102 Unity Colleges spread across the country. These schools were set up to provide education for young Nigerians in an atmosphere that would provide total education, promote mutual understanding and tolerance amongst people from varying ethnic, religion and cultural background; entrench the values of patriotism and national unity and the pursuit of excellence in academic achievement and moral virtues. It is unfortunate, according to Kanno, (2001) that public opinion revealed that the school system has failed in achieving these.

The principle of equal educational opportunity has been credited for its ability to remove traditional structural obstacles to achievement so that each person can rise as far as his talents will allow. According to Oyebade, Oladipo and Adetoro (2007), it de-emphasizes such accidental factors as family and ethnic background, social class, colour and region, so that individuals can rise by merit alone.

The basic idea behind this principle is that, it is only accidental that a child's father is poor, or that he is of a particular religion or ethnic group/race. If equalization of access to education means that no one should be denied access to education because of any of the aforementioned accidental factors, how fair is it to indirectly base admission on child's family status or religion not withstanding the candidate's performance in the entrance examinations to some private schools? How else can one explain the commercialization of education as a result of the emergence of private schools that charge very exorbitant fees, which in most cases are beyond the reach of the masses. A situation where parents have to pay as much as #60,000.00 ($8,000.00) per annum on a primary or secondary school child and above #500,000.00 per annum on university undergraduate means that children and wards of wealthy parents who could afford such expensive education are eligible for quality education especially at the primary and secondary level. This is rather unfortunate since "the confidence being reposed in the public schools is gradually being eroded due to their poor quality instruction and unequipped facilities" (Oyebade, Oladipo and Adetoro, 2007). The failure of private schools to promote access and equity due to exorbitant fees defeats the aim of education as vehicle for social mobility while perpetuating positions of advantage in life for those who are born into high status families. It is in the light of this that the Federal Government of Nigeria sought for a reform in this sector.

Omolewa (2007) observed that reform are by no means a novelty, rather they have always been with us and are motivated by a desire for change and the zeal to search for progress and development via alternative modes.

The Public-Private-Partnership in the education sector have been used extensively and successfully in many parts of the world as a means of bringing together various stakeholders in the education system to deliver innovative solutions to school problems.

Striking Reforms in the History of Education in Nigeria

The Wikipedia Encyclopedia (2008) describes reform as a phenomenon which possibly a reversion to what is perceived to be a pure original state. It is however used for any change to thought to positive.

Major reforms have always taken place during critical periods of the nation's educational development. In Nigeria, the earliest educational reforms were jump-started by the visitation team of six from the United States led by Thomas Jesse Jones and financed by the Phelp-Stokes Foundation. They reported in 1922, that there was the need to draw up an education package that will be adapted to the local needs and train African leaders through the activities of secondary schools.

The education reforms of 1926-1929 saw many schools closed down and new government secondary schools established in Ibadan and Enugu. Before 1954, the number of years spent in primary school, secondary school, higher school certificate and university was 8, 6, 2, 3, respectively. The movement for self-government and independence advocated for a reduction in number of years spent in school, so, that Nigerians will all be opportuned to make contributions to the system and so became 6, 5, 2, 3 for primary, secondary, higher school certificate and higher education respectively.

The massive reforms in education were epitomized by the National Curriculum Conference of 1969. This actually culminated in the formulation and adoption of the National Policy on Education in 1976.

The policy provided for a 6-year primary, 3-year junior school, 3-year of senior secondary school and a 4-year tertiary education. The structure was widely misunderstood and poorly implemented.

The introduction of the Universal Basic Education in 1999 automatically changed the structure from 6-3-3-4 to 9-3-4 educational system, i.e., nine years in Junior Secondary School, three years Senior Secondary School and four year Tertiary education.

The latest initiative (when this research was been carried out) has shifted focus to producing a system that will be sufficiently credible to launch Nigeria into a competitive and increasingly globalized world. Some 'bold' educational programmes such as Operation Reach All Secondary Schools (ORASS), Tracking Assets for Progress (TAP), Adopt-a-Public School, Community Accountability and Transparency Initiative (CATI) and the Public-Private-Partnership (PPP) were put in place.

Public and private organizations, no doubt, have always owned schools individually, but in this arrangement, both government and private bodies are involved in the administration and management of the so called Unity Schools.

Statement of the Problem

With the implementation of the Universal Basic Education (UBE) and the high level of enrolment in schools, it has become unrealistic for government alone to provide all necessary infrastructures and facilities, textbooks, pay teachers salary, as well as meet all such required costs for quality and productivity. There is a need therefore to adopt a policy that will bring the private sector into partnership.

However, the Federal Government of Nigeria, due to an unprecedented increase in the cost of provision of education, generally introduced the reform that involves partnership with private individual or groups in the management of Federal Government Colleges which are referred to as Unity Schools.

In the light of the above, this study therefore focuses on the reform as it affects the entire management of secondary schools and the role of school administrators in the Public–Private-Partnership (PPP) model with particular reference to the unity schools.

Research Questions

The following research questions guided the study:

1. What are the propositions of the PPP model in the Nigerian context?
2. How is the status of this reform influenced by reform success indicators such as:
   (a) pre-introduction of the reform?
   (b) consultation with stakeholders?
   (c) acceptability of reform by target groups?
   (d) sustainability of the reform?
3. How do Secondary School Principals' rate the quality and adequacy of Educational Resources?
4. What is the position of the school administrator in the model now that the organizational context is complex?

Methodology

The study adopted the descriptive research design and the population consisted of the 52 Unity Schools spread across the South-South, South-West and South-East geographical zones of the nation. Out of this number, only 10 colleges from each geographical zone were randomly sampled. In addition to the ten colleges sampled from the South-West geographical zone, one 'boys-only' college and one 'girls-only' college were added to the sample. In all, 32 (57.1% of Unity Schools located in Southern Nigeria) unity colleges were sampled. A self-constructed eight item questionnaire, tagged, the Principals Perception of Secondary Education Reform Questionnaire (PPSERQ) were used to solicit information from the principals. The items were designed to evaluate the potency of the PPP reform success indicators. In addition some governments documented and proposed structure were analyzed.

Results

Research Question 1

What are the propositions of the PPP model in Nigeria?

In Nigeria, the structure of the PPP model is presented in Figure 1 below:

Figure 1: Public-Private-Partnership Model for Secondary School Management in Nigeria

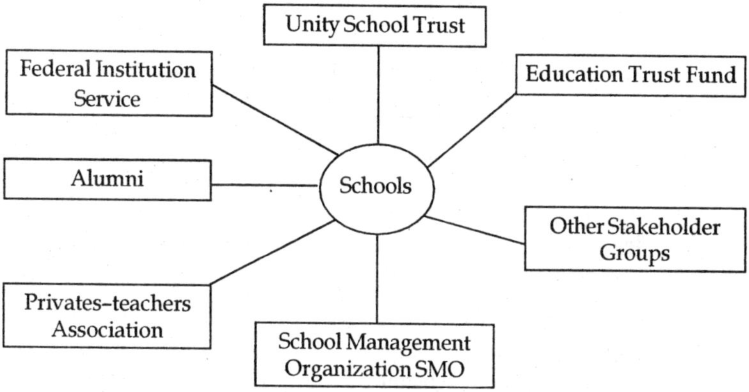

Source: Federal Government Education Bulletin (2006).

In Figure 1 above, the Unity Schools Trusts now replaces the Federal Ministry of Education, which existed as the sole manager before the reform. The Trust provides general guidelines using international best practices in standands and assessment. The Trust also disburses funds through Education Trust Fund. The general guidelines cover not only core ideology, vision, mission and goals, but are also directed to governance, leadership and management system in school governance, structure, ethical, legal and regulatory compliance, systems, human resource management, financial management and reporting systems.

The typical private stakeholders group will include the Parent-Teacher-Association, school alumni; School Management Organization (SMO), Educational Non-Governmental Organizations (NGOs) and charity and local community groups. They are the proposed operators and managers of schools and are expected to mobilize non-government funding to augment resources provided by Federal Government, employ school management and staff, and are responsible for achievement of standards and goals.

The unity schools will be managed by Education Management Trust (backed by law) and referred to as School Management Organisations (SMO). The SMO manages the academic and administrative affairs of the schools and each SMO will be overseen by a Board of Governors selected according to the general guidelines.

Research Question 2

What is the status of the PPP reform in Nigeria as it is determined by reform success indicators?

Table-1
Secondary School Principals' Evaluation of PPP Reforms Success Indicators

Sl. No.	*Reform Success in Dicators*	*Rated very High*	*Rated Highly*	*Rated Average*	*Poor Rating*
1.	Careful study of the reform before it was launched	6 (18.7)	10 (31.2)	05 (15.6)	11 (34.3)
2.	Wide consultation to ensure ownership by the stake holders	02 (0.62)	01 (0.03)	08 (25.0)	21 (65.6)
3.	Sober reflection to confirm that there could be possible and better alternative approaches	03 (9.3)	07 (21.8)	10 (31.2)	12 (37.5)
4.	Commitment of reform to genuine promotion of the development of the entire populace	14 (43.7)	12 (37.5)	03 (9.3)	03 (9.3)
5.	Assurance of the sustainability of the reforms	02 (0.62)	01 (0.03)	15 (46.8)	14 (43.7)
6.	Adoption of appropriate legal instrument to legitimatize the reform	04 (12.5)	03 (9.3)	21 (65.6)	12 (40.6)
7.	Adequate time for reform to be nurtured and nourished	07 (21.8)	07 (21.80)	07 (21.8)	11 (32.3)
8.	Clear perception of what the reform is all about	05 (15.6)	02 (0.62)	05 (15.6)	20 (62.5)

Table 1 above shows the sample principals evaluation of the reform success indicators. One the preconditions for a successful lunch and acceptance of a reform innovation is the need to adequately study and understand the potentials of change ingredient to bring out a positive and desired change. This result reveals that 34.3 per cent sampled principals feel very strongly that the reforms were not given enough time for considerable study before it was lunched. A larger number of principals (65%) by their evaluation, also confirm that consultation to ensure ownership by stakeholder was poor. Consequently, very few (0.03%) had assurance of sustainability of the reforms. It is characteristic of a political government to be too much in a hurry to want to impress his/her electorate and in the process, not allow for adequate time for clean perception of a reform. Majority (62.57%) of sampled principals reported that the reform indicator failed to allow for clear perception of what the reform is all about.

Research Question 3

What are Secondary School Principals' opinions on the Quality and Adequacy of Educational Resources?

Table-2
Secondary School Principals' Opinion on the Quality and Adequacy of Educational Resources

Educational Resource	*Available and Adequate*	*Available not Adequate*	*Not available*
Infrastructure	–	22	10
Teaching staff	–	29	03
Non-teaching staff	24	6	02
Student matters	–	–	–
Governance and Administration	08	20	04
Finance	–	01	31

The data generated revealed that majority of the unity schools are starved of required and adequate infrastructure. Human resources in unity Schools are of two categories, the teaching and the non-teaching workforce. In almost all sample schools, it was observed that the number of non-teaching staff is usually over bloated and have served longer years than the teaching staff. Finance has also become the most crucial, as almost all respondents were not favourably disposed to the issue of finance. Financing institutions continue to remain a perennial problem for the principal, sourcing for a legitimate fund becomes imperative.

Research Question 4

What is the relative position of the school principal in the PPP Model?

Figure 2: Government Proposed Management Structure of Secondary Education in Nigeria

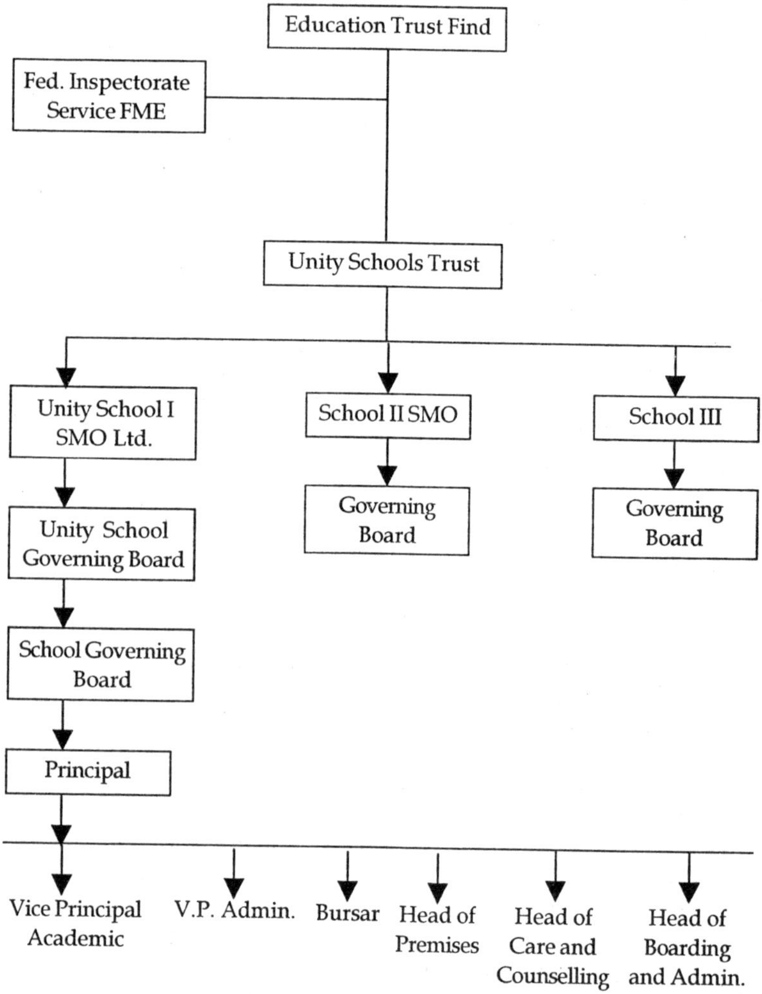

The school management will be led by the school principal who will be accountable to the Unity Schools Trust. The Board of Governors will be the employer of staff in individual schools. The school principal, therefore, occupies a central position in management in the PPP model.

At the level of each school, the implication for management of the government proposed structure is as below:

Figure 3: Government Structure at Each School Level

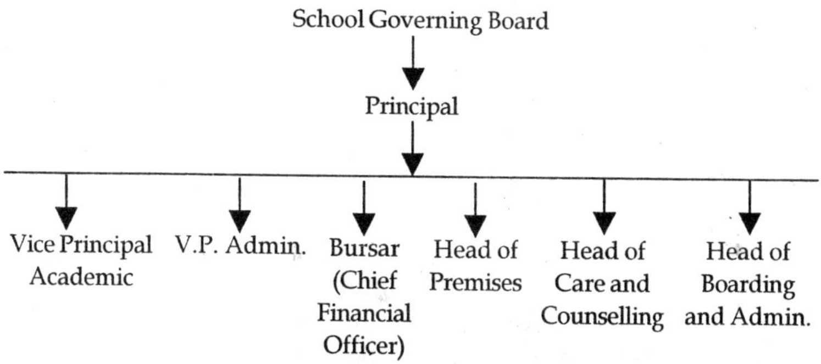

The above structure shows that the principal is directly responsible to the Governing Board of his school. Before the reform, the principal was directly responsible to the Ministry of Education. The principal is also accountable to the Unity School Trust.

It is necessary to further exploit the role of the principal *vis-à-vis* other members of the grassroot implementation school team.

Table-3

Governing Board Membership

Sl.No.	*Position*	*Tenure*
1.	Parents Representative	Rotational – 3 years
2.	Alumni Representative	Rotational – 3 years
3.	Two sponsors Representative	Permanent
4.	Principal	Permanent
5.	Representative of Senior Staff	Permanent
6.	Community Representative	Rotational – 3 yeas
7.	Federal Ministry of Education	Tenured – 3years
8.	Bursar	Permanent not rotating member
9.	School and Board Secretary	Permanent not rotating member

Position of the Secondary School Principal in the PPP Model

The principal is directly responsible to the superior Governing Board whose membership is a total of 11. The officers' composition of the Board rather creates a more complex problem for the school principal because of the wider coverage of stakeholders.

The challenges that this might pose for the principal is that he/ she may not have adequate time to be fully involved in what is taught and learnt in school. The overall effect may spill over to affect the quality of school and therefore its productivity.

There are too many people groups in the board and so the more the number, the more time will be required to resolve the challenges for effective school management. The statutory permanent tenure of five out of the eleven board members, however provides for relative continuity in long term plans for the school.

The school principal, under the arrangement of rotational 3 years of parents representative, must be prepared to work with a new set of parents each time because as the students graduate, new parents come on board. There may also be problems with principal's interaction with two sponsors unless there are strict regulations on the level of involvement by both parties; the adage that says "he who pays the piper dictates the tune" may explain the relative positions of both the principal and the sponsors.

It is mandatory for a principal of a secondary school to become quite familiar with the primary assignment of leadership and management and so the schedule of Vice Principal (academic and admin.), Bursar, Head of Premises etc. come under direct supervision and guardian of the school administrator.

The need to build structures that will ensure accountability, transparency and due process is central to the realization of the Public–Private-Partnership Model. The Chief Accounting Officer, the bursar, must work closely with the principal as a matter of necessity.

The larger responsibility of managing secondary schools falls on the principal who must have a larger than life size to be able to cope with the pressure from the different people groups.

Suggested Innovations and Best Practices for Effective School Management

The Public-Private-Partnership Model for Secodary School administration must be studied adequately and test-run before it is applied on the larger School Society Nigeria. With a structure that places the school administrator at a focal point, the involvement of subordinates will create a cordial relationship and development of programme in a supportive school climate. The school principal needs to delegate authority to execute the many functions that are mandatory and to ensure participatory administration.

The secondary school principal is faced with the challenge of moving both human and material resources to achieve school goals. The employment of modern facilities that will aid best practices is therefore necessary. Advancement in technology has not only produced more and improved machineries, it has improved human societies and management techniques. Moreover, Modern organizational systems are driven by electronic and computerized Information Communication and Technology (ICT) for speed and accuracy in the phase of massive information to be made available to large members, the principal must be ICT – compliant. He/She is expected to go beyond the awareness level into the stage of development and utilization of skill needed for operating the facilities.

A facility sharing and networking plan is proposed to enable the school administrators maximize the utilization of educational resources where facilities are available and highly insufficient quantity. For maintenance, private firms can be partners with institutions for updating, repair and replacement of functional equipment.

To improve finances, the development/upgrading of some of the technical departments to produce goods and services in exchange for funds for the immediate community is proposed.

Conclusion

The Unity Schools were established to propagate knowledge and skills relevant to development of secondary school pupils so that they can become self reliant and adequately prepared for tertiary education in addition. One of their goals is to unite Nigerians in diversity. The reform in education has placed the school principal in a focal point for effective administration which may be possible by using innovative and best practices strategies.

REFERENCES

Adepoju, T.L. (2003). Locational factors and academic performance of students in senior school certificate examinations.

Adesina, S. (1977). Planning and Educational Development in Nigeria. Lagos: Educational Industries Nigeria Ltd.

Coffey, E. and Lashway, L. (2002). Trends and Issues: School Reform. Message posted to http://weux,yiewfib,wsy/rewbsanaaywa/reform/

Ehiametahor, E.T. (2004). Issues of Access, Equity and Priavte Sector Participation in the Deregulation of Education. Lead paper presented at NAEAP conference UNIJOS September, 28-30.

Fafunwa, A.B. (1991). *History of Education in Nigeria Ibadan*: NPS Educational Publishers.

Fagbamiye, E.O. (1986). Possible predictors of students' academic performance at WASSCE African Journal of educational Management, 1(1), 88-93.

Federal Republic of Nigeria, (2004). *National Policy on Education.* Lagos: NERDC.

Federal Republic of Nigeria, (1999). *The Nigerian Constitution.*

Federal Government Education Bulletin, (2006).

Kanno, T.N. (2001). Students performance and curriculum implications. In Aghenta, J.A. and Lassa, P.N (Eds.) Academic Congress publication. The proceedings of the 16th Annual Congress of the Nigerian Academy of Education.

Obemeata, J.O. (1995). Education: *An unprofitable industry in Nigeria. A postgraduate school interdisciplinary Research Discourse,* University of Ibadan.

Omolewa, Michael (2007). Education reform for what? Being a keynote address at the meeting of committee of Deans of Education of Nigerian Universities, University of Lagos, Lagos, Nigeria.

Oyebade, S.A.; Oladipo, S.A.; and Adetoro, J.A. (2007). Access and equity in university education: A Status Report in Nigeria and Sub-Sahara Africa. Being a paper presented at the annual national conference of the Nigerian Association for Educational Administration and Planning (NAEAP), Enugu State University, Enugu.

Taiwo, C.O. (1980). The Nigerian education system: Past, Present and Future. Lagos: Thomas Nelson (Nigeria).

The Unity College PPP Initiative, Public presentation 31st – 2nd February, 2007. Federal Ministry of Education Publication.

Wikipedia Encyclopedia (2008).

7

Managing Student's Unrest in Institutions of Higher Education in Nigeria

Dr. Austin Njiribeako Nosike, Spain
Nkasiobi S. Oguzor, Nigeria
Prof. M.O.N. Obagah, Nigeria

Introduction

Although students' unrest or uprising has existed for quite sometime, its impact has never been felt as was the case since the 19th century. Many students today are concerned not just with their immediate adjustment, but also increasingly concerned with the societal and environmental factors or forces which seem to impinge on them as member of human race. Consequently, they participate actively and sometimes aggressively in societal reconstruction and reformation.

Across the globe, students have been known to have shaken their political systems for one reason or the other. In sub-Saharan Africa, students' activism or rebellion has been known to have threatened governments in Tanzania, South Africa, Liberia, Ghana, and Nigeria just to mention but a few. It is clear that student discontent with institutional authorities, government and the society at large is as old as the institutions. If is not a phenomenon limited to a particular area, rather it occurs all over the world but the form if takes may vary from place to place depending on the cultural, economic and socio-political situation prevailing in the area in question (Ajayi, 1989). Our concern in this chapter is to examine the phenomenon of student's crisis in Nigerian higher educational institutions with the view of reflecting on some of its causes, with a view to recommending some solutions.

Causes of Students Unrest in Nigeria

Young people within the age range of 16, and 30 years being in the prime age are the most exuberant, impulsive, vocal, impetus and radical group. This is also the group which nature has endorsed with undaunted creativity, ingenuity, inventiveness, initiative and disposition towards adventure and discovery. The period is that of great possibilities and opportunities and self assertiveness. Students of this age group take active interest in the political, social and economic events taking place around them. Regrettably there have been too many instances when these positive characteristics for so many reasons, have been misdirected with unfortunate results of outright confrontation with both institutional authorities and Government which always led to violence and wanton acts of vandalism. The causes of student unrest are discussed under the following rubrics:

Inadequate Students Support Service

Apparently because of the high demand for education all levels in Nigeria, it has been difficult for the institutional authorities or even the governments to provide certain basic support services needed for the full realization of the goals of education. These short comings are reflected in the unrealistic ratio of the available services to the population of the students in tertiary institutions. It is a known fact that most institutions are faced with inadequate financial allocations for quite sometime now due to mis-management of the economy and decreased revenue due the world oil glut. Consequently, most of the institutions could not provide services needed for the ever increasing enrolment in schools.

Some of the identified needs of the student support services programme which are seriously affected are transportation, sanitation facilities, food services, recreational facilities, better advising systems, the need for better dissemination of information and for more meaningful dialogue between the authorities and students as well as finance and services. Of particular emphasis here, and which have been one of the main sources of conflict between students and institutional authorities in Nigeria is welfare services.

In the recent past, Nigerian students in tertiary institutions demonstrated for different reasons. In May, 1976, University of Benin students demonstrated violently for non provision of transportation from halls (dormitories) to lecture rooms. While Auchi Polytechnic and Abraka College of Education students also demonstrated for shortage of lecturers, poor food and accommodation.

Unresponsiveness of the Governance

Unresponsive governance constitutes a major instrument of student crisis. Failure by the Governments and or individual institutions to implement policy statements results to anger and frustrations which naturally follow with equal consequences. No doubt, when students fail to recognize the effectiveness and viability of an administration, they become suspicious of all authorities and are resentful of institutions structures in which they find themselves. For instance, in 1978 and 1988 there were nation-wide strikes by students of tertiary institutions in Nigeria. At a time when the National Economy was considered to be better (1978), Government introduced new University fees and students reacted violently. Similarly, in 1988, the Federal Government withdrew the oil subsidy and introduced Structural Adjustment Programme (SAP). These policies, the students argued that they were not necessary at the time in point and it did not favour the common-man. At the institutional level, there had been various strikes for one reason or the other (accommodation and instructional materials and shortage of lecturers and many other instances).

Major among the causes of student unrest external to the University is government policies. University students have taken to the streets in reaction to what they say as government policies which are not in their interest. Such past polices as the introduction of the NYSC Scheme, increase in boarding and lodging fees, withdrawal of government subsidies of catering services and increase of Petroleum products prices (Madu, 1987).

The higher institutions of learning have a large concentration of some of the most intelligent young people in the society who are exposed to a wide range of knowledge with unlimited freedom of expression. The radical and eloquent among them portray government polices as injustice and literally mobilize the other students and demonstrate against government policies. In the past, Nigerian students have expressed their dissatisfaction over government policies in so many ways (writing to the media, traditional rulers, talking to senior government officials and discussing with influential personalities in the society).

Societal Gap

The youths posses traits in several respects. The youth try to demonstrate their coming of age and they seem to revolt against certain established norms to prove to the adults that they have arrived. This is mainly due to the fundamental changes within the social system which are manifested in the current craze of dance, songs, dress, and social activities of the youths that not only challenge but obliterated the accepted moral values of the society. However, the failures of the adults to understand these traits often lead to conflict between them, and consequently their explosion at the slightest suggestion that they do not know what they are doing. This notion of general gap when carried to the tertiary institutions could serve as a potent source of student unrest, especially if the institutional leadership tends to be conservative and strict with students.

The society no doubt should lay claim, to some of the blames for student's crisis in our tertiary institutions. Student's conduct in Nigeria can only be seen against the general background of the complex social changes which are taking place in it. This is because the higher institutions are expected to mirror the larger society of which it is a sub-system. Hence, the higher institution is easily affected by the psychological, social, economic and political factors within the larger society and over which the institution has no control. As students feel justifiably aggrieved and resort to tactics resulting to their alleged misbehaviour.

The general causes for the student unrest are deeply rooted in our society. Since the University - including the student body is part and parcel or the larger society in which the University is situated in the reflection of the society, the socio-political and religious maneuvers in the larger society are experienced in the campus. The case in point was the 1990 religious disturbances in Kaduna State where Ahmadu Bello University and Bayero University, Kano students took to the street in reaction to what one would have thought as complete extra University affair (Madu, 1987).

The Mass Media

There is no doubt that the mass media has somewhat being a factor which is known to have facilitated students unrest, through their manner of reporting. When a report is in citing or not balanced enough, it can easily set the students on motion, thinking that they have the support of the press. This can help to fuel or spread the protest out of proportion. Exposure to films, and television programmes of all sorts from foreign countries could have considerable influence on students and help to stimulate the tendency to have liked the students of the foreign countries even when the cultural settings are quite different. The mass media has not helped matters at all in containing student unrest. If anything they have contributed in escalating the unrest. The sensational and instigating coverage of students led to the controversy of the University of Maiduguri in 1983. The students of University of Maiduguri demonstrated against their Vice-Chancellor over suspension of their union president and demanded for his release. Although student unrest was not peculiar to the University, the unbalanced comments from certain quarters - especially the media, generated into a national issue. A responsive media is a necessity for solving the perennial incidence of student unrest in a plural society such as Nigeria.

Institutional Leadership and Management

One major challenge confronting the Nigerian tertiary institutions is that of poor management. The greatest a challenge facing Nigerian tertiary institutions however is that of effective leadership. This is because the right leadership is crucial to the solution of the hitherto enumerated problems. Leadership is the element that makes the difference between success and failure in organization. The importance of leadership in Nigerian Higher Institutions cannot be over emphasized. To a large extent, it affects motivation and job satisfaction, productivity, organizational success and student unionism.

Leading can be looked upon as a subset of the management function. However, it seems to occupy a critical niche in the diagnosis of the problems of Nigerian tertiary institutions to justify a separate treatment. Ironically, Nigerian tertiary institutions seem to have shunned the idea of the need for organized management training especially for the academics. Instead of encouraging the cultivation of administrative and leadership skills for its managers, our tertiary institutions traditionally emphasize technical and academic proficiencies. The result is that some academics assuming important administrative positions rarely have leadership training or administrative experience. The assumption is that a professor would make a good Vice-Chancellor, Dean, Director or a Provost. Little accepted is the notion that academic competence may not necessarily confer leadership and administrative capability. The culture of higher institutions the world over seems to exaggerate the importance of the accumulation of knowledge and research skills per-se over leadership or management abilities. Specialism is often pursued at the expense of broad mindedness and realism. Expectedly, if there were any relation between theory and practice (and the tertiary institutions exist to show that there is) then some measure of management and leadership training must be advantageous for potential and practicing academic leaders in assisting them to perform their duties more effectively.

The Way Forward

To effectively avert student's unrest, it is essential that they should constantly seek, create and utilize all possible strategies for dialogue with tertiary students generally and student activities in particular, so as to gain a better understanding of the basic characteristics of and factors conducive to student activism, irrespective of whether or not any specific issue is currently at stake. An understanding of the characteristics of activist protest will lead to more effective methods of averting potential unrest.

Government (public and institutional authorities) should give positive consideration to and utilize student avenues for student participation in institutional decision-making and management at the heist levels and opportunities, authorities should exploit to the full all communication and dialogue facilities with their students, and provide for continuous review. Government should continuously examine with institutional authorities, student unions and all other envisaged participants, projects, programme and new avenues with which students can voluntarily, or by persuasion participate and contribute to the socio-economic and political life of the Nigerian society generally and specific communities in particular on a regular and systematic basis. The experiment of the NYSC is pertinent. All such avenues of participation on contribution should include systems and awards of public recognition.

Considering the potential or student activism for spontaneous violence and disruption, government and institutional authorities should approach such violence first, at the preventive level. The preventive level will include communication and feedback of full available information, thus pre-empting rumour and speculation, consultation with systematic basis, through predetermined mechanisms and channels. The curative stage must include a well regulated system of discipline and sanctions, the use of well equipped law enforcement agents such the police but not the army, the application of available sanctions under the institutions as well as under the state, including any specific lawful modifications existing at the time against incidents of "creative vandalism".

As a strategy for improved dialogue, government and institutional authorities need effective systematized and operational mechanism of communication in which student concerns when formally petitioned, will receive appropriate and reasonably prompt responses, in which established channels will function and be respected, and to which exceptions are only deliberately, temporarily and exceptionally made. Such mechanisms should seek to provide for the development and maintenance and time scales, and recognized the importance of the "generation gap" between student's perspectives and adult's systematic attitudes which may need to be bridged. The mechanisms should also be turned to take note of the "the silent majority" which may be influenced by "the activist minority's" mobilization skills. Such mechanisms, at the institutional, federal and state levels should also encourage student consultation as a matter of routine be able to adjust its quality and tempo in times of levels after ensuring full participation of all relevant persons or bodies.

In the institutional context, a committee should be set up, where one does not already exist, to perform the task of overall "positive interaction", under the Vice-Chancellor's Rector's, Provost's and Principal's office, with the student union of the institution, on a regular basis. There should be personal contact of the student body with the institutional Head. It should be chaired by the officer holding overall student affairs responsibility. Such an officer should be a senior academic who has the psychology of the institution-preferably a graduate of the same institution (an alumni). Details of its composition and operational disposition should be worked out in the light of the institutional characteristics.

Summary and Conclusion

Students' uprising at the tertiary level in Nigeria could be attributed to lack of adequate provision of certain support services. These are traceable to personal factors (home circumstance, and financial worries), academic factors (inadequate schooling, unsuitable choice of course, poor teaching strategies, and facilities, and inadequate options for courses, unsuitable residence, poor transportation, poor communication, lack of recreational facilities, unclear institutional structure and policies and undefined regulations), and external factors (socio-political, in equalities, government infringement of institutional governance and policies, and students being increasingly better informed of standards and practices elsewhere). It should therefore, be upper most in the minds of all concerned (i.e., the parents, institutions and the government) as to how to provide suitable environment through which each individual within the system can develop to the fullest of his abilities and capabilities in terms of democratic ideals. When adequate support services are provided in all our tertiary institutions, it will not only assist in increasing the students feelings of satisfaction, belongingness, identification and achievement both in the present to reduce if not totally eliminate unrest in Nigerian institutions of higher learning.

The support services which tertiary institutions should strive to lay emphasis on are admissions, registration, records, orientation of new students, counseling, housing, food and health services, student's activities and conduct (Gomez, 1980 and Edge, 1981). When these are provided, it will no doubt help to facilitate the optional coordination and integration of the academic and non academic needs of the students. Besides, since the needs of the students are not likely to be met all times, they too should shun violence in the bid to seek better solutions to whatever problems that might be confronting them. These suggestions would facilitate conducive for teaching and learning. This will also encourage students to feel free in choosing any institution of their choice and pursue course(s) they like. In the past, prospective students try to avoid institutions like the Ahmadu Bello University (ABU), Lagos, and Ibadan at the point of entry even though their courses are obtainable in these universities due to the fact that historically, these institutions have had more incidents demonstration/unrest compared to other institutions in Nigeria. They also assumed that they might not graduate on time due to these claims. Among other things, these institutions are considered peaceful by both parents and students. If these recommendations are considered, our tertiary institutions would be a better place for students, staff and institutional authorities.

REFERENCES

Ajayi, T. (1989). Managing Students Crisis in Nigerian Educational System. *Management in Nigeria.* Nigerian Institute of Management, March/April.

Akpofure, E.E.O. (1995), "Student Activism and Federal Government Policies in Nigerian Tertiary Education 1967-78." *Unpublished Ph.D. Thesis,* Department of Education, University of Wales, Cardiff.

Aminu, J. (1986) Quality and Stress in Nigerian Education. Selected Addresses and papers 1975-85, Northern Nigerian Publishing Company, Maiduguri and Zaria.

Baldridge, *et al.,* (1980). *Policy Making and Effective Leadership: A National Study of Academic Management,* Jossey–Bass Publishers, San Francisco, California.

Beckett, T. (1977). *Education and Power in Nigeria, A Study of University Students",* TH & S, London.

Denga, D.I. (1982). *Students Counseling: A Major Solution to Campus Unrest,* Lagos: Orit Egwa Publishers Ltd.

Edge, E.D. (1959)."The College Influence on Students Character", Washington: American Council on Education.

Flack, R. (1967) "The Liberated Generation: An Exploration of Roots of Students Protest." *Journal of Social Issues.* 5(2) 5-18.

Gomez, J.R. (1980)."Student Perception of Student Services at the Michigan State University" *Dissertation Abstract,* 42 (12) 48-52.

Hoy, W.K. and Miskel, C.G. (1978). *Educational Administration: Theory Research and Practice,* Random House New York.

Oshagbemi, T. (1989)."Management Practices and Problems in Nigerian Universities, *Management in Nigeria,* Nigerian Institute of Management January/February.

Woolf, D. (1953). *Student Personnel Programme.* New York: McGraw Hill Ltd.

8

Is Education to Fill the Pail or Light the Fire?—A Study on Higher Education in Ethiopia

Dr. R. Dayanandan, Ethiopia

Introduction

Development is both a physical reality and a state of mind in which society has through some combination of social, economic and institutional process, secured the means for obtaining a better life. Development must be conceived as a multidimensional process involving major changes in social structures, popular attitudes and national institutions, as well as the acceleration of economic growth, minimize inequality and the eradication of absolute poverty. Education is a prerequisite to building a food-secure world, reducing poverty and conserving and enhancing natural resources. In the last few decades, the world is swinging here and there between different methods of education. There has been tremendous development in the field of higher education in Ethiopia in recent years. International agencies are pouring millions of currency in this area. Still the country has not started enjoying the fruits of this just because of the lacuna prevailing in the educational methods which is not in accordance with the country's demand. This research paper is to bring up the scarcities in the universities which impede the education system, which is crucial for the national development in spite of massive international aids.

Ethiopia, a country with diversified and dense population of animals and birds, it harbors a variety of diseases which really reduce the production capacity of the livestock. With all the insufficiencies, universities are now concentrated in launching postgraduate programmes in almost all the fields regardless of the basic facilities required for the programmes. The nation is fast moving towards

Millennium Development Goals and the field of education has been given greatest emphasis. How far is this going to be effective for the nation? Will it be really fruitful for the country? This study is an attempt to assess the outcome of the various reforms in the field of education with special reference to university education.

Ethiopia, one of the ancient countries in the world had a glorious past. The history of Queen Sheba is even now enthralling the mass. But what happened in the field of education is something that demands serious discussion. Even though the general silhouette of the country is still lagging far behind other countries with an enormous pouring of international funds, it is thriving very hard to regain the past glory in all fields. Before analyzing the educational set up of the country. It is better to have a general out look of the country, it is essential to know the overview of the economy since education lays the first stone for the development of any country in the world.

General Profile

The country's economy is largely based on agricultural as well as animal husbandry sectors and there was a drastic decline in the agricultural output before two decades which has exacerbated the food crisis and contributed to the permanent label for the country which expressed the image of one showing the under nourished children with bulging abdomen and thin limbs, in the international portfolio. The performance of the non-agricultural sectors has been better; but less than impressive. The growth rates for the industrial and service sectors were 3.8 per cent and 3.9 per cent, respectively, far below the plan targets. The social infrastructure along with the economic status were both insufficient and in poor shape. For example, the road network of Ethiopia is the lowest even by the standards of Sub-Saharan Africa, with a road density of 29 km per 1000 square km or 0.48 per 1000 persons (in 2001/02). It is currently estimated that 70 per cent of the country's land area is not served by modern transport system. Access to safe potable water in the year 2000 for urban areas was 72 per cent and if Addis Ababa is excluded the figure drops to 38 per cent. Access to safe potable water for rural Ethiopia is about 24 per cent. Except for Addis Ababa and a few urban centers, sanitation facilities are basically non-existent. The current access to electricity in the country is estimated at 13 per cent of the population. Constraints include insufficient generation of power, unsatisfactory quality of supply, and weak customer service.

Widespread unemployment is a national crisis which is growing serious year by year. Urban unemployment is said to be over 30 per cent and underemployment i.e., disguised unemployment in rural and urban areas. While labor, undoubtedly, is the most abundantly available resource for populated developing countries like Ethiopia, if it is not properly used for productive purposes the opportunity cost would be high. Here is the education play its most important role. By educating this biggest resource properly enable the country to move fast to its goals of food security and self reliance. The socioeconomic infrastructure is at a lower level of development when compared with other Sub-Saharan African countries, which are regarded as the least developed countries of the world. Many factors have contributed to the poor socio-economic realities of the country some of the major reasons are outlined below.

- For a longer period the country maintained a traditional economic base that has missed the benefits of modern scientific and technological revolution.
- Despite its huge potential, the agricultural sector has remained sluggish due to inappropriate policies and practices.
- For an extended period in the past, Ethiopia has been a land of social upheavals, civil war and other forms of instability.
- The low productivity and saving rate (capital formation) coupled with unsound utilization of the country's available resources have resulted in the deterioration of the standards of living of the population.

All these factors directly or indirectly influence the education standards or from this general silhouette, one can get an outline of the present state of higher education in the country.

Developments in Higher Education

Improvement of a country's human capacity for productivity is a must for social and economic development in this ancient nation. Many Ethiopian universities have emerged very recently as a part of the new education policy of the Federal Government. It was only a half century ago modern higher education started with the founding of the University College of Addis Ababa in 1950. The University College had less than 1,000 students and less than 50 teachers in the late 1950s. Most of the teachers were foreigners. The College of Agriculture and Mechanical Arts, College of Engineering in Addis Ababa, Institute of Building Technology, Gonder Public Health College, Theology College of Holy Trinity, Kotebe College of Teacher Education, and the Polytechnic Institute at Bahir Dar were opened in the 1960s. In 1961, most colleges in the country were reorganized under the Haile Selassie I University. With the beginning of a socialist revolution in 1974, the name of the university was changed to Addis Ababa University (AAU).

Among the Universities and Institutes offering higher education in various subjects, Addis Ababa University is the most prestigious and attracts students not only from Ethiopia but from other African countries as well. Other universities are Alemaya University, Bahir Dar University, Dilla University, Mekelle University, Jimma University and Debub University. Recently as part of universalisation of education policy of the government, fifteen additional universities are also established. Institutes offering studies in specialized subjects are Arbaminch Water Technology Institute (AWTI), Nazareth College of Technical Teacher Education, Gondor College of Medical Sciences (GCMS) and Openo Technical School, Gambela. The Unity University College in Addis Ababa, a private institute, has also earned good name in recent years. According to the available statistics, the number of university students in 2000-01 was about 46,000. This figure excludes those students who are enrolled in the extension (night classes) and postgraduate programmes, which could be around 20,000. The total number of enrolment would, therefore, be roughly about 66,000 students. The enrollment system also has changed to help more students into the higher education institutions. The cut off marks of the entrance examination has brought down in this procedure. But this has led the way towards reducing the standard of higher education.

A country that honors it's highly skilled and educated force and invests on and wisely utilizes it, lays a groundwork that guarantees the success and betterment of its future. It may appear that the university faculty is one of the government's highly paid communities in the country. But that falls far short of fulfilling the basic needs and necessities of the academic community. Ethiopia, as poor as it may be, should promptly address these pressing issues of its higher education institutions, if its development plans to bear fruit. The key for this to materialize rests on promoting trust and cooperation and encouraging constructive engagement between the government and the university community.

Essential Components of Education

In the quest for education for all, it is possible that the full potential of education for development is being overlooked in favour of a 'quick fix' statistical achievement. This may not only lead to a waste of valuable resources, but could inadvertently erode future confidence and investment in education for development. For education to be successful in achieving itse development intentions it must be contextually located and not treated as an isolated variable. An investment in education is an investment in human capital, but this is of limited utility in the absence of a supportive environment. The prominence of the knowledge industry is more critical now as the economic archetype of the 20th century that was largely dependent on natural resources has appeared to have shifted toward a knowledge and information-based economy. The main components of education have to be in accordance with the country's demand. Now let us analyse the essential prerequisite for smooth teaching learning process in an ordinary university and the existing facilities in the Ethiopian universities.

The Learning Environment

To achieve universal education at global standard, a university classroom must be equipped with necessary facilities like comfortable chair and desk for the students, computer, beamer and a screen for lecture presentation, overhead projector, flip chart, white board etc. These are some of the essential things even an LDC (Less Developed Country) can afford. Here in the Ethiopian conditions, all the above prerequisites are missing. The teachers even now depend on blackboards and chock pieces. This is a paradox when the universities are spending unlimited amount for buying stationeries and nobody bothers where these materials really go.

The Class Strength

There should be an optimum number of students in a classroom for effective and interactive teaching learning process. But here every class has more than 70 students. And some times goes unto 120 and that too sitting in very congested and the back benchers will never hear the teacher unless She/he breaks open his/her vocal cord! This has generated short comings in the thorough and sincere evaluation method. Examinations become name sake and teachers find it difficult to submit the results of such a huge number of students in time.

The number of students being admitted to each faculty is also not based on the capacity of the faculty. The ministry of education pushes the lot students to each university and the departments are naturally obliged to bear all of them on their head irrespective of their teaching facility. Another miserable feature is the methods following to admit the students. It is not based on their choice and interest but the discretionary power of the university to direct a student to choose the specialization. So most of the time this has sited one reason by the students for not having interest in their studies being forced to study a boring subject for them.

Faculty Position

The scarcity of teachers is an important crisis in the higher education sector. It is still dependent on expatriate staff from Asian and other African countries in almost all the faculties. Here comes the need of discussing the so called brain drain. "In 25 years, Africa will be empty of brains", Dr. Lalla Ben Barka of ECA has rightly put. It is found that Ethiopia lost 75 per cent of its skilled workforce during 1980-91. Analyzing all these together, one can conclude that this is a major problem tackled by proper government policies alone. Even though the Ministry of Education has directed to start postgraduate programmes at all the departmental levels, the feasibility of starting such programmes has to be worked very precisely and with long-term planning.

The present education policy is encouraging to employ Graduate Assistants immediately after their graduation to reduce the scarcity of teaching staff. It is a fruitful strategy of getting students just after their graduation to the teaching field. But the way of deploying them to conduct classes should be done very carefully. They should not be given the responsibility of an entire course but sharing course with some senior staff. In my observation, the lion parts of the instructors are too young to deliver classes. The findings of the study pointed out that such condition some times has led to many malpractices and even reducing the motivation of the students in attending classes.

The teaching staffs are appointed on contractual basis while the administrative staff has been given permanent positions. This has led to a sort of disappointment among the instructors and they are waiting for an opportunity to go for better chances. Another problem due to this style of appointment is that once an instructor is appointed is no controlling mechanism over this member. His credentials are never attached to his appointment. So he is free to leave anytime from his position. Many times the head of the department has shoulder the burden for a replacement in the middle of the semester.

Remuneration for Teaching Staff

Universities have to pay attention to attract graduates to teaching profession. At present the salary norms are not attractive when compared to other sectors. The only attraction for the graduates is to get scholarships for higher studies in abroad. In my observation this had negative impact in one way or other taking better brains off the country. The wide disparity in terms of payment between the local and the expatriate staff have created an unsound cheated feeling among the local staff. Another observation is the disinterest of the teachers to work in rural areas. All the local staff members are fascinated to work in the capital city, Addis Ababa. So other universities run short of qualified teaching staff. In the eve of Ethiopian Millennium, the government doubled the salaries for the university teachers and announced special incentives to the staff who are working in rural settings. Even then the situation is not changed.

The Syllabus/Curriculum Structure

As far as curriculum structure is concerned, so far there is no strict control over the syllabus. Concern course Instructor can develop whatever he/she is interested and there is no monitoring system for the syllabus that is used. Many instructors don't even finish the syllabus that they have prepared and the students are forced to write the examination with the very limited lessons they have been taught. Students welcome this situation since many of them are interested in their grades alone. There should be an examination board to monitor the questions prepared for the examinations and see that the portions are well covered in the stipulated time. The present university syllabus is adapted mostly from western universities which are not fitting to the national requirements. This creates confusion among students when they understand what they learned is not what they observe in the surrounding society. At least in some of the faculties serious attempts are taking place to modify the curriculum. Movements are going on to have a nationally unified syllabus for all universities.

Each department enrolls students for summer classes and some for distance learning. These programmes are well accepted by all the instructors since these give very good remuneration to them. But the disappointing factor is that the quality of contents given to the summer students is deplorable. The students also not concerned about the quality but only in the certificate provided to them at the end of the day which will bring promotion or additional increment.

Field Practicum

The ministry of education in the country started eight universities all on a sudden in the year 2002 and not it become 23. This has created a revolutionary change in the history of higher education. As much as twenty thousand students as regular and around five thousand in-service students are studying in each university. But the practical exposure for these students is far behind. Lack of farm land to learn farming activities, inadequate poultry/dairy farms and lack of field visits are all part of the problems. Most of the courses need field visits and these are part of the curriculum. Students can learn many things in live conditions; rather depending on models or dummies, especially the course involving clinical practices like veterinary the field visits occupy paramount importance.

Ethiopia stands first in Animal population but the production potential is much low when compared to other African countries. There are many reasons attributed to this paradox. The major one being acute shortage of skilled man power in the field of animal management and disease control. When coming to the veterinary science, pathology is one of the connecting links between the clinical and non clinical subjects and so it is the basic of veterinary medicine and a student should have thorough understanding about etiology, pathogenesis course and sequel of important diseases. Teaching methods in Pathology, be it any branch of it, will have to be effective only when the learners understand the condition by actually seeing or feeling it and not just by reading the textbooks or browsing the websites. Of course these methods help them to support their knowledge and make it sturdy. One incidence of outbreak in the Mekelle University poultry farm killing hundreds of birds during a period of two weeks showed all the pathegnomonic lesions of

Infectious Bursal Disease on necropsy examination. But as the samples were sent for confirmatory diagnosis to the laboratories, the result came as New Castle Disease. Here the method of teaching by actually showing the lesions could not be supported by laboratory evidences. This kind of paradoxical situation arises in many occasions! When the whole world is frightened by the scary pandemic, people may consider death of birds as similar one, so a false diagnosis may lead to unnecessary worries and expenses to the nation.

Laboratory Facility

Laboratories are the milestones of any higher education institutions. As far as Ethiopian system is concerned they never give due importance to laboratories or practical! Practical sessions are there in almost all the faculties in the schedules. But what actually being done in the practical class is no body's concern. The most desperate situation is in the case of veterinary and medical faculties. The practical sessions are the indispensable part of these two. But the clinical facilities are extremely poor and the laboratory classes are only for name sake. Even in the postgraduate classes the story is not different. In my observation very few instructors take pain to give the practical sessions. The disappointing factor is that the labs in the universities have enormous facilities in term of equipments, instruments and chemicals in all the fields. Sophisticated equipments costing billions of dollars have been donated by international communities. But some of those equipments are still in the store rooms without being touched! No initiative being taken to train the staff for the activation of those equipments.

Library Facility

The continuous flow of funds has encouraged the universities to construct beautiful buildings for libraries. The out put from these are yet to be shown its effect really in the education system. It has no system to attract students and the functioning has to be improved. It should be opened round the clock accommodating all the students with most advanced treasure of knowledge. At present there is scarcity of textbooks in most of the disciplines, and the books available are also not exhibited properly for the students. Most of the time students are relying on handouts supplied by the instructors which restrict their wide reading for widening the knowledge. Any way positive changes are seen as time passes. But the pace is still at lower rate.

Evaluation System

The present evaluation system is not a scientifically prepared one and there is no standard evaluation method for the universities. Those who have a system also do not follow it strictly. For instance the grading system is different for different faculties. Within the faculty it is unique for each instructor. This has created dissatisfaction among the students. Here is the need for the external evaluation to see that the students have been taught the syllabi completely and this also will make teacher more aware of the need of completing the portions. Another interesting finding was the gender discrimination in evaluation. Though one can not generalize this, sometimes affect the quality of higher education where in males getting higher grades and the number of female drop outs increasing in those departments who follow strict evaluation methods. Generally the female students do not take much effort for studying the courses since there is a "superstition" that they can get higher grades by other means. But this will not work out all the time. Many girl students could not cope up with the cut off grades due to their weak background and forced to leave the university premature.

Students Attitude

The most important component, the students render the bright scope as far as higher education in Ethiopia is concerned. The attitude of the students has changed a lot from the previous years. They have ardent interest towards learning and try their best to go much higher with a motto of going abroad. Education is one of the important means for them to visit other countries. The doors are wide open for them in all the countries around the globe for higher education. Some times ago there was a tendency for those who go out, not interested in coming back. So the country has made strict policies so that they have to come back and serve the home country after their studies. Another interesting thing is their preference of choosing the country for higher education. They are all after prestigious institutions to gather knowledge as well as money and to bring a car while coming back.

Medium of teaching should compulsorily be English in Universities. But it is found that most of the young teaching staff prefers to teach in national language, Amharic in their classes though they are comfortable in English. Some students appreciate this while some others indicate the difficulty of expressing things in the answer papers, since the question papers always in English.

Youth, the Hope!

Education and culture go hand in hand. The best example is in the ancient history of Indian culture. But in the case of Ethiopia such a linkage is difficult to see. It had a glorious past, which could not harmonize with the education standard. Learned from experience and external world, the Ethiopian youth have imbibed the real enthusiasm of higher education. Supported by the education policies, their dream has no end nowadays. They have all doors opened to them for higher education abroad. When compared with other developing countries, the Ethiopian youth are blessed with their chances of going abroad for higher education. This remains only a day dream for an Indian graduate who has neither government nor financial assistance. The Ethiopian graduate has the right to teach in a University as soon as he graduates. Then all his efforts will be to earn money not by sincere teaching but by muscle power, the whole time in the University is spent for internet search till get a university to get admission. Now-a-days the faculty has to facilitate his study to get scholarship and also leave with all the salary and allowances! Of course this encourages the young generation to get higher education. On the other hand the current tendency is to get out of the country and settle wherever possible. This has been the motto of getting higher education of the present generation. Exceptions are there only counted by fingers. This period in the history is going to be the era of foreign education.

Other Scarcities Observed

Boarding and Lodging

Whether it is student or staff, accommodation is a problem in these Universities, where the most beautiful palace like buildings are erected inside and out side the campus! The local instructors are given fixed allowance for accommodation and for expatriates the university has been arranging private accommodation outside as per the contract. But the university even after bringing expatriates for the last one decade, put them in rented houses and most of them complain about this and that. Such a hue and cry will adversely affect the quality of education.

Condition of students is even more pathetic. One cannot imagine how the students can study in such a small dormitories exactly like caged birds! There are buildings built all around the campus without proper planning and architectural quality. To add oil to the fire, scarcity of water is a constant problem with improper sewage treatment. Whatever the university holds high about its achievements these insufficiencies will plunge all those in a split second. One use to wonder even with all the funds and awareness, these problems are never addressed by anyone and not even complained at least once!

Food for the soul is not to be given in an empty stomach. An unfilled stomach cannot afford even a small bit of knowledge! Coming to food for the students, there was students' unrest emerged due to poor quality food given to them and the corruption associated with the purchase of food materials. The "Injera", the most essential food for Ethiopians is made out of teff, a very small grain grown in the country. Many top officials had to quit their position due to the scandals associated with purchase of not only food materials but many other things in the University. Students' council started strong agitation against corruption and they came out with success along with the removal of some officials by the Ministry of Education.

Computer Access

In the era of computer revolution, it is unfortunate to mention that the university students are not fully accessed with computers for their day to day academic activities of writing assignments, preparing Practical Attachment Reports etc. and applying statistical packages in their analysis. Even though they have to study one compulsory course on 'Computer and its Application', their computer literacy is far below because of lack of computer accessibility.

Access to Internet

As the world has shrunk in to a global village, information is to be on fingertips. Students and staff need to enjoy the freedom of learning things at their will through the electronic world! In Ethiopian universities this has not become a regular service yet. Presently students are relying only on the handouts and available textbooks as well as classroom teaching. This limits their connectivity with other sources of information.

Conclusion

Ethiopia is growing faster outside the country! Outflow of skilled man power is not yet controlled while inflow of international funds is also in full swing! There should not be any scarcity while evaluating the magnitude of external aids. Still why these controversies exist in Ethiopia is some thing that calls for global interests. While there are still poorer countries which need educational aids for their developments why the developed countries pump this much money to Ethiopia alone? Have they ever examined the results of their help? Have they ever thought that the country has the means of utilizing these funds effectively? Have they ever extended the help to manage these funds effectively? For all these queries the answers we get is not that satisfactory. It may not satisfy your quest for knowing the details.

The development of a dear and near working relationship between the government and the university communities is a vital step to bring about meaningful solutions to the deplorable situation. In an environment where each often watches the other in suspicion, forging a meaningful relationship to address the problems remains distant. Government policies should be strictly adhered with financial allocation while establishing the classrooms and laboratories. For this, long-term plan should be formulated. In order to lead the nation towards light, the basic thing is to make good for the present scarcities to march towards the millennium development goals. If necessary, the policies of the government need to be changed or to be elaborated according to the present requirements.

The main objective of higher education is to serve as a tool in the development of and its way forward to development. To achieve this, there is a need for decentralization of power at faculty level, close monitoring and controlling mechanism both academic as well as administrative side, accountability and responsibility at instructors side, proper periodical assessment at government and donor agency side. Above all responsible citizenship is more vital in achieving all the above. It enables individuals to take lead role in all fields of social, political, cultural, scientific and technological arenas. Ethiopia is getting revolutionized in the field of Higher Education. It has the will power and the human resource. The existing gap can be filled by the right vision in the right place in which the role of donor communities is vital. They should have the machinery to evaluate the utilization of funds. There should be proper direction and invigilation on higher education. Education is not only to fill the stomach; it should also light the fire and the Ethiopian higher education system needs that enlightenment. It is the right time to act and show the effect of international fraternity to give the spark for the fire which will definitely pilot its way forward for creativity and a bright future.

REFERENCES

Vasanda Desai and Robert B. Potter (Ed.), The Companion to Development Studies, Oxford University Press, New York, 2002.

Michael P. Todaro and Stephen C. Smith, Economic Development, Pearson Education Limited, England, 2006.

Tim Allen and Alan Thomas (Ed.), Poverty and Development in to the 21st Century, Oxford University Press, Oxford, 2000.

9

The Ethics of Care and Education: Cultivating a Culture of Care in PAREF Schools

Emylou C. Visaya, Philippines

When we think of people who know how to care, next to parents and people involved in charity or religious work, we normally single out teachers. For many, the idea of having an uncaring teacher is unthinkable since we presume that it is because people care that they go into teaching. Unfortunately, just as there exist uncaring parents in this world, we also meet uncaring teachers, and among those teachers who say that they do care for their students, some may do so without actually establishing a personal relationship of trust with the students, hence these students do not really feel cared for.

Dr. Nel Noddings is closely identified with the promotion of the ethics of care. A Lee L. Jacks Professor Emerita of Child Education at Stanford University and a Professor of Philosophy and Education at Columbia University, she believes that the first job of the schools is to care for its children, and that the school's main educational aim should be to encourage the growth of competent, caring, lovable and loving individuals (Noddings, 1997). For Noddings, it is imperative that schools educate students to develop the attitudes and skills required to sustain caring relationships and to create learning environments which teach students to care.

The importance of establishing caring relationships in schools can never be undermined. With the increasing aggression and violence we see in schools and beyond, there is a need to educate students to care and to practice caring in school, at home and in their community. Studies show that virtually all learning happens within the context of human relationships. The contacts teachers have with individual students affect how the students feel about themselves and what they are learning (Cohen, 1999). The extent to which students perceive teachers as caring is found to be predictive of motivational outcomes or how much effort students evince. The 1997 Add-Health study of over 90,118 adolescents in a stratified, random sample of 80 middle schools and high schools in the United States found that parent-family connectedness (i.e., a feeling of closeness to parents and family) and connectedness to school (i.e., a feeling of closeness to people in school) were protective factors against emotional distress, suicidal thoughts and behaviour, violence, delinquency, use of cigarettes, alcohol and marijuana and early sexual experimentation (Lickona and Davidson, 2005). Such relationships do not cure the problem but potentially they do make a profound difference.

In describing resilient children, Segal writes: "From studies conducted around the world, researches have distilled a number of factors that enable children of misfortune to beat the heavy odds against them. One factor turns out to be the presence in their lives of a charismatic adult—a person with whom they can identify and from whom they can gather strength. And in a surprising number of cases, that person turns out to be a teacher."

Our own experience tells us that feeling uncared for, unsafe and alone affects one's ability to think of others and to care for them. We all experience the need to have meaningful relationships and encounters with others, to be part of a group, to belong in order to be recognized and loved, and to defeat the terrible effects of loneliness. A person who is lonely feels that whatever happens to him has not the tiniest importance to anyone else; that what he thinks or says will never be heard with interest by anyone else, and that if he ceases to exist, everything would continue as before and no one would notice (Ferrucci, 2007). We all have experienced that when we are hurt, sick or wounded, we are prone to be engrossed in ourselves, to think more of our pain, and our need for healing and care. In these situations, a certain level of maturity is needed for someone to learn how to go beyond the hurt, and to think of and to care for others.

Nature of Caring Relations

Noddings explains the nature of caring relationships by examining how caring is actually experienced, that is, what are we like when we engage in caring encounters:

The phenomenological analysis of caring reveals the part each participant plays.

The one caring (or carer) is first of all attentive. This attention is receptive; it receives what the cared-for is feeling and trying to express. It is not merely diagnostic, measuring the cared-for against some pre-established ideal. Rather, it opens the carer to motivational displacement. When I care, my motive energy begins to flow towards the needs and wants of the cared-for. This does not mean that I will always approve of what the other wants, nor does it mean that I will never try to lead him or her to a better set of values, but I must take into account the feelings and desires that are actually there and respond as positively as my values and capacities allow. In a caring relation or encounter, the cared-for recognizes the caring and responds in some detectable manner. An infant smiles and wriggles in response to its mother's caregiving. A student may acknowledge her teacher's caring directly, with verbal gratitude, or simply pursue her own project more confidently. The receptive teacher can see that her caring has been received by monitoring her students' responses. Without an affirmative response from the cared-for, we cannot call an encounter or relation caring (Noddings, 2005).

Noddings explains that caring involves connection between the carer and the cared-for and a degree of reciprocity; that is, that both gain from the encounter in different ways and both give. Caring is a relation involving dialogue and exchange.

Noddings also highlights the distinction between caring-for and caring-about. Caring-for involves face-to-face encounters in which one person cares directly for another. Caring-about is something more general and takes us more into the public realm. We learn first what it means to be cared-for, then gradually we learn both to care for and, by extension, to care about others. We learn to care-about through our experience of being cared-for (Smith, 2004).

Care theory starts with an ideal home and moves outward—learning first what it means to be cared-for, then to care for intimate others, and finally to care about those we cannot care for directly (Noddings, 2002). Placing a special emphasis on the home as a site for educational encounter, Noddings views the home as the primary educator. As a consequence, she believes that every child should live in a home that has at least adequate material resources and attentive love, and that schools should include education for home life in their curriculum and should use the sort of methods found in the best homes to educate (Noddings, 2002).

Noddings has argued that education from the care perspective has four key components:

(a) Modeling where educators have to show in their behavior what it means to care?

(b) Dialogue where educators have to talk directly about their caring and help people to critique and evaluate their attempts to care?

(c) Practice where educators provide students with opportunities to practice caring and to reflect on that practice?

(d) Confirmation which is an act of affirming and encouraging the best in others? Noddings explains:

When we confirm someone, we identify a better self and encourage its development. To do this, we must know the other reasonably well. Otherwise we cannot see what the other is really striving for, what ideal he or she may long to make real. Formulas and slogans have no place in confirmation. We do not posit a single ideal for everyone and then announce "high expectations for all." Rather we recognize something admirable or at least acceptable, struggling to emerge in each person we encounter. The goal or attribute must be seen as worthy both by the person trying to achieve it and by us. We do not confirm people in ways we judge to be wrong (Noddings, 1998).

A Culture of Care in PAREF Schools

Established in 1977, PAREF stands for Parents for Education Foundation, Inc. After more than thirty years, it has established ten schools in different parts of the Philippines and continues to help other schools which have adopted some of PAREF's educational practices.

PAREF schools are single-gendered schools and affirm the importance of having healthy and caring family relationships as a foundation to better educate children. In PAREF, the school environment is that of a bright and cheerful home, where parents, students and school staff treat each other as members of a family.

Like Noddings, PAREF believes that parents are the primary character or moral educators of their children, that their home is the first school, and that parents recognize and value teachers as their partners. PAREF stresses the need for home-school collaboration. A good PAREF education is based on a healthy and caring family and school environment where the values of home and school are strengthened and harmonized, and where possible conflicts between home values and school values are avoided.

In a way, PAREF schools can be described as an ethical learning community where teachers, parents and students try to work collaboratively in order to help students succeed and do the right thing, and where all their curricular, co-curricular and extra-curricular programmes, practices, school traditions and activities are aligned to the integration of excellence, ethics and character (Lickona and Davidson, 2005).

PAREF schools try to ensure that each student is known, loved and cared for as a precious jewel. Teachers, parents, school staff, learning specialists, and youth professionals work collaboratively to help address the needs of each individual child. PAREF schools encourage a collaborative and caring culture where space for social and spiritual education, youth development programmes, parenting education, mentoring, family support and community development is provided.

Engaging Parents to Care More

PAREF believes that parents are the single strongest influence on their children's character and that it is the parents' primary responsibility to raise good, moral, respectful and caring children. This implies that parents should be equipped with the essential parenting knowledge and skills so they are able to build a home filled with moral rectitude, attentive love and care, and be able to demonstrate this love and care to their children.

To help parents be better parents, PAREF schools provide space, resources and create positions for family liaisons and coordination. An Office for Parent Activities and Formation managed by the Coordinator for Family Orientation takes care of organizing and coordinating activities where parents are involved. Parenting literacy courses are organized to make parents feel that they are cared-for and valued like the School for Parents, Family Visioning, Parents' Get-together or Forum, Mother-Daughter Activities, Father-Daughter Activities, Family Day, Family Outreach etc. Parents realize that the time they allot for these parenting activities offered by the school is an investment in their children's future as they learn how to care for themselves and their children better. The better and more caring parents they become, the better and more caring children they will raise with the hope that their children will, in turn, build stronger and more caring marriages and families later on.

Aside from parenting literacy courses, some parents are tapped to take an active role in school by being Parent Coordinators who serve as communication links between the families and the school, or as parent volunteers for committees on sports, academic and library programmes, outreach etc. Parents are also encouraged to come up with initiatives to help in the social and emotional education of their children and their children's friends. Some parents with their friends have banded together to set up girls' clubs offering activities that will enrich what is being offered in school; they are normally offered after school hours, beyond schooldays, at week-ends or during school holidays. These are opportunities for parents to care about others, not just for their own families.

The active involvement and physical presence of parents in these activities signal to their children that they care for them and care about others, and that they are worth their time and attention. Active parent involvement in PAREF schools is not a mere add-on but is an essential part of the instructional core because to be able to develop caring students, there is a need to have caring parents and teachers.

Teaching Students to Care

As mentioned earlier, care theorists believe that before anyone can care for and about others, one has to experience being cared for. The feeling of being cared for has to be fostered at home and strengthened in school.

A concrete way to make students in PAREF schools feel cared for is the presence of a mentoring programme. Research shows that mentoring is an effective strategy for working with young people. Studies have shown the effectiveness of mentoring in promoting resiliency and helping kids overcome adverse circumstances (Freedman, 1993).

The PAREF notion of mentoring follows the classical definition. A mentor is an older experienced guide who is acceptable to the young person, and who can help ease the transition to adulthood by a mix of challenge and support. The mentor is normally an unrelated adult, and the relationship between the mentor and the mentee is essentially private.

The PAREF Mentoring Programme is a programme of planned relationships where a student is paired off with an adult, normally a teacher or a school staff, who helps the child identify and draw out his or her hidden potentials, face difficulties, and reflect on his or her experiences and learnings. In PAREF schools, there is a mentor for each student, not just for those who have difficulties. Mentoring in PAREF has been mainstreamed as all students from Grade I to Year IV have access to this educational resource. The mentor individually chats with the student at least twice a month, and with the student's parents at least four times a year. In the chats with parents, the mentor talks about the child's personal development and academic performance: Her strengths and weaknesses, interests, work skills, study habits, achievements, failures, emotional difficulties (immaturity, confusion, personal conflicts, low self-esteem), family circumstances and climate (family warmth, affection, reasonable expectations and limits), interpersonal gifts or problems, school problems, helpful or unhelpful coping strategies the child has acquired etc. These face-to-face conversations help facilitate knowing the child more, and addressing his or her needs.

Since teenagers are more discriminating, high school students in most PAREF schools like Woodrose where I work as an academic coordinator normally get to choose their mentor. However, grade school students are assigned a mentor although requests for particular mentors on the part of the parents and students are usually accommodated depending on the availability and loading of the teachers and staff.

The PAREF idea of mentoring can be considered as a social and educational intervention. A PAREF mentor is, in a way, a youth professional based in school who serves as a guide and adviser for the child. The mentor also acts as a single point of contact as she works closely with the child's parents, teachers, class adviser, learning and support service specialists so the needs of each child are met in a focused and integrated way. Mentoring in PAREF is also meant to facilitate the communication of shared thoughts, feelings, caring acts, understood agreements and disagreements. It is meant to lead to a communion of minds and hearts where there is no fear of deception or misunderstanding. It also tries to facilitate the building of friendship by keeping the mentor and the student paired together for several years through mutual consent, and by providing time in school for dialogue to happen and for the relationship to mature.

Young people who were interviewed in a study identified key elements of good mentoring: Trust, confidentiality, reciprocity, mutual respect, support and challenge. They also listed the factors that inhibit a good mentoring relationship: An authoritarian approach, a lack of respect, taking control away from the person, intrusiveness and forcing the pace (Philip, K. and Hendry, L.P., 2000).

Trust is important in establishing a truly caring relationship. To establish trust entails spending time with the person and giving him or her attention. Establishing a relationship can never be hurried. It takes time and requires hard work to know the other person and recognize the person as someone unique. Attention is a form of care while inattention, a lack of it. Attention is warm and caring; inattention, cold and hard. If there is no attention, there is no caring, there is no trust, there is no relationship.

To establish trust, empathy is also needed. Unfortunately, in many relationships, judgments, not empathy, reigns. Judgment is normally linked with the desire to control or to feel superior. In caring relationships, being judgmental is avoided. Young people normally just want to be with someone who listens to them and whom they can open up to without being judged.

Mentoring in PAREF schools facilitates that each student in school feels cared for. It can be better understood under the light of Noddings' idea of a caring relationship which serves as the best foundation for pedagogical activity and stresses moral interdependence and responsibility for another's moral perfection. As the mentors listen to the students, engage them in dialogue, and show them that they care for them through their words and actions, they are able to gain their trust. Hence the students will more readily accept what the mentors suggest or advise them to do because they do not see their mentors' efforts to help them as interference.

Aside from mentoring, the school also provides opportunities for the students to practice caring. It offers spiritual literacy courses as a way to develop a loving and caring relationship and friendship with God. It also creates partnerships with youth organizations and community development programmes to provide more opportunities for the young people to establish caring relationships with other persons and to care about others by contributing useful service in a variety of ways. Partnerships with youth organizations lead to the establishment of friendship and care camps, outreach activities, service learning, study and cultural tours etc. which help the students form caring relationships with other young people and learn how to care about others in need. The school also encourages initiatives among high school students to come up with programmes and activities meant to serve the less-privileged and the sick. Monthly visits to the sick and dying in the hospitals, academic tutorials to the less-privileged, visits to the aged are organized.

Caring for the Mentors and Teachers

Mentoring is not only limited to students. Each teacher and staff also has a mentor, usually a staff member chosen for his or her understanding and appreciation of the PAREF philosophy. The mentor is different from the subject head or coach that each teacher has in school since the latter focuses more on honing the teacher's professional competence. PAREF realizes that mentoring as a strategy to form caring students will not be effective if it is implemented by teachers who have a negative mind-set and who do not truly understand and appreciate the PAREF philosophy. PAREF believes that teacher-mentors should be reliable sources of authority whose behaviour is worth modeling since the attitude of teachers often determines the success or failure of school programmes.

Similar to the parenting courses offered to parents, training courses for teachers to be effective and caring mentors are offered like courses on the PAREF philosophy, mentoring, guidance and counseling, communicating with parents, developmental psychology, philosophical anthropology, etc. Mentors are also supervised and guided by a coordinator in each level (i.e., primary, intermediate and high school). In the Management Committee and School Board level, there are also similar positions for this task to ensure the smooth functioning of the programme.

School administrators also take time to talk with each teacher and staff to get to know them more and to ask for their feedback on how the school is run so that each one feels valued and cared for. There is also a provision for a staff dialogue where the staff can discuss issues and concerns with management. To facilitate bonding and friendship among teachers and staff, activities like Teachers' Day Celebration, Summer Outing, Milestone Awards,

Christmas Celebrations, Birthday Celebrations, Directors' Day Celebrations have been institutionalized. Teachers and staff are also encouraged to come up with outreach activities or "volountourism" activities during holidays to facilitate the cultivation of caring relationships in school and to help them practice caring for and about others.

To implement these programmes and networks of care, the school tries to provide strong administrative support by providing appropriate time, personnel and resources as it believes that "effectively educating minds and hearts rests on quality relationships between the parent and the child, between the teacher and the student" and that these relationships should be characterized by a genuine and loving concern for the lives entrusted to their care (Udani, 2006).

Schools should provide schooling not only for the head but also for the heart. They should make as their moral priority the challenge to care for their students, parents and teachers and help them to practice caring for and caring about others. As Noddings puts it: "We should want more from our educational efforts than adequate academic achievement, and we will not achieve even that meager success unless our children believe that they themselves are cared for and learn to care for others."

REFERENCES

Cohen, Jonathan (1999). Educating Minds and Hearts: Social Emotional Learning and the Passage into Adolesence. Teachers College, Columbia University.

Ferrucci, Pierre (2007). The Power of Kindness. New York: Penguin.

Freedman (1993). The Kindness of Strangers: Adult Mnetors, Urban Youth and the New Voluntarism. San Francisco: Jossev-Bass.

Halford, J.M. (1998). "Longing for the Sacred in Schools: A Conversation with Nel Noddings."

Lickona, Thomas and Davidson, Matthew (2005). Smart and Good High Schools: Integrating Excellence and Ethics for Success in School, Work and Beyond. New York: Center for the 4th and 5th Rs (Respect and Responsibility). Washington,D.C.: Character Education Partnership.

Noddings, Nel (1997). "A Morally Defensible Mission for Schools in the 21st Century." Transforming Public Education: A New Course for America's Future." New York: Teachers College Press, 27-37.

Noddings, Nel (2005). "Caring in Education," the encyclopedia of informal education, www.infed.org/thinkers/noddings.htm. Last updated December 28, 2007.

Philip, K. and Henry, L.P. (2000). "Making sense of mentoring or mentoring making sense? Reflections on the mentoring process by adult mentors with young people," Journal of Community and Applied Psychology.

Smith, M.K. (2004) "Nel noddings, the ethics of care and education," the encyclopedia of informal education, www.infed.org/thinkers/noddings.htm. Last updated" April 17, 2005.

Udani, Delia (2006). "Message from the Executive Director," Phases.

10

Developing an Indigenous Science Curriculum for Kindergarten in the Philippines

Greg Tabios Pawilen, Philippines
Dr. Manabu Sumida, Japan

Background of the Study

All people live in a culturally diverse society characterized by a variety of culture defined by race, ethnicity, gender, socio-economic status, religion, and family background (Stremmel, 1997). Thus, culture has become one of the most interesting topics of local and international discussion and research because of the growing importance of understanding culture particularly its indigenous knowledge component in enhancing researches and other disciplinary studies (Abueva, 1999), and it has always been an essential component of all social activities even for science (Gardner, 2000; Pertierra, 2004; Roncoli, 2004). In fact, the UNESCO Universal Declaration of Cultural Diversity (2001) advocates that cultural diversity should be *preserved encouraged* and *shared* among people and nation through curriculum and other educational programmes.

This study discusses the process of developing an *indigenous science curriculum* for kindergarten in the Philippines. It is inspired by a vision to utilize the rich experience and indigenous knowledge of the people to enhance and enrich the science curriculum for the kindergarten level. This study aims to make the kindergarten science curriculum more relevant and responsive to the daily-life culture of the learners and to make culture a part of science. In this chapter, important data from the socio-cultural systems of selected communities are analyzed and discussed in order to determine the context in which the curriculum is situated.

In this study, the development of an indigenous science curriculum for kindergarten is viewed as one way of making education more relevant and responsive for young children from different cultural background. In this chapter, the term *indigenous* is viewed as synonymous to the terms like *community-based, ethnic,* or *local.* Consequently the term *indigenous people* refer to a group of individuals sharing a common ancestry, culture, history, and language.

What is Indigenous Science?

In this study, Indigenous Science (IS) is defined as a body of knowledge that consciously or unconsciously uses scientific process skills to support its claims. The process of indigenous science is guided by the peoples' culture and values such as ethics, spirituality, sense of responsibility, and love for nature. Indigenous science is also composed of traditional knowledge that is product of peoples' interaction with nature and daily-life experiences in the community.

One way to define indigenous science is by understanding the unique, traditional, and local knowledge that exist within, and developed around the specific conditions of people in a particular geographic area. Communities have their own indigenous methods for imparting knowledge and ways of deriving a livelihood from the environment, and information, insight, and techniques that are passed down and improved in every generation that cover different areas of knowledge.

What is an Indigenous Science Curriculum for Kindergarten?

The indigenous science curriculum for kindergarten consists of learning experiences, process skills, and concepts that are responsive, relevant, appropriate, and compatible with the culture of the learners. This type of curriculum is based on the principle and framework advocated by Bransford, Brown and Cocking (2000) on learner-centered curriculum that pays attention to the learner's knowledge, skills, attitudes, and beliefs. It clings to the idea that teaching science is a cultural activity that includes what Stigler and Hiebert (1999) called *cultural scripts*—that composed of beliefs, knowledge and views about the world that are shared among the learners.

Ideally, an indigenous science curriculum for kindergarten is a kind of curriculum that reflects Dewey's (1859-1952) idea of *democratic education* that enables the learners to perceive meaning in their culture and experience. This type of curriculum enables children in indigenous communities to learn science in a meaningful way by connecting science knowledge with indigenous knowledge. It is a way of letting young children know and remember that over centuries, human beings have been producing knowledge and strategies enabling them to survive in a balanced relation with their natural and social environment.

It develops and equips children with scientific knowledge and useful life skills, and presents the community as a perfect laboratory for conducting science observations. It adheres to the idea of Kuhn (1962) that science and society are inseparable since science is a part of a social and personal history thereby making science as a cultural and intellectual activity.

The indigenous science curriculum for kindergarten advocates a different perspective of looking at the world of science and it emphasizes that scientific knowledge is valued in different ways base on a particular cultural context. This curriculum advocates the use of the local language as the medium of instruction in science, and it solely believes that science curriculum, as pointed out by Michie (2000), should facilitate a two-way exchange of scientific knowledge and cultural understanding.

Furthermore, the indigenous science curriculum for kindergarten connects what children learned in school science with issues and problems that arise in other disciplines and especially with the society's culture and history. Linking indigenous knowledge and science in kindergarten provides the following dimensions that serve as a framework for the development of the indigenous science curriculum for kindergarten:

1. *Construct knowledge* so that young children understand how experiences, personal views and how other peoples' ideas influence the development of science concepts and scientific knowledge.
2. *Use instructional strategies* that promote academic success for children of different cultures.
3. *Integrate contents and activities* that reflect the learners' culture, history, traditions and indigenous knowledge in the science curriculum.
4. *Utilize community's cultural, material and human resources* in the development and implementation of the science curriculum.

These ideas are relevant to the curriculum framework of a developmentally – appropriate practices (Bredekamp and Copple,

2006; NAEYC, 2005) and are important factors in designing early childhood curriculum.

Why is it Important to Develop an Indigenous Science Curriculum in the Philippines?

The Philippines is an archipelago and most Filipino children belong to different indigenous cultural communities. However, many teachers have had very little training on how to effectively instruct such cultural diversity in the curriculum and there are insufficient indigenous instructional materials particularly for preschools (Barsaga, 1988; Lupdag, 1999) particularly for science. Most preschool institutions in the country are influenced by western education by using imported instructional materials. Constantino (1982) referred to this western-oriented education as miseducation of the Filipinos. Arinto (1996) also opines that that type of knowledge learned in school often alienates people from their culture and their communities. Therefore, this type of situation challenges schools to meet the needs of the growing population of kindergarten learners from different cultural communities in the country.

The Philippines also face the challenge to develop strong science and schools are entrusted with the task to develop a culture of science starting from young children. Science is taught as a subject in the kindergarten curriculum however, the problem of teaching science to kindergarten children in the Philippines is its inability to present science knowledge in the context of the learners. Science is a universal theme however its applications vary from different context and culture so educators need to link science concepts and the application of science skills in the context of the learners especially among young children who are beginning to study science. This kind of situated pedagogy hopes to increase the chance for learners to feel ownership of their education and reduces the conditions that produce their alienation in learning scientific knowledge and skills.

Theoretically, young children come to formal education with a range of prior knowledge, skills, beliefs and concepts that significantly influence what they notice about the environment and how they organize and interpret it (Bransford, Brown, & Cocking, 2000). In relation to this, Hartman and Glasgow (2002) postulate that children's ideas in science are personal and social constructions that are affected by their personal experience and the culture they live in. It is essential then that science should be taught in the context of the Filipino learners' culture, conditions, needs, and history. Indigenous science knowledge also influences children's prior knowledge.

This prior knowledge, the indigenous science curriculum for young children is a liberating force to broaden the understanding of the learners about the relationship of science, culture, and daily life experience. Furthermore, the study to develop an indigenous science curriculum for kindergarten can serve as model for developing an indigenous curriculum and in promoting science literacy for public and private kindergarten schools in the Philippines and in other countries with indigenous group of peoples.

Methodology

The study includes three phases. Figure 1 shows the procedure in order to gather vital data that are imperative for the whole process of developing the indigenous science curriculum. Phases 1 and 2 constitute the important phases of curriculum planning that help define the content of the. Phase 3 constitutes the design phase of the curriculum emphasizing culturally – relevant and responsive science concepts and skills in the kindergarten curriculum.

Figure 1: Research Procedure

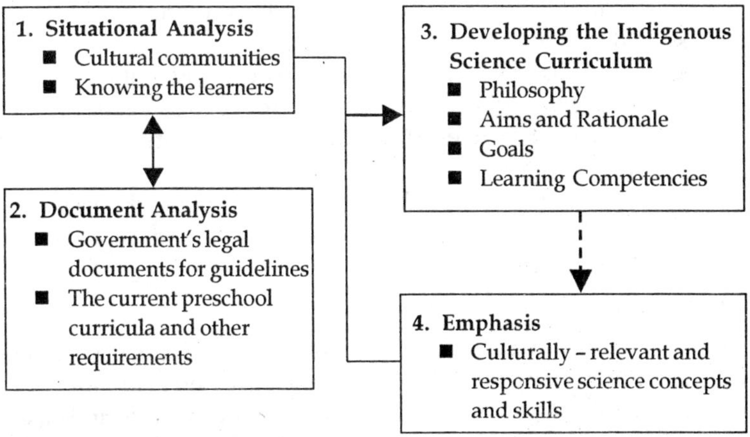

Phase 1 - Situational Analysis

1. A survey questionnaire and actual community visit were used to gather important data from the communities. An open discussion was also done to introduce and to exchange

ideas with the people regarding the proposed indigenous science curriculum for kindergarten, and to develop awareness of community folks of their possible role in curriculum development.

2. An open and guided interview was conducted for young kindergarten children with the help of the teachers during the children's circle time so that the children will not feel shy to express their answers to the questions. The interview focuses on activities they enjoyed most in school, and the topics of their interest. To supplement the result of the interview from young children, teachers were asked to answer a survey questionnaire about the socio-economic status of the children and some perceived problems in the education of kindergarten children.
3. Science educators, preschool teachers, and administrators were invited to give their insights on the study to develop an indigenous science curriculum for kindergarten. Purposive sampling was used in selecting the participants for the colloquia.

Research Participants

1. *Community Elders*: Randomly selected from people who hold socially responsible positions such as community officials and community elders.
2. *Young People*: Randomly selected from the identified cultural communities with an average age of 18 to 25 years.
3. *Teachers*: Science educators, preschool teachers, and administrators.
4. *Kindergarten Children*: Around 81 kindergarten children from selected schools. 48 are female and 32 are male. Their age ranges from 5 to 6 years old.

Research Locale

The research involves 30 different cultural communities located in northern Philippines. Purposive sampling was used to identify local communities that were visited. The communities are selected based on the following criteria:

(a) They must be a representation of an agricultural community, fishing villages, and upland villages where indigenous or cultural communities are located.

(b) They must share a common local language.

(c) They must have either an existing kindergarten school or a day-care center.

Phase 2 - Documentary Analysis

Existing documents and studies from the Department of Education and from the local government office are gathered and analyzed to examine the profile of Filipino kindergarten learners particularly in the selected local communities. The government requirements and guidelines on early childhood education in the Philippines were also examined.

III. Findings and Results of the Study

1. Result from the Situational Analysis

Two curriculum sources were examined through an interview using a survey questionnaire: (1) the community– that includes the needs, problems and concerns, and community resources and cultural aspects, can be utilized to support the development of an indigenous science curriculum; (2) the learners–that include learners' profile, interest, and attitudes towards schooling. According to Tyler (1949), knowledge about the community and the learners are essential curriculum sources.

Part I–Immediate Concerns and Problems of the Communities

The result of the survey questionnaire answered by community elders, teachers, and young people shows that the immediate concerns and problems of their communities are still the basic effects of poverty. These are: (1) Poor health services; (2) Inadequate water supply; (3) Insufficient energy supply; (4) Environmental destruction and (5) Poor transportation facilities. In relation to these problems and concerns, the result of the survey questionnaire reveals that all the respondents from different communities believe that science education can help solve the problems in their communities.

Their responses to the questionnaire show that all the respondents believe that science develops skills that are needed in their daily life. They also believe that science provides knowledge by offering alternative solutions and strategies to address their problems and concerns. The community elders express optimism that their lives could have been better if they have sufficient knowledge about science and technology. All the community folks believe that scientific knowledge is one of the reasons why other countries are progressive.

This result shows that people give high regard to science and technology's power to transform their living conditions. All the respondents strongly believe that the transformation of the society is predominantly shaped by scientific knowledge and by technical change. The responses from the people support the claim of Nowotny, Scott and Gibbons (2001) that there is a growing urgency and convictions among communities that science determines and shapes not only technical processes and economic systems but also social structures.

Another important result from the situational analysis is the identification of community resources and cultural aspects can be utilized to support the development of an indigenous science curriculum for kindergarten. Based on the result of the questionnaire, some communities serve as trustees or guardians of communal lands (mostly forest/mountains) they inherited from their ancestors and these are classified as public property. These communal forest reserves sometimes serve as laboratories of students for science and other classes in elementary and secondary schools. These properties contain various species of plant and animal life that can be good for student to do science observations and investigations. The communities have other natural resources such as farmlands for agricultural purposes, and rivers and streams that are sources of water for agricultural and household purposes. Some families also maintain fishponds for propagation of fresh water fishes. All of these resources are useful for studying ecosystem, plant and animal habitat, and earth science.

The result of the survey questionnaire also shows that there are several cultural practices and traditions that are still used in the community like: Dances, literatures (stories and poems), songs and chants, superstitious beliefs, festivals, games and sports. These cultural practices and traditions are concrete and creative expressions of how human beings view nature in relation to their observation and experiences. The songs and chants for example contain language metaphors of how people view certain objects in the environment in relation to their daily life. The music of dances, the poems and other stories are dense with meaning, combining metaphoric reference to nature in descriptions of human action. Taylor (1995) claims that science encompasses all other topics, and is found in relationships, in the environment, art, music, movements, and language. Hence, science can be found in these activities. These are valuable and useful in the indigenous science curriculum for kindergarten.

According to the respondents, although modernity is now taking its place in the lives of the people, indigenous knowledge composed of *practices, tools, skills, values, beliefs* and *institutions* are still observed by people in their daily lives. This indigenous knowledge is very useful and is already embedded in their daily lives. These indigenous knowledge are parallel to some areas in science like: (1) *Classification*—understanding of specific elements of factors in the environment, such as plants, animals, soil, water, air, weather, and other environmental phenomena; (2) *Technology and Management of Resources*—the development and use of traditional technology in daily lives, and management of resources for the present and future generations; and (3) *Ecology, Evolution, and Systems*—the understanding and awareness of the life processes—this includes origins, interrelatedness of living and non-living things in the environment.

All of the teachers and young people support the idea of the community elders that indigenous knowledge should be transmitted to the younger generation to maintain their cultural identity and historical heritage. They believe that indigenous knowledge could serve as guide for the people to live in harmony with nature and other human beings. The indigenous knowledge also provides moral lessons and values among the people to enable them to behave as good stewards of the natural resources. Understanding indigenous knowledge system as an integral part of the cultural heritage of the people is essential in determining the aims, objectives, and contents of the indigenous science curriculum for kindergarten.

Part II–Learners' Profile

Information about the learners is an important source of curriculum goals and objectives. Hence in this part of the study, the socio-economic profile of young children, their feelings about schooling and their activities and topics of interest in school were analyzed.

The result of the survey questionnaires from teachers shows that only 60 per cent of the total number of young children in each cultural community attends preschool classes. These young children enroll in either a Daycare center or in a private kindergarten school. Children who do not attend preschool classes have several reasons like: (1) Parents can't afford to pay their tuition fees; (2) Children are not motivated to go to school; (3) The school is to too far from children's homes; or (4) Parents see preschool education as not necessary for their young children.

The children who attend preschool classes in community schools belong to either poor or middle class families. Those families who can afford to pay tuition fees send their children to big schools in the town or city proper. Most of the children who attend preschool classes in the community schools go to school by walking (with accompanying parent) or through a tricycle that serves as their school service in lieu of a school bus.

In relation to how young children feel about schooling, the result of the open and guided interview for young kindergarten children, during the children's circle time, reveals that 71 out of 81 kindergarten children in 3 local schools responded that they feel happy and excited and they enjoy going to school because of the following reasons: (1) They are excited to meet friends; (2) They enjoyed listening to stories; (3) They enjoyed playing and doing class activities e.g. writing, drawing, doing experiments, field trips; and (4) They want to meet their teachers everyday. The other 10 pupils responded that they feel tired and bored in school because they do a lot of school works such as: Answering workbooks, doing assignments, and reading.

The children were also asked what activities they enjoyed doing and what topics or lessons they are interested to learn in school. Tyler (1949) suggests that learners' interest must be identified so that they can serve as focus for educational attention. Based on the responses, all the 81 kindergarten children like the following activities most in school:

1. *Play time*: They like toys and they want to play with their best friends.
2. *Story time*: They like listening to stories, fables, and legends.
3. *Fieldtrips*: They like going to the beach, visiting farms and see what the farmers do, visiting museums, and going to far places.
4. *School festivals*: They enjoyed eating foods, doing traditional sports and games, participating in different contest, and joining song and dance presentations.
5. *Art activities*: They like drawing pictures of plants, animals, and other objects.

These could suggest the use of local toys or artifacts in teaching science concepts, the use of local stories as spring board for science lessons, the possibility of conducting a science festival highlighting several science projects and science-related activities, and the use of art to illustrate science concepts.

Table 1 shows that young children have a lot of topics of interest. It is surprising to note that most of these topics are all related to science. Therefore, it is possible that these topics can be included in the indigenous science curriculum.

Table–1
Summary List of Kindergarten Children's Topics of Interest in School

Plants especially fruits and flowers	Transportation (cars, jeep, airplane, motorbikes, cart)
Weather (rainbows, clouds, rain, winds)	Music (songs and dances)
Stories (Bible stories, fables, fairy tales, legends)	People (history, culture, heroes, heroines)
Water formations (sea, river, streams, falls)	Land formations (mountains, fields, valleys, volcanoes)
Celestial bodies (sun, moon, stars)	Communication (TV, radio, telephone)
Animals (farm animals, zoo animals, pets, insects)	

In the process of the interview, the children were also asked what science-related activities they enjoyed most in school? The responses are:

1. Doing simple experiments.
2. Observing things like insects and plants.
3. Going to the farms to observe plants and animals/insects habitats.
4. Making fruit salad during their lesson on "fruits and food nutrients."
5. Field trips.
6. Drawing plants, different objects, and animals/insects.

These further strengthen the claim that children are passionate to learn science in school. They want to move, to observe, to do things, to experience the adventure of exploring the natural environment and to experience the joy of finding out things to satisfy their curiosity. It was observed that kindergarten children love activities where they can move or manipulate something and they are always curious of finding out new things especially on those that are related to their immediate environment.

To add more substance to the interview with young children, kindergarten teachers were also interviewed if there are opportunities available for children to see and explore the context of their daily life and culture in the present science curriculum. In response, several examples were enumerated by the teachers like: (1) Using local children's literatures like stories and poems as motivation to young children during science lessons; (2) Identifying examples of indigenous technology used by people in the community; (3) Inviting community elders as resource person during class sessions; and (4) Field trip around the community. These existing practices are very important and could be a good start to support in the development of an indigenous science curriculum for the young children.

2. *Results from the Consultative Colloquia*

Three groups of people ranging from community elders, kindergarten teachers, and young people were invited to share ideas related to the study. First, the respondents were asked to answer a questionnaire containing five questions. After that, a discussion was done based on the responses.

Question No. 1: Do you Agree that Indigenous Knowledge should be Part of the School Science Curriculum?

The result shows that 75 out of the 90 respondents agreed on the development of indigenous science curriculum for kindergarten, and 15 from young people's group did not agree. The main reason of those who agree is that, this is one way to keep their cultural heritage alive and to continue the cultural traditions that molded their lives as a group of people. Part of their indigenous knowledge are important skills, values, and thoughts that influence their understanding of the environment and to other ideas like scientific ideas. Those who disagree simply believe that local communities should adapt itself to the global changes and they believe that patronizing indigenous knowledge is a hindrance to modernity. These results are necessary to understand the sentiments of the different sectors involved about the possibility of integrating indigenous knowledge in the school science curriculum.

Question No. 2: What Community Values and Beliefs should be Included in the Indigenous Science Curriculum for Kindergarten?

All the respondents (community elders, the young people, and the kindergarten teachers) agreed that some local cultural values like: Conservation of resources, industry, diligence, cooperation with others, and perseverance should be included and developed in the kindergarten science curriculum.

Reflecting on these responses, these community values are relevant or consistent with the scientific attitudes, attitudes in science, and attitudes to science identified by Johnston (2000). Johnston grouped these set of attitudes into four types namely:

1. Motivating attitudes;
2. Cooperating attitudes;
3. Practical attitudes; and
4. Reflective attitudes.

Accordingly, these attitudes can be developed alongside with science process skills and conceptual understanding. Likewise, the community values identified by the respondents can develop learners' curiosity about the natural world and in understanding scientific phenomena.

The community elders also suggest that some of their cultural beliefs should be taught in the kindergarten science curriculum such as:

1. The land is a source of life. It is a precious gift from the creator.
2. The earth is revered as "Mother Earth". It is the origin of their identity as people.
3. All living and non-living things are interconnected and interdependent.
4. Human beings are stewards/trustee of the land with a responsibility to preserve it.
5. People should conserve natural resources. Nature is a friend to human beings – they need respect and proper care.

These beliefs are relevant to science. Lederman (1998) postulates that science is a way of knowing, and there are values and beliefs inherent to the development of scientific knowledge. Hence, these identified cultural values and beliefs can be good foundation for developing positive values towards science. However the idea of having a "creator" who creates things is a religious matter that needs careful consideration in science.

Question No. 3: What Skills should be Developed in the Indigenous Science Curriculum for Kindergarten?

The community elders do not have any specific answer to this question. Their lack of to learn science when they are young and their lack of knowledge of what is taught in kindergarten are some factors that hinder them to identify skills to be developed. However, the group of young people identified two important skills that they want young children to learn in school–science like: Life skills and critical thinking skills. The kindergarten teachers also added the importance of developing science process skills among young children.

Question No. 4: What Language should be used in Teaching Indigenous Science to Young Children?

Table–2
Perceptions of Community Peoples and Kindergarten Teachers on the Medium of Instruction for Teaching Indigenous Science

Language	*Ilocano*	*English*	*Filipino*
Teachers (N = 30)	16	5	9
Community Elders (N = 30)	30	0	0
Young People (N = 30)	6	24	0
Total = 90	**52**	**29**	**9**

The result of the questionnaire as shown in Table 2 reveals that majority of the respondents prefers the used of the local language *Ilocano* as the medium of instruction. They explained that this language is easier to understand for young children because they speak Ilocano at home and they express their ideas and feelings using this language. Furthermore Ilocano language is part of their cultural heritage. While they recognized the importance of learning English, still they maintain their view that English is foreign to young children. They suspect that the reason for the failure of teaching science is because children cannot express their ideas in English, which is the medium of instruction for science in school in the Philippines. According to them, using Ilocano as a medium of instruction for science enables the learners to relate their daily-life experiences to what they learn in science.

Those who agree for the use of English in teaching science argued that English is important for children to learn and master specially those government officials in the Philippines stress the use of English as a medium of instruction. They also believed that mastering English language is an important tool to understand the ideas of science. Since all the materials in schools are in English, it is therefore necessary that children should master the use of the English language.

The respondents who believed that science should be taught in Filipino gave a simple reason that, Filipino is the national language, and therefore using Filipino as a medium of instruction for science is one way of enriching the use of the language in the academe. This small group raised the issue of nationalism. According to them using Filipino for teaching science is a patriotic act.

Reflecting on the result in Table 2, the dominant acceptance of using the local language as the medium of instruction provides a good foundation for learning indigenous science curriculum. Based on the innovative literacy efforts documented in the *IK Notes* (Leauter, 2004), instruction in the local language and the use of teaching materials based on local language tend to be more successful in achieving higher literacy rates. The use of local language is not only more effective, it underscores the value of cultural norms and practices in development planning and practice. Using the local language also gives meaning and context to the scientific ideas learned in school. It embodies the genius perspective and identity of the indigenous people to any idea. Language is a reflection of the people – their lives and culture.

Question No. 5: How Indigenous Knowledge or Cultural Practices Should be Included in the Indigenous Science Curriculum for Kindergarten?

Based on the questionnaire, all the 90 respondents opine that lessons containing cultural content, themes, and perspectives should be integrated in the kindergarten science curriculum while several cultural elements such as foods, holidays, and existing practices should be featured in the science curriculum to make the science curriculum relevant to the context of the learners. During the discussion, the respondents suggested strategies that can be use in integrating indigenous knowledge in the science curriculum are:

1. Integrating indigenous knowledge in the curriculum content.

2. Community immersion to do observation and hands-on experience.
3. Inviting elders from the community in school to serve as resource speaker.
4. Using cultural artifacts and crafts in the classroom.
5. Using folklores and literatures whenever it is relevant to the lesson.

3. *Results from the Documentary Analysis*

Several public documents related to the study were reviewed and analyzed. The result of the analysis found out that several laws in the Philippines provide requirements and prerequisites for developing any educational programme for indigenous local communities. Article II, Section 22 and Article XIV, Sections 2, 4, and 17 of the 1987 Philippine Constitution, and the Republic Act No. 8371 also known as "The Indigenous Peoples Rights Act of 1997" advocate a curriculum for indigenous communities/indigenous people that: (1) respond to community needs; (2) within the framework of national unity and development; (3) preserves and develops the cultures, traditions, and institutions of the people; and (4) promotes cultural integrity.

Republic Act No. 8980 also encourages the organizing and developing of a curriculum that focuses on children's total development according to individual needs and socio-cultural background (Sec. 5 a.). According to this law, the curriculum should: *Integrate local learning experiences and indigenous learning materials* (Sec. 4. c), and *shall use the child's first language as the medium of instruction* (Sec. 5 a.).

The Department of Education (DepEd) in the Philippines also provides a policy that any curricula that are developed and offered to Indigenous Peoples (IP) should be: *Flexible without undermining the balance between the attainments of the core learning competencies that every Filipino learner should master in the community and the indigenous culture* (DepEd Order 42 S. 2004).

The Department of Education provides suggested contents of the different subjects. Science is identified under the subject "Sensory-Perceptual Skills". Under this subject are nine different themes or topics: (1) Personal identification; (2) Personal cleanliness and safety; (3) Plants; (4) Animals; (5) Matter; (6) Water; (7) Light; (8) Weather; and (9) Time. The curriculum emphasizes basic skills in observing, describing, comparing and classifying. The lessons in this subject are designed using simple science and health as its content (DECS Order No. 107, S. 1989).

4. The Contents of the Indigenous Science Curriculum for Kindergarten

In selecting and developing the curriculum contents, the researcher draws implication from the results of the situational analysis and the interviews conducted in the communities. Likewise, the nature of the society, and the interest and needs of the learners are carefully considered in selecting the contents. The aims, goals, and content of the indigenous science curriculum for kindergarten emphasize on the importance learning science in relation to the nature of the learner - his/her interest, prior knowledge, concerns, language, and socio-cultural background.

Table-3
Aims and Goals of the Indigenous Science Curriculum for Kindergarten

The indigenous science curriculum for kindergarten aims to:

1. Develop science basic process skills, knowledge, and values among the kindergarten learners for deeper understanding of their community environment.
2. Develop a strong foundation and interest for learning science.
3. Develop appreciation of the role of science in enhancing the quality of life in the community.
4. Make science culturally responsive, compatible, and relevant to the learners by utilizing science-related indigenous knowledge in the curriculum.

The goals of the curriculum aim to develop a learner who:

- Learns basic science concepts that revolve around daily-life experiences.
- Applies scientific concepts and skills in a given socio-cultural environment.
- Develops science attitudes and desirable values in relationship with nature.
- Understands the practical application of science in real-life situations.

The content of the curriculum is organized into different themes related to: (1) life science (2) physical science (3) earth and other heavenly bodies. Table 4 shows the summary of the content of the indigenous science curriculum for kindergarten. It also shows how the identified curriculum themes of the indigenous science curriculum are relevant to the science curriculum contents for preschool provided by the Department of Education. The contents of the curriculum are also organized in a way that it should meet the suggested contents of the science curriculum for preschool in the Philippines.

An important way of setting appropriate context to the content or themes of the indigenous science curriculum is to understand the peoples' culture. For example, the Ilocano people always regard themselves as one family or one group. They value cooperation and unity in accomplishing their tasks and other responsibilities. This provides a framework for organizing the themes of the curriculum by emphasizing the relationship of science to the community as a group of people doing science and learning science: "*science and us*" that is why the themes start with either "*we are*" or "*we can*".

Table–4
Content Themes of the Proposed Indigenous Science Curriculum for Kindergarten

Science Areas	*Themes of the Indigenous Science Curriculum*	*Related Topics in the Science Curriculum for Kindergarten in the Philippines*
Life Sciences	■ We are Special (Human Body/Health)	■ Personal identification; Personal cleanliness and safety
	■ We Can Recognize Different Plants and Animals Around the Community (Plants and Animals)	■ Plants and Animals
Physical Sciences	■ We can Recognize Different Things Around Our Community (Non-living Things/Materials/Air/Water).	■ Matter; Non–living Things
	■ We can Recognize the Importance and Use of Energy in Our Community	■ Energy; Light; Force; Air
Earth and Other Heavenly Bodies	■ We Live in Planet Earth (Seasons/Climate/Weather/Water & Land Formations)	■ Weather; Time; Earth
	■ We Can Recognize Heavenly Bodies in the Sky (Sun, Moon, Stars, Planets)	■ Heavenly Bodies

consortium where the main problem usually is the bureaucratic (and legal) task of recognition of the qualifications and degrees of the other universities as owns (because students of one university who have taken the universities courses in the other universities are registered in the original one).

The map in Figure 1 shows the territory covered by the nine Spanish public universities belonging to the G9 group (www.uni-g9.net), and covering 50 per cent of all the Spanish territory.

Figure 1: The G9 Catchment Area, with Over 240,000 Potential Students

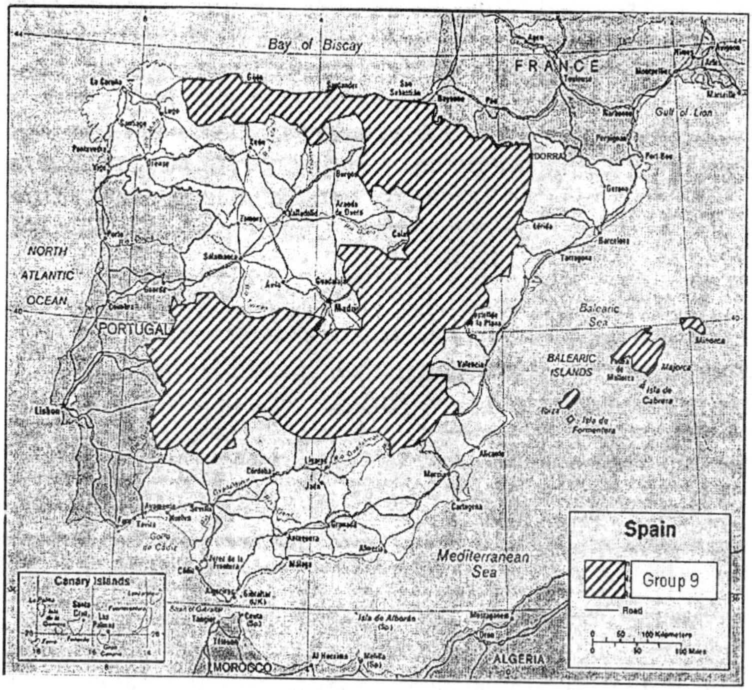

The group, with over 240,000 potential students, was created in 1997 with the common objective of "promoting the co-operation among university institutions belonging to the group in activities regarding teaching and research as well as management and services", but at the same time maintaining the autonomy of each individual university. Mobility of students and recognition of the studies done at other universities of the group are promoted. Its "Shared Virtual Campus" for eLearning allows students from any university in the group to study certain subjects of the other universities on-line. Table 1 gives some figures on its actual size:

Table–1
Numbers of Subjects and Students in the G9 Virtual Campus

Academic Year	*2001-02*	*02-03*	*03-04*	*04-05*	*05-06*	*06-07*	*07-08*
Subjects	15	23	42	61	68	72	86
Students	390	945	1800	2500	3800	3950	4744

Teaching materials and mid-term evaluations are supplied through the Internet from any computer that is connected. Most subjects are grouped into 3 itineraries: "eEnterprise", "ICT in Education", and "Environment and Sustainable Development." Completing 18 credits in at least three different modules of one same itinerary grants the student a "University Diploma." Another highlight of these policies is the 2nd edition of the "University Master in Information and Communication Technologies and Virtual Training Environments", open to students from any part of the world, and studied entirely on-line.

The two main advantages of this initiative over presential teaching at university level are: *(a)* Any student from a university in the G9 group may register and study subjects from other universities in it without having to move from his/her own home; *(b)* Every university will legally recognize the subjects taught at the Virtual Campus –which implies acknowledging the capacity of professors from other G9 universities to evaluate one's own students at distance.

An Experience in the G9 Shared Virtual Campus: The Subject "Introduction to C Programming" and its Moodle Implementation

In the academic year 2002-03, the one-semester subject "Introduction to C Programming" started to be taught by some professors of the Department of Applied Mathematics at the Superior Technical School of Engineering of Bilbao, belonging to the UPV/EHU (Spain).

The average rate of students per professor is around 40. Due to the continuous evaluation of students, and because of the massive use of e-mail and the Moodle platform for sending exercises, questions and answers, evaluation results, etc., the time demanded from professors is very high, and not only in the first year when documentation, exercises, links, etc. must be generated.

The big effort is, nevertheless, appreciated by students: Surveys made at the end of each course show a high degree of satisfaction, with 80 per cent of opinions being "very satisfactory."

At the beginning of each course, the list of registered students is sent to the professor by each university. On the list, an e-mail address of each student appears, being the primary way to communicate with them. A first e-message gives the student the login and password to access the Moodle course. It is also advisable to include a short video presentation.

Moodle allows to organize contents by theme blocks or by weeks; in our case, the former was chosen. After each block, some tasks must be completed by the student and sent to the professor for evaluation. Working "at home", the ability to organize one's working times at will entails the danger of sometimes "parking" the subject for too long. Therefore, block contents are hidden and revealed only shortly before they must be studied (about a week before). The objective is that students acquire an adequate working rhythm and never fully leave the subject.

Three kinds of Moodle activities are basically used for this subject: Forums, Tasks and Wikis.

Forums are used in two modalities. The news forum is used by the professor only, providing day-to-day guidelines. Another forum is used by students to clear out their doubts, both regarding practical issues (assignment deadlines, etc.) or theoretical or practical questions related with the subject content itself. Both professors or other (supervised) students can answer these. Another way to solve doubts are direct messages to the teacher (almost always through the Moodle platform). These forums create the everyday link in the "virtual classroom" and give life to the subject.

The tasks presented at the end of each block represent a percentage of the final mark. Each student is informed of the errors or possible improvements in their assignments, as well as the mark obtained in each task. If several people similar mistakes, that can be explained in the general subject forum.

Finally, we regard Wikis as a very useful tool in Moodle to promote students' participation. In our case, a tutorial for the compiler used in the subject to solve the exercises had to be written.

All these activities promote students' participation by being part of their evaluation (under known weights). The continuous evaluation counts as more than half of the final mark.

Finally, and apart from the continuous evaluation, every student must take a final presential exam, which is done at the computer. The exam is just a special Moodle task that must be solved and sent within a strict time frame, and typically consists in writing a C programme with the aid of all the on-line manuals available in Moodle and the free-distribution compiler used throughout the course. Each student does this at his own university's premises, without any need for displacements or travel expenses.

Conclusions

The present industrial engineer responds perfectly to the framework socio-industrial. The society benefits from the existence of professionals with multipurpose and generalist formation.

The present state of the implantation of new compatible models with the convergence varies from one country to another one. Thus, there are countries that have already done it in all the degrees, like Austria, Estonia, Italy, Latvia, Liechtenstein and the Netherlands. Others, like Germany, Belgium (French-speaking community), Hungary and Finland, are doing it of progressive form. On the other hand, there are countries like Spain, Portugal and Sweden, which have not defined completely the model yet.

Some studies of engineering receive a special treatment in certain countries. For example, the French Grandes Écoles will maintain the traditional integrated title of five years of Diplome d'Ingenieur. Something similar happens in Norway, where the corresponding degree expresses that engineering stay to the margin of the reform, so institutions as Norges Teknisk Naturvitenskapelige Universitet (NTNU) maintain their integrated title of five years.

The predominant model in the new European Higher Education Area is the commonly denominated "3 + 2", even in those countries in which legislation allows them to choose between 3 and 4 years for the Bachelor, as the case of Germany. Few countries, such as Bulgaria, Croatia, Greece, Scotland and Turkey, have duration of 4 years for the Bachelor. Spain will take the "4 + 1" model.

In the case of Masters, duration is usually of 120 ECTS credits, although exceptions exist. Thus, in United Kingdom it consists of 60 ECTS credits.

European higher education institutions, for their part, have accepted the challenge and taken up a main role in constructing the European Area of Higher Education, also in the wake of the fundamental principles laid sown in the Bologna Magna Charta Universitatum of 1988. But sometimes decisions can be improved, that is, all around the world models of education are different, for Engineering too; then copying some models, like the American one, cannot be the best option and although educational system is of very high quality it has proved in industrial world that generalist engineers have much more value than the specialists.

Moreover, educational institutions must cooperate among them to improve the preparation of their students, to adequate programmes and the own institutions to the new global world, and to obtain new students when the birth-rate is diminishing. In this case, one experience that has several years and where the success is increasing is the Spanish G9 Group of Universities.

REFERENCES

Sorbonne Joint Declaration: Joint Declaration on Harmonisation of the Architecture of the European Higher Education System by the four Ministers in charge for France, Germany, Italy and the United Kingdom. Paris, the Sorbonne, May 25, 1998.

The European Higher Education Area: Joint Declaration of the European Ministers of Education. Convened in Bologna on the 19th of June 1999.

Magna Charta Universitatum. Bologna, Italy. September 18, 1988.

Graz Declaration 2003. Forward from Berlin: The Role of the Universities. Graz, September 2003.

Towards the European Higher Education Area. Communiqué of the meeting of European Ministers in charge of Higher Education in Prague on May 19th 2001.

Realising the European Higher Education Area. Communiqué of the Conference of Ministers Responsible for Higher Education in Berlin on 19 September 2003.

The European Higher Education Area: Achieving the Goals. Communiqué of the Conference of European Ministers Responsible for Higher Education, Bergen, 19-20 May 2005.

Bilbao, J.: E-Learning Experiences and Projects. Engineering Education 2004 Int. Conf. Wolverhampton (UK), (2004).

Bilbao, J., Bravo, E., García, O., Varela, C., Rodríguez, M., González, P.: Future Quality in the Emergent European Higher Education Area Involves the Use of Informatics. Informatics in Education, Vol. 7, Nos. 1, 3-16, 2008.

12

Emergence of Research and Entrepreneurial Activities of Universities in Korea

Ki-Seok Kwon, U.K.

Introduction

In general, the university is regarded as an institution that is highly entrenched within the society, and consequently the boundary between them is not distinct. Therefore, before analysing the characteristics of universities in a given national innovation system, it is necessary to look into some idiosyncratic properties of institutions and their environments. In this vein, this chapter aims to analyse the characteristics of the Korean university system. A description of the historical development of Korean higher education institutions should help us to understand some specific characteristics of the current Korean university system. Against this background, the emergence of the second and third missions of the Korean universities is delineated.

Firstly, in terms of longitudinal perspective, section 2 provides a brief history of Korean universities from the fourth century to the mid 20th century. Based on this historical background, some specific characteristics of the Korean academic system are suggested in the later sections.

Secondly, in section 3, we focus on the development of the policy environment of the Korean higher education system according to the different stages suggested in section 2. Then, the longitudinal changes in the research and entrepreneurial activities of Korean universities are investigated. Based on these results, the interaction between the responses of universities and institutional settings is also examined. The data discussed in this section mostly come from secondary sources such as previous studies and published national

R&D statistics, as well as from primary sources such as interviews with Korean academics.

Finally, as a conclusion, section 4 summarises the findings from the previous sections. Based on these findings, at the three levels (system, organisation and individual) several stylised facts characterising the two Korean academic revolutions compared to those of developed and developing countries are suggested.

Brief History of Korean Universities

This section briefly introduces the historical development of Korean higher education system broken down into a number of periods from the 4th century to the 1950s.

Before the Opening

Generally, the origin of the formal public Korean education institutions can be traced back to the 'Tae-hak' established by a King of the Goguryeo dynasty (BC 37-AD 668) in 372 based on the oldest existing literature of Korean history written by Kim (Kim, 2004: 49). According to this work (Kim, 1145), entrance to the 'Tae-hak' was only open to children of aristocratic bureaucrats and the main aims of this institution were to provide literacy in Chinese and to be well versed in Confucianism.

Afterwards, throughout the Unified Silla (668-918), Goryeo (918 - 1392), and Choson dynasties (1392-1910), the Korean education system became more systemised and opened up to the wider class of people (Byeun, 2007). For example, the Choson dynasty established a three-stage (primary, secondary and post secondary) education system integrated with an entrance exam to become a high-rank bureaucrat based on academic performance. Furthermore, even common people were allowed to become a student at the highest level education institution named as 'Sung-kyun-kwan' incorporating 'Tae-hak' (Shin, 2000). However, the merit-based system in hiring bureaucrats had become corrupted by the ruling class by the end of the 19th century. In spite of some reformation efforts on the educational system, the dynasty and its education system collapsed in the face of Japanese imperialism in 1910 (Byeon, 2007).

Western Missionaries (1885-1910)

After the opening of Kangwhado Island near Incheon to Japan in 1876, the existence of Korea began to be widely recognised by the western world (Byeon, 2007). Responding to this new era, the Choson dynasty created a modern public school named 'Youkyungkongwon' in 1886 providing a western curriculum in English, but this school closed in 1894 because of the corruption of bureaucrats and the political intervention of Russia and China (Umakoshi, 1997).

In contrast, in the private sector, western missionaries contributed significantly to the establishment of the modern institutions of education of Korea after the opening up the country (Lee, 2006). In 1910,2,250 private schools were recognised by the Ministry of Education, and thirty seven per cent (823) of these schools were established by religious organisations and missionaries. Seventy one per cent (574) of these religious schools were created by US missionaries (Sohn, 1987).

Moreover, American missionaries began to establish 'seed' institutions of higher education such as House of Universal Grace in 1885, Underwood School in 1885, Pai Chai College in 1886, Ewha School in 1887 and Pyeng Yang Academy in 1897, which has developed into Severence Medical School [Yonsei University], Yonhee College [Yonsei University], Pai Chai High School [Pai Chai University], Ewha Womans College [Ewha Womans University] and Soongsil University respectively around the 1910s (Yoo, 2000). Umakoshi (1997) maintains that it was the 'college of liberal art' type of US university in the late 19th century rather than land grant universities and research-oriented universities that was influenced the Korean higher education system as a model.

The Colonization Period (1910-1945)

After the occupation by the Japanese imperialists in 1910, the Korean people could not develop the educational system in their own way. Under the control of the colonial authority, the Japanese made use of education policy as a major means to control the Korean people. Lee (2004: 149) maintains that the education policy in this period can be characterised as one of 'denationalisation', 'vocationalisation', 'deliberalisation' and 'discrimination'. In the same vein, Lee *et al.*, (1997: 347) concluded that 'practicality' and 'simplicity' are the key words to understand the education system under the Japanese rule.

'Vocationalisation' and 'practicality' mean that education was allowed mainly for the training of lower-level skills and it focused on primary schools (Kim, 1997). Furthermore, until 1924, the establishment of higher education institutions by Korean people was hindered and none of the tertiary schools was recognised as a university by the colonial authority (Kim, 2000). These two characteristics also related with regard to the supply of 'simplicity' for minimal education opportunity and 'discrimination' between Japanese and Koreans. For example, the number of private schools (1,973) in 1910 decreased to 604 in 1919 (Umakoshi, 1997). Furthermore, in 1939, only 1.3 Korean students out of every 1,000 Koreans were enrolled at secondary schools, whereas 32.7 Japanese students out of every 1,000 Japanese were enrolled at secondary schools (Kim, 1973). The Kyungsung [Seoul] imperial college of Japan was established as university in 1924; however, the majority (more than 60%) of the students were Japanese and the quality of faculties was far lower than that of Japan (Kim, 2005). The competition for admission to Kyungsung imperial college and its operation style has influenced the Korean higher education system in terms of the preference for a state-run university and centralised system (Lee, 2004).

The US Military Government Period (1945-1948)

After the liberation in 1945, in spite of strong aspirations for education, the illiteracy rate was 78 per cent and only two per cent of Koreans over 14-year old finished their secondary education partly due to the previous Japanese education policy (Kim, 1997). However, from 1945 to 1948, the number of institutions, students and faculties increased abruptly as shown in the below table. Some of them were newly created, and some of them were accredited by the civil government after 1948. Lee (2004) interprets this sudden increase as an 'eruption of education fever', which has been oppressed during the colonisation period.

Table–1
Increase in the Number of Higher Education Institutions Under the US Military Government

	1945 (Just after the Liberation)	*1948 (Establishment of the Government)*
No. of HE institutions*	21 (1 university**)	42 (4 universities)
Students in HE institutions	7110	24000
Faculties in HE institutions	753	1256

*Higher education institutions just after the liberation is tertiary schools after 6-year primary ('botong') and 5-year secondary ('godeung-botong') schools, and the US Military Government recognised these institutions as four types of HE institutions: Universities consist of several colleges, colleges granting bachelor's degree, junior colleges and miscellaneous schools.

**Only Kyungsung university (Kyungsung imperial college) was recognised by the US Military Government in 1945.

Source: The Monthly Report of Ministry of Education (1948) cited in UNN (2005), The 50 years History of Korean Universities, UNN (University News Network).

In addition to this quantitative growth, the Korean educational system as well as the university system has been exposed to substantial US influence after escaping from the Japanese model during this period. Emulating the US higher education system, the authority reformed the Korean education system in terms of the period of study, the semester system, the categorisation of universities and the status of faculty. The Japanese duplicative system for the period of study based on discrimination (6-5 for Japanese and 4-4 for Korean) and a three-semester system beginning in April was replaced by the unified 6-3-3-4 system and the US two-semester system beginning in September respectively (Lee *et al.*, 1998). Categorising higher education institutions (see the note in Table 1) and providing qualifications for faculties, the authority introduced a four-year undergraduate system granting bachelor's degree, while in the previous period, the tertiary schools under Japanese rule had provided a three-year course and had not conferred degrees (Lee *et al.*, 1998). Moreover, the Korean Association of Colleges and Universities which was organised by the military authority established a system of quality control based on the US model for institutions of higher education (Lee, 2004).

US Educational Aid (1952-1967)

Lee (2004) maintains that in terms of the higher education system, the US influence on Korean system after the Korean War (1950-1953) is more significant than in the period between 1945 and 1948 during the reconstruction of the country. The US spent more than 19 million dollars from 1953 to 1967, with a great number of aid programmes for the reconstruction of Korea (Dodge, 1971: 199-201).

The biggest programme in terms of the level of expenditure was the 'Minnesota project' between 1954 and 1958. Based on this project, three hundreds academic faculty members (particularly, in the fields of agriculture, engineering and medical science) in Seoul National

University were invited to be trained as a Ph.D. in Minnesota University in the US (Dodge, 1971: 199-210), and facilities and equipment of Seoul National University were enhanced to an international level (McGinn *et al.*, 1980: 91).

Based on another programme, some prestigious private universities in Seoul such as Yonsei University and Korea University entered a contract with Washington University to support their faculty training, curriculum development, library enhancement and research programmes (Lee, 2004). Between 1954 and 1967, these kinds of aid programmes enabled 2,883 Koreans to receive advanced training in the US and the other western countries (Dodge, 1971: 199-201).

Against the background mentioned above, the US-trained scholars at Korean universities had a leading role in development of Korean higher education system (Lee, 2004). However, these programmes created the inequality issues in the Korean university system between the public and the private and between the different regions, and a strong preference was established for overseas training, particularly in the US institutions (Umakoshi, 1997).

Explosion of Research and Entrepreneurial Activities: The First and Second Korean Academic Revolutions

This section focuses more on the Korean university sector in the last half century, while the previous section described the history of Korean higher education. The main aim of this section is to investigate the interactions between the government's university policies and the activities of universities. In order to do this, this section consists of two major subsections. On the one hand, section 3.1 addresses government policy and the institutional settings influencing universities' activities broken down into different periods. On the basis of these conditions, various quantitative and qualitative changes in the activities of Korean universities are presented in section 3.2.

Policies and Institutional Changes of Universities: Characteristics of Different Periods

During the last half century, Korean universities have experienced tremendous changes both quantitatively and qualitatively. The number of universities, academic faculties, and students increased at a rapid rate compared to other developing countries as well as developed countries. For example, according to the rate of enrolments of each stage, Trow (1974) suggested three stages of development of higher education: Elite (less than 15%), mass (between 15% and 50%) and universal (more than 55%) the higher education. Based on his definition, Korean higher education has moved from the 'elite phase' to the 'universal phase' within only three decades as shown in Figure 1. This rapid development is also confirmed by appendix Figure 1 that is comparing different countries' situation.

Figure 1: Trajectory of Educational Expansion

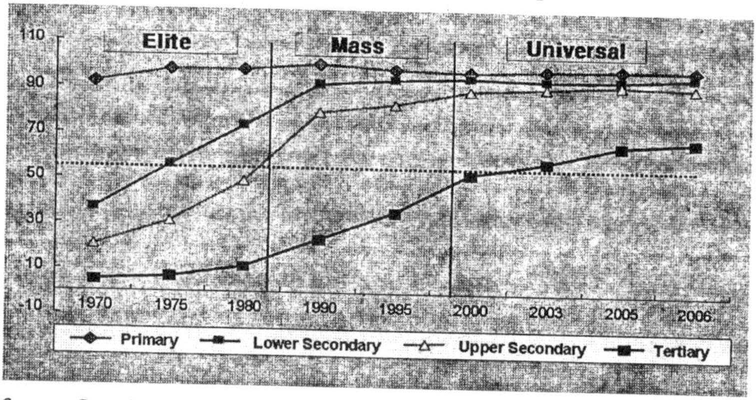

Source: Supplemented to MOE (2005), *Brief Statistics On Korean Education,* MOE.

From the early stage of catch up, the Korean Government has been a dominant actor influencing the growth of the university system as well as industry. Particularly, through the provision of technically skilled labour as well as qualified scientists and engineers, Korean universities have been continually encouraged to play a role as human resource supplier for economic growth up to now. In the 1990s, the government adopted a series of policies for strengthening universities' research activities, and recently Korean universities began to be recognized as one of the direct contributors to local economic development.

In this vein, this section follows the same categorisation of periods introduced in the previous section, because this categorisation mostly centres on the development of Korean firms as encouraged by the government's industrial policy. The various responses of universities according to their different policy environments as well as the evolving stages of the Korean national innovation system are suggested in this section as summarised in Table 2.

Table-2
Characteristics of Korean Universities in Three Main Periods

	Strong Regulation (1960-mid-1970s)	*Massive Expansion (late 1970s-1980s)*	*Academic Revolutions (1990s-present)*
Major policy orientation	Strong regulation over numbers	Policy to meet the needs of the masses	Deregulation and diversity are strengthened
	Medium-skilled labour	Establishment of research infrastructure	Encouragement of research and its economic usefulness
	Focus on vocational education		
Responses	Limited access to universities	Expansion of higher education system	On-line universities, Credit bank system etc.
	Focus on teaching	Open universities and junior colleges	Invigoration of research and cooperation with industry
	Research as an individual activity		

Source: Based on the material compiled by the author and described in this chapter.

Strong Regulation Over Education System for Economic Take up (1960s–mid 1970s)

In the aftermath of Park Chung-Hee's military coup in 1961, strong regulation over the national system as well as the education sector characterises the 1960s and 1970s (Lee *et al.*, 1998). In this period, acting as a supplier of technical labour was regarded as a main role of the secondary and tertiary education system in particular through vocational education and training, while access to universities was limited (Kim and Lee, 2006; Lee *et al.*, 1998). In particular, in addition to encouraging an increase in the supply of human resources in the field of science and engineering to industry, overall governmental control over public universities as well as private universities was based on strong policy measures such as fixed numbers of students.

On the other hand, in this period, the government chose public institutes such as KIST (Korea Institute of Science and Technology) created in 1966 as the main national R&D supporter for industry instead of existing universities. Based on the successful operation of KIST, a series of public institutes have been established in order to support 'six national strategic industries' (e.g., iron, chemical, non-metal, machinery, shipbuilding and electronics) (Kim, 2006). For example, KORDI (Korea Ocean Research and Development Institute) was created in 1973 in order to support the shipbuilding industry and KIMM (Korea Institute of Machinery and Materials) in 1976 for the machinery sector. Moreover, the quality of the working condition (e.g., three times higher salary than for professors) of these public institutes attracted a large number of highly qualified scientists and engineers trained in industrialized countries throughout the '70s, the '80s and the '90s, in a process known as the 'reverse brain drain' or 'brain gain' (Moon, 2004).

After the liberation in 1945 and the Korean War between 1950 and 1953, the reestablishment of the Korean higher education system continued until the '60s as described in section 2. A 5-year economic development plan drafted by the government in 1962 was implemented through various policy measures. At the same time, the government recognised certain problems arising from the '50s 'laissez-faire' education policy: The heavy concentration of students in the Seoul area, 4-year universities, private universities and disciplines such as humanities and social sciences (Umakoshi, 1997). To address these problems, the 5-year education reconstruction plan and the act of advancement of industrial education were drawn up in 1962 and in 1963 respectively. In 1966, the 5-year plan of advancement of science and technology was drafted. Based on this plan, the office of science education was established in the ministry of education.

The implementation of these plans and laws launched an era of strong government control of the education system. Particularly, according to the presidential order no. 2332 in 1965, the fixed number of the students enrolling in tertiary education institutions was to be determined by the minister of education. Based on this order, the government could control the number of graduates not only in a given university but also in specific disciplines of the university; therefore, the university system could be easily mobilised to provide increasing human resources in science and engineering, with decreasing numbers of students in humanities and social science.

For example, in 1963 the majority of students enrolled in tertiary education were those in humanities and social science (50.8% in humanities and social science, 39.6% in science and engineering and 9.6% in teacher training), whereas in 1973, the largest number were those in science and engineering (42.0% in science and engineering, 35.1% in humanities and social science and 22.9% in teacher training). Considering the number students in 4-year universities only, the proportion of the students in science and engineering amounted to 59.7 per cent, whereas those in humanities and social science was 38.7 per cent and those in teacher training was 1.6 per cent in 1972 (MOE, 1963; KNCESI). Furthermore, the specific disciplines of these students mostly coincided with the main strategic industries chosen both at the national and regional levels in the 5-year economic plan (Cho *et al.*, 2002). Umakoshi (1997) evaluates this change as 'an abrupt transition of humanities centred country to science and engineering centred one in ten years.'

Along with the increase in the number of students in science and engineering, the government established new forms of institutions such as 'a 5-year higher specialised industrial school' in 1963 in order to 'support the efficient provision of field specialists of industry workforce' (the promotion of industrial education act in 1963). This institution can be seen as an integrated form of 3-year upper secondary schools with 2-year tertiary school. In 1969, the number of these schools amounted to 23, while the number of the enrolled students increased to 20,741. In the 1970s, following a recommendation of the International Development Association, the last two-year course of this school was separated and established as an independent 'specialised industrial school'. This school developed into 2-year junior colleges in the 1980s to meet the explosive demand for higher education (Cho *et al.*, 2002).

Based on the fixed number policy, big national universities in the regions were strongly supported. As mentioned above, the government regarded the imbalanced development between the capital area and other regions as a serious problem stemming from the 50's policies with regard to the economy and education. Therefore, by increasing the quota for enrolled students of regional universities, the government aimed both to reduce the concentration of students in the capital area and to attract them to regional universities. For example, between 1968 and 1978, while the quota of the capital area increased 1.4 times, that of the other regions increased 2.8 times. Moreover, this increase was concentrated in the fields of science and engineering in order to meet the needs of regional industry. This concentration coincided with support for strategic local industry in the third 5-year economic plan (1972-1976) (Umakoshi, 1997).

In terms of highly qualified scientists and engineers, the strong dependence on overseas institutions started during this period. In 1950s, the government began to encourage overseas training supported by foreign scholarships and initiated an official supporting programme for students to study abroad in 1954. These were possible due to US aid just after the Korean War (see section 2). In the 1960s and 1970s, the training of highly qualified scientists and engineers was motivated by both the government initiatives and by individual demand for higher education at overseas institutions (Kim, 1997). Half of these students were in the field of science and engineering, and most of students went to the institutions in the US, as shown in Table 3.

Table–3

Number of Students Going Abroad by Discipline and Country

Periods	*1953–1960 (%)*	*1961-1973 (%)*
Humanities/Social Science	2,183 (44.7)	3,588 (47.9)
Natural Science/Engineering	1,614 (33.0)	3,177 (42.4)
Medical/Pharmaceutical Science	651 (13.3)	247 (3.3)
Agricultural/Maritime	124 (2.6)	127 (1.7)
Education, Etc.	312 (6.4)	347 (4.7)
The United States	4,391 (89.9)	6,398 (85.5)
Germany	160 (3.3)	246 (3.3)
The others	333 (6.8)	842 (11.2)
Total	**4,884 (100.0)**	**7,486 (100.0)**

Source: MOE (1974), Report on students studying abroad, Ministry of Education.

Massive Expansion of Higher Education System (late 1970s - 1980s)

In the aftermath of the coup in 1980, General Chun Doo-Hwan succeeded Park Chung-Hee. In the light of the vulnerable political legitimacy of the government, a series of distinctive reformation of the education system as well as in the other areas were implemented (Lee *et al.*, 1998). The most significant characteristics of this period are the massive expansion and the relaxation of previous strong

regulation of the university system in order to meet the explosive demand for higher education (Kim and Lee, 2006). However, the expansion occurred mainly in terms of the number of students in non-technological disciplines such as humanities and social science, whereas in the previous period, vocational training in the fields of science and engineering was stressed (Cho *et al.*, 2002).

At the same time, the public institutes were mobilised for several national R&D projects operated by the government since the early 80's, whereas they had enjoyed a measure of institutional and financial autonomy for supporting domestic industry directly in the previous period (Kim, 2006; Moon, 2006). Moreover, there were efforts to establish not only several organisations but also broader institutions in order to stimulate high quality knowledge creation activities, which later functioned as a positive condition for the 1990s' vitalisation of university research. In 1977, KOSEF (Korea Science and Engineering Foundation) was established to support basic research activities. In 1979, the act on the advance of academic research was passed. Based on this law, in 1981, the KRF (Korea Research Foundation) was created in order to support mainly university research.

Around the end of 1970s, the strong regulation policy based on fixed numbers of students faced a few challenges due to the explosion of demand for higher education. For a long-time, personal education had been considered as a significant factor for the success of members of Korean society, something which can be traced back to Confucianism (Lee, 2006). Furthermore, as the national economy grew, households accumulated enough wealth to pay for tuition fees, and industry needed more qualified human resources. Therefore, the demand for higher education increased throughout the society (Lee *et al.*, 1998). Responding to these increasing demands, the quota or fixed number of students in higher education institutions was increased from 78,615 in 1978 to 185,065 in 1979 a 250 per cent increase (Kim and Lee, 2002). Considering the much smaller increase from 45,000 in 1969 to 66,000 in 1977, this was a remarkable increase. During the 1980s, the number of students enrolled in higher education institutions increased from 0.57 million to 1.49 million and 10 new universities were established. Moreover, the form of the control policy focused on fixed numbers shifted from the number of entrants to the number of graduates in 1981, allowing the number of freshmen for each university increase.

With the increase in the number of students and institutions, structural changes in the university system became possible. In the 1980s and 1990s, new forms of higher education institutions were created, whereas in the 1970s, the need for higher education was met mainly through increasing the size of pre-existing institutions. For example, the 2-year air and correspondence colleges and 2-year teacher-training colleges were upgraded to 4-year national universities. The specialised higher schools aiming to provide qualified industrial labour which had been established around 1970, upgraded to formal short-term higher education institutions in order to meet the demand from both citizens and industry (Umakoshi, 1997). New forms of institutions such as open universities were introduced in 1982 and exams for the various bachelor degree launched for students opting for the self-study route.

In particular, various science education institutions for the gifted young linking secondary to tertiary education were set up by the government in the early 1980s: For example, Science High Schools, KIT (Korea Institute of Technology) and KAIST (Korea Institute of Science and Technology). On the other hand, industry also began to be aware of the importance of highly innovative knowledge. In this vein, POSCO (Pohang Steel Company) established a research-intensive university POSTECH (Pohang Institute of Science and Technology) in 1986. The establishment of these organisations stimulated existing prestigious universities to strengthen their research activities and to upgrade graduate education (Cho *et al.*, 2002). For example, Seoul National University initiated several programmes in order to strengthen graduate education especially in the field of science and technology such as upgrading the research facilities in the university laboratories, an initiative that was partly supported by the government through a World Bank loan (Woo, 2002).

Around the late 1970s, certain conspicuous changes started with regard to the graduate education (Woo, 2002). The number of graduate students was abruptly expanded as show in Table 4. In 1970, the number of students enrolled in graduate schools was only 6,640, which amounted to 3.7 per cent of all students in higher education institutions. However, in the 1980s, the increase of postgraduate students in domestic institutions was faster than that of undergraduate students, whereas in the 1970s, most doctoral degrees had been earned abroad except for medical doctor

(Umakoshi, 1997). Furthermore, certain changes in military service speeded up these trends. For example, shorter military service as an officer for graduates of masters programme was introduced in 1981, and highly qualified scientists and engineers were exempted from the military service from the same year. As a result, the proportion of postgraduate students in higher education institutions increased to 6.6 per cent in 1993. This formed part of the background of the 1990s' invigoration of academic research of Korean universities.

Table-4

Increase of Number of Postgraduate Students

Year	*Master Programme*	*Doctoral Programme*	*Total*
1970	6,112	518	6,640
1975	12,351	1,519	13,870
1980	29,901	4,038	33,939
1985	57,698	10,480	68,178
1990	72,417	14,494	86,911
1995	–	–	113,836
2000	–	–	229,437
2005	238,753	43,472	282,225

Source: MOE (2005), Annual Report on Educational Statistics, MOE.

Invigoration of Research and Direct Contribution to Economy (the 1990s –Present)

In 1988, the direct vote system for the presidential election resumed following popular pressure, and in 1993 a leader of the democratic movement, Kim Young-Sam was elected as president. Following this, a series of educational reforms as well as political one was implemented. The 90's democratization speeded up the deregulation of education policy, so it was easier than before to establish higher education institutions. In other words, the previous 'permission' policy was replaced by minimal 'condition' policy for the establishment of new higher education institutions.

For example, one of the most distinctive educational reforms was the abolition of the quota system for higher education institutions (except for those in the capital area) in 1995 (Kim and Lee, 2006). This leads to numerous higher education institutions being created, not only typical small-and medium-sized private universities in local areas but also new forms of institution such as graduate schools without undergraduate students and on-line universities. On the other hand, this reform encouraged big private universities in Seoul to create a dozen of local autonomous campuses. This increase can be regarded as the second explosion in the number of universities as well as in the numbers of students enrolled (see the second peak in figure 2). Between 1990 and 1993, twenty new 4-year universities were created.

In terms of higher education policy, the government took note of the 1980s' oversupply following the massive increase in university graduates. Therefore, the focus of the fixed number policy switched back from the number of graduates to the numbers of entrants to universities in 1987, and the increase in university graduates was focused on science and technology instead of in humanities and social science (Cho *et al.*, 2002), as shown in Table 5.

Table–5
Number of University Graduates Overall and in Science and Engineering

	Graduates–Overall (A)	*Graduates-Science and Engineering (B)*	*B/A*
1976	34,725	10,266	29.6
1981	55,846	18,527	33.2
1986	137,846	48,099	34.9
1991	175,586	61,781	35.2
1996	184,212	75,150	40.8
2001	239,702	98,150	40.9
2005	268,833	105,860	39.4

Source: Korean National Center for Education Statistics and Information. (http://cesi.kedi.re.kr)

Several new research-oriented universities were also created: For example, GIST (Gwangju Institute of Science and Technology) in 1993, KIAS (Korea Institute for Advanced Study) in 1996 and ICU (Information and Communications University) in 1998. In order to provide highly qualified scientists and engineers, overseas postdoctoral programmes were implemented for domestically trained Ph.Ds in the field of science and engineering in 1996. On the other hand, new universities more specialised in university-industry cooperation have been created by the government. In 1992, KUT

(Korea University of Technology and Education), which aimed to 'educate human resource development facilitators and vocational training instructors' was established by the Ministry of Labour. Moreover, in 1998, KPU (Korea Polytechnic University) was founded by the government in several major industrial parks 'to produce outstanding industrial engineers and improve the nation's competitive edge in industrial technology' through strong university-industry linkages.

Research Invigoration: 'The First Korean Academic Revolution (?)' in the 1990s

Research has begun to be stressed as one of their main missions of universiteis since the early 1990s by the science and technology policy community, which consists of public officials, scientists and academics related to the field. Accordingly, the government began to establish policy measures encouraging universities to provide innovative knowledge in order to raise the level of Korean industry. Simultaneously, the main role of public research institutes was re-oriented to 'future oriented large complex advanced technology development' (Yim and Kim, 2006). Furthermore, national R&D programmes were diversified and expanded by individual ministries without strong coordination among the ministries (Song, 2002). This section summarises various policy measures to support research activities in universities, including laws, R&D and its supporting programmes, and the other institutional changes.

Firstly, in order to establish an infrastructure for basic research, the government enacted 'the basic science advancement law' in 1989. According to this law, 'the master plan for advancement of basic research' was drafted. On the other hand, in its final report to the president, the PACST (Presidential Advisory Council on Science and Technology) maintained that national science policy goals needed to be re-oriented to invigorate basic research capabilities (1990, PACST). This led to the creation of 'the implementation plan for innovation in science and technology' in 1991, which suggested various policy measures such as fostering excellent research groups and establishing university laboratories.

Secondly, in addition to the establishment of the infrastructure mentioned above, the research activity of academics was strongly supported through various programmes implemented by KOSEF (Korea Science and Engineering Foundation). Some of the most successful programmes to support academic research are: SRC (Science Research Center) / ERC (Engineering Research Center) and RRC (Regional Research Center) created in universities by KOSEF and MOST (Ministry of Science and Technology). On the other hand, the creation of university laboratories was encouraged by the MOE (Ministry of Education) through financial support, and the MOIC (Ministry of Industry and Commerce) established TIC (Technology Innovation Center).

Furthermore, as briefly mentioned in the previous section (see table 4), the massive increase in postgraduate students is another characteristic of this period. The 'Brain Korea 21' programme (hereafter, BK 21) was launched based on 'performance contracts' in order to support university researchers, particularly postgraduate students. 1.2 billion dollars were invested over seven years (1999-2005) in this programme. Moreover, the major outputs were the increase in the numbers of SCI papers from 4,414 (in 1999) to 7,477 (in 2003), and the increase in patents from 103 (in 1999) to 261 (in 2003) (KRF, 2008). However, some worry that the funding principle of 'selection and concentration' may have aggravated the poor conditions of the non-selected graduate schools (Lee, 2000).

Thirdly, in order to support various R&D programmes, huge amounts of funding have been invested in the university system through national R&D programmes operated by the ministries. Furthermore, the way of allocating the funding of these programmes has changed since 1990. University researchers have to compete not only with their colleagues in academia but also with researchers in governmental institutes to obtain the funds and to carry out the research proposed by government, whereas in the previous period research funds were allocated based on the number of academics in each university (Cho *et al.*, 2002).

Stress on Direct Contributions to the Economy: The 'Second Korean Academic Revolution' in the 2000s

There have been a large number of policy measures supporting cooperation between universities and industry including various government programmes and laws since the 1960s. However, the policy measures before 2000 were mainly focused on the training of industry-oriented human resources and were based on government-initiated R&D programmes (Park *et al.*, 2007). Around 2000, as the research capacity of universities increased, various governmental and university efforts particularly focused on the exploitation of academic potential have been implemented. Against this background, this subsection examines the efforts of both government and university authorities to invigorate university-industry linkages. These efforts can be categorised into several areas: Enactment of laws, national R&D programmes, national plans and the other institutional changes including those to the university system.

First of all, the government created new laws and amended existing laws in order to encourage the exploitation of academic potential. The specific laws invigorating university-industry cooperation are as follows: The promotion of industrial education and the university-industry cooperation act (1963), the promotion of technology transfer act (2000) and the promotion of invention act (1994). Including these, eight ministries have enacted or partially amended a total of eleven laws since 2000.

Based on the amendment of the 'promotion of industrial education and university industry cooperation act (1963)' in 2003, legally autonomous organisations such as university-industry cooperation foundations have been established on university campuses since 2003; as a results, Korean universities have been permitted to create for-profit companies based on academics' inventions. Moreover, a Korean version of the US Bayh-Dole Act, the 'promotion of technology transfer act' was enacted in 2000. This act enforces public research institutes to create technology licensing offices; moreover, in 2001, the range of this enforcement was extended to forty six public universities. 'Promotion of invention act' has been enacted in 1994, and subsequently revised to set out to jurisdiction of Intellectual Property Rights (IPR) of academics in public universities in 2001; therefore, the agencies affiliated to universities can manage their IPR and the transfer of university inventions.

Secondly, the government implemented a series of R&D programmes to stimulate the commercial exploitation of academic research as well as to strengthen university-industry linkages. According to Sohn *et al.*, (2006), the level of funding for university-industry cooperation programmes consists of 25 per cent (1.8124 trillion won) of all national R&D projects (0.72283 trillion won) in 2006. Moreover, most of them have been started since 2000, and from around 2004 they have been implemented actively (Park *et al.*, 2007). In terms of size and importance, these are four major programmes of particular importance: The second phase BK21 project, the NURI (New University for Regional Innovation) project, the CK (Connect Korea) project and the HUNIC (Hub University for Industrial Collaboration) project. In addition to these, eleven ministries were operating 50 similar projects in 2006 (Cho *et al.*, 2007).

The BK21 project in its second phase (2006-2012) is focused on university-industry collaborative research, while the first phase (1999-2005) was concerned with the overall research capability and the training of students at universities (KRF, 2006). In order to contribute to balanced regional growth across the country, the NURI project (2006-2010) encourages universities located outside the Seoul metropolitan area to achieve three goals: Enhancing the disciplinary specialisation of regional universities, providing regional human resources and 'establishing' the regional innovation system. In order to 'connect' the demand side [industry] and supply side [university], the CK project (2006-2010) has focused on invigorating technology transfer to industry by strengthening the TLO (Technology Licensing Office) capacity. The HUNIC project (2004-2009) is aiming to strengthen the R&D activities of existing industrial clusters by encouraging regional universities to cooperate with industries nearby through various channels such as cooperative research, training human resources and sharing research infrastructure.

Table–6
Four Major National R&D Projects Focusing on University-Industry Cooperation

Ministries	*Supporting Agency*	*Projects*	*Year Starting*	*Budget 2006 (Bil. Won)*
Ministry of Education	KRF (Korea Research Foundation)	The second Phase Brain Korea 21	2006	290
		New University for Regional Innovation (NURI)	2004	260
		Connect Korea project (University TLO supporting project)	2006	5.8
Ministry of Industry and Commerce	KOTEF (Korea Industrial Technology Foundation)	Hub University for Industrial Collaboration (HUNIC) Project	2005	20

Source: Revised from KRF (2006), pp. 399-436.

Thirdly, the government has drafted several national plans embracing the university-industry cooperation strategy, such as the 'plan for university-industry cooperation to establish the national innovation system (February, 2002)', the 'vision and strategy for new university-industry cooperation (September, 2003)' and the 'plan for the expansion of university-industry cooperation under the MOE, MOIC and MOL (May, 2005)'. In 2002, the 'plan for university-industry-government cooperation to establish national innovation system' has been jointly drafted by 15 ministries including MOE in order to coordinate ministries' university-industry-government cooperation projects. According to this plan, an associated body for coordinating each ministry's projects has been created, and the incentive system for participants such as professors and researchers in the projects has been strengthened. To upgrade this plan, the 'vision and strategy for new university-industry cooperation' has been announced in 2003. This plan identifies key implementation tasks such as supporting hub universities for university-industry cooperation, enhancing the evaluation system for universities involved in university-industry cooperation, and encouraging universities to create companies. Following these plans, the 'plan for expansion of university-industry cooperation under the MOE, MOIC and MOL' was published in 2005, and the three ministries have started the 'expansion of university-industry cooperation programme' including the HUNIC project.

On the other hand, in response to the government's strong emphasis on invigorating university-industry cooperation, university authorities have not only established an incentive system benefiting the professors involved in entrepreneurial activities by modifying performance evaluation indicators, but they have also implemented various programmes such as the operation of incubation centres, commissioned training for industrial labour, internships in companies and consultancy for regional industry. According to a survey of 26 Korean universities on changes in the performance indicators for university-industry cooperation (Cho *et al.*, 2006), all of them reported that patents performance has been considered, and 16 universities (62%) had adopted this indicator by 2000. Moreover, 35 per cent of universities were using the number of technology-transfer agreements as a performance indicator, and recently the proportion has grown rapidly. Another similar survey (KRF, 2007) reported that 100 out of 129 universities were reflecting industrial collaboration activities in their performance evaluation, and 99 universities weighted an international patent as 16 per cent of a SCI paper.

Table-7
Inclusion of an Industrial Collaboration Indicator in the Performance Evaluation of Academics

	Patent Performance	*Equal Weighting of Patent and int'l Paper*	*Technology Transfer*
First year	1974	1982	1998
Last year	2006	2007	2007
Before 2000	16	9	1
After 2000	10	10	15
No of university	26 (100%)	19 (73%)	16 (62%)

Source: Revised from Cho *et al.,* (2007), p. 27.

In terms of the government's efforts with regard to university-industry linkage, most of the laws were created and revised after 2000, and the R&D and supporting programme started between 2002 and 2004, while the major plans were published after 2002. Furthermore, the universities strongly adopted government's policy after 2000. Therefore we may conclude that the 2000s is a period of invigoration of university-industry cooperation in the Korean academic system.

Change of the Korean Universities' Activities During the Last Half Century

Against the background of the governmental policies and institutional changes described in section 3.1, Korean universities have experienced considerable developments in terms of their activities during the last five decades. This section focuses on the quantitative and qualitative changes of Korean universities in terms of the three main activities: Teaching, research and entrepreneurial activities.

Teaching Activities: Enrolment of Students

The growth of enrolment of students in higher education has been enormous as shown in Figure 2. In terms of the enrolment of 4-year colleges, there have been two explosions during the last four decades: The first one was in the early 1980s while the second was in the late

1990s. These two peaks are closely related to the different higher education policies of each period as presented in section 3.1. The late 1990's increase in the enrolment of graduate school was also influenced by both higher education policy partly and science and technology policy aiming to produce more highly qualified human resources.

Figure 2: Expansion of the Korean Higher Education System Over the Last Four Decades

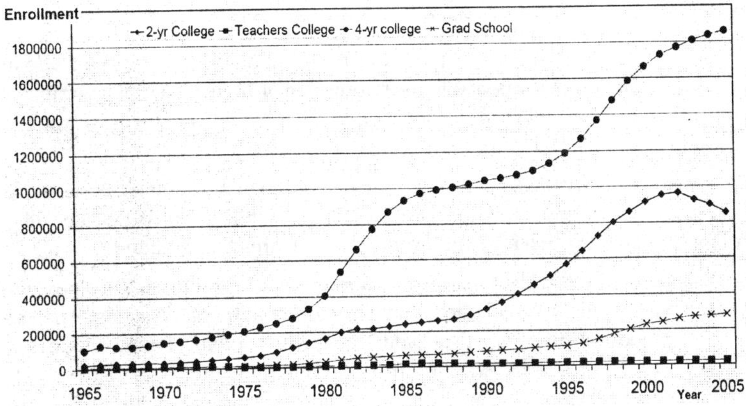

Source: Data from the website of the Korean National Center for Education Statistics and Information.

On the other hand, in terms of the overall enrolment 'rate', only 0.05 per cent of the total population was enrolled to higher education institutions in 1945. In the aftermath of the Korean War, the percentage increased steadily: From 0.40 per cent in 1955, to 0.49 per cent in 1965 and 0.69 per cent in 1975 (Lee, 2006: 145). As shown in Table 8, an explosive increase in enrolments to higher education institutions has been observed during the last three decades. Since 1980, the enrolment has increased enormously: From 11.4 per cent in 1980, to 36 per cent in 1995, 52.5 per cent in 2000 and 65.6 per cent in 2005.

The rapid growth of enrolment in Korea had already surpassed even that of Japan by the mid 1990s as shown in Table 8. Compared to OECD and other countries, the speed of catch-up was remarkable. As shown in appendix Figure 1, the percentage of Korean population of the 25 to 35-year-old group attaining at least tertiary education ranked in the fourth position in 2005. Furthermore, the percentage gap between the two age groups is the largest of the countries investigated, which means that the fastest change has been achieved by Korea.

Table–8
Comparison of the Enrolment Rates* to the HEIs in Korea and Japan**

	1970	*1975*	*1980*	*1985*	*1990*	*1995*	*2000*	*2005*
Korea	5.4	6.7	11.4	22.9	23.6	36.0	52.5	65.6
Japan	23.6	38.4	37.4	37.6	36.3	32.2	49.1	51.5

*The enrolment rate is defined as the ratio of the number of enrolled students graduating in the previous year to the population of 18-years old (the number of students who completed lower secondary schools and the lower division of secondary school three years ago).

**For comparison, the HEIs (Higher Education Institutions) include 4-year universities and 2-year vocational junior colleges, while the specialised training colleges in Japan which have no counterpart in Korea are excluded.

Sources: MOE & HRD (Ministry of Education & Human Resources Development) and KEDI (Korean Educational Development Institute) (2005), Analysis on Educational Statistical Data, KEDI; MEXT (2006), Japan's Education at a Glance 2006, MEXT (http://www.mext.go.jp/english/statist/07070310.htm).

Due to the faster increase of enrolments compared to that for the recruitment of professors, the student-professor ratio increased from 22.6 in 1966 to 35.8 in 1985, according to data obtained from the website of the Korean National Center for Education Statistics and Information. Therefore, this situation adversely affected the quality of teaching and research (Kim, 1997). Until the end of the 1980s, most Korean universities remained "primarily undergraduate teaching-oriented rather than graduate research oriented" institutions (Kim and Dahlman, 1992: 446). However, more recent programmes such as NURI (New University for Regional Innovation) and BK (Brain Korea) 21 have been initiated by the government in order to boost the quality of teaching facilities and to encourage recruitment of new academic staff.

Research Activities

In terms of the number of publications in SCI (Science Citation Index) journals, a sharp increase can be observed after the early 1990s, as shown in Figure 3. This change is likely to be closely related to the policy measures regarding Korean universities as one of the main actors providing knowledge in the national innovation system as presented in section 3.1. Furthermore, the contributions of industry as well as public research institutes to this have also increased since the 1990s.

Figure 3: The Number of Publications on SCI (Science Citation Index) Journals by Sectors

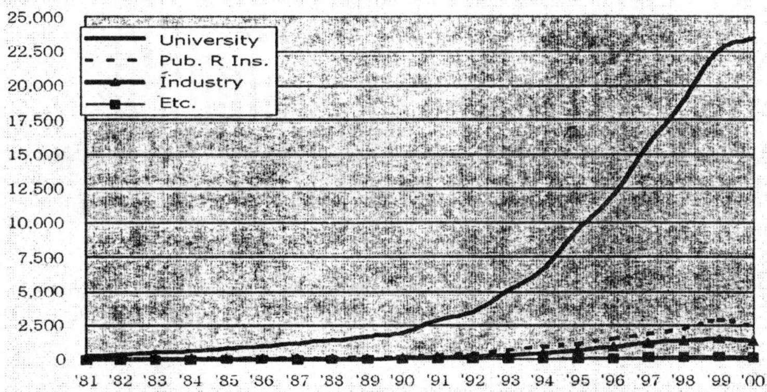

Source: Yun and Ahn (2002), *The characteristics of structure and science activity in Korea: An analysis by SCI.*

While the policy changes in the 1990's for universities can be regarded as one of the main indirect conditions, a more direct driver is the massive increase of resources in terms of research personnel as well as funding. Figure 4 shows that university research expenditure substantially increased in terms of both absolute level and as a share of total university expenditure after the 1990s. Moreover, the number of university researchers has nearly doubled every five years after the 1970s, as shown in appendix Table 1.

In particular, the increase in expenditure was driven mainly by government funding after the early 1990s, as shown in Figure 5. Furthermore, the funding by universities themselves decreased after the late 1990s, while funding from industry increased after the 2000s.

In the early catch-up stage, Korean universities were widely regarded as teaching institutions for providing qualified human resources, while research and development were mainly allocated to publicly funded research institutes (Kim, 1999: 7). The government chose the public institutes as an applied research institution providing technological assistance for industry. On the other hand,

Figure 4: R&D Expenditure of Universities and the Ratio to Total Expenditure (unit: mil won)

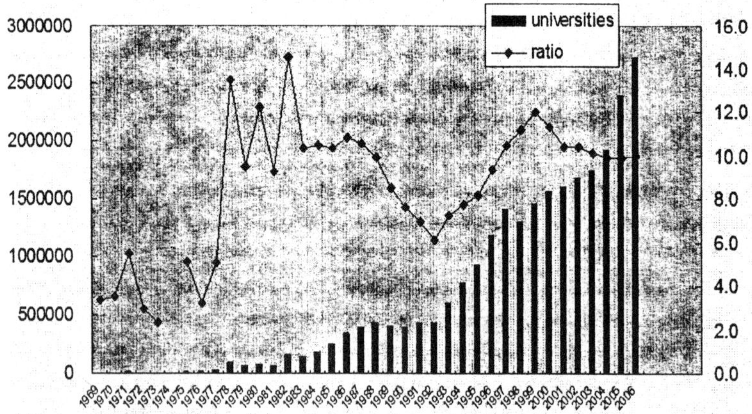

Sources: MOST(2007), Report on the Survey of Research and Development in Science and Technology, MOST, MOST(1999), Report on the Survey of Research and Development in Science and Technology, MOST.

Figure 5: Sources of Korean Universities R&D Expenditure (unit: billion won)

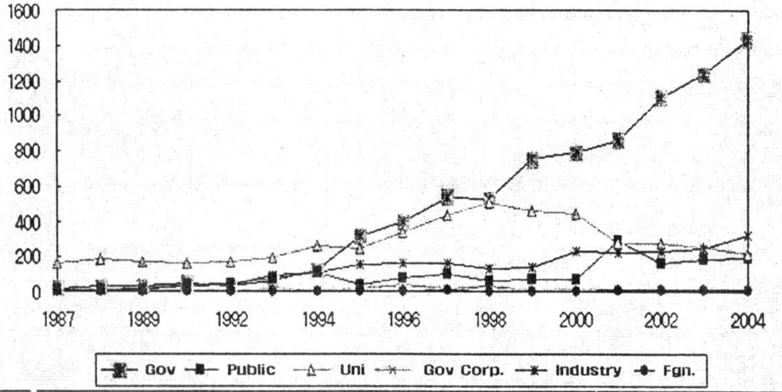

Sources: MOST(2005), Report on the Survey of Research and Development in Science and Technology, MOST, MOST(1999), Report on the Survey of Research and Development in Science and Technology, MOST.

universities in the period of the early catch-up could not attract external research resources, not only because the government was mainly dependent on publicly funded institute in term of research activities, but also because the needs of the industry sector were not developed enough to encourage research in the universities.

Furthermore, research used to be regarded as a private activity for Korean academic staff until the 1960s (Bak, 2006b: 68). In 1963, the Ministry of Education started to support Korean academics through 'the academics research support programme', which was the only programme for funding the research activities of academics until the late 70's. However, the amount of funding was mostly too small to support 'research', so this support was often regarded as little more than another type of salary for academics (Kim *et al.*, 2000).

In contrast, since the early 1990s, research has begun to be recognised as an essential part of academics' every-day life. According to several interviews with Korean academics, an academic with no research activities (particularly, in the field of science and engineering and among the younger generation) is likely to be regarded as an indication of incompetence in the Korean academic community.

Direct Contribution to the Economy

Since 2000, providing direct economic contributions has begun to be strongly recognized as one of the main missions of universities in particular. This subsection describes the invigoration of the third mission of Korean universities in three terms: Patent applications, technology transfer and company spin-offs.

Figure 6: Increase in Number of Domestic Patents Applications and the Ratio to the Total Applications by Universities

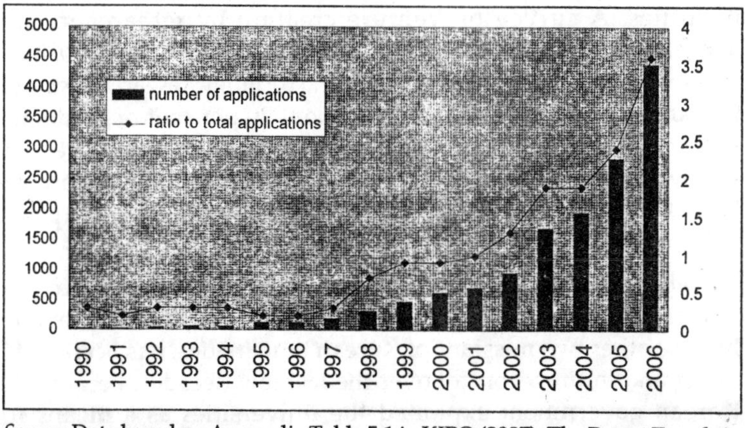

Source: Data based on Appendix Table 5.1 in KIPO (2007), The Patent Trends in Korea 2007, KIPO.

Firstly, as shown in figure 6, the number of domestic patent applications and its ratio to total applications have increased very considerably since the early 2000s. The timing of the abrupt increase coincided with the government policy change on strengthening universities' linkages to industry, as explained in section 3.1.

Secondly, in terms of the technology transfer activities of universities, the performance after 2003 is distinctive compared to that in previous period. As shown in Table 9, about two thirds of royalties have been created after 2003, and four fifths of the numbers of technology transfer agreements have been implemented after 2003.

Table-9
Royalties from Technology Transfer by Universities
(unit: million won)

	2002	2003	2004	2005	2006
Royalties	11,191	2,250	3,177	6,878	9,033
– no. of trans.	(410)	(210)	(243)	(587)	(563)
– no. of univ.*	(34)	(47)	(45)	(50)	(66)

*Number of universities reporting that they transferred technology to industry.

Sources: MOCIE (2006), *A Survey on the Technology Transfers of Public Research Organization* MOCIE; KRF (2007), *White Paper on University-Industry Cooperation* KRF.

Thirdly, in the 2000s, a large number of spin-off companies were established by academics and researchers in public research institutes. A survey on venture creation by researchers and academics was conducted by SMBA (Small and Medium Business Administration) for 219 universities and 51 public research institutes in 2007. According to this survey, about 70 per cent of academics who created companies have done so after 2001. Moreover, the survival rate of the companies created by professors and researchers (72.7%) is higher than that of other small or medium-sized companies within five years (55%) (Kim, 2005).

The qualitative change in the third mission of Korean universities can now be considered. First of all, the third mission like the other two missions of Korean universities, has been under direct and indirect control over the last few decades, because the Korean government exploited the universities as a means for pursuing their industrial and science and technology policies. Therefore, some may maintain that the third mission of Korean

Table-10
Number of the Professors and Researchers Created Spin-off Companies

	2000	*2001*	*2002*	*2003*	*2004*	*2005*	*2006*	*2007*	*Total*
Created	348	118	113	77	70	105	90	82	1003
- profs.	263	99	99	72	64	90	82	74	843
- reschrs.	85	19	14	5	6	15	8	8	160
Closed*	43	33	48	31	36	33	33	17	274
Going-on	305	390	455	501	535	607	664	729	729
Survived		85	65	46	34	72	57	65	**72.7%

* Number of alienated companies is included.

**Survival rate is calculated the ratio of the going-on (729) to the created (1003).

Source: Press release on the website of SMBA (Small and Medium Business Administration), http://www.smba.go.kr/ accessed on 11th May, 2008.

universities was not totally new when it emerged in the 2000s. However, the mode of implementation of the third mission has certainly changed. In other words, the channels of contribution to the economy have extended from human resource provision to direct practical research and even to some profit-making activities.

Conclusion

Based on the history of Korean universities and the development of the Korean university system and their activities as presented in the previous sections, the main characteristics of the Korean academic system are summarised in this final section. To do this, the characteristics are discussed at three levels: The overall system, the organisational and the individual.

Firstly, at the system level, until the early 1990s, the Korean government regarded the university as a provider of practical human resources for industry rather than as an important research base in the national innovation system. Recently, the third mission of making a 'direct contribution to the economy', has been added to 'research' and 'teaching'. Furthermore, the revitalisation of university research and their efforts to make a direct contribution to the economy have been dependent not only on government initiatives but also on funding from government as well as recent increase in industry funding. This suggests that the two Korean academic revolutions were strongly controlled in a 'top-down reformation' by government rather than in a 'bottom-up revolution' by university.

According to typology of Martin (2003: 14), the university model that has prospered in Korea is closer to the 'technical university', which mainly trains human resources and provides useful knowledge for society than, 'classical university', which is highly autonomous and involved in research for its own sake. In terms of strong state control, the Korean universities are also somewhat similar to the Humboldtian model, although in terms of their focus on the practical needs of the society, they are perhaps closer to the technical university and to *Fachhochschulen* in Germany. Therefore, recent higher education policy encouraging Korean universities to become 'entrepreneurial universities' is not so 'revolutionary', while the 'entrepreneurial' activities are more in response to government guidelines than to the needs of the market and industry.

The strong governmental involvement based on the historical development path of Korean universities may remain as an important factor in analysing the research and industrial collaboration activities for the moment. At the system level, some close coupling phenomena can be observed in terms of the similarities between the performances of academe and industry. This characteristic is also closely related to the peculiarity of the behaviour of Korean universities at both the organisational and the individual level, as we see below.

Secondly, the poor resource endowments of the state and the short history of modern universities have created several special characteristics of Korean universities at the organisational level. Historically, the state has been regarded as a central provider and stakeholder, so higher educations have been supported mainly by the government over a long period of time. However, during the last century, due to the limited national supply and the explosive demand, private higher education institutions made up the majority of Korean universities. They are too, under strong government control, although government support has focused more on public universities.

The locations of individual universities are also an important factor in considering the imbalanced development of higher education across the country. A traditional preference for the capital area has influenced the heavy concentration of national resources on the area. Therefore, there have long been issues of inequality between universities in the capital area and those outside. The inequality issue may also be related to the size and age of the universities. The bigger and the older universities are likely to attract more and higher quality resources such as funding and researchers.

Thirdly, at the individual level, until the 1990s, Korean academics have not been generally recognised as important actors for innovative knowledge production but as a provider for human resource training, whereas the engineers and scientists in governmental institutes were instead mobilized for research to meet industrial needs. In other words, the central missions of Korean academics have changed over the last few decades. Therefore, in explaining the behaviour of individual academics, it is important to look for any difference between the older and younger generation.

The strong influence of the government on individual academics with weak organisational buffering is also another characteristic to understand the Korean academic system. The government has influenced the orientation of the performance evaluation system for individual academics through indirect interventions such as the allocation of research funding for each university. Furthermore, due to policies focused on the usefulness of the research output, variation with discipline is expected to be quite high even in the same science and engineering field. Therefore, the discipline of individual academics is likely to be an important property to understand their behaviour. Finally, academics trained in overseas institution (particularly in the U.S.) have been leading the Korean academic community, so whether individuals belong to this group may be an important property in analysing their activities.

REFERENCES

Bak, Hee-Je (2006a), Commercialization of Science and Changing Normative Structure of the Scientific Community, *Journal of Korean Sociology*, Vol. 40 (4), pp. 19-47.

Bak, Hee-Je (2006b), The Characteristics of Korean Universities' Research in terms of Structural Change: Analysis on the R&D Expenditure after the 1980s, Conference of Korean Association of Science and Technology Studies 2006, 30th June, 2006.

Byeon, Taesup (2007), *Korean History*, the 4th edition, Samyoungsa Publishing: Seoul.

Cho, H., Lee, E., Lee C. and Kim S. (2002), *Review of S&T Human Resource Policies in Korea*, STEPI (Science and Technology Institute): Seoul.

Crow, M.M. and Nath S.A. (1992), Technology strategy development in Korean industry: An assessment of market and government influences, *Technovation*, 12 (2), pp. 119-136.

Dodge, Herbert W. (1971), *A history of U.S. assistance to Korean education, 1953-1966*, Unpublished doctoral dissertation, George Washington University.

Kim, Busik (1145), translated by Lee, Kang-Rae (1998), *History of Three Kingdoms*, Hangilsa Publishing: Seoul.

Kim, Geun Bae (2005), *The Emergence of Modern Work Force in Science.*

Kim, Gui-Sung (2004), Foreign Curtural Relations of Koguryo and School Education: Focused on Tae Hak, *Journal of Korean History of Education*, No. 2, pp. 49-74.

Kim, Hoil (2000), Efforts of establishment of the university under the Japanese rule, in Association for Studies for University History (2000), *Universities in the Turning Point*, Hangilsa Publishing: Seoul.

Kim, Hyun Suk (1997b), Technological Innovation System and Science and Technology Policy of Korea, Chapter 4 in Lee *et al.*, (1997), Technological Capability and Competitiveness of Korean Industry, Kyungmoonsa: Seoul.

Kim, Jin-Eun (1973), *An analysis of the national planning process for educational development in the Republic of Korea, 1945-1970*, Unpublished doctoral dissertation, University of Pittsburgh.

Kim, Ju-Hoon (2005) (eds.), *The role of SMEs in the innovation-driven Economy*, KDI (Korea Development Institute.

Kim, L. and Dahlman, C. J. (1992), Technology policy for industrialization: An integrative framework and Korea's experience, Research Policy, 21, pp. 437-453.

Kim, Linsu (1997) *Imitation to Innovation: The Dynamics of Korea's Technological Learning*, Harvard Business School Press.

Kim, Linsu and Yi, Gihong (1997), The Dynamics of R&D in Industrial Development: Lessons from the Korean Experience, Industry and Innovation, Vol. 4, No. 2. pp. 218-233.

Kim, Pil-Dong *et al.*, (2000), *A Preliminary Research on the Structural Change of Institutions of Universities*, Ministry of Education.

Kim, Seok-Hyeon (2006), Public Research Institutes: Universality and Peculiarity, Science and Technology Policy, Vol. 16, No. 5. pp. 102-114.

Kim, Seong-soo (1999), Promotion Policy of the University Research in Korea, STEPI (Science and Technology Policy Institute).

Kim, Seung-Soo (1999), Promotion Policy of the University Research in Korea, STEPI.

Kim, Sunwoong and Lee, Ju-ho (2002), Promoting Innovation- Role of Education—Korea s Economy 2002, *Korea Economic Institute*, 2002.

Kim, Sunwoong and Lee, Ju-ho (2006), Changing facets of Korean higher education: Market competition and the role of the state, *Higher Education*, 52, pp. 557-587.

Korea National Center for Education Statistics & Information (http://std.kedi.re.kr/).

KRF (2006), *White paper on the university-industry cooperation*, KRF.

KRF (2008), The achievement of Brain Korea 21 programme, the website of Korea Research Foundation (http://bnc.krf.or.kr/home/eng/bk21/achievement.jsp) accessed on the 25th Apr., 2008.

Lee, Gilton Eun-Jun (2000), Brain Korea 21: A Development-Oriented National Policy in Korean Higher Education, International Higher Education, Spring 2000.

Lee, H. Yoon, J. and Ryu, B. (1997), *A Study on the History of Modern Education During Japanese Rule*, Korea Education Development Institute.

Lee, H., Choi, K., Yoon, J. and Kim G. (1998), *A study on the History of Modern Education after Liberation from Japanese Rule*, Korea Education Development Institute.

Lee, J.K. (2006), Educational fever and South Korean higher education, *Revista Electrónica de Investigación y Educativa*, 8 (1).

Lee, Sungho H. (2004), Korean Higher Education: History and Future Challenges in Altbach and Umakoshi (eds.), *Asian Universities*, The Johns Hopkins University Press: Baltimore and London.

Lee, Sungho H. (2006), *Korean Higher Education: Its Emergence, Development and Future Challenges*, Hakjisa Publisher: Seoul.

McGinn, Noel F. *et al.*, (1980), *Education and development in Korea*, Harvard Univeristiy Press: Cambridge, MA.

MOE (1963), *Annual Report of Education Statistics*, Ministry of Education.

Moon, Manyong (2004), Reappraisal of the Establishment of KIST: U.S. and Korea's Role, *The Korean Journal of History of Science*, 26 (1), pp.57-86.

Moon, Manyong (2006), Change in the R&D Activities of KIST: 1966-1980, *The Korean Journal of History of Science*, 28 (1), pp. 81-115.

Park, K., Kwon, K., Eun, J., Han, D, Han, Y. and Han, S. (2007), *Analysis on the impact of university-industry collaboration policy on research activities and patenting activities in Korean universities*, KRF (Korea Research Foundation).

Shin, Haesoon (2000), The History of the Highest Level Education Institution, Sung-kyun-Kwan', in Association for Studies for University History (2000), *Universities in the Turning Point*, Hangilsa Publishing: Seoul.

Sohn, B. *et al.*, (2006), Current situation and prospect of Korean university-industry cooperation, *Venture Creation Study*, Vol. 1 (1), pp. 31-32.

Sohn, Insoo (1987), *History of Korean education*, the 2 edition, Muneumsa: Seoul.

Song, Sung-Soo (2002), A Study on the Characteristics of Science and Technology Policy in Korea, *Korean Journal of Study of Science and Technology*, Vol. 2 (1).

Trow, M. (1974). Problems in the Transition from Elite to Mass Higher Education, in *Policies for Higher Education*, from the General Report on the Conference on Future Structures of Post-Secondary Education, 55-101. Paris: OECD.

Umakoshi, T. (1997), The Establishment and Development of Korean Modern Universities, Nagoya University Press: Nagoya.

Webb, M. (2007), *South Korea: Mass innovation comes of age*, DEMOS.

Woo, Jong-Chun (2002), Infrastructure of Research and Development and Human Resource in Korea, in Shin, Gi-Wook, *A Study on Innovation toward University-Industry Networking*, STEPI.

Yim, D.S. and Kim W.D. (2005), The Evolutionary Responses of Korean Governmental Research Institutes in a Changing National Innovation System, *Science, Technology and Society*, Vol. 10, Issue 1, pp. 31-55.

Yoo, Youngreul (2000), The first Modern University: Soongsil University, in Association for Studies for University History (2000), *Universities in the Turning Point*, Hangilsa Publishing: Seoul.

APPENDIX

Figure 1: Population that has Attained at Least Tertiary Education (2005)

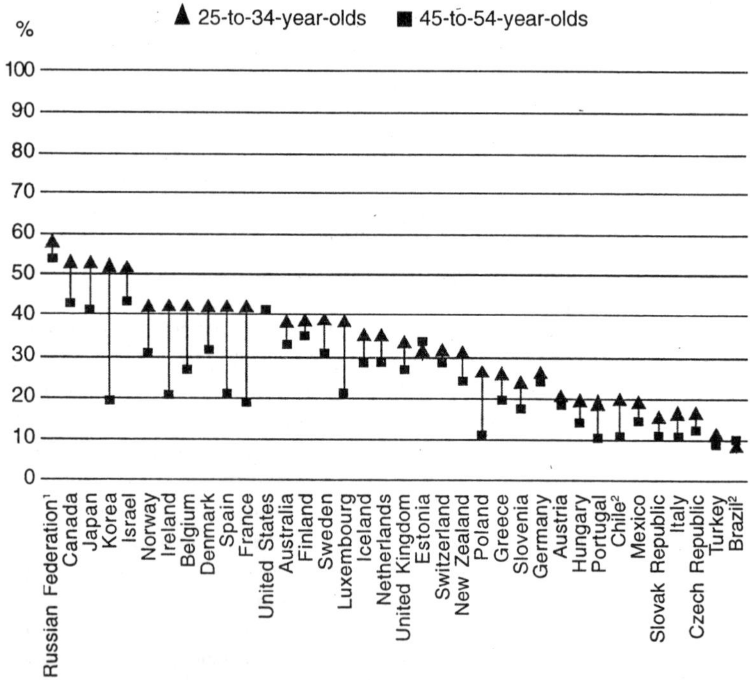

1. Year of reference 2003.
2. Year of reference 2004.

Countries are ranked in descending order of the percentage of 25-to-34-year-olds who have attained tertiary education.

Source: OECD (2007), Education at a Glance 2007, Chart A1. 3, p. 29, OECD: Paris.

Table-1
Some R&D Indicators of Korean Innovation System (1965-2005)

Year	*1965*	*1970*	*1975*	*1980*	*1985*	*1990*	*1995*	*2000*	*2005*
R&D Exp.*	2.1	10.5	42.7	211.7	1,155.2	3,210.5	9,440.6	13,848.5	24,155.4
-Public	1.9	9.2	28.5	109.2	231.3	510.5	1,780.9	3,816.9	5,877.2
-Private	0.2	1.3	14.2	102.5	923.9	2,700.0	7,659.7	10,023.4	18,106.8
Pub. vs. Pri.	90:10	88:12	67:33	52:48	20:80	16:84	19:81	28:72	24:76
R&D/ GNP	0.26	0.83	0.42	0.57	1.58	1.95	2.51	2.40	2.98
Rese-archers	2,135	5,628	10,275	18,434	41,473	70,503	128,315	159,973	234,702
-Govt.	1,671	2,458	3,086	4,598	7,542	10,434	15,007	13,913	15,501
-Univ.	352	2,011	4,534	8,695	14,935	21,332	44,683	51,727	64,895
-Industry	112	1,159	2,655	5,141	18,996	38,737	68,625	94,333	154,306
R&D Exp**	967	1,874	4,152	11,486	27,853	47,514	73,574	86,568	102,920
Rese-archer***	0.07	0.17	0.29	0.48	1.01	1.64	2.85	3.38	4.86
Industry Lab.	0	1****	12	54	183	966	2,152	4,194	7,368

*Unit: billion won, **R&D Expenditure Per Researcher (Unit: thousand won), ***Number of Researchers per 100,000 population, **** Data in 1971. Sources: MOST (1998-2006), Report on the Survey of Research and Development in Science and Technology, MOST (Ministry of Science and Technology).

13

Strategies in Reading Instruction

Dr. Marlow Ediger, USA

The reading instructor needs to use a variety of strategies to encourage student reading achievement. Strategies used must meet learner needs. Meeting diagnosed needs assists the teacher in providing adequately for each student in the classroom. The needs of each student may differ from that of others; however, there will be some overlapping. Students need to achieve as optimally as possible. It is salient then for the reading teacher to possess excellent knowledge and skills in how to assist students to attain relevant objectives in the curriculum.

Strategies of Teaching and Learning

Strategy instruction has received much emphasis in professional literature. Teachers should assist students to use different strategies in ongoing learning activities in assisting learners to attain more optimally (Ediger, 2006). This is especially true for students who experience difficulty in learning such as in reading and writing. Difficulties in learning may be ameliorated with effective instruction. Early teaching to use each strategy well is needed. Systematic teaching also needs to be in evidence. Explicit teaching may not be adequate to help certain pupils learn to use these tools effectively. Students may use specific strategies during explicit teaching, but fail to use them during independent study time. They also need guidance to apply each strategy. Tools of the trade may be taught through the use of *physical objects* such as

- looking for the word on the word wall.
- finding a word which will assist in spelling and in word identification such as could-should.

- locating the word in a dictionary.
- noticing if the word is in print in the classroom environment, in addition to the word wall.

Tools of the *mind* include the following used strategies:

- saying the word slowly and listening for sounds heard.
- thinking of different spelling patterns that can spell the sound one hears, *out* vs *down*.
- say the word slowly and listen for parts that are known in spelling, *and* in *candy*.
- think about the word and notice if it can be seen mentally.
- think of a word which rhymes that one is attempting to spell, (Williams and Lundstrom, 2007).

The tools of the trade may be used in both reading and writing. For example, an unknown word may be recognized by looking on the word wall in the classroom for a similarly spelled word. Each student needs to be cognizant of monitoring his/her own achievement in reading. The monitoring must be ongoing as the leaner evaluates continuously if subject matter read is understood.

Retelling what has been read is one approach to the monitoring one's own progress. Merely reading words without comprehension does not suffice in monitoring the self in an ongoing reading activity (Ediger, 2007).

Monitoring vocabulary growth and development aids the student to ascertain which words are meaningful or lack understanding. Those vocabulary terms not understood become objectives to achieve. With the use of context clues or dividing an unknown word into syllables helps the learner to read meaningfully. Skipping over unidentified words may add to increased reading difficulties later on.

Growth and development needs to be sequential and continuous. Thus, the student in monitoring the self notices if subject matter and vocabulary terms are understood. Teaching and learning strategies must emphasize students monitoring their very own individual achievement and progress (See Reis and Fogarty, 2006).

Second, self efficacy needs to be achieved by learners. Here, the student develops confidence in the self through sequential progress experienced in reading. Success in learning is sequential and continuous, making for an increasingly positive self concept. Feelings of being able to successfully read/comprehend well and do things to achieve relevant goals are inherent in feelings of self efficacy. How is this to be done?

- sequence learnings in reading so that the student perceives progress, not failure.
- adjust the reading curriculum to the present achievement level of the learner and then optimize successful progress.
- assist the student to experience subsequent progress.
- provide adequate feedback of student progress so the latter receives knowledge of results in order to benefit from the ensuing activities.
- have the learner experience appropriate readiness activities in reading to benefit fully from the ensuing experiences.
- help the student to relate previous learnings to the new subject matter to be acquired (Ediger and Rao, 2007).

Success in learning helps the student to become more confident in his/her abilities. Growth in achievement assists the student in developing a more adequate self concept. He/she leans more upon the self to solve problems and answer questions. The student then has had numerous opportunities to have esteem needs met. Recognition for progress made in order to benefit fully from the ensuing activities, should promote feelings of confidence. Feeling confident with a good self image makes for positive attitudes in being successful in the new and novel tasks which abound (See Noyagam, 2006).

Third, metacognition strategies used assist the learner to review, rehearse, evaluate and come up with a new synthesis of ideas. In having read subject matter, the student may think about what was acquired in terms of facts, concepts, and generalizations. Clarity of ideas might have been missing and the learner notices what needs additional clarification. Problems may be identified through metacognition. An hypothesis may be developed pertaining to the identified problem, resulting in information sought from a variety of reference sources. The hypothesis is then tested.

Factors involved in metacognitive thinking include the following:

- analyzing one's own comprehension from reading, discussions, and group work.

- using the instructional component according to one's analyzed needs.
- determining background information necessary for acquisition of ensuing ideas.
- selecting and utilizing a specific strategy for learning.
- clarifying each strategy.
- monitoring the effectiveness of strategy used.
- evaluating strategies used.
- assessing subject matter achieved (Savithiri, 2006).

For the teacher of reading, the above metacognitive strategy involves helping the learner to use critical thinking to appraise his/her ideas gained from the ongoing activity. Then the student needs assistance to choose a method of procedure such as reading to secure an answer to a question. The learner must retrieve background information in order to benefit from the ensuing reading activity. The learner needs to possess clarity on the strategy to be used in securing answers to questions or problems. The student should monitor his own effectiveness in the strategy used. Reading involves comprehending ideas and evaluating secured subject matter.

Metacognition may also be stressed in transcript analysis. Here, for example, the reading teacher tapes a segment of student discussion pertaining to subject matter read. He/she asks questions pertaining to content discussed in the tape. The questions extend thinking. Thus, answers to questions provided by learners presently become more indepth inclined. Students think about thinking in that the answers to questions given on the tape form a basis for elaboration. They review what was said on the tape and then bring in additional and new ideas. The relationship between the old and then new make for a synthesis (op. cit. Savithiri, 2006).

Fourth, a student centered reading curriculum may be emphasized. Here, goals of instruction stress input from learners in the classroom. For example, pupils may present ideas for subject matter to be read in beginning reading instruction. Objects on an interest center may provide for encoding while pupils watch the process of linking the objects (the concrete situation) with the abstract (words recorded). Pupils present the ideas from observations made of these objects. The teacher then types the commands using the word processor, resulting in words seen on a screen. Pupils might then see talk recorded. They practice reading the ideas as the teacher points to each word in the read aloud. The read aloud may be stressed as often as desired. Many times, pupils like to hear the same content read aloud more than once. It should, however, be read aloud frequently enough as pupils observe each word being read in order to develop a basic sight vocabulary. This is a learner centered reading programme in that

- pupils present the content for encoding which stresses familiarity of subject matter read.
- pupils sequence their very own ideas to be read as they are being presented from objects viewed on the interest center.
- pupils practice reading aloud their own thinking pertaining to observations made.
- pupils rehearse the read aloud until abstract words are recognized which become a part of their own reading progress (See San Antonio, 74-79).

Reading programmes on any age/grade level need to emphasize questions to discuss which come from learners. These questions tend to be of interest to students. Elementary school reading programmes which stress learner input into selecting and sequencing achievement in addition to the above asterisked item include individualized reading, sustained silent reading, the accelerated reader, and the Big Book approach, among others. Teachers of reading need to select those programmes which involve considerable learner choice in terms of objectives, learning activities, and appraisal procedures (See Keefe, 2007).

Conclusion

Students need to experience strategies of instruction which engage, meet needs, optimize achievement, and promote perceived purpose. Reading programmes and strategies of instruction must provide for individual differences (See Clarke and Holwadel, 2007).

REFERENCES

Clarke, Lane W., and Jennifer Holwadel (2007), "Help! What is Wrong with these Literature Circles and How can we Fix them?" The Reading Teacher, 61 (1), 20-31.

Ediger, Marlow (2006), "Administration of Schools," College Student Journal, 40 (4), 846-851.

Ediger, Marlow (2007), "Teacher Observation to Evaluate Achievement," Journal of Instructional Psychology, 34 (3), 137-139.

Ediger, Marlow, and D. Bhaskara Rao (2007), Reading Curriculum and Instruction. New Delhi, India: Discovery Publishing House.

Keefe, James W. (2007), "What is Personalization?" Phi Delta Kappan, November issue, 217-223.

Noyagam, Soosai, (2006), Constraints and their Impact on the Academic Achievement of the Santal Tribal 12th STD Students in Jharkhand State. Ph.D. thesis evaluated by the writer for St. Xavier's College of Education, Palayamkottai, India.

Reis, Sally M., and Elizabeth Fogarty (2006), "Savoring Reading, Schoolwide," Educational Leadership, 64 (2), 32-36.

San Antonio, Donna Marie (2006), "Understanding Student Strengths and Weaknesses," Educational Leadership, 65 (7), 74-79.

Williams, Cheri, and Ruth P. Lundstrom (2007), "Strategy Instruction During Word Study and Interactive Writing," The Reading Teacher, 61 (3), 204-211.

Savithiri, V. (2006), Impact of Metacognitive Strategies in Enhancing Perceptual Skills Among High School Students on Learning Geometry. Ph.D. thesis evaluated by the writer for Alagappa University, Karaikudi, India.

14

Professionalization in Physical Education

Ogunleye, S.B., Nigeria

Introduction

Love of teaching and service are essential elements for those who wish to enter this noble profession—PHYSICAL EDUCATION. Happy people are usually loving people, and to be content in educating, one must be in harmony with self, with others and with the outside world.

This paper focuses on PROFESSIONALISATION IN PHYSICAL EDUCATION. The meaning of physical education and profession were briefly explained.

Physical Education

Physical Education is an integral part of education through a well-planned programme of physical activities that aims at developing individuals physically, mentally, and socially. In other words, it is the development of a well integrated individual having a sound mind and body, and socially sound. In short, physical education is the building of the body and mind of individuals. Physical education is defined by Nixon and Jewett as the art and science of voluntary, purposeful human movement. It focuses on selective aspects of the realm of experiences in voluntary, purposeful human movements. The physical educator basically is interested in all human movements, but because this (term) is so encompassing, formal studies and programmes of physical education today are generally concentrated in movement designated by such terms as sports, dance, gymnastics, aquatics, and exercise (Nixon and Jewett, 1980, p. 3).

A common view of the totality of physical education's scope holds that it is both an academic discipline and a professional field having many programme outlets such as in schools, hospitals, parks, beaches, forests, rivers, cities, mountains, on and in the water, and so on. Many public and private agencies sponsor programmes of physical education, sport and dance in a wide variety of environments (Vendien and Nixon, 1985).

Profession

Profession is an occupation usually involving relatively long and specialised preparation on the level of higher education and governed by its own code of ethics. Therefore, in this paper profession was defined as a work which needs long special professional training, mental skills, specialised knowledge and other scientific foundations which are essential to the adequate performance of the services. Physical education may be described today as a discrete academic discipline with a unique body of knowledge and an educationally based profession (Nixon and Jewett, 1989 p. 18).

Physical Education as a Profession

Physical Education is completely a profession which possesses most of attributes required of a profession. The following are some of the features of Physical Education Profession:

1. Physical Education renders unique, definite and essential services to the society. It provides education through physical activities which enable the individuals to be physically fit, acquire physical skill, possess an understanding of human body, motivating good health habits and meaningful social experience.
2. Physical Education specialists are specially qualified by long period of training and experience relative to their unique responsibilities. The period of specialised training ranges from one year for certificate courses, two years for Diploma courses to three years (though Joint Admission Examination is four years) for Bachelors' Degree.
3. Physical Education claims to form Associations which includes:

   (i) Nigeria Association for Physical, Health Education and Recreation, Sport and Dance (NAPHER-SD).

   (ii) Nigeria Association for Sports Science and Medicine (NASSM).

   (iii) Sport Psychology Association of Nigeria (SPAN).

(iv) Nigeria Association for Comparative Physical Education and Sports (NACPES).

4. The services rendered by Physical Education practitioners is largely intrinsic. In other words, they desire to serve others and their satisfactions come primarily from the opportunity to serve rather than from external incentives such as high salary or public recognition.
5. Physical Education service can only be provided by somebody who has undergone specialised training in the profession. For example, given firstaid treatment to victim, organisation and administration of competition and sports, weight control clinics, coaching etc.
6. Members of Physical Education profession regulate the conduct of each other and insist on high behaviour of all concerned. This covers the code of ethics, that is, regulates the professional conduct of members, the relationship between the profession and its client.
7. Physical Education as a profession involves a specialised body of knowledge. Some of this specialised body of knowledge are movement education, physiology of exercise, psychology of education, kinesiology, method and materials for teaching physical education etc.

What Constitutes Professional Preparation?

In physical Education, some factors determined the professional constituent of physical educator. These factors are:

(a) Qualities of the teacher.
(b) Recognition of problems.
(c) Preparing to meet problems.
(d) Duties and services rendered.
(e) Groups to which physical education is accountable.
(f) Teacher's evaluation.

Qualities of a Teacher

Professional Education

In attaining a professional attitude, it required a long period of training which ranges from one to four years before a certificate is awarded. Physical Education possesses the following:

(i) Professional Diploma Certificate in Physical Education (Dip. P.E.)

(ii) Nigeria Certificate of Education (NCE).
(iii) B.Sc.(Ed)/B.Ed.

Appearance

Physical Educators should distinguish themselves from clients and students who are not professional. As a professional, the mode of dressing would be moderate, smart and sportish when officiating at athletics and any other games and sports. Unlike non-professional who officiate in flowing outfit and unsportish dresses. Good appearance of physical educators would promote both dignity and respect for the profession.

Health

The teacher of physical education must be in shape, not only to set an example, but also because the nature of the work necessitates excellent health at all times (Greyson and Lewis, 1979). In addition, Bucher (1975) also stated that teacher should be able to establish standards of healthful living in order to meet the challenges of teaching physical education. The teacher should care for skin, teeth, eyes, ears, chest, heart, feet and posture, and show personal health history, mental health and emotional stability.

Personality

It means the gait and posture of an individual as a person. Greyson and Lewis (1979) in their opinion stated that successful teachers are friendly, extroverted, and able to relate to students. No longer can embittered or unfriendly teachers produce the types of programmes necessary for quality education. The ability to establish harmonious relationships and rapport with differing individual students; co-workers, administrators, and parents is one desirable as a physical education instructor.

Dedication

Physical Education teachers need to be dedicated to their profession by making sure that the enthusiasm and aggressiveness necessary for teaching is maintained. He has to avoid neglects of the many little details involved in day to day class management and teaching. Devotion to physical education profession is very vital for effective teaching.

Emotional Stability

This is one of the most important attribute physical educators should possess. Lack of emotional stability would picture a physical educator as unqualified and unfit to be in the classroom and this should not be so. Physical educator must have a good emotional stability. He should be well adjusted, happy, enthusiastic, and understanding, usually develop the buoyant and relaxed atmosphere essential for effective teaching.

Individual Differences

Physical Educator should respect the students and allow for individual differences. Students of Physical Education classes are different physically, mentally and emotionally and this should be considered when planning their programmes. This is because students progress in acquisition of skills and procedures must be developed to provide opportunity for each student to learn at his or her own pace.

Leadership

Good leadership is very essential to any physical education programme. A well-prepared and creative physical education is extensive and more effective than most expensive equipment. Good leaders are energetic individuals with socially valuable objectives who assume a sense of responsibility to create an excellent teaching, learning experience, (Greyson and Lewis, 1979).

Professional Interest and Dignity

Physical Educator should seek to improve himself through research, study, and participation in professional efforts which will make him superior in the profession. He should be current with the latest developments in learning theories and the best methods for teaching skills, so as to achieve the expected performance required of him.

Awareness of the advance base of knowledge in sport psychology, sport sociology, exercise physiology, kinesiology and perceptual motor skills should bring about a new emphasis in professional interest and dignity (Greyson and Lewis, 1979).

The prestige of the physical educator means a lot in the profession and, therefore, the successful physical education leaders should be well-articulated, have a command of English Language, and leave a good impression with their fellow teachers.

Recognition of Problems

Recognition of problems by physical educators is very vital in this profession. This will help him prepare well in offering something unique to students during or after physical activities.

Preparing to Meet Problems

Professional physical teacher who has the ability to recognise problems still need to prepare to meet such problems that are uncalled for. The following questions comes-up; what does physical educator do after confirming the problems? Does he run-away? Was he embarrassed? How does he go about solving it? The answer is 'No'. As a professional, he has committed himself and well-prepared to meet and solve any problem that might arise. Maturity, good judgement, and a professional etiquette help him to function properly as a professional and this shows professional preparedness.

Duties and Services to be Rendered

Physical Education professional perform the following duties and render services expected of him diligently when called upon.

1. ***Teaching:*** A physical educator teaches in school like any other teachers in their field of discipline by applying appropriate methodology for effective teaching.
2. ***Special Duty:*** He also renders services as specialist to the handicapped. That is service for the blind, deaf and dumb, crippled, mentally retarded, emotionally disturbed, gifted children etc.
3. ***Health Services:*** He renders health services and safety education to people in clinics, camps and health centres.
4. Coaching and training of athletes is part of his services.
5. ***Business and Industry:*** He renders services to business organisations (Catholic Youth Organisation, Church or Mosque). Serves as personnel for the development of fitness programmes.
6. ***Counselling:*** He renders counselling services to people on how to go about their lives.

Groups to Whom a Physical Educator is Accountable

According to Bucher and Thaxton (1976), a physical education teacher performs duties for

1. The Students
2. The Department
3. The Faculty and School
4. The Community
5. The Profession

In addition to the above, physical education also performs duties for himself for lifetime professional development. Mediocrity is not welcome in physical education profession rather the profession requires a well-prepared and creative physical educator.

Teacher Evaluation

Bucher, (1975), said that evaluation of teacher is very important in determining the level such as promotions, in-service training, tenure merit, salary increase and the improvement of teaching.

The criteria for the evaluation of teachers include the following:

1. Personal qualification—emotional stability, appearance, control of English Language, dedication etc.
2. Class management—competence in class organisation and use of teaching aids/materials.
3. Teacher-pupil relationship—attitude of class and how they relate.
4. Techniques of teaching—knowledge of subject matter, attending to course of study, daily preparation.
5. Professional attitude—professional conduct, in-service training, parent relationship.

Conclusion and Recommendations

1. Physical education leaders should have strong personality that reflects integrity, character, and emotional stability.
2. They professionally prepared to teach physical education by involving in specialised physical education courses which varies in duration.
3. Government and the professional bodies in physical education should flush out non-professional individuals and business organisations who are on the field. Laws should be made to penalise offenders/violators.
4. Adequate facilities and equipment/materials/supplies should be provided right from the primary schools to secondary and higher institutions.
5. Government should lift any embargo on importation of sports facilities and equipment/materials/supplies and the Agro-industries in the country should be encouraged by a way of subsidising them financially in improving locally made equipment and facilities.
6. The requirements for admission into physical education schools should be improved and schools should comply to

the necessary requirement before giving admissions. English language, Physical Education, Biology, Physics, Chemistry should include some of the required subjects at credit level form the applicants.

7. The importance of Physical Education should be inculcated in the learner right from the onset. Physical Education as a career; its branches of specialised discipline and its industrious values.

Professionlisation in Physical Education is the understanding of the profession itself, what is entails to be a professional. Physical Education require "good leaders who are well prepared and creative, generally energetic individuals with socially valuable objectives who assume a sense of responsibility to create an excellent teaching-learning experience" (Greyson and Lewis, 1979).

Preparation is the key word for Physical Education. This noble profession (Physical Education) is now gaining much ground everyday because people in the society are now realising and having interests by participating in sports and games.

In addition, students of Physical Education should avoid shyness and inferiority complex in their profession. They should stand as mirror of their noble profession and ready to defend it at any point in time. They should be able to talk and enlighten peoples on what their profession entails, and that it is not just "jumping up and down" or "Ajiserepa" as it is normally referred to by innocent and non-professionals.

REFERENCES

Hornby (1974). *Oxford Advanced Learner's Dictionary of Current English.* 3rd (Ed.) E.L.B.S. London.

Bucher, (1975). *Foundation of Physical Education,* (7th Ed) C.V., Mosby Company, St. Louis.

Bucher and Thaxton (1976). *Physical Education and Sports*: Changes and Challenges, St. Louis: Mosby and Company.

Greyson and Lewis (1979). *Effective Teaching Strategies in Secondary Physical Education* Philadelphia, W.B. Saunders Company.

Nixon, J.E. and Jewett, A.N. (1980). *Introduction to Physical Education* (9th Ed.). Philadelphia. Saunders College.

Vendien, C.L. and Nixon, J.E. (1985). *Physical Education Teacher Education: Guidelines for sport pedagogy.* New York, Macmillan Publishing Company.

15

Integration of Vocational Agriculture Education for Effective Citizenship Development in Nigeria

Onanuga, P. Abayomi, Nigeria

Introduction

There is hardly any school subject that commands the same public attention as agriculture science because of its importance and contribution to national economy. Two aspects of agriculture make its study a very challenging concern to education and the society. First, is the fact that food is the most basic human need that it must be laboured for. The second is that any nation which cannot meet with its food requirement is jeopardized politically and economically. Krishna Sastry (1987) reported an agriculture teacher as saying that agriculture is part of human behaviour and culture; an intrinsic component of human existence, which people must learn to appreciate if they must understand and contribute to human conditions of existence. The study of agriculture is expected to meet the needs of any society.

In Nigeria, education has been adopted as an instrument "par excellence" for effecting national development (FRN, NPE 2004). The Nigeria's philosophy of education, therefore is geared towards "self-realisation, better human relationship, individual and national efficiency, effective citizenship, national consciousness, national unity, as well as toward social, cultural, economic, political goals which derive from the philosophy of education hinged on the acquisition of appropriate skills and the development of mental, physical, and social abilities and competencies as equipment for the individual to live in and contribute to the development of his society".

To achieve this, the government has stated that education will continue to be highly rated in the national development plans;

because it is the most important instrument of change as any fundamental change in the intellectual and social outlook of any society has to be preceded by an educational revolution (FRN, NPE 2004); Ubahakwe (1999) have suggested that one way of meeting this is to reposition our cultural values at the very core of the leasing process itself.

The study of vocational agriculture is expected to meet the needs of the society (Olaitan 1993) so it can be a desirable tool for the revolution. The National Policy on Education shall be to "give training and impart the necessary skills to individual who shall be self-realiant economically" (FRN, NPE 2004:31).

Education for development is a veritable factor for socio-economic emancipation and politico-cultural inculcation of a nation. This type of education must be capable of fostering in the individual those values that make for good and responsible citizenship. In consequence to the national educational goals, the quality of instruction at all levels has to be oriented toward inculcating the following values:

(i) Respect for the worth and dignity of the individual;
(ii) Shared responsibility for the common good of society; and
(iii) Acquisition of competencies necessary for self-reliance among others.

In addition, another provision of the policy document under the secondary education stressed that youth clubs, organizations and school societies are important instruments for character training and shall be positively encouraged" (NPE 2004:24).

On the other hand, for education to be actually relevant to the development process of any nation, it must seek to meet the following objectives among others: (Obasanjo and Mabogunje 1991).

(i) Training the individual to relate to and interact meaningfully with other individuals in the society and to appreciate the importance of effective organization for human progress;
(ii) Fostering in the individual those values, which make for good citizenship, such as honesty, tolerance, selflessness, dedication, hard work and personal integrity, all of which, provide the rich bases for good leadership.

A search through the developmental stages of education in Nigeria reveals the dimensions of the societal dynamism. Following increased nationalist activities and agitation for independence, the general outlook of the curriculum in school was modified to reflect some basic knowledge in civics and principles of self governance (Boateng 1991).

Except the various enlightenment programmes designed to mould the citizen's values and moderate their behaviour patterns, such as Shagari's Ethical Revolution (1982), Buhari/Idiagbon's War Against Indiscipline (1984) and the Babangida's Mass Mobilization for Social Justice and Economic Recovery (1986), not much efforts have been achieved (Ogunyemi 2001).

That is, a critical look at educational system in Nigeria shows that not enough emphasis is given, to the essence of developing practically responsible citizenship in individuals while going through all the levels of education. This is implying that inadequate emphasis has been placed on the aspect that constitutes a factor of vital relevance to national development and survival. Therefore, it becomes pertinent that a model be evolved focusing on individual citizens at developing the nation hence the advocacy of integration of vocational agriculture education for effective citizenship development.

Perspectives of Integration in Agriculture Education in Nigeria

Integration is not a new concept in the Nigeria education system. Social studies and primary school science at the primary school level, and integrated science, introductory technology and business studies at the junior secondary school level, are clear examples. The idea of bringing together topics from various related subjects under the same umbrella has been the most popular practice of integration in the Nigerian school system.

In agricultural education, integration is viewed in two perspectives, namely;

(a) Concept integration, and
(b) Subject integration (Olaitan, 1993).

Concept integration refers to the collection of topics from all areas of agriculture science, that is, crop production, animal production, soil science, agricultural economics, plant and animal protection and so on, all of which are under a single course or programme. Subject integration on the other hand refers to the teaching of all disciplines related to agriculture with an agricultural tinge.

Within the framework of these perspectives of integration are various approaches namely;

(*a*) The "pure science" approach;
(*b*) Modular approach;
(*c*) Integration of the three major components of the study of agriculture;
(*d*) The integration of the study of agriculture with social life;
(*e*) Integration of all agricultural subjects and experiences into a unified single package; and
(*f*) Institutional affiliation.

Meanwhile for the purpose of this chapter the focus is integration of the three major components of the study of agriculture viz-a-viz effective citizenship development.

Integration as Concept in Agriculture Education Curriculum in Nigeria

For many years agriculture has been defined variously and the meaning has undergone overwhelming elaborations. The simplest definition of agriculture as the growing crops and rearing of animals for man's use is really being replaced by a school of thought viewing agriculture as a system with many interrelated components. Hence, it is thus classified as a field of knowledge rather than as a mere subject.

In the real sense of it, agriculture as a field of study is a combination of knowledge and skills in biology, chemistry, physics, geography, economics and any other subjects found necessary in order to facilitate the growing of crops and rearing of animals for man's use. As noted by Olaitan (1993) the knowledge from these subjects are organized around concepts and units or occupational areas such as crop production, animal production and soil management. It further explained that singly, these areas can be studied on their own but effective practical utilization of agriculture knowledge demands that the learner be familiar with all the occupational areas in the field.

The primary level of agriculture education in Nigeria is offered as an integration of various units needed for a well rounded occupational awareness in agriculture. The primary agriculture curriculum consists of topics in soil science, crop science, animal science and general agriculture. Essentially, the main focus of the programme is to enable the student to view agriculture as a meaningful holistic area of study where a student could find a comfortable living as he explores this broad area subsequently for a choice of career.

Ever since the emergence of agriculture as a subject of study in Nigerian secondary schools in 1963, concept integration has been the practice. However, the present junior and senior secondary curricula are organized around the three major concepts of production, protection and economics. The curricula content of agriculture at the two tiers of secondary education had been further clustered into six units thus: Basic concept; crop production; animal production, agricultural ecology and system, agricultural engineering and agricultural economics (Olaitan and Uwadiae, 1993).

At the tertiary level, agriculture education had also adopted the concept of integrative approach. Most tertiary institutions in Nigeria offer agricultural science courses of a general nature up to their final year. In a typical Nigerian University, for instance, students of crop production, soil science, animal production, agricultural economics and agricultural extension and rural sociology usually offer more or less similar courses up to the end of their third year when they proceed for internship or industrial attachment. During the final year, meanwhile, the courses offered are taken from the student's area of specialization in the earlier enumerated areas.

Integration of the Components of Agriculture Education Curriculum

Vocational agriculture education has three major components, namely;

(a) Classroom and Laboratory instruction,
(b) Supervised Occupational Experience, and
(c) Leadership development through youth organizations.

These three components make input into the curriculum objective, and evaluation, hence the need to synchronize class work with laboratory and field experiments becomes compelling. Apart from these, Olaitan (1993) Olaitan and Uwadiae (1993) stressed that the other components of agriculture education (occupational experience and leadership) must be closely interwoven with formal instruction for a well-rounded vocational skills development. Olaitan (1993) pointed out that in United States of America, vocational agriculture programmes are designed to embrace these three components complementing one another.

At any time a curriculum revision is advocated, evidence that the proposed innovation is advantageous over the previous one is usually demanded. The same applies to the case presented in this chapter but the manifestation of the advantages of integration would definitely take time. Therefore, it requires that the approach recommended be implemented first so its advantages can be apparently judged. Rao (1987), however, justified the integration of relevant courses around agriculture from a philosophical argument, saying;

> *"... the barrier between academic knowledge and applications need to be broken down. A body of knowledge which is not useful is of no value. The problem area should therefore have a central position in the curriculum whether they concern food and agriculture or any other topic."*

Thus, the much desired stimulation of students' interest in agriculture as reflected in the national curriculum lies in integrating vocational agriculture into teaching of essential aspects of relevant body of knowledge. This is in agreement with Olaitan's (1993) position that the much desired relevance in tertiary level training in agriculture can be achieved by integrating the three components into the study of vocational agriculture at the penultimate secondary school level.

Citizenship Development

Lack of functional literacy and technical know how deprive the citizens of the necessary confidence, knowledge and skills to assert their rights, embrace their responsibilities and participate effectively in public life, Adedoyin (2001). Galadina (2000) identifies poverty as a threat to responsibly effective citizenship development and the democratic process. He therefore recommends that people should be empowered through functional and competence-based education to challenge the status quo so as to secure fundamental political and social change. The scholar also linked the inability of the people to resist voting for corruptly enriched political office seekers to poverty.

Development should be people-oriented rather than institution oriented. According to Amucheazi (1980), development should focus attention on individual citizen, thinking of what he needs at a particular time and how he can combat the forces that hold him down. This is probably why Adedoyin (2001) defines development as a situation whereby every citizen is able to meet the basic needs of life and has steady access to means of decent livelihood.

Obasanjo and Mabogunje (1991) define development as a process concerned with people's capability in a defined area over a defined period to manage and induce positive change and reduce or eliminate unwanted or unwarranted change. Thus, the more people develop themselves, the more they would become instruments for further change.

Taking a cursory look at a society where poverty is the bedrock of living and there has been the intent of gearing several efforts to make political and social change achievable in her people had become pretty difficult. There is thus, need to ask the question "how can change be managed or induced in such a society or nation?". This situation calls for skill and entrepreneurship training as a motivator to effective citizenship development and survival.

Relationship between Vocational Agriculture Education and Citizenship Development

(a) Apart from making inputs into the curriculum objectives and content, the three major components of an agricultural curriculum, individually or collectively, are veritable strategies for helping students acquire relevant agricultural knowledge and skills.

(b) Appropriate skills facilitate the willingness, ability and capacity of man to meet the challenges of a dynamic political and socio-economic environment. Skills and occupational competence predispose human beings to the development of good and effective citizenship.

(c) Education, especially vocational agriculture education is vital as a component of any democratic society, the object being to produce citizens who are self-reliant, independent, questioning and analytical in their disposition, yet deeply familiar with the precepts and practices of democracy and effective citizenship.

(d) As far as development is the ability of every citizen to meet the basic needs of life and their steady access to means of decent livelihood. It is also the capacity to manage and induce change in a positive direction. Citizens must develop

Figure 1: Integrating Vocational Agriculture Education Model for Attaining Effective Citizenship Development

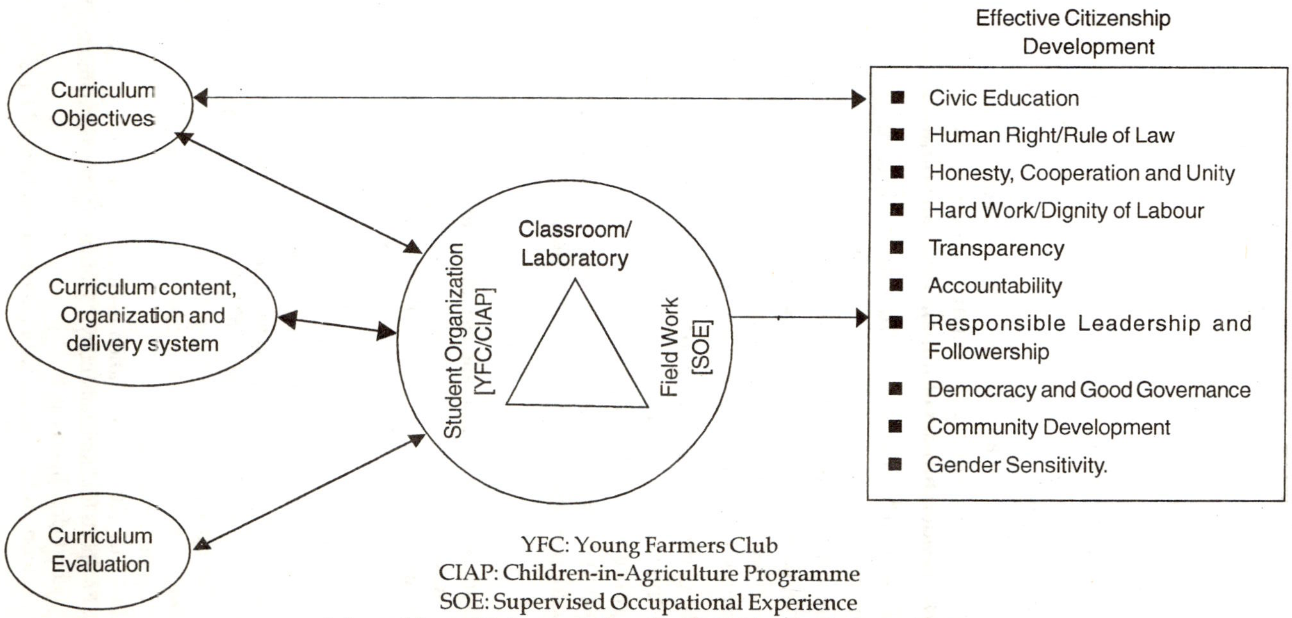

YFC: Young Farmers Club
CIAP: Children-in-Agriculture Programme
SOE: Supervised Occupational Experience
Adopted from Olaitan and Uwadiae (1993) and Adedoyin (2001).

the skill and capacity that will stimulate in them the culture of responsible and effective citizenship through which they will become active participants in the overall national development.

Conclusion

Agriculture education at all levels in Nigeria has not been able to incorporate the three major components required in vocational agriculture thus;

(i) Classroom and laboratory instruction,
(ii) Supervised occupational experience, and
(iii) Leadership development through youth organizations.

The Young Farmers Club and Children-in agriculture Programme are non-existent in most of the schools blaming their failure on different factors; prominent is the perception of these groups as extra-curricular rather than co-curricular. So also the supervised occupational experience has not been operationalized in many schools for both the known and unknown reasons.

In order to harmonize the Nigeria's philosophy of education with the national goals the curriculum must evolve a model of integrating vocational agriculture education geared towards effective citizenship development in advancing and enhancing social, cultural, political, scientific and technological progress.

REFERENCES

Adedoyin, S.F. (2000). "JDPC and its Participatory Intervention Approach." A survey report. JDPC, Ijebu-Ode, Nigeria, p. 12.

Adedoyin, S.F. (2001). "Vocational and Technical Education Culture of Enterprise-Responsible Citizenship-National Development: A path to Self-Reliant Economy in Developing Nations". Lead Paper presented at the 1st National Conference organized by the School of Vocational and Technical Education, TASCE Ijebu-Ode, 11-15 June 2001.

Amucheazi, E.C. (1980). *The problem of National Development.*

In; Readings in Social Science: Issues in National Development. Fourth Dimension Publishers, Enugu Nigeria pp. 1-10.

Fafunwa, A. Babs (1967). *New Perspectives in African Education.* Lagos and London, Macmillian.

Galadina, H.S. (2000). "Evaluation in current democratic process in Nigeria; Prospects for its sustainability." Human rights programme report, JDPC, Ijebu-Ode, Nigeria, p. 8.

Krishna Sastry, K.S. (1987). *Food Production and General Education,* In: Rao.

A.N. (ed.) Food Agriculture and Education Pergamon Press, New York pp. 45-50.

Federal Republic of Nigeria (2004). *National Policy on Education* 4th Edition. NERDC Press, Lagos, Nigeria, p. 47.

Obasanjo, O. and Mabogunje, A. (1991). *Elements of Development.* A4 Publications, Nigeria pp. 1-55.

Ogunyemi, B. (2001). *University General Studies and Provisions of Civic Education in Nigeria.* In proceedings of the 12th Annual General Association of SSAN.

Olaitan, S.O. (1993). *Integration in Agricultural education,* In; Adaralegbe A. (ed.) Integration and Innovation in Nigeria Education. Jas Publishers, Lagos Nigeria pp. 116-125.

Olaitan, S.O. and Uwadiae, S.A. (1993). *Developing Curriculum in Agriculture.* In; U. M. O. Iwowi (ed.) Curriculum Development in Nigeria. Sambook Publishers, Ibadan pp. 248-257.

Rao, A.N. (ed.) (1987). *Food Agriculture and Education.* Pergamon Press, New York.

Ubahakwe, Ebo (1999). *Curriculum Recycle Theory. A new dimension in curriculum development.* In; J.O. Obemeata, S.O. Ayodele and M.O. Araromi (ed.), Evaluation in Africa. Stirling Horden Publishers (Nig) Ltd. Ibadan pp. 211-223.

16

Cultivating the Culture of Reading for Effective Communication and Sustainable Development in Nigerian Schools

B. Oluwakemi Adekola, Nigeria

Introduction

Reading is one of the four basic communication skills, others being: speaking, listening and writing as indicated in the following Figure 1 :

Figure 1: Hierarchy and Interrelationship of the Four Language Skills (Lawal, 1990)

WRITING

READING

SPEAKING

LISTENING

Ngwoke (2006) defines it as the recognition and conscious reproduction of written or printed symbols letters words, word group and sentences either mentally or vocally by means of eye or finger contact. It can also be seen as one's ability to acquire information by identifying written symbols. Here, *"eye contact"* relates to humans that have no visual impairment whereas finger contact relates to the blind who make use of the Braille writing.The *Webster's Dictionary of English Language (2002)* defines *"to read"* as "to look at and understand the meaning of written or printed words or symbols: to go through written or printed words etc. silently or aloud."

Reading is a complex channel of communication which involves an interaction between the encoder and decoder (writer and reader). Although a number of important technological developments have taken place in the area of communication and teaching recently, nevertheless deriving information from print has remained the most important mode through which young people learn most subjects in schools. As Lawal (2008) rightly observes, the ability to read is the most important aspect of education. One of the basic ways of learning is by reading. Reading is not only ability to give correct answers to the questions that follow after reading a passage. Such questions center on the explicit content of reading selection. Oyetunde (2001) opines that for learners to become effective they must be trained to handle both explicit and implicit meanings of a passage. Learners must possess the skill to decode and absorb information. Udosen (2004) asserts that "reading is not a simple matter." Of course the reader has to learn to perceive and interpret accurately all the various symbols that are involved in written language and to build in the necessary skills, such that they function automatically. This is why Omojuwa (2001) considers reading to be a constructive thinking process. In this sense, reading is developmental in nature. In Fakuade (2001) words, reading is an exchange of ideas between an author and the reader. He also agrees that reading is developmental in nature a point that reveals why the numerous components of reading cannot be mastered all at once.

The State and Status of Reading in Nigeria Today

In Nigeria to day, the reading level is very low and this is in spite of the increasing volumes of materials that surface everyday begging for reading. In an interview granted by Ausbeth a writer in THE SUN of Saturday November 25, 2006, she revealed that the reading rate of Nigerians is very poor and this affects zealous writers negatively. "I would say that sadly, that not many Nigerian like to read: most people read because they need to pass their examination especially students. The reading culture is generally poor. People do not engage in active reading anymore and it is painful." According to Agwu (2004):

> *Reading is one area that is particularly problematic for children within the school system. A great majority of them are failing to learn to read and many more are unable to read to learn.*

He warns that "... there are many children at risk and unless we come to their rescue, the age of darkness might recur." Lawal (2008), summarizes the state and status of reading in Nigeria as follow:

1. Most of the communities in Nigeria, especially the rural ones which constitute the bulk of the populace, are largely preliterate, with most of their languages (not less than 200)

yet to be reduced to writing. This makes reading to be generally seen as an elitist activity done mainly through the medium of English.

2. Contradiction in values—increasing urge for formal education but unwillingness to read and study hard. This paradoxical situation manifests itself in the "Reluctant Reading and Learning Syndrome" (Unoh, 1983), the "Higher Illiteracy Syndrome" and a steady reversal of illiteracy.
3. Hazy and tongue-in-cheek bilingual education policy:
   (*a*) Language policy devoid of systematic planning leading to lack of functional reading competence in either reading or a Nigerian language for most learners across the educational ladder;
   (*b*) Absence of political will which manifests in escape clauses in the language policy in education; and
   (*c*) Crisis in implementation, all of which has led to confusion in the teaching of reading.
4. Poor teaching-training programmes relative to reading. This makes teachers to abandon children with reading problems to their fate; while for other children they teach reading for recitation and recall rather than for reflective, critical and creative thinking.
5. An epileptic book industry and a weak book production policy especially as regards reading both in English and the local languages.
6. Poor and sometimes non-existent library facilities at school and community levels, not to talk of majority of homes, which are non-supportive to reading.
7. The cumulative impact of these dimensions of the status and state of reading can be palpably felt in the poor reading habits of a large portion of the populace and the narrowing down of the relatively little reading that is done to the formal school setting where intensive reading is done to cram ill-digested facts, which are regurgitated in examination rooms, to be forgotten immediately after. In more recent times, rote learning is even fading out as students are now demonstrating intriguing dexterity in examination malpractice.
8. The current unmanaged contest among the books, the computer, the home-video and the use of texts in mobile

telephone communication further worsen the parlous situation.

Aspects of the Reading Culture

The reading culture is a construct comprising several interlocking variables with cognitive, affective and psychometric dimensions. The cognitive and affective dimensions of the reading culture is the foundation for the overt physical behaviour. A pervasive awareness of the following values of reading in the modern world is therefore the bedrock of this culture.

1. *The Linguistic Value:* Reading is the medium of learning to read, and of learning the other skills of language, as well as the different aspects of grammar - spelling, punctuation, pronunciation, vocabulary, word and sentence structures.
2. *The Educational Value:* Beyond mastery of language, reading is not only the tool for mastering other subjects in the curriculum, but also a window through we peep into the outside world. Against this background, one would easily appreciate the full significance of the English epigram: "Reading maketh the man" and the Chinese proverb: "The world cheats those who cannot read."
3. *The Didactic Value:* Reading is also an instrument of behaviour modification through the projection and celebration of Virtue and the condemnation of Vice, in using worthy books and adjunct materials. This, however, underscores the importance of judicious and balanced choice of reading materials for all categories of people. The question is therefore about why and what to read, if reading must perform its didactic function.
4. *The Therapeutic Value:* Reading is a tension reliever and a form of leisure through which we come to know, in addition, that we are not alone in our problems.
5. *Aesthetic Value:* Reading is pleasure and leisure.
6. *Heuristics Value:* Reading has problem-solving value.

The level of awareness of a person or people determines to a large extent their reading attitudes which in turn influence and are influenced by their reading interests, which concomitantly affect and are affected by their reading problems towards the development of specific reading skills. "Reading habits" thus describes the totality of a person's attitudes, interests, problems and skills relative to

Figure 2: The Dynamics of Reading Habits (Adapted from Lawal, 1989)

Reading Habits

Reading Attitudes	*Reading Interests*	*Reading Problems*	*Reading Skills*
(*a*) Intensive Reading	(*a*) Romance	(*a*) Recitation	(*a*) Literal
(*b*) Literary Reading	(*b*) Crime and Detective	(*b*) Reflection	(*b*) Inferentia
(*c*) Extensive Reading	(*c*) Historical	(*c*) Ramification	(*c*) Critical
	(*d*) Adventure	(*d*) Creative	
	(*e*) Science fiction		
	(*f*) Religious		
	(*g*) Current Affairs		
	(*h*) Professional, etc.		

reading. In relation to the reading culture, the attitudes to the three types of reading are positive and balanced, rather than being negative/ambivalent or lopsided, the reading interests are varied and robust, while the reading problems are constantly and consistently corrected or remedied as the case may be, from grade to grade to enhance functional reading skills. Conversely, in a society, such as Nigeria where the reading culture does not thrive, the attitudes are mostly negative or sometimes ambivalent towards all the three forms of reading, reading interests are largely non-existent for most of the higher literates and reading problems hamper the development of effective and efficient reading skills, especially across several basal and intermediate grades of the literate populace.

Significance of Reading in Nigerian Schools

Whatever is our tradition, norms and values, we are living in a reading world today. The outstanding educational skills in the whole world are reading and writing. But reading takes precedence because one has to learn through reading before one knows what to write.

Reading is one of the most important literacy skills. It is the major key to progress and success in learning. It is said that one has to learn to read in order to read to learn.

Reading is the window through which a literate person can see the world far above his physical reach. According to the new Webster Dictionary of English Language, reading is the act of understanding the meaning of symbols, signs, gestures, etc. by looking at them and assimilating them mentally. It is the method by which a percentage of symbols bring some effective reasoning in the mind of the reader. Reading is the ability to recognize and comprehend graphic codes and symbols occurring individually or in groups.

Reading is an important skill that should be emphasized and normally acquired at the primary school level. It constitutes the foundation of primary school curriculum because it makes immediate learning possible and also enhances the study of other subjects. Learning of any subject in the curriculum depends largely on the reading ability of the learner.

Reading is fundamental to literacy. Those who do not read get lost from the world of knowledge and the happenings in the world. That is why Okoro, (1999) argued that they do not live who do not read.

For effective literacy to be achieved, effective reading skill must be developed in the pupils at the primary school level. This makes such pupils able to achieve maximally from printed materials.

All success in academic pursuit is hinged on effective reading habits. Reading serves as one of the language skills employed for effective academic pursuit, as such for reading to be meaningful, children must be able to comprehend and learn from text. Children must be taught reading properly in order to make it meaningful.

Reading involves prediction and construction of meaning. Reading proficiency is the royal road to knowledge. It is essential to the success in all academic subjects. Learning depends largely upon the children's ability to interpret the printed page accurately and fully. In other words, reading is the key to leading.

Reading as an entrance into almost all vocations. It is needed to keep pace with new development. Lawyers, Engineers, and Physicians claim that reading is essential. One is successful if he/she keeps up-to-date (Strang, 1978). For a quality reading in science, there must be a path to new experience.

Reading often relieves emotional tensions and gives insight into personal problems. The reader has time to reflect on the ideal he meets and give play to the imagination.

Suggestion for Improving the Reading Culture in Nigeria

Having analyzed the complex dynamics of the reading culture and its glaring absence in Nigeria, it would be appropriate and useful to proffer some suggestions to ameliorate the unhealthy situation.

1. There is urgent need for a more pragmatic, realistic and feasible language policy in education as a prelude to conscious and conscientious planning for the involvement of more and more Nigerian languages in the literacy development of the populace.
2. The gaps among educational policy, planning and implementation would also need to be urgently bridged so that education can be more purposeful, meaningful and functional, and reading can be accorded its pride of place within the framework.
3. Since the reading culture has been found to be a multi-systematic and inter-relational phenomenon, there is the need for strong networking among the key systems and institutions especially with regard to the interdependence of family, school and community literacies.
4. Educational institutions should place greater premium on the teaching of reading which should be approached both as a personal and social activity. Emphasis should be given to both the cognitive and meta-cognitive aspects of reading, i.e., not only are learners to be taught how to understand what they read but also how to know that they are gaining from reading. In this regard specific reading and study skills should be cultivated in learners to stem the tide of examination malpractice.
5. Government should intensify adult literacy campaign so that it can have positive backwash effect on family literacy, which is he veritable foundation of the reading culture. This would make it possible for parents to appreciate the values of the family library and home literacy activities in general.
6. Teacher-training institutions would have to constantly evaluate their language education programmes as they relate to reading pedagogy so that pre-service teachers can be well grounded in the right knowledge, attitudes and skills that can foster the reading development of various categories of learners.
7. Finally, since it is the individual that is the ultimate focus of

literacy development, learners need to realize that any skill such as reading can only be mastered through constant practice, commitment, abiding interest and a lively attitude. Without the individual learner or citizen striving to become a functional and proficient literate, the dream of any society to cultivate the reading culture would be a mere mirage.

Recommendations

It is considered important to make the following recommendations to the stakeholders:

(i) Teachers and pupils should be encouraged to see reading henceforth as the most important language skill to be developed since reading is the gate way to functional literacy.

(ii) Teachers should know that reading lessons should be activity based thereby making reading as pleasurable as possible by introducing into it varieties of activities.

(iii) School and class libraries should be provided and stuffed with materials that can be of interest to the pupils.

(iv) Parents should provide reading materials for their children and encourage extensive reading at home.

(v) English language teacher-trainees should as a matter of necessity be given varieties of courses in reading to make them acquire the skills, interest and the methods of teaching reading.

(vi) Government and non-governmental organization must organize reading programmes and competition for primary and secondary schools to promote reading culture.

(vii) Schools should map out separate period outside the timetable as a school—wide reading period when all teachers and pupils will be made to engage in reading. It could be done at least three days in a week. This will enhance the development of reading skills and culture in the pupils and students in the schools.

Conclusion

Great people are those who read and reading maketh a man so says an adage. There can never be functional literacy without extensive and intensive reading. The reading culture of the people must be improved if functional literacy will not be only a lofty dream in Nigeria.

School teachers should themselves be good readers in order to impart such culture into their pupils. Children should always be motivated to read by the teacher providing varieties of materials of their interest. Teachers to emphasize reading for pleasure rather than reading for learning. They should be given varieties of positive reinforcement when they make even a little effort at pleasure reading. This will help them develop a good reading culture, for if a solid efficient reading culture foundation is laid at the school the rate of educated illiterates in Nigeria will come to the lowest ebb or even be fully eradicated. A number of suggestion for promoting reading culture were given. It is the belief of the author that if these suggestions are carried out, effective reading in Nigeria will be highly promoted.

REFERENCES

Agbada J.O.J. (2001) Use of English for Tertiary Education; John Jacob's Classic Publishers Ltd.

Agwu, S.N. (2004). Teaching in Nigeria – A Dynamic Approach: Cheston Ltd. Enugu.

Fakuade, G. (2001) A hand book for Reading Comprehension and Summary Writing Skills. Yola; Paraclete Publisher.

Lawal Adebayo (2008). Cultivating the culture of reading in Nigeria. A Guest Lecture delivered at Fountain University Oshogbo.

Lawal, Adebayo (1989). An Analytical Study of the Reading Habits of Some Secondary School Students in Oyo, *Literacy and Reading in Nigeria,* (4), 288-213.

Lawal, Adebayo (1990). *English Communication Skills for Teachers* (Unpublished Mimeograph), Institute of Education, University of Ilorin.

Ngwoke, I.R. (2006). Fundamentals of Reading Comprehension: Cape Publishers Int. Ltd., Owerri.

Omojuwa, J. (2005). Laying a Strong Foundation for Higher Level Achievements: Problems and Prospects. *Journal of Applied Literacy and Reading,* Vol. 2, 7-14.

Opara C.G. (2007) The teaching of reading at pre-primary level in the public schools in the rural and urban areas in imo state. *Journal of Applied Literacy and Reading,* Vol. 3 (special edition).

Oyetunde T.O. (2001). Teaching learning to read and reading to learn.In Agwu S.N. (ed.) Learning in Nigeria a Dynamic Approach. Enugu:Cheston Limited.

The Sun Newspapers, November 25, 2006.

Udosen, A.E. (2004). Reading instruction in Secondary schools: Implication for sustainable development. Nigeria Journal of Curriculum Studies, 1.

Webster's Dictionary of English Language (2002) USA: Trident Press International.

17

Marketing Practices in Thai Higher Education Competing in Recessive Environments for Domestic and International Students

Dr. Paul TJ James, Thailand

Introduction

Marketing for Thai higher education institutions now involves both a domestic, and also and international focus, although this wasn't always seen as necessary or desirable (Gray, 1991). The competition between universitites in Thailand (Foskett, 2002) resulting in the need for universities to differentiate themselves from the competition (Cubillo *et al.*, 2006) thus changing the important role of stakeholder/ student marketing (Kotler and Fox, 1995) in terms of recruitment strategies (Canterbury, 1999). Adding to increased competition is the spectre of another recession that not only contributes to less student numbers but also challenges Thai universities to make more effective strategic choices relative to programme offerings. Consequently, external pressures resulting from recessive pressures constructs difficult situations within which Thai university marketing managers must manage competently and expertly. To exacerbate the issue, many Thai higher education institutions have experienced consistent declines in their enrolments (MacGregor, 2000), further emphasising the important role of student marketing for recruitment purposes (Tagwireyi, 2000; and Smith *et al.*, 1995). Consequently, stakeholder perceptions of university programme offerings (Eagle and Brennan, 2007) and the brand image conveyed needs to be managed appropriately (Ivy, 2001; and Nicholls *et al.*, 1995). Mass media also plays an important role in developing stakeholder/student choice at a time when many universities are facing increasing financial pressures and heightened competition. Consequently, it has become and operational imperative for universities to market themselves to interested stakeholders—the most important of which are students and their opinions (Lancaster and Reynolds, 2002)—directly through contemporary marketing techniques using modern technologies such as mobile media and focused database marketing (Tapp *et al.*, 2004).

Until recently, higher education in Thailand has managed to avoid the need for full-scale strategic marketing efforts (Morgan, 1991) through a wide variety of reasons that include demand outpacing supply for university places—especially at under-graduate level-for well-established universities. This initiates new challenges for Thai university management because of an increasingly competitive higher education environment (Binsardi and Ekwulugo, 2003). However, many universities in Thailand have now also begun to realise the importance of having sound marketing strategies to stay competitive (Ho and Hung, 2008). However, marketing practices traditionally involved the utilisation of specific techniques (Caruana *et al.*, 1999), such as advertising, market research and low-level branding. Nevertheless, newly emerging private and public-funded universities tend to build their marketing strategy around the philosophy of production (Naude and Ivy, 1999) and are therefore enacting an efficiency/bureaucratic orientation. This university management behaviour relating to the partial adoption of a carefully managed branding strategy is designed to enhance the university's overall image and overall market and is consistent with behaviour changes reported from past research findings into the competitive advantage of service industries (Aaker, 1991). Additionally, potential changes to Thai governmental educational policy, which has reduced funding for public universities, has led to an increased need for marketing initiatives in order to encourage increased student recruitment through an opportunistic privatisation agenda (Meek and Wood, 1997).

The international higher education student market is approaching maturity in the West (Mazzarol and Hosie, 1996) as international education brands have started to evolve (Gray *et al.*, 2003; and Mazzarol, 1998). Consequently, for western universities competitive pressures preclude large-scale openings for western international alliances. However, in Thailand the international higher education student market is perceived by many to be in the developmental stage (Maringe, 2005) and opportunities for western universities thus exist as there can be a varied approach to such alliances ranging form short programmes associations to full-degree granting practices that go beyond collaboration to strict partnerships. Mazzarol (1998) found that reputation, available resources, and collaboration to be important for the successful recruitment of international students. In this respect, reputation comprised characteristics such as market profile, financial resources, and an appropriate range of pedagogic programmes; while collaboration related to any engaged international strategic alliance. The most common factors found influencing international student choice (Mazzarol and Soutar, 2002) were knowledge of the host country; perceived quality of education; recognition of prior qualifications; and the reciprocal recognition of the host country qualifications in the student's home country. However, many international students visiting Thailand do so as part of their degree programme presumably through unmet home-demand and thus issues revolve around the efficacy of the arrangements to capture appropriate quality demands by the international institutional partner as few international students engage in Thai domestic full-degree programmes.

Changing the Marketing Brand Image Focus

Internationalisation starts at home, and in essence, a strategic marketing focus on domestic students should start with actioning changes away from *whole-institution* activities and more towards the development of *programme-brands* that match adopted marketing segments. However, there appears to be a lack of awareness of the marketing process required to develop a focused programme-brand, such as an MBA (Nicholls *et al.*, 1995). By focusing marketing effort on programme brands, the student's demands will be mirrored more closely to match what it is that they want from the selected academic programme. It will also mean less budget constraints as targeting practices become more efficient due to technological developments and gains would also result in increased student numbers for targeted programmes. However, it has been recognised and reported by some researchers (Pine *et al.*, 1995) that universities creating more choice for students do not necessarily assimilate student demand effectively as this leads to unacceptable levels of stakeholder confusion (Mitchell and Papavassiliou, 1999). For example, in an attempt to diversify the educational offering some universities have realised that doing so reduces the overall numbers of students interested in any specific degree programmes specialisation. Thus, giving student's more choice actually reduces the overall efficacy of the university educational provision. In times of recession, many universities are often advised to rationalise/reduce their offering (Kelly, 1999; and Quelch and Kenny, 1994) to coincide with the expected overall drop in student numbers as a consequence of stakeholders/students reducing personal cost. It is the timing of such advice and actions that facilitates and enhances a university's equitable future marketing outcomes.

Higher education marketing managers need to be aware that stakeholders/students suffering from information overload, inadequate, ambiguous, conflicting and misleading information often take the easy route (if they can afford it) and make a choice based on the whole-university brand image (Mitchell and Papavassiliou, 1999). This may shed light on why student rationale often reflects that any *affordable degree* is OK, as more students move from more expensive universities to less expensive ones. Consequently, strategic marketing effort should be directed to stakeholders/students in ways that make it easy for them to make their choices—and that means diversifying and focusing the methods of marketing, not diversifying the university pedagogic offering. Consequently, in order to create a more unified university marketing approach, particular attention must be given to brand building by university marketing managers.

Programme Brand Building and Management

An increasingly global educational arena has influenced how Thai universities develop and use marketing activities (Abdullah, 2006; and Prugsamatz *et al.*, 2006). However, much of the brand development in Thai education comes from a local university source, as universities have become historically known for their academic rigour and innovation. Gray *et al.*, (2003) indicated that little research had been conduted on positioning in Thai university markets although overseas markets are generally considered highly competitive where there is an increasing emphasis on overall branding development. Thai higher education brand *images* have often been strongly developed as an *whole-institution,* as sector marketing activities of higher education tend to communicate specific whole-brand identities (Lowrie, 2007) rather then specific programme or even particular personnel, as in the West. As a consequence, Naude and Ivy (1999) suggested that older and more nature Universities with long-standing reputations carry out less marketing effort than less well-established universities as a brand image with an established reputation reduces stakeholder/student perceived risk (Levitt, 1986)—giving rise to movements of students from less well-known universities to better-known universities in times of recession. As a result, those universities who are not perceived by ordinary stakeholders—including prospective students—to be part of the older fraternity of universities need to engage with strategic marketing techniques with more vigour than their more established counterparts.

Those universities seeking international associations and partners need to utilise the same marketing techniques as overseas universities and Thai universities are therefore left with no choice other than to embrace these new and remarkably effective operational conceptions of marketing. Of continuing concern though are the costs associated with possible new marketing developments for Thai universities. In the beginning, managers other than marketing managers at university may relate marketing costs in terms of sunk costs—similar to machine/production treatments. This would be a mistake, as marketing costs should be seen as future investment, not as past costs. In this way, derivative outcomes from marketing activities can generate the optimum perspective for long-term developments in associative university marketing practices.

Branding—A Service Package in Development

Many universities now realise that brand management and image (Nicholls *et al.*, 1995) requires careful consideration (Park *et al.*, 1986) as it is an important condition; that the business perception is that there is no longer a singular product or service but service package; and that this service package results in grater *business* emphasis than the specific attention to the development of an overall brand image. A brand represents a coherent relationship that customers have come to know and value with a specific service package but the branding and positioning of an educational service is even more difficult because of its intangibility (Dibb and Simkin, 1993). In this respect, a service package can be seen as a whole-institution or as a specific programme of study. This service package contemporarily surrounds a brand and all that it means to the stakeholder/student. Consequently, brands refer to singular educational products (degree), services (administration), or families of such products and services (contained in the pedagogic provision). When a university asks what is a brand? they actual mean what does our service package mean to the stakeholder/student—present, potential or even an understanding of the meanings/attributes/needs of their competitor's cients.

Usually, university branding development consists of three main, but plausible and reasonable, features:

1. *The Service Package—The Brand*

This corresponds with the perception that already exists in the stakeholder/student mind. In terms of a university brand image, it is a combination of recognition, past experiences and stated or implied promises from present or previous marketing effort. This is perhaps why many older universities have an advantage on newer universities, as the marketing effort takes time to filter through to the stakeholder/student population and onto present or prospective segments. Lesser known universities therefore have to manage their marketing effort to ensure a consistent and continuous stream of promotion so that targeted stakeholders receive appropriate messages which will help them develop stronger links via appropriate university brand awareness within the contemporary context that stakeholders/students are no longer passive consumers in this environment (Maringe, 2006).

2. *The Brand Strategy*

Universities that the engaged in better brand marketing practices and activities have a greater opportunity to generate an accepted position in the marketplace. Every service package comes with it a marketing related promise—however ill-conceived or mismatched with the intended target segment. Brand strategy is simply known as positioning and re-positioning which is built around the specific perceptions of stakeholders/students as consumers (Ho and Hung, 2008; and Parasuraman *et al.*, 1990). Every university can develop and understand their positioning and this is done through marketing research practices. In this regard, contemporary methods include cluster analysis (Churchill and Iacobucci, 2007) which is considered a very useful market segmenting tool to identify groups of similar characteristics in terms of their responses to the university brand image.

What does the university service package stand for? The most important is that the university name will often begin to be associated with a specialty as a university becomes known and recognised—leaving target segments with a positive postion in the stakeholder/student mind.

Additionally, marketing effort will become better focused, as the target segment becomes easier to place through enhanced marketing research practices. However, there is a continuing issue in higher education—that of change (Deem, 2004; Boxer, 2005; and Halbesleben *et al.*, 2003). The main focus of university activity is on change through teaching and learning practices. In this way, most stakeholders/students also change as they engage with the university operations over time. University marketing managers therefore need to continually understand the university service package offering and respond and deliver appropriate brand strategies that will interest and engage present and prospective stakeholders/students. This is a very difficult task to undertake consistently. Consequently, universities need to employ qualified and experienced marketing managers and not just individuals who understand advertising, but those individuals who have developed a complete picture of marketing and its positive influences in higer education. This leads the university to professionalising the management of the direct relationship between university and the stakeholder/student. Inevitably, this professionalization will also be seen by the competition who will need to *upgrade* their personnel also, as more effective marketing strategies give rise to increased numbers of students who are able learn what they want to learn because the university ensures it continues to meet their specific and varied demands.

3. *The Brand Identity*

This is the visual expression of the brand, through media digitally or such as, print, or TV. The key to marketing a service package image is its consistent placement in all appropriate markets—relative to each target segment. This includes any visual element in packaging, colours, design and the consequent service package's total image. Consequently, a well-designed service package campaign will establish consistent core branding elements where the most critical step in delivering service quality is knowing what the stakeholder/student expects (Parasuraman *et al.*, 1990) whilst providing flexibility in terms of operational university requirements. Through careful service package management, the on-going success of the university programme brand will be enhanced. Further, care most be used to ensure harmonisation and coherence of the programme brand image with the overall brand image of the university (Nicholls *et al.*, 1995) resulting in a symbiotic co-branding environment.

Why is a focus on a service package even necessary when it constitutes only a single product? The simple answer to this is that service failure has the greatest impact on the stakeholder/student brand image (James, 2005). Consequently, university managers need to make changes to their marketing mind-set—that of understanding that the management of an overall brand image entails the successfull management of the service package resulting in a greater focus of the totality of the stakeholder/student experiences. Further, this focus must be designed at the on-set and developed over the long-term, as it takes time to influence stakeholder/student behaviour. A useful notion for university marketing managers when considering brand value is that strong brands can command premium prices, which not only leads to grater profits but also enhances stakeholder/students satisfaction.

Issues Surrounding University and Programme Brand Management

Some of the issues surrounding brand management reflect a university management's inability to understand the service package they offer. The university may be run by individuals who don't know what good service package management involves and therefore most branding activities are left to the marketing department that focus more on traditional activities such as attempts at changing customer mind-sets through advertising campaigns and employ other mass-media strategies and processes. Management consequently never appear to go beyond what is traditionally expected, and this results in reduced returns of marketing effort. They focus on the whole university as a brand, rather than the specific service package for any given offered programme. This raises the notion that unless university management continuously changes to connect and respond to stakeholders/students in the most appropriate way for them as clients-profits and service package appeal will be limited. University management who follow this strategy are doomed to failure, for failing the very people who could make their service package the envy of the educational sector—the specific stake-holder/student segment.

In order to develop and apply a successful branding strategy, university managers need to be convinced that moving from a *whole-university-centric* focus to *stakeholders/centric* focus and on to a *service package* focus will result in enhanced stakeholder/student relationships. This means realising that managing the entire university stakeholder/student experience through programme brands can be one of the most significant drivers to increasing university brand value which is personified by enhanced stakeholder/student contact with the university and added-value transactions—over time.

How do you build or enhance a university's programme brand images in terms of its present service package? The old way was through one-way communication: mass-media via TV, print, broadcast, web-cast and word-of mouth. The contemporary way is through two-way communication: including mass-media via TV, print, broadcast, web-cast and word-of-mouth plus 1-to-1 relationship by communicating with stakeholders/students through the creation of purposeful dialog—stakeholder student needs bounded by university marketing capability.

Further analyzing financial transactions will clearly lead to a better understanding of the net worth of a university's current stakeholder/student portfolio and through this analysis help to determine which stakeholders segments of focus marketing efforts on. This means that some service packages (programme brands) can be used as cash-cows, whilst development into more progressive areas and brands continues.

University management should think about branding each specific service package by:

1. Making the brand strategy a way of doing business—not just actioning a marketing activity to some generalised university objective.
2. Developing and shifting emphasis from *acquiring* stakeholders/students to *retaining* clients.
3. Training staff well enough so they can usefully anticipate, engage with and enhance stakeholder/student service package experiences.

Consequently, university management need to review and adjust brand-development processes, practices, tools and promotional strategies in order to ensure coverage of appropriate programme brands and thus targeted segments (Maringe, 2006).

Conclusion

The brand image a university develops and portrays plays a crucial role in developing public attitudes towards the university as an institution (Yavas and Shemwell, 1996). In order to attain an effective programme brand strategy, university management will need to communicate *with* rather than *to* stakeholders/students, which will result in better managed stakeholder/student client expectations. Active branding campaigns constitute an important element for any university seeking to participate in international markets or compete effectively in domestic markets, and this will require focused strategic leadership from top management (Chapelo, 2007; and Hammond *et al;* 2007) in order to secure a competitive advantage (Mazzarol and Soutar, 2007). Getting the promotional platform correct is seen as essential and helps in successful stakeholder/student recruitment (Education and Skills Committee, 2005).

It is clear from the literature that the nature and substance of marketing practices in Thai higher education is undergoing considerable change and university management are possibly best placed to initiate appropriate marketing related mechanisms that support brand management (university and programme) to ensure that stakeholders/students receive what it is that they want and need from Thai higher educational service provision.

BIBLIOGRAPHY

Aaker D.A. (1991). *Managing Brand Equity: Capitalizing on the Value of a Brand Name,* The Free Press, New York, USA.

Abdullah F. (2006). *Measuring Service Quality in Higer Education: HEDPERF Versus SERVPERF,* Marketing Intelligence and Planning, Vol. 24, No. 1, pp. 31-47.

Binsardi A. and Ekwulugo F. (2003). *International Marketing of British Education: Research on the Students's Perception and the UK Market Penetration,* Marketing Intelligence Planning, Vol. 21, pp. 318-27.

Boxer L. (2005). *Discourses of Change Ownership in Higher Education,* Quality Assurance in Education, Vol. 13, No. 4, pp. 344-52.

Canterbury R.M. (1999). *Higher Education Marketing: A Challenge,* The Journal of College Admission, Vol. 165, pp. 22-30.

Caruana A., Ramaseshan B. and Ewing M.T. (1999). *Market Orientation and Performance in the Public Sector,* Journal of Global Marketing, Vol. 12, No. 3, pp. 59-75.

Chapleo C. (2007). *Barriero to Brand Building in U.K. Universities,* International Journal of Nonprofit and Voluntary Sector Marketing Vol. 12, No. 1, pp. 23-32.

Churchill G.A. and Iacobucci D. (2007). *Marketing Research: Methodological Foundations,* 9th ed., Peking University Press, China.

Cubillo J., Sanchez J. and Cervino J. (2006). *International Student's Decision-making Process,* International Journal of Educational Management, Vol. 20, No. 2, pp. 101-15.

Deem R. (2004). *The Knowledge Worker, the Manager-academic and the Contemporary UK University: New and Old Forms of Public Management?*, Financial Accountability and Management, Vol. 20, No. 2, pp. 107-28.

Dibb S. and Simkin L. (1993). *The Strength of Branding and Positioning in Services*, International Journal of Service Industry Management, Vol. 4, No. 1, pp. 25-35.

Eagle L. and Brennan R. (2007). *Are Students Customers? TQM and Marketing Perspectives*, Quality Assurance in Education, Vol. 15, No. 1, pp. 44-60.

Education and Skills Committee. (2005). *UK e-University*, House of Commons, available at: www.publications.parliament.uk/pa/cm200405/cmselect/cmeduski/205/205pdf.

Foskett N. (2002). *Marketing*, in Bush T. and Bell L. (Eds.) *The Principles and Practice of Educational Management*, Paul Chapman, London, pp. 241-57.

Gray L. (1991). *Education Marketing*, Open University Press, Buckingham, UK.

Gray B. Fam K. and Llanes B. (2003). *Branding Universities in Chinese Markets*, Journal of Product and Brand Management, Vol. 12, No. 2, pp. 13-30.

Halbesleben J.R., Becker J.A. and Buckley M.R. (2003). *Considering the Labour Contributions of Students: An Alternative to the Student-as-customer Metaphor*, Journal of Education for Business, Vol. 78, No. 5, pp. 255-57.

Hammond K.L., Harmon H.A. and Webster R.L. (2007). *University Performance and Strategic Marketing: An Extended Study*, Marketing Intelligence and Planning, Vol. 25, No. 5, pp. 436-459.

Họ H. and Hung C. (2008). *Marketing Mix Formulation for Higher Education*, International Journal of Educational Management, Vol. 22, No. 4, pp. 328-340.

Ivy J. (2001). *Higher Education Institution Image: A Correspondence Analysis Approach*, The International Journal of Educational Management, Vol. 15, No's 6-7, pp. 276-82.

James P.T.J. (2005). *TQM in Asia*, Perason Education, Singapore.

Kelly J. (1999). *Lapses in Concentration*, The Grocer, 3rd May.

Kotler P. and Fox K. (1995). *Strategic Marketing for Educational Institutions*, (2nd ed.,), Prtentice-Hall, Englewood Cliffs, NJ., USA.

Lancaster G. and Reynolds P. (2002). *Marketing – The one Semester Introduction*, Butterworth-Heinemann, Oxford.

Levitt T. (1986). *The Marketing Imagination*, The Free Press, New York, USA.

Lowrie A. (2007). *Branding Higher Education: Equivalence and Difference in Developing Identity*, Journal of Business Research, Vol. 60, pp. 990-999.

MacGregor K. (2005). *Dire Results Slash Numbers*, The Times Higher Education Supplement, 28th January, p. 15.

Maringe F. (2005). *Interrogating the Crisis in Higher Education Marketing: The CORD Model*, International Journal of Educational Management, Vol. 19, No. 7, pp. 564-578.

Maringe F. (2006). *University and Course Choice*, International Journal of Educational Management, Vol. 20, No. 6, pp. 466-479.

Mazzarol T. (1998). *Critical Success Factors for International Education Marketing*, International Journal of Educational Management, Vol. 12, No. 4, pp. 163-75.

Mazzarol T. and Hosie P. (1996). *Exporting Australian Higher Education: Future Strategies in a Maturing Market*, Quality Assurance in Education, Vol. 4, No. 1, pp. 37-50.

Mazzarol T. and Soutar G.N. (2002) *The Push-pull Factors Influencing International Student Selection of Education Destination,* International Journal of Educational Management, Vol. 6, No. 2, pp. 82-90.

Mazzarol T. and Soutar G.N. (2007). *Strategy Matters: Strategic Positioning and Performance in the Education Services Sector,* International Journal of Nonprofit and Voluntary Sector Marketing, Vol. 13, Issue 2, pp. 141-151.

Meek V. and Wood F.Q. (1997). *The Market as a New Steering Strategy for Australian Higher Education,* Higher Education Policy, Vol. 10, No's 3-4, pp. 253-75.

Mitchell V. and Papavassiliou V. (1999) *Marketing Casues and Implications of Consumer Confusion,* Journal of Product and Brand Management, Vol. 8, No. 4. pp. 319-39.

Morgan N.A. (1991). *Professional Service Marketing,* Butterworth-Heinemann, Oxford, UK.

Naude P. and Ivy J. (1999). *The Marketing Strategies of Universities in the United Kingdom,* International Journal of Educational Management, Vol. 13, No. 3, pp. 126-34.

Nicholls J., Harris J., Morgan E., Clarke K., and Sims D., (1995). *Marketing Higher Education: The MBA Experience,* International Journal of Educational Management, Vol. 9, No. 2, pp. 31-38.

Parasuraman A., Zeithaml V.A. and Berry L.L. (1990). *Delivering Quality Service: Balancing Customer Perceptions and Expectations.* The Free Press, New York, USA.

Park C.W., Jaworski B.J. and MacInnis D.J. (1986). *Strategic Brand Concept-image Management, Journal of Marketing,* Vol. 50, October, pp.135-45.

Pine B.J., Peppers D. and Rogers M. (1995). *Do You Want to Keep Your Customers Forever?,* Harvard Business Review, Vol. 73, No. 2, pp. 103-8.

Prugsamatz S., Pentecost R., and Ofstad L. (2006). *The Influence of Explicit and Implicit Service Promises on Chinese Students' Expectations of Overseas Universities,* Asia Pacific Journal of Marketing and Logistics, Vol. 18, No. 2, pp. 129-145.

Quelch J.A. and Kenny D. (1994). *Extend Profits not Product Lines,* Harvard Business Review, Vol. 72, No. 5, pp. 153-60.

Smith D., Scott P. and Lynch J. (1995). *The Academic Service Provider: Is the Customer Always Right?,* Journal of Higher Education Policy and Management, Vol. 21, No. 2, pp. 193-203.

Tagwireyi S. (2000). *Decline in Students Hits Universities,* available at:

wwwsn.apc.org/wmail/issues/ooo128/news40.html(accessed 24th May, 2008).

Tapp A., Hicks K. and Stone M. (2004) *Direct and Database Marketing and Customer Relationship Management in Recruiting Students for Higher Education,* International Journal of Non-profit and Voluntary Sector Marketing, Vol. 9, No. 4, pp. 333-45.

Yavas U. and Shemwell D.J. (1996). *Graphical Representation of University Image: A Correspondence Analysis,* Journal of Marketing Higher Education, Vol. 7, pp. 75-84.

18

Manpower Development and Lecturer's Productivity in Tertiary Institutions in Nigeria

Prof. V.F. Peretomode, Nigeria
Dr. R.A. Chukwuwa, Nigeria

Introduction

The central idea underlying manpower development in any sector, including the education sector, is how best to keep the employees current, vibrant and versatile so that they can continuously perform their roles effectively in this age of rapid socio-economic, political, scientific and technological changes and globalization. As Lassa (1992) rightly emphasized, in education teachers are the foundation of quality; they hold trust for the implemented curriculum of formal education and therefore, are at the centre of the educative process. In fact, no education system can rise above the quality of its teachers (NERDC, 2004). This is even all the more important with the institutions of higher learning whose mission include research – the expansion of the frontiers of knowledge, teaching, and community services.

Manpower development has become an accepted phenomenon in organizations. In tertiary institutions, lecturers development programmes are considered very critical. They are planned activities which focus on increasing and enlarging the capabilities, improving the technical and conceptual skills of lecturers so that they can posses the necessary abilities to handle complex situations and better perform their job. Through renewal activities, lecturers avoid becoming rustic.

The need for lecturers to improve their knowledge, skills, attitudes and behaviours while on the job is even more critical now in developing nations than ever before for a number of reasons. For instance, academic programmes in our universities rarely adequately prepare candidates as "finished" products for their future positions and their accompanying responsibilities (Heis 1970, Peretomode and Peretomode, 2001). There is also the issue of knowledge explosion. Tertiary institutions are also in constant flux and there are willing and unwilling lecturers to be trained and retrained on regular basis (Johnson 1976) as globalization and the economy and competition for talents is becoming worldwide (Fanny, 2001).

The above situation implies that lecturers need to keep abreast of the time and the trends of knowledge development in their discipline so as not to become obsolete and made redundant. The ultimate goal of self-development is the enhancement of individual's job satisfaction and the optimization of skills, talent and task accomplishment.

Jones (1994) stressed that manpower development of lecturers in tertiary institutions should be geared towards acquiring or sharpening the capabilities of lecturers required to perform various obligations, tasks, and functions associated with or related to their present or future expected roles. Similarly, Peretomode and Peretomode (2001) identified the benefits of training and development of lecturers to include increase in knowledge, skills and the development of positive behaviour and attitude to work, increased personal and organizational productivity, and quality services. It can bring about improvement in morale, inculcate sense of belongingness, reduce absenteeism and turnover rate among lecturers, and importantly lead to better coordination of both human and material resources within institutions of higher learning.

Statement of the Problem

The importance of lecturers professional renewal in tertiary institutions cannot be over emphasized. In spite of its apparent merit, there are still many employers particularly in the education industry who do not commit sufficient funds to the development of their employees. They consider staff development as a waste of mager resources because of the high cost involved although most employees appear to have positive feelings about the usefulness of training and development and would want to engage in them.

In Delta State of Nigeria, there are a number of tertiary institutions with lecturers of different academic status. The principal criterion for promoting lecturers from one level to the other is the lecturer's productivity defined in terms of research output or publications in referred national and international journals and textbooks. Some of these lecturers have participated in self-sponsored development activities and few others have benefited from their institution's sponsored staff development progammes.

One thing that is not certain or that has not been determined empirically is whether those who have participated in development programmes are more productive than their counterparts who have not. In other words, how has development efforts enhanced the productivity of lecturers?

Research Questions

1. What a difference exists, if any, in the productivity of lecturers before and after development activities?
2. How does productivity after training compare between lecturers in College of Education and the University?
3. How does manpower development relate to the productivity of male and female lecturers?
4. How does productivity of lecturers after development activities compare amongst those in the faculties of education, humanities, social sciences, and the sciences?
5. What relationship exists, if any, between manpower development and lecturers' productivity?

Research Hypothesis

There is no significant relationship between manpower development and lecturers' productivity based on gender, faculty and type of tertiary institution.

Method and Procedure

This study is an expost-facto design in nature. In this study, the independent or predictor variables such as manpower development, gender, type of institution and type of faculty and the dependent or criterion variable which is lecturers' productivity had already occurred and cannot be manipulated.

Population of the Study

The population of this study comprised all the 1,021 lecturers from the tertiary institutions in Delta State of Nigeria. These institutions are the Delta State University Abraka with campuses at Oleh and Asaba (470 lectures - 365 males and 105 females), College of Education, Warri with 274 lecturers (163 males and 111 females), the College of Education Agbor, with 183 lecturers (143 males and 40 females) and the College of Education (Technical) Asaba with 94 lecturers (60 males and 34 females). This information was obtained from the Personnel Department or Establishment Departments of the various institutions.

Sample Size and Sampling Method

The sample size of this study was 205 lecturers selected based on proportional stratified random sampling technique. This represented 20 per cent of the population. The sampling was done in such a way that twenty per cent (20%) of the entire lecturers in each of the four selected institutions were selected through random sampling (see Table 1).

Table-1
Selection of Lecturers by Proportional Stratified Random Sampling

S. No.	*Institution*	*Population of Lecturers*	*20% of the Population*
1.	Delta State University, Abraka	470	94
2.	College of Education, Warri	274	55
3.	College of Education, Agbor	183	37
4.	College of Education (Tech), Asaba	94	19
		1,021	205

From the data in Table 1, the sample of the study consisted of 94 lecturers from the Delta State University, Abraka; 55 from the College of Education, Warri; 37 from the College of Education, Agbor, and 19 lecturers from the Federal College of Education (Technical), Asaba.

Instrumentation

A survey instrument titled 'Manpower Development and lecturers' Productivity Questionnaire (MDLPQ) was developed by the researchers to obtain data for the study after an extensive review of the related literature on manpower development and productivity. The questionnaire consisted of three sections. Section A compromised seven items on demographic variables. Section B consisted of 29 items based on publications made before and after staff development activities. Section C consisted of 15 items based on manpower development structured on a four-point likert-type scoring scale of 1-4 with 4 = Strongly agree, 3 = Agree, 2 = Disagree and 1 = Strongly disagree.

Validity and Reliability of Instrument

The validity of the survey instrument was established using professors in the Faculty of Education to evaluate the suitability and appropriateness of each item and the adequacy of the instrument. Their useful comments, corrections and suggestions for improvement were taken into consideration in preparing the final survey instrument for the study.

The reliability of the instrument was determined by the test-retest method. The instrument was administered to 20 lecturers, ten of whom were from the university setting and the others from the Colleges of Education. After two weeks, the same survey instrument was again administered on the same lecturers. Thereafter, the test-retest reliability coefficient was calculated using the Pearson Product Moment Correlation and 0.734 Coefficient was obtained.

Administration of Instrument

The copies of the research instrument were personally administered on the respondents and retrieved the same day after they have been completed, in each occasion.

Data Analysis

Descriptive Statistics – percentage, mean, Pearson Product Moment Correlation and the multiple regression statistical tools were used in analyzing the data. The analysis of data has been presented according to the specific research questions and hypothesis.

Research Question 1

Determining whether there is a difference in the productivity of lecturers before and after development activities.

Table–2
Mean Score of Lecturers Productivity Before and After Manpower Development N = 196

Variable	--*X*	*SD*
Productivity before Training (Manpower Development)	15.82	5.40
Productivity After Training	18.80	5.94

The data in Table 2 show that the mean scores for the respondents on productivity before training was 15.82 and the standard deviation was 5.40 while the mean score on productivity after training was 18.80 and the standard deviation was 5.94. This shows that the mean score for lecturers productivity after manpower development was higher than that before training. This implied that training positively affected lecturers productivity. This result is also illustrated in Figure 1 below.

Figure 1: Productivity of Lecturers Before and After Manpower Development

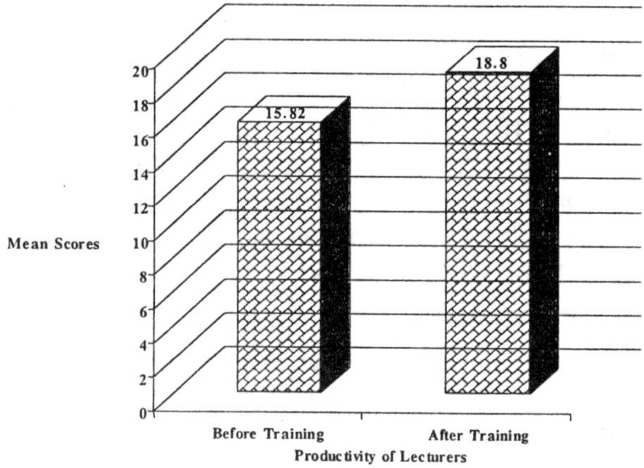

Research Question 2

Compared the productivity after training between lecturers in the Colleges of Education and those in the University.

Table–3

Comparison of the Productivity Mean Scores of Lecturers in University and Colleges of Education, N = 196

Institution Type	*–X*	*SD*
Colleges of Education (N = 110)	17.472	5.15
University (N = 86)	20.470	6.51

The data in Table 3 show the mean scores of productivity of lecturers after manpower development in the University and Colleges of Education. The mean score on productivity for lecturers in Colleges of Education was 17.47 and the standard deviation was 5.15 while the mean score on productivity of lecturers in the University was 20.470 and the standard deviation 6.51.

From the above analysis, it is evident that the mean score on productivity of university lecturers after manpower development was higher than that of lecturers in Colleges of Education.

Research Question 3

Was raised to determine if there is a difference in the productivity of male and female lecturers after manpower development and involvement in training programmes.

Table-4

Mean Scores of Productivity of Male and Female Lecturers After Manpower Development N = 196

Gender	*Productivity*		*Manpower Development*	
	X	*SD*	–X	*SD*
Male (N = 142)	18.95	6.35	24.11	4.09
Female (N = 54)	18.39	4.75	23.81	3.84

Table 4 shows the mean score for the male respondents on productivity to be 18.95 and the standard deviation 6.35, while the mean score for female respondents was 18.39 with a standard deviation of 4.75. On manpower development, the mean score for male lecturers was 24.11 and the standard deviation 4.09. The mean score for the female respondents on this variable was 23.81 with a standard deviation of 3.84. The above analysis shows that the mean scores of male respondents was basically similar to that of their female counterparts on both productivity and manpower development.

Research Question 4

Compared the productivity mean scores of lecturers by faculty.

Table-5

Comparison of the Mean Scores of the Productivity of Lecturers by Faculty After Development Programmes N = 196

Faculty	–X	*SD*
Education (N = 32)	23.16	3.63
Humanities (N = 55)	23.29	4.52
Social Sciences (N = 34)	24.62	3.28
Sciences (N = 75)	24.67	3.70

The mean scores as shown in Table 5 for the respondents' productivity by faculty are; 23.16 for Education; Humanities = 23.29; Social Sciences = 24.62, and Sciences was 24.67. This shows that there were relatively very small differences among the mean scores of the respondents from the various faculties. However, the faculty of sciences has the highest mean score of 24.67 followed by social sciences with a mean score of 24.61. The result is illustrated in Figure 2 below.

Figure 2: Bar Chart of Productivity of Lecturers in Four Faculties After Training

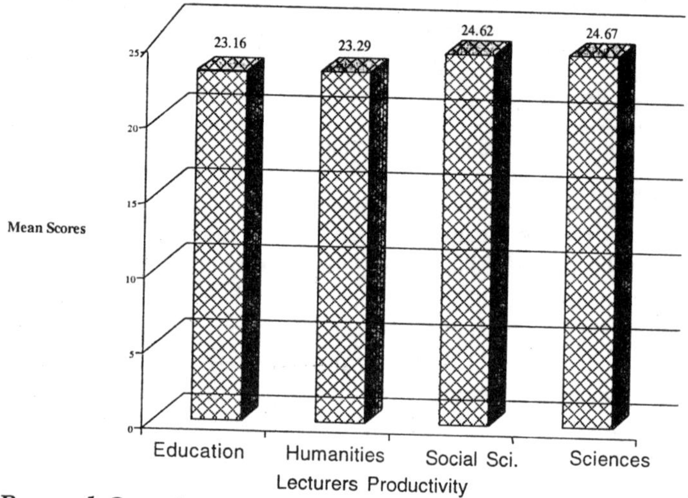

Research Question 5

Determined relationship between manpower development and lecturers' productivity?

Table-6

Person r Between Manpower Development and Lecturers Productivity N = 196

Variable	*X*	*SD*	*N*	*df*	*Cal. r Value*	*Critical r Value*
Manpower Development	24.03	4.02	196	194	0.446	0.195
Productivity	18.80	5.94	196			

The data in Table 6 show the relationship between manpower development and lecturers' productivity using the Pearson Product Moment Correlation. The correlation coefficient was .446, and the critical r was .195 with degree of freedom (df) as 194. Since the calculated r which is .446 is greater than the critical r (.195), we state that there was a positive relationship between manpower development and lecturers' productivity.

Hypothesis 1

Hypothesis 1 stated that there was no significant relationship between manpower development and productivity of lecturers considering gender, faculty, and type of tertiary institution. Multiple regression statistical tool was used to analyse the data relating to this hypothesis.

Table–7
Multiple Regression Analysis of the Predictor Variables (Gender, Faculty, and Type of Institution) and the Criterion Variable of Lecturers' Productivity

Multiple R = 0.278
R Square = 0.077
Adjusted R^2 = 0.063
Standard Error = 5.7536

Group Variable	*Sum of Square*	*Df*	*Mean Square*	*Observed F. Ratio*	*Critical F-Ratio*	*Level of Signature*
Regression	513.804	3	177.268	5.355	2.65	0.05
Residual	6356.033	192	33.104			
Total	6887.837	195				

Table 7 shows the application of the multiple regression analysis to determine the relationship between manpower development, gender, faculty and type of institution when combined together and related to productivity of lecturers. The analysis shows the multiple R to be .278 which is a low correlation. The multiple R^2 was .077, implying that the predictor variables combined were able to explain only approximately eight per cent of lecturers productivity in institutions of higher leaning.

The data in Table 7 also show that the calculated F-ratio was 5.36 with df of 195 and the critical table value of 2.65 at the .05 level of significance. Since the observed f-ratio (5.36) is greater than the F-table value (2.65), we concluded that the predictor variable of manpower development and productivity of lecturers based on gender, faculty and type of institution were significantly related.

Table 8 presents the Beta weights for each of the predictor variables. An examination of the table shows that type of institution with a Beta weight of 2.463 was the highest and this was followed by faculty with a Beta weight of .677. The Beta weight for gender had a negative value of -.146 showing that it predicted the criterion variable (lecturers' productivity) in a negative direction. In the regression equation, therefore, the type of tertiary institution is a better predictor of lecturers' development and productivity than gender and faculty.

Table–8
Multiple Regression Analysis Showing Beta Weight, Standard Error, t-Value for Predictor Variables and Criterion Variable of Productivity

S.No.	*Variables*	*Beta*	*Standard Error*	*B*	*T-Value*	*Sign*
1.	Faculty	0.677	0.386	0.126	1.753	0.081
2.	Gender	-.146	0.933	0.011	0.156	0.876
3.	Institution Type	2.463	0.800	0.219	3.078	0.002

Discussion of Findings

The findings of research questions 1 and 2 revealed that the productivity of lecturers was higher after development activities but that of university lecturers' productivity was higher than their counterparts in Colleges of Education. This finding could be attributed to the fact that admission requirements and criteria for promotion are higher and more rigorous in universities than in Colleges of Education whose course contents and scope are also lower. In most cases, publications in the Colleges of Education, particularly books, are of lower quality, locally printed most a times without peer review. It is little wonder, therefore, Nwadiani (2003) lamented that most publications these days in tertiary institutions in Nigeria are of low quality geared towards promotion in a context of publish or perish. Locally, self printed books and in-house, low quality journals have proliferated everywhere.

The result of data analysis relating to research question 3 showed that both male and female lecturers do not differ significantly in terms of manpower development and productivity. This finding should not be surprising because in tertiary institutions in Nigeria, equal opportunity is given to both male and female lecturers to attend staff development programmes. Since female lecturers recognize that promotion criteria are the same, they work just as hard as their male counterparts, their additional domestic burden not withstanding. This finding seem to support that of Haggerty (1994), Balogun (1994) and Quandzi (1994) who expressed the view that intelligence or hard-work has no gender, and in fact found that females tend to show more intrinsic interest than males in matter of life, education and people, although did not see it from productivity point of view.

The findings of research question 4 showed that the four faculties - education, humanities, social sciences, and science - do not differ significantly in terms of manpower development and productivity. This finding can be attributed to the fact that lecturers from the various faculties and institutions attend seminars, workshops and conferences which they recognize as means towards self renewal in their respective discipline and also a requirement in most tertiary institutions. As McConnel (2001), Bamidele (2003) and McDermott (1997) pointed out, in recent years, like ever before, the reward or promotion of lecturers has come to be based on the amount and quality of their work-papers presented in conferences, articles published in referred journals, national and international books published by renowned publishers. Consequently, lecturers have come to recognize the importance of self-renewal in this age of knowledge explosion and the internet.

The analysis of research question 5 showed that the observed r-value (.446) was greater than the critical r-value (.195). This implied that there was a positive significant relationship between manpower development and lecturer's productivity. This finding supports the personal experience of the researcher whose performance, over the years has been improved upon and enhanced by active participation in seminars, workshops, conferences and self development efforts through reading of current and related articles in journals. The findings also lend credence to the results of the study by Georglades (1980), Kuma (1991), and Yang (1999).

Georglades (1980) in his study, for instance, pointed out that with age human beings suffer from diminished vitality, creativity and flexibility. Ageing lecturers, he added, can be assisted to remain once again to become vibrant, vital and productive through training and development. Kuma (1991) also found that in tertiary institutions where lecturers have the opportunity of training or self renewal on the job, while such development efforts do not ensure automatic promotion, it however, does increased lecturers productivity. Similarly, Yang's (1999) findings led him to assert that manpower development seeks to address, enhance and transform the work environment and improve the productivity of the workforce.

Conclusion

Based on the results of this study, it was concluded that manpower development enhances lecturers productivity, irrespective of gender, faculty, and type of institution, and that both lecturers in Colleges of Education and Universities engage in similar manpower development programmes.

From the above conclusions, it has been recommended that management of tertiary institutions and the National Universities Commission (NUC) should continue to encourage lecturers to actively participate not only in local development efforts but also international seminars, workshops, conferences and short courses outside the shores of Nigeria by providing funding for sponsorship of lecturers to such international development activities. Because of paucity of funds on the part of lecturers resulting from poor earnings, it has been difficult for them to personally fund such activities within the country let alone overseas. The institutions of higher learning should, as a policy, set aside certain percentage of internally generated revenue to argument government funds *earn marked* for research and staff development.

REFERENCES

Ayeyalemin, C.N. (2002). "Education and Manpower: Don calls for quality teacher education programmes." *Vanguard* (November 21) pp. 15-17.

Balogun, T.A. and Qandzi L. (1994). Gender issues in the teaching of Science, technology and mathematics." In S. Erinosho (ed.) *Perspective of Women and science and technology in Nigeria*. Ibadan: university Press.

Bamidele, C. (2003). "Legendary History" *Vanguard* (October 27): pages 7-9.

Fanny S.O. (2001) *Education and Manpower Bureau in Hong Kong*. Hong Kong: Kong Press.

Georglades, W. (1980). "Renewal: A must for the principal and instructor leader." *Thrust for Educational Leadership* 2(1): 37-45.

Haggarty, S.M. (1995). "Gender and Teacher Development: Issue of Power and Culture." *International Journal of Science Education*, 17, 1:47-58.

Hallstain, T. (1990). *Human Resource Development*. New York: Renhort Winston.

Hammond, J.C. (1997). "Merit-Based Pay Wont Motivate Faculty." *Journal of Higher Education*, XIII, 2, 13 – 21.

Heis, A. (1970). *Changes of Graduate Schools*. New York: Jossey-Bass.

Johnson, T.N. cited in Ejiogu, A. (1990) *A human resource Management: Towards Greater Productivity*. Lagos: Generation Press Ltd.

Jones, M. (1994) "The tide is now turning in the favour of the Unions". *The Sunday Times* August 28, 7-11.

Lassa, P.N. (1992) *Maintaining Quality in Higher Education*. London: Routledge and Keegon.

Nigeria Education, Research and Development Council (NERDC) (2004) *National Policy on Education* 4th Ed. Abuja: NERDC.

Nwadiani, M. (2003) "Preparation of Acceptable Seminary Journal Papers" (A Paper presented at the one day seminar organized by Women in Colleges of Education (WICE), College of Education, Agbor, 28th May).

Peretomode, V.F. and Peretomode, O. (2001) *Human Resources Management*. Lagos: O and O Publisher Ltd.

Yang T. (1999). "Manpower Development in Singapore under a new paradigm". (Conference paper presented at the National Conference on Manpower Development, June 15).

19
Building School Capacity in Indonesia

Dr. Raihani, Indonesia

Introduction

The building of school capacity has been identified in research as essential in terms of both school reform implementation and whole school improvement (Caldwell and Spinks 1992; Cosner 2005). This capacity building is often related to leadership roles at every level of education authority, namely central and provincial or district authority, school council, and school principal (Leithwood and Riehl 2003; Massell 2000). The leadership of these parties plays different roles so that effective school capacity building is more likely enhanced through simultaneous and integrated programmes and strategies.

In terms of the roles of principals in building school capacity, which is the focus of this chapter, Martinez (2003) identified two types of functions of principal leadership. First, instructional [leadership] functions are enacted in assisting teachers to develop their professionalism and expertise in the provision of quality instruction for better student outcomes (Hill 2002; Lahui-Ako 2001). Second, transformational [leadership] functions describe the principal's roles in building school conditions such as school culture and structure, collaboration or cohesion amongst teachers, and other school organisational conditions which in turn create quality instruction to achieve better outcomes (Gurr 2002; Leithwood and Jantzi 2000; Leithwood *et al.,* 1999). As research has shown, both types of function are inarguably important in the context of school improvement. Confirming this importance, Leithwood (1999) found these two functions of leadership those mostly referred to in the Journal of Educational Administration during the period 1985-1995.

This chapter is based on a study of successful school leadership in Indonesia, which was inspired by an international study of successful principalship in eight different countries (Australia, Canada, Denmark, China/Hong Kong, England, Norway, Sweden, and the USA). This international study, called the International Successful School Principalship Project (ISSPP), has suffered from a lack of representation of Asian countries, which are assumed to be different from the Western contexts in terms of socio-cultural, economical, and education systems. Therefore, the current study of Indonesian school leadership is important in order to provide knowledge about successful leadership practices in the given context and to contribute to the shaping of a worldview of successful school leadership. This paper presents particular findings of the principals' leadership practices in school capacity building from an Indonesian perspective.

Successful School Capacity Building

School Capacity Concept

School capacity is referred by most scholars as the ability of the school community to continue learning. Stoll, Fink, and Earl (2002, p. 61) define school capacity as '[t]he power to get involved in and sustain the learning of everyone within the school community with the collective purpose of enhancing pupil learning'. Similar to this, Cosner (2005) puts a greater emphasis on human capital as the most important dimension of school capacity through the development of teacher learning. It is vital to develop teacher learning in order to provide better quality instruction in school, which in turn will enhance pupil performance (Cosner 2005).

Although school capacity has a goal of influencing quality instruction, similar to Stoll, Fink, and Earl's (2002) and Cosner's (2005) concept, King and Newman refer school capacity to broader organisational features. In some ways, their dimensions of school capacity are parallel to Mitchell and Sackney's (2000) school capacity categories as follow:

- Personal: The active and reflective construction of knowledge;
- Interpersonal: Collegial relations and collective practice, building the learning community climate and team;
- Organisational: Building structures that create and maintain sustainable organisational processes, opening doors and breaking down walls, sharing leadership and

sharing power, and making it happen (Stoll and Earl 2003, p. 492).

More broadly, Martinez (2003) prefers a concept of school capacity which includes social, economic, and symbolic and human capital. She states that school capacity is 'the interaction of teacher knowledge, professional community, resources, programmes and leadership' (2003, p. 4).

In this present chapter, school capacity is defined as referenced to school culture, school structure, and school resources. All of these school components have been convincingly found in school leadership studies as conditions contributing to the improvement of school capacity (Caldwell and Spinks 1992; Leithwood 2005; Leithwood *et al.,* 2004). School culture includes interactions of school members' values, norms, and symbols which are supportive of school improvement, which provides a foundation for the development of learning community. It may encompass the networks and alliances with school community in both limited and broader perspectives (Gurr *et al.,* 2003). School structure is a hierarchy within the school system including how decisions are made, and what and how job and responsibilities are distributed (Beck and Murphy 1996; Leithwood 1994). School resources cover issues of personal and professional capacity and school economic and financial capacity. In this concept of school capacity, the principals' leadership of this current study is reviewed and discussed.

School Capacity Building Practices from the ISSPP Perspectives

The international research on successful school leadership—ISSPP—was inspired by the work of Day *et al.,* (2000) on the head-teachers' leadership in the context of successful schools in the UK. Using qualitative methodology, Day *et al.,* interviewed many different members of the school community—a multiple perspective, which provided rich sources of evidence in the research. This particular approach is important, as Gurr (2003) argued that reliance on principals as the primary sources of data about school leadership not only limits the understanding about the phenomenon, but may also lead to ill-founded conclusions. This is because leadership is a perceived quality (Law and Glover 2000), and so good leaders are those who have meaningful relationships with other school stakeholders including teachers, staff, students, parents, school governors, and the education authority (Leithwood and Riehl 2003).

The ISSPP expanded to incorporate other seven countries in addition to the UK, namely Australia, China, Denmark, Hong Kong, Norway, Sweden, and USA. Using the same methodology and approach, the researchers in each participating country selected schools, both primary and secondary, based on the following criteria:

1. Schools that had received a 'positive' school review report ... particularly with regard to the leadership provided by the principal.
2. Schools that, on the basis of statewide test and examination results, could be shown to be improving their performance overtime at an exceptional rate.
3. Schools in which the principals are widely acknowledged by their professional peers as being 'successful' leaders (Gurr *et al.*, 2003, p. 23).

According to Day *et al.*, (2001; 2000), such criteria answered the need for the provision of a wide range of school contexts and leadership challenges. In practice, the ISSPP selected schools from different communities (urban/suburban/rural, different socio-economic groupings, regional spread) (Day *et al.*, 2001; Jacobson *et al.*, 2005; Mulford and Johns, 2004).

The findings of the ISSPP, as synthesised by Leithwood (2005), have provided knowledge of common characteristics and practices of leadership in the studied schools across different countries. With significant variety due to contextual demands, the leadership practices portray three basic and generic dimensions of successful school leadership developed earlier by Leithwood *et al.*, (Leithwood and Jantzi 2000; Leithwood and Riehl 2003). They are *setting direction, developing people*, and *redesigning the organisation* [original emphasis]. Setting direction includes building a shared vision, developing consensus about goals and priorities, and creating high performance expectations. Developing people includes providing individualised support, offering intellectual stimulation, and modelling important values and practices. Redesigning the organisation includes building a collaborative culture, creating and maintaining shared decision-making structures and processes, and building relationships with parents and the wider community (Leithwood and Riehl 2003; Yu *et al.*, 2002).

The ISSPP findings strongly suggest that each of the principals studied showed outstanding ability in building school capacity in the respective context. Two of the three dimensions of Leithwood's concept of successful school leadership—developing people and redesigning the organisation—that the principals showed confirmed this. In detail, for example, the principals of the Victorian schools showed interventions at developing the personal, professional, organisational, and community capacity of the schools. Gurr *et al.*, (2003, p. 34) explain:

Interventions aimed at building individual capacity of teachers included professional development activities directed towards enhancing skills and knowledge, as well as strategies to improve self awareness through reflective practice and networking with other schools. At the professional level, teachers were encouraged to work as teams and develop as teacher leaders [...] In terms of organisational capacity, each principal changed existing hierarchical structures and put into place more collaborative decision-making structures and processes. In addition, there was a significant focus on building community support by developing networks and alliances with community, business groups, improving parent-school relationships, and actively encouraging greater community participation and ownership.

In the UK context, the principals (headteachers) built their school capacity by demonstrating high professionalism which was based on their strong personal beliefs and values. These strong values were translated through strategies for developing self-esteem and restoring self-confidence in which both were linked closely to the issue of staff's professional development and their potential maximisation. The professional development of staff was fostered through in-service, visits to other schools or peer support schemes with the principals' major concerns of morale and motivation maintenance and capacity building (p. 44). Moreover, they successfully promoted collaborative cultures. Day *et al.*, (2001, p. 45) said: '[t]he most important aspect of leadership for all the principals was working successfully with people'. These collaborative cultures were enhanced through the establishment of good relationships with their staff in which they demonstrated care, support, and knowledge.

[T]he principals led both the cognitive and the affective lives of the school, combining structural (developing clear goals), political (building alliances) and educational (professional development and teaching improvement) leadership... (p. 52).

Working on culture and structure was also shown by principals in the Norwegian and Swedish school contexts (Hoog *et al.*, 2005; Moller *et al.*, 2005). They have successfully built supportive cultures and cohesive structures in order to achieve more meaningful improvement of the schools. In the Norwegian context, for instance, two aspects of school culture were among the main concerns of the principals—learning and collaboration. The learning culture was promoted in respect of the individual potentials of student and staff. This has three aspects:

1. Concern for the individual student's learning process;
2. The development of conducive learning environments and teacher-student relations; and
3. Guided by the curriculum visions and goals (Moller *et al.*, 2005, p. 592).

The collaborative culture was created through structural change, namely distribution of jobs and responsibilities and through formation of teams of teachers. Teachers were working with significant responsibilities and decisions in their daily tasks (Moller *et al.*, 2005).

To sum up, the school principals in every context demonstrated ability in, and concern with, school capacity building. They successfully established a learning organisation where members improved their understanding, competences, and professionalism in a supportive school culture. The successful school leaders inarguably exercised transformational leadership qualities to build school capacity.

The Yogyakarta Case Studies

Indonesian School Context

In general, there are two types of school in the Indonesian education system in terms of ministerial affiliation (MNE 2003b; National Office of Overseas Schools Recognition 1995; Poerbakawatja 1970; Raihani 2001). This includes schools affiliated to the Ministry of National Education (MNE) and schools affiliated to the Ministry of Religious Affairs (MRA). The MNE and MRA administer public and private schools, and provide education at kindergarten, elementary, secondary, and tertiary levels. Both the MNE and MRA manage their own schools and develop the curriculum (Hasbullah 1995; MNE 2003a; National Office of Overseas Schools Recognition 1995;

Tilaar 1995; Yunus 1979). The number of the MNE schools constitutes about eighty per cent of the total number of Indonesian school (EMIS 2002; Hartono and Ehrmann 2001; MNE 2002). The main differences between these school types are found in the curriculum content in that there is a stronger focus on religious teaching in MRA compared to MNE schools (Mastuhu 1994; Raihani 2001), with about thirty per cent of the whole curriculum of the MRA schools being religious (Islamic), whereas it is less than five per cent in MNE schools.

The Indonesian Government has conducted two major school reforms in the last decade. First, School-Based Management (SBM), both in primary and secondary levels, was introduced in 1999 (Jalal and Supriadi 2001; Jiyono *et al.*, 2001; Umaedi 2001). Second, Competency-Based Curriculum (CBC) was trialled in 2004, and will be implemented in 2006 in both primary and secondary schools (MNE 2003a; Penabur 2003; Setiawan 2000; Umaedi 2001). Although these reforms have been criticised[1], they do reflect the major government policy of political decentralisation begun in 1999, shortly after the fall of the Soeharto regime (Jalal and Supriadi 2001; Jiyono *et al.*, 2001; MNE 2001). Another initiative is to have the larger community involved in the school education processes through the empowerment of local education councils (dewan pendidikan) and school committees (komite sekolah).

School Selection

Three successful public senior secondary schools (SMAN) in Yogyakarta were selected on the basis of two following criteria:

1. Schools that, on the basis of provincial wide test and examination results, could be shown to be improving their performance at an exceptional rate.
2. Schools where the principal had been in the principalship position at least for two years at the school.

For instance, Stuart Weston, a Chief of Party of the Managing Basic Education (MBE) Project, a project funded by USAID, in his e-mail said: 'It is official [Indonesian] government policy to encourage school based management, but the roles of the various levels in the education system under decentralised government are not adequately defined. This means that many local governments intentionally fail to support school-based decision making, particularly by retaining many procurement activities (to support their corruption)'. As indicated by Bjork Bjork, C. 2003. "Local Responses to Decentralisation Policy in Indonesia." Comparative Education Review 47(2):184-216, a lack of knowledge and conceptual basis of improvement programmes has been a problem in Indonesia.

These two criteria partly followed those set in the ISSPP. Consultation was held with an official of the Education Office of Yogyakarta regarding the two criteria to see whether the criteria were contextually acceptable and to see which schools best met the criteria. The schools selected are under administration of MNE. They are:

SMAN A: Located in an outskirt of the Yogyakarta city, this was a school of 857 students in 2004, mostly from middle to lower socio-economic backgrounds. The principal, a male in his forties, was in his third year at the school, and instituted significant changes, particularly in terms of academic improvement programmes and the development of school facilities. Under his leadership, the school had achieved outstanding performances, both academically and non-academically. The school had been ranked for the last two years among the top ten schools in Yogyakarta, whilst previously it was below twenty.

SMAN B: This school is located outside the city of Yogyakarta, and had 712 students in 2004. The students mostly came from middle to lower socio-economic backgrounds, with more than fifty per cent of students having parents who were farmers. The principal was a male in his forties. Under his leadership, the school focussed on improving its teaching and learning facilities, particularly the use of information and communication technology (there was the Internet available in the school library for students to use, and multimedia provision in every classroom). There had been continuous improvement over a three year period (the school was ranked ninth, fifth and third in the years 2002, 2003 and 2004 respectively), with the school regarded as one of the best secondary schools in Yogyakarta. There had also been outstanding achievements by students in non-academic programmes in sports and arts.

SMAN C: This had been regarded as the best secondary school in Yogyakarta for many years. The school is located in the city of Yogyakarta, and had 781 students enrolled in 2004. Most of the students came from middle class families, in that most of the parents worked in public services. The principal was a male in his fifties. Under his leadership there had been some innovative changes implemented including the establishment of classes with internationally-standardised curriculum and accelerated classes.

High student academic and non-academic achievement had been maintained or improved. For example, in 2003 95 per cent of graduates were accepted into prestigious universities, whilst in 2004 96.5 per cent of its graduates were accepted, with some receiving scholarships from universities in Singapore, Japan, and the Netherlands.

Data Collection Techniques and Analysis

The research was modelled on the multiple perspective case study approach of the ISSPP. In each school, individual or group interviews were conducted with the principal, vice-principal, three teachers, one support staff, two groups of students, one group of parents, and the school committee president. All the interviews were recorded on audiotapes and transcribed, with the transcripts sent to the respondents for checking, amendments and additions as necessary. After all the data were collected from each school, they were analysed case by case. Each case was treated as a comprehensive case in and of itself—within-case analysis. Once the analysis of each case was accomplished, cross-case analysis started (Merriem, 1988, pp. 194-5). The within-case analysis comprised the procedures of transcribing, coding and categorising, and interpreting (Miles and Huberman, 1994; Patton, 2002; Poland, 1999).

School Capacity Building: An Indonesian Perspective

One of the imperatives of a successful school, according to Beck and Murphy (1996), is the leader's ability to build school capacity. The relationship between leadership and school capacity building is significant, and it is convincingly articulated in the body of literature, though some scholars believe that leadership itself is even one aspect of school capacity (Cosner, 2005; King and Newmann, 2001; Martinez, 2003). As mentioned previously, Gurr *et al.*, (2005; 2003) found that successful school leaders intervened in the school capacity which included personal, professional, organisational, and community capacities that support the school improvement as a whole. In this paper, findings of the school capacity themes of the study are discussed using the framework mentioned previously, that is school culture, school structure, and school resources.

School Culture

Organisational culture is defined as a manifestation of beliefs and values that organisational members share (Jenkins, 1991). The process of creating culture in an organisation is affected through the establishment of norms and values, the articulation of philosophies, the creation of symbols, ceremonies, rituals, parental and community interaction patterns (Jenkins, 1991; Caldwell and Spinks, 1992; and Bush and Middlewood, 2005). Through this process, successful school leaders are able to create organisational culture supportive to the achievement of school objectives (Leithwood *et al.*, 1999; Leithwood *et al.*, 2004; Leithwood and Riehl, 2003; MacBeath, 1998; Mulford and Johns, 2004).

Findings of this current study confirmed the above theories in that each of the principals was able to create a school culture that supported the attainment of better school performance. Amongst the most important cultures to each school were collaborative and learning cultures.

Each of the principals valued the importance of collaboration amongst the school community members, and created accordingly symbols and rituals to support the creation of such a culture. There are methods that they employed to create this particular culture—formal and informal. In formal ways, for example, each of the principals involved teachers, staff, parents, students, and the school committee members in the school-decision making process.

> I think the most important strategy that the principal has applied is coordinating endeavours among the school community. Everyone feels united and together. When good coordination is established, every policy can easily be implemented (SMAN A School Committee President).

> Internally, the principal has assistance such as vice-principals, teachers, and staff. They have regular meetings, and the decisions of major issues are brought to the school and the committee meeting. Parents through the school committee may agree or not with such decisions. Some revisions sometimes are needed (SMAN B Parent Group).

The involvement of stakeholders in each case was underpinned on value concepts of respect and openness and on a belief in the importance of the broader community partnership. Each of the principals articulated these values in his leadership by being eager to listen to others' opinions and by respecting them.

Formal methods do not always work in facilitating the school principals to achieve the objective of the creation of a collaborative culture. Sometimes, a formal approach even hinders school members from being collaborative (Leithwood, 2005; Rubin, 2002). Each of the principals was aware of this, and, therefore, in anticipating this, he employed informal methods to create collaboration. These ways, for instance, included staff recreations, arisan haji[1], sporting activities, and religious and social occasions, which were intended to build emotional closeness amongst them upon which a collaborative culture was easily created.

Two interchangeable value concepts appeared which underpinned collaborative culture. These are 'kebersamaan' (togetherness) and 'kekeluargaan' (family-like relationship). These concepts indicate the importance of every member of the school in working together in carrying out the school tasks. This togetherness comprises some family values such as being open to each other, caring for each other, helping each other, and not being too formal and bureaucratic. The symbols of 'kebersamaan' and 'kekeluargaan' have helped the principals in promoting trust amongst them. Trust is a pivotal foundation for long lasting collaboration (Gurr *et al.*, 2005).

The learning culture is another concern for each of the principals in enabling the creation of a learning organisation of the school. This creation of a learning organisation is repeatedly mentioned in the body of literature as a vital component in school capacity building (Tomlinson, 2004). Each of the principals strived to create this learning culture by promoting and fostering professional growth amongst teachers and staff, and showing appropriate examples of how he was doing so for himself. Each of them also suggested the value of a competitive culture by providing rewards for well performing teachers and staff. In the case of students, the learning culture was created through motivating processes, discipline reinforcement, high expectations of their outcomes, and school academic strategies.

School Structure

Each of the principals demonstrated his ability to work on another aspect of school capacity building that is redesigning the school structure. According to each principal, the school structure redesign was intended to meet the need for changes and improvement by putting each school matter into the right division in the school. Parallel to the creation of collaborative school culture, each of the principals put additional coordinators under the principal structure to cater for the needs for personnel specified to deal with certain areas. Included in this was a common additional structure across the cases: The formation of Musyawarah Guru Mata Pelajaran (MGMP), meaning subject teacher consultancy, in which subject teachers shared ideas, showed their creative and innovative thinking, collaboratively solved their problems of instruction, and so on.

Every year, we have workshops of subject teachers discussing what and how to teach in the coming semesters (Sarmila, An SMAN A teacher).

Also for the purpose of professional development, I added to the structure an MPP (learning and teaching development consultancy). In this board, teachers of the same subject sit together and discuss what needs to be discussed (SMAN B Principal).

MGMP teachers meet regularly and discuss issues related to the teaching and learning processes of their own subject. They solve problems together. Sometimes, we have invited experts to talk about contemporary issues in the subject so that our knowledge is up to date (the interviewed vice-principal of SMAN C).

Another method was by redefining the job description within the existing structure so that each staff member was aware of his or her own rights and responsibilities. For instance, a radical change was made in the case of SMAN B where the principal firmly suggested that a vice-principal position is not a life-long job as perceived conventionally by his staff, but is subject to assessment and change. However, changing or replacing staff in general was found to be a very sensitive issue for the principals to undertake, particularly in the early period of their principalship. If not calculated carefully, as all the principals said, it could be counter-productive to the improvement efforts and strategies developed.

In addition, there was an indication from the interviews that the principals were concerned with the establishment of, and supports for, a variety of student organisations. They generally involved students in making school decisions, particularly in relation to their needs through representative body that was clearly set up as part of the school structure.

The efforts by the principals to distribute power and promote a shared decision-making process were intended as well to empower staff, teachers, and even students particularly in terms of leadership development, as was also found in other contexts (Gurr *et al.*, 2005; Leithwood *et al.*, 1999; Leithwood and Riehl, 2003). Yet, empowerment is beyond the mere sharing or collegial decision-making process, and requires a sincere distribution of power from principals to teachers or other staff (Jenkins, 1991). In each of the cases, there seemed to be a little resistance to such leadership distribution from staff, which might result from the long-time centralist culture[2] (more than three decades under the centralist cultural mindset) (Bjork, 2003; Jalal and Supriadi, 2001; Rubiannor 2003).

School Resources

School resources are also an important component of school capacity with which school leaders were concerned. There are two vital aspects of this component—human resources and financial resources. Each of the principals in the study showed an outstanding ability to manage these two resources in order to support school capacity building.

(a) Human Resources Development

The management of human resources or professional development is a key to successful organisation (Moorhead and Griffin, 1998; Riley and MacBeath, 1998; Smith, 1995). Well-programmed professional development will be highly likely to contribute to effective processes of organisation, particularly in the support of the creation of a learning organisation. In this current study, each of the principals showed a high concern for in professional development of himself, his teachers, and staff. He believed in the importance of long-life learning, and accordingly showed examples of learning continuously to foster personal and professional growth. Besides undertaking training relevant to his profession as a principal, each of the principals was keen on exchanging knowledge and information amongst the school principals in Yogyakarta and amongst teachers. The principal of SMAN C was studying at a doctoral level, while those of SMAN A and B expressed their willingness to continue their formal education to a higher level.

As to teacher and staff professional development, each of the principals considered motivation as an important factor for their better performance. Many methods to motivate them were employed, including the provision of rewards and individualised support, the emphasis on the school performance in every meeting, and the ongoing monitoring and evaluation of their performance. Each of the principals provided types of rewards for teachers and staff including compliments when they did jobs well, material rewards such as bonuses, wages increases, etc. In the respondents' words, these rewards were referred as 'kesejahteraan' (welfare), which encompassed psychological, spiritual, physical, and financial welfare.

The principal was concerned with the staff and teachers' welfare. He improved it. I was involved in calculating the increase. I was asked about my income and expenditure so that he knows how much I need (the interviewed support staff member of SMAN B).

On many occasions, he [the principal] often praises staff and teachers for their good jobs. He always says that staff and teachers here are competitively selected persons, so we have to prove that we are really rightly selected (the interviewed vice-principal of SMAN C).

The provision of individualised supports, a characteristic of successful school leadership across contexts (Leithwood, 1999), is a feature of the principals' leadership of this current study. The principals paid attention to teachers as individuals, asking about their personal and family conditions (found as well in Jacobson *et al.*, 2005), as well as their professional problems. They were keen on providing advice to solve problems. Each of them was also open and visible for teachers to see him and discuss any matters with him.

In regard to the context of Indonesian education, the teacher salary was very low (Asia Times, 2000; Bjork, 2003; Sutjipto *et al.*, 2001). Consequently, many Indonesian teachers worked also as part-timers in other job areas, such as ngojek [motorcycle drivers for public transportation]. Therefore, salary increases are important in order to provide teachers and their families with a better living standard. Some teachers interviewed in this study confirmed that since this current principalship they did not have to find a part-time job to fulfil their financial needs since they already received better salary from the school. Accordingly, they could concentrate more effectively on their teaching work.

Simultaneous with the above welfare improvement, each of the principals was concerned with further education of his teachers and staff-in-service training. Many forms of meaningful in-service training were developed for teachers, including sending them to further education, workshops and courses such as the Competency-Based Curriculum (CBC) preparation course, English courses, computing skills, etc. Another was training for teachers about how to use ICT in their instruction. In addition, each of the principals encouraged teachers to be involved in MGMP. All of these were intended to equip teachers with better knowledge and skills in curriculum and instruction.

Another important means of professional development that each of the principals was concerned was empowering teachers and staff through the exploration of their creativities and innovative ideas. Each of the principals was described as frequently having deliberately provided intellectual stimulation (Jacobson *et al.*, 2005; Leithwood *et al.*, 1999; Leithwood and Riehl, 2003) for their teachers and staff and challenged them to perform better in their job. The respondent teachers said that they were asked to come up with fresh ideas for the school improvement, classroom teaching strategies, and other issues.

(b) Financial Resources Management

Each of the principals was capable in managing his school's financial resources. He was described as diligent in seeking various sources of school funds and establishing partnerships with such sources for the benefits of the school. As a result, not only has the government offered regular funding, but also private sources such as business companies from both national and international bases have provided funds. The key to this effort in seeking funds is the communication skills that each of the principals mastered outstandingly (Leithwood, 2005).

This is really courage bythe principal in lobbying the general director [of elementary and secondary education] in Jakarta. We fully support this. Last night, there was also a meeting with Singaporean education authority officials. I attended this meeting, which discussed the partnership between the school and the Singaporean Government (Syarif, An SMAN C Parent).

What appeared to be a distinctive feature in each case was its accountability in the use of the funds. This was enhanced through the involvement of various school stakeholders in the process of school development planning, which was held every year. Another regular meeting, particularly between the school and its community including parents and the school committee, was held in order to evaluate the implementation of school programmes. Reports on school funding were given, and were open to questions or internal audits.

Each of the principals ensured that the use of the school funds was intended to build school capacity. There were at least three areas on which the funds were used: staff professional development, student scholarships, and school maintenance and facilities. As to staff professional development, each of the schools for instance provided financial supports for staff undertaking further education and other professional development programmes such as seminars and training sessions/packages. The principals were also reported to have sought some funds directed to the provision of scholarships for students.

The funds were also used to improve school maintenance and facilities. Most respondents of each case confirmed that since this current principalship there has been considerable improvement in school facilities. A range of the facilities included new school buildings, multimedia in each classroom, the Internet connection in the school library, religious facilities, and other school accessories such as school gates and gardens. The teacher and student respondents expressed their happiness about this improvement, and they had become more confident that their school was one of the best in Yogyakarta.

Concluding Remarks

The three Indonesian school principals have demonstrated their ability in building school capacity. They were diligently working on the three related areas of school capacity: School culture, school structure, and school resources. They had successfully identified and created two pivotal cultures—collaborative and learning—that gave rise to wider possibilities of creating a learning school organisation. Within these cultures, members of the schools were motivated and highly supported to learn, while working, continuously and collaboratively. The creation of these cultures was simultaneously supported through the redesign of school structure, which was intended to ease changes promoted in order to achieve maximum school improvement. The school structure redesign such as putting in new programme coordinators was also able to meet the needs for job distribution and staff learning and empowerment. It is obvious that staff professional development was being fostered through regular and non-regular programmes, whilst financial resources were managed to support school improvement programmes.

The Indonesian principals have exercised the two functions of leadership as mentioned in the body of literature to be important in the process of school capacity building—instructional and transformational. Instructional functions were shown in their concern and work on teacher professional growth in order for them to practise better quality instruction. This was supported through the enactment of transformational functions in which the principals created supportive school conditions including culture, structure, financial resources, and facilities. In Leithwood *et al.*, (1999) term, this is called 'second order changes'. Above all, through these transformational functions, they successfully raised staff and students' motivation towards learning and hence enhanced school capacity.

Beyond the instructional and transformational functions, the three principals founded their leadership on strong and enduring beliefs and values, and on interpersonal skills. These beliefs and values in particular included openness and respect, and 'kekeluargaan' and 'kebersamaan', whilst interpersonal skills included most importantly communication skills. These particular findings confirmed further the importance of personal and professional beliefs and values in successful school leadership practices.

REFERENCES

'Arisan Haji' is **a regular gathering** where members contribute to and take turns at winning an aggregate sum of money for doing hajj or pilgrimage to Mecca. Hajj is the fifth pillar of Islamic belief. This programme continues for many years until all the members are able to perform hajj.

As explained briefly in the methodology section, Indonesian education has changed from the centralist approach to school management to a decentralist one following the fall of Soeharto in 1998 since which time decentralization of politics and governance has been implemented. It is difficult, however, to shift the centralist culture of government officials including school staff and teachers to a new one.

Asia Times. 2000. "Indonesian Education Fails in Face of Crisis." In Asia Times Online.

Beck, L.G. and J. Murphy. 1996. The Four Imperatives of a Successful School. Thousand Oaks, California: Corwin Press, Inc.

Bjork, C. 2003. "Local Responses to Decentralisation Policy in Indonesia." Comparative Education Review 47(2):184-216.

Caldwell, B. J. and M. Spinks. 1992. Leading the Self-Managing School. London: The Falmer Press.

Cosner, S. 2005. "Toward a Human Capital Development Strategy." In Educational Leadership and Reform, eds. Wayne K. Hoy and Cecil G. Miskel. Greenwich: IAP.

Day, C., A. Harris and M. Hadfield. 2001. "Challenging the orthodoxy of effective school leadership." International Journal of Leadership in Education 4(1):39-56.

Day, C., A. Harris, M. Hadfield, H. Tolley and J. Beresford. 2000. Leading Schools in Times of Change. Buckingham: Open University Press.

EMIS. 2002. Statistik Pendidikan Islam. Jakarta: Education Management Information System, The Ministry of Religious Affairs Republic of Indonesia.

Gurr, D. 2002. "Transformational Leadership Characteristics in Primary and Secondary School Principals." Leading and Managing 8(1):78-99.

Gurr, D., L. Drysdale and B. Mulford. 2005. "Successful Principal Leadership: Australian Case Studies." Journal of Educational Administration 43(6):539-551.

Gurr, D., L. Drysdale, E. D. Natale, P. Ford, R. Hardy and R. Swan. 2003. "Successful School Leadership in Victoria: Three Case Studies." Leading and Managing 9(1):18-37.

Hartono, D. and D. Ehrmann. 2001. The Indonesian Economic Crisis and its Impact on Educational Enrolment and Quality. Singapore: Institute of Southeast Asian Studies.

Hasbullah. 1995. Sejarah Pendidikan Islam di Indonesia. Jakarta: Rajawali Pers.

Hill, Peter William. 2002. "What All Principals Should Know About Teaching and Learning." In The Principal Challenge, eds. M.S. Tucker and J.B. Codding. San Francisco: Jossey-Bass.

Hoog, J, O. Johansson and A. Olofsson. 2005. "Successful Principalship—The Swedish Case." Journal of Educational Administration.

Jacobson, S.L., L. Johnson, R. Ylimaki and C. Giles. 2005. "Successful Leadership in Challenging U.S. Schools: Enabling Principles, Enabling Schools." Journal of Educational Administration 43(6):606-618.

Jalal, Fasli and Dedy Supriadi eds. 2001. Reformasi Pendidikan Dalam Konteks Otonomi Daerah. Yogyakarta: Adi Cita.

Jenkins, H.O. 1991. A Handbook for Successful School Leadership. Oxford: Basil Blackwell Ltd.

Jiyono, Fasli Jalal, A. Syamsuddin, D. Syafruddin, R. Suparman, Ajisuksmo and Rumtini. 2001. "Menuju Desentralisasi Pengelolaan Pendidikan Dasar." In Reformasi Pendidikan Dalam Konteks Otonomi Daerah, ed. Fasli Jalal. Yogyakarta: Adicita.

King, M.B. and F.M. Newmann. 2001. "Building School Capacity Through Professional Development: Conceptual and Empirical Considerations." International Journal of Educational Management 20(1):86-94.

Lahui-Ako, B. 2001. "The Instructional Leadership Behaviour of Papua New Guinea High School Principals." Journal of Educational Administration 39(3):233-265.

Law, Sue and Derek Glover. 2000. Educational Leadership and Learning: Practice, Policy and Research. Buckingham: Open University Press.

Leithwood, K. 1994. "Leadership for School Restructuring." Educational Administration Quarterly 30(4):498-518.

Leithwood, K. 2005. "Understanding Successful School Leadership: Progress On A Broken Front." Journal of Educational Administration 43(6):619-629.

Leithwood, K. and D. L. Duke. 1999. "A Century's Quest to Understand School Leadership." In Handbook of Research on Educational Administration, eds. J. Murphy and K.S. Louis. San Francisco: Jossey-Bass Publishers.

Leithwood, K. and D. Jantzi. 2000. "The Effects of Transformational Leadership on Organizational Conditions and Student Engagement with School." Journal of Educational Administration 38(2):112-129.

Leithwood, K., D. Jantzi and R. Steinbach. 1999. Changing Leadership for Changing Times. Philadelphia: Open University Press.

Leithwood, K., K.S. Louis, S. Anderson and K. Wahlstrom. 2004. "How Leadership Influences Student Learning." New York: The Wallace Foundation.

Leithwood, K. and C. Riehl. 2003. "What Do we Already Know About Successful School Leadership?".

MacBeath, J. ed. 1998. Effective School Leadership: Responding to Change. London: Paul Chapman Publishing Ltd.

Martinez, M.C. 2003. "One Principal Developing School Capacity Through Building Social Capital." Rutger University.

Massell, D. 2000. "The District Role in Building Capacity: Four Strategies." GPRE Policy Briefs (September):1-8.

Mastuhu. 1994. Dinamika Sistem Pendidikan Pesantren: Suatu Kajian Tentang Unsur dan Nilai Sistem Pendidikan Pesantren. Jakarta: INIS.

Merriem, Sharan B. 1988. Case Study Research in Education: A Qualitative Approach. San Francisco: Jossey-Bass, Inc.

Miles, Matthew B. and A. Michael Huberman. 1994. Qualitative Data Analysis. Thousands Oaks: SAGE Publications.

Mitchell, C. and L. Sackney. 2000. Profound Improvement: Building Capacity for a Learning Community. Lisse, The Netherlands: Swet & Zeitlinger.

MNE. 2001. "Programme Pembangunan Nasional (Propenas) Tahun 2000-2004: Pembangunan Pendidikan." The Ministry of National Education.

MNE. 2002. Indonesia Educational Statistics in Brief. Jakarta: The Ministry of National Education Republic of Indonesia.

MNE. 2003a. "Pusat Kurikulum Balitbang." Kurikulum Berbasis Kompetensi.

MNE. 2003b. "Undang-Undang Sistim Pendidikan Nasional Tahun 2003." Ministry of National Education the Republic of Indonesia.

Moller, J.A. Eggen, O.L. Fuglestad, G. Langfeldt, A Presthus, Skrovset, S. Stjernstrom and G. Vedoy. 2005. "Successful School Leadership—The Norwegian Case." Journal of Educational Administration 43(6):584-594.

Moorhead, Gregory and Ricky W. Griffin. 1998. Organizational Behaviour: Managing People and Organisation. 5th Edition. Boston: Houghton Mifflin Company.

Mulford, B. and S. Johns. 2004. "Successful School Principalship." Leading and Managing 10(1):45-76.

National Office of Overseas Schools Recognition. 1995. Indonesia: A Comparative Study. Canberra: Australian Government Publishing Service.

Patton, Michael Quinn. 2002. Qualitative Evaluation and Research Methods. 3rd Edition. Newbury Park: Sage Publications.

Penabur, BPK. 2003. "Kerangka Dasar Kurikulum Berbasis Kompetensi." BPK Penabur Online.

Poerbakawatja, Soegarda. 1970. Pendidikan Dalam Alam Indonesia Merdeka. Jakarta: Gunung Agung.

Poland, Blake D. 1999. "Transcription Quality as an Aspect of Rigor in Qualitative Research." In Qualitative Research, eds. Alan Bryman and Robert G. Burgess. London: Sage Publications.

Raihani. 2001. "Curriculum Construction in the Indonesian Pesantren." In Learning and Educational Development. Melbourne, VIC: The University of Melbourne.

Riley, K. and J. MacBeath. 1998. "Effective Leaders and Effective Schools." In Effective School Leadership: Responding to Change, ed. J MacBeath. London: Paul Chapman Publishing Ltd.

Rubiannor, Taufik. 2003. "Peran Kepala Sekolah SMU 1 Marabahan Dalam Perspektif Pengembangan Manajemen Berbasis Sekolah di Kabupaten Barito Kuala." Yogyakarta: Universitas Negeri Yogyakarta.

Rubin, H. 2002. Collaborative Leadership: Developing Effective Partnerships in Communities and Schools. Thousand Oaks: Corwin Press, Inc.

Setiawan, C. 2000. "Relevansi Kurikulum Pendidikan Masa Depan." In Membuka Masa Depan Anak-Anak Kita: Mencari Kurikulum Pendidikan Abad XXI, ed. Sindhunata. Yogyakarta: Kanisius.

Smith, R. 1995. Successful School Management. London: Cassel.

Stoll, L. and L. Earl. 2003. "Making It Last: Building Capacity for Sustainability." In Handbook of Educational Leadership and Management, eds. Brent Davies and John West-Burnham. London: Pearson Longman.

Stoll, L.D. Fink and L. Earl. 2002. It's About Learning (and It's About Time). London: Routledge/Falmer Press.

Sutjipto, Dedi Supriadi, B. Musthafa, H. Mansyur, E. Soenarya, E. Suwarni, R. Yunus, A.A. Wahab, F.A. Hamied and H. Muhammad. 2001. "Rekomendasi-rekomendasi Untuk Pemberdayaan Guru dan Tenaga Kependidikan." In Reformasi Pendidikan Dalam Konteks Otonomi Daerah, eds. Fasli Jalal and Dedi Supriadi. Yogyakarta: Adicita.

Tilaar, H.A.R. 1995. 50 Tahun Pembangunan Pendidikan Nasional 1945-1995. Jakarta: PT Grasindo.

Tomlinson, Harry. 2004. Educational Leadership: Personal Growth for Professional Development. London: Sage Publications.

Umaedi. 2001. "Manajemen Peningkatan Mutu Berbasis Sekolah." Ministry of National Education.

Yu, H., K. Leithwood and D. Jantzi. 2002. "The Effects of Transformational Leadership on Teachers' Commitment to Change in Hong Kong." Journal of Educational Administration 40(4):368-389.

Yunus, Mahmud. 1979. Sejarah Pendidikan Islam di Indonesia. Jakarta: Mutiara.

20

Hermeneutics and Disciplinary Perspectives of Education: The Education-Socio-Cultural Perspectives in Relation to Research Trend in Indian Academia

Rajarshi Roy, India

Introduction

Education is a broader connotation. Good many scholars defined education in different ways, in different approaches and from different perspectives. It is closely related with society as well. Professor **Feinberg**, the eminent western sociologist and educationist, categorically establishes the function of education and its close association with the society in his well-known book "Understanding Education: Towards a Reconstruction of Educational Inquiry" (1983). According to professor Feinberg, "... *Education is best understood by recognizing that one of the functions of any society is that of maintaining intergenerational continuity – that is, of maintaining its identity as a society across generations and even in the context of many possible and significant changes, and that is the activity and institution of education, both – formal and informal, that carries on this function.*"

To be more precise, education is a social process. Nowadays it is widely accepted that any inquiry into educational process necessarily incorporates the society within which the process of education takes place. The present practice of social science research is oriented towards positivistic approach, resulted due to mere imitation of the west.

Shifting its attention from positivism, social science research in our country needs to emphasizes much over the *humanistic approach* where interrelationship between values, interests, actions and power of the social atom (i.e., human individual) is taken into consideration along with the process of change in society. Humanism is usually considered as an integrated approach of humankind and society.

This integrated approach helped a lot for the advancement of new research perspectives and methodologies, including *symbolic interaction, action research, ethno-methodology, ethnography, historical materialism, participatory research, cultural anthropology, social phenomenology, and critical social science,* apart from a number of other forms of research methodology, mostly practiced in the first-world countries. Since the outset of the last decade, many alternative approaches to study the social processes and research in the field of education have emerged, across the globe, giving rise to numerous confusions and conflicts, as they have competed against one another to establish their superiority and in search of acceptance from scholars and researchers.

Education and Culture

The famous educational thinker ***Whitehead (1962)*** wrote in his book entitled, 'The aims of education and other essays', *"...Culture is activity of thought, and receptiveness of beauty and human feeling. Scraps of information have nothing to do with it. A merely well informed man is the most useless bore on God's earth. What we should aim at producing is men who possess both culture and expert-knowledge in some special direction. Their expert-knowledge will give them the ground to start from, and their culture will lead them as deep as philosophy and as high as art."*

Whitehead (op. cit.) also considered culture as the basic aspect of education, which is obviously having its root in the society within which an individual is born and is grows up. This advocates that the process of education as well as the product coexist with society. Irrespective of societies, culture possesses its own value. Being a component of education, it adds value to education. Therefore, in respect of educational research in social sciences, the attempt to carry out value-free research is hardly possible. An attempt of quantitative research on social aspects of educational process may contribute specific information, but may hardly contribute to knowledge. However, one has to agree about the restriction of imposing personal values in the process of observation and recording the findings of social research in education because of the reason of ethical consideration. Ethnocentrism often influences the social aspects of educational research and it is more true in our country. The tendency should be avoided.

Way back in 1974, **in the context of the research-trend in sociology of education in Indian social fabric,** Tirtha, N.V., and

Mukhapadhyay *remarked,* ".... Indian society is passing through a silent transformation and is awaiting a bigger revolution. Education happens to be, and is the most instrumental one in it. There is no alternative to empirical and depth studies in education, using sociological models and methodologies for bringing about relevance of educational process and product to the changing conditions of modern Indian society. Education in India has been far too long programmatic and imitative of advanced countries. The sooner does it becomes sensitive to the responses of society on it's own function, structure and process, the better it will be for education in terms of purposes laid down by architects of Indian nationhood."

Since then exactly three decades have passed, during which Indian social system and structure pursued sequels of changes. The same is, though in a comparatively restricted sphere, however, reflected in the field of research in Education in Indian academia. Research in the area of sociology of education dates back to the mid of last century with a systematic base. During this wide time span, good many significant trends emerged in various dimensions, which incorporate sociological aspects of education too. A number of institutions and organizations came up with a prime objective to assist the process of research in social aspects of education. Among them, Indian Council of Social Science Research (ICSSR), New Delhi shoulders the largest share. Apart from ICSSR, The University Grants Commission (UGC) and other funding agencies, including non-governmental efforts, have also extended their helping hand to carry on educational research in social aspects. Higher education in India witnessed a phenomenal growth during the last thirty years and the extent of growth is much more in the recent past. As a result, the scope of research in India has expanded a lot. [Experience says that this expansion has helped to enrich other related disciplines such as sociology, social anthropology etc., much more, as compared to that of education]. A number of training organizations are also available in almost each part of the country today, extending training programmes to enrich the human effort to pursue research in educational sociology with sophisticated methodologies. Expansion of higher education in course of time helped people interested in education to pursue formal research programmes and training (i.e., M.Phil. etc.) in education. Right now, as many as eighty-four higher learning institutions, if not more, across the nation are extending the scope of such training to the scholars, emphasizing over various dimensions of education, with largest share towards sociology of education. In spite of all these efforts, unfortunately the field of educational research failed to establish *'education'* as an *independent discipline of study*. This may be due to the nature of interpretation of 'education,' where the cognitive set of the researches in the field are mostly enriched by the other allied disciplines than that of education. The basic requirement of establishing a discipline, as we all know, depends upon the number and quality of research in the field, which, in its turn, enrich the number of theories of the discipline, help in evolving stable methodology and offers (more or less specified) boundary for the discipline. Statistics says that as many as two hundred and -seventy-two (272) research studies (up to March, 2008) hinge over the area of educational research in relation to the social process during the preceding five years. However, except a very few, none of those contributed either for forming theory or for evolving methodology. It is crystal clear that almost all the researchers are habituated to adopt methodology from the allied disciplines. The result reveals a dearth of sound methodology, less number of theories and lack of more or less specified boundary for the discipline *'education'*, which are the pre-requisites for the emergence of a discipline. Apart from the exceptions, to be more frank, the domain has become an attractive platform for those who failed in their respective disciplines and thereby oriented themselves with this very platform for their own survival as an 'academician'. Neither they are inclined to contribute for developing theory and evolving methodology of education, nor are they capable enough of doing so. Another trend is also noticeable which reveals that a handful number of eminent educational researchers perceive pedagogy and education synonymous. As a result, 'education' remains an inter-disciplinary approach in which a Ph.D. is produced in every eighteen (18) hours (or may be even less than that). Controversial issues prevail without any feasible solutions.

Social Process in Education

History advocates that up till the onset of the nineteenth century, 'psychology' was the major dominant discipline over the field of education in the West. The trend of West was imitated by India which resulted in an 'individualized' approach to interpret the social process. Since the beginning of the twentieth century, sociology expanded its root to education. Since then individualized interpretation of education perused a paradigm shift towards the 'group-approach' with the underlining fact that education is a process, which takes place in society. Individual's existence depends on the group within which he lives and grows on. In fact, individual is a part of group, i.e., a *social atom*. Therefore, it was quite inevitable to accept the social aspects in educational process which holds that any study on educational system must go beyond the individual and is supposed to pay sufficient consideration to the complex factors and forces of I-G (i.e., Individual - Group) interactions, both within and outside the formal education system. The process of imparting and imbibing education is in no way a non-directional process. Rather, it is a 'both-way' process, a social process, in which two or more individuals, with either similar or differing socio-economic situation, communicate with similar or differing consequences. Famous sociologist and educationist *Durkheim (1985)*'s comment is worthnoting in this context. In the volume entitled "The evolution of educational thought", he categorically traced that education is essentially a *social process*, so far as its origin is concerned. Simultaneously, it is a social function too. He opines that there is, however, no one ideal type of education for all: it differs from society to society, from group to group, within a given society, and within the same society at different times, because of different socio-cultural environments and differing needs of different societies and groups. Famous educator *John Dewey (1899)* also echoes the very concept when he says, "*... If the school is to be effective, it must be a social institution. Closely related to the community.*" Another sociologist from West, *Professor Ward (1883)* in his book entitled "*Dynamic sociology*", expressed his views saying, "*...Education is the proximate means of progress of society*". *Herbert Spencer* in his book, entitled '*What knowledge is most worth?*", established the rationale of accepting education as a social process. He stressed over the basic function of education to develop the system of society through socializing social atoms.

In the early phase of development, the very dimension of education was enriched and influenced by the thoughts and ideas of famous sociologists like *Ward (1883), Goode (1926), Ellwood (1927)* and *Kinneman (1932)*, followed by *Finncy (1927), Clement (1927) and Peters (1935)*, who regarded it as a basis for a scientific analysis of the aims and objectives of education. They were further followed by *Payne (1928), Smith (1928), Brown (1947), Robbins (1953), Mukherjee R.K. (1960)* and so on.

Here it is worth mentioning that not only the process of education is regarded as a social process. But the system, within which the process of education takes place, is also considered as a social system related to the total social system. In other words, it is to be accepted that the system of education acts as a subsystem of the society to execute certain functions for the improvement of the society as a whole. The goal of 'social aspects of educational process' is, therefore, to observe and to analyze the existing structure of the educational system, to evolve knowledge about the pattern of its elements, and the roles played by various factors and forces, and thereby to acquaint the level of achievement of the functional sets, which are active within and outside the system. It is also essential to study the magnitude and effect of such factors and thereby to identify the basic factors, intervening factors, as well as obsolete factors, obviously in relation to the educational system itself, and also as a system of social relationships among the human components.

Both the processes - i.e., the process of socialization and the process of advancement of knowledge in the field should be the basic focal point of researchers, apart from identifying their interrelationships. It may also be examined through researches to what extent the process of education is becoming instrumental for furthering the development of knowledge and controlling, managing or assisting information-explosion in this direction.

The subsystems of any society are supposed to be interrelated and interdependent. Consequently, the other major sub-systems viz., *political situation, economic condition, policy perspectives, religious institutions or the like,* also pose a tremendous impact over the process of education. At present, while the societies are undergoing a rapid change, research in education, as it appears from the trend, is aimed to explore the interrelationship of these major social systems. Polities, among those, draw the interest of a handful number of scholars, although as a peripheral factor. Frequent changes as well as an absolute stability of governance across decades, both have tremendous impact over society and its system of education. Unfortunately no scholar has identified the very area for their study, as yet, which may be studied by future researchers. The area is still remaining as a virgin one for educational research. This very area demands high attention because of the fact that Indian academia has been facing the question of qualitative degradation for the last two decades. During the period, the quantitative expansion surely touched its apex. Experience reveals that an attempt of destroying any society is easily possible through destruction of the system of education of the very society. Penetration of politics in the arena of academics is the easiest method to destroy the system and the process of education and thereby to cripple the entire society in due course of time. Assured absolute stability of governance extends a synergic impact and the task becomes easy accessible. If the situation appears in a democratic country (or even a small part thereof), it questions the very process of 'prevailing democracy' itself. Laterally, it expands its arm to cripple the economic situation. Cheap-populism in policy-formulation-process may aggravate the extent of threat towards democracy in such a situation. Therefore, once the quality of education is under question, prevailing political situation, and its interrelationship with the other allied factors are supposed to receive proper attention from multiple angles. Researches focusing on *'societal aspects of the educational process"* need to emphasize the cumulative impact of major social subsystems on the educational system in various regions of the country. A perusal of the abstracts of educational research on social aspects reveals lack of research in this dimension. The gap of knowledge in these aspects needs urgent and in-depth team-research. " Team research" in connection with educational research in Indian academia is yet rare. For the empirical research, to evolve the grounded theories, team research is quite indispensable. In fact, the polity, economy, society, culture and education are various facets of one and the same reality, and any attempt to isolate them would absolutely be arbitrary. These are all social (and to be more specific, major social) factors and should be studied in a holistic perspective. Educational researchers should focus upon the process of education and the product thereof, obviously taking into account, other major factors, too. This will enable them to develop a realistic outlook on one hand and on the other hand, will help to enrich education.

The 'Boundary Dispute' between Educational Sociology and Sociology of Education

It has already been mentioned that the major share of educational research comes under the broader category, which incorporates both society and the process of education. However, controversy remains even now so as to term the very area: Whether sociology of education, or the educational sociology.

Sociology is the study of social relationship, as defined by the famous sociologist *Giddings (1984)*. He says, *"... a number of like minded individuals, who know and enjoy their like mindedness and, therefore work for the common goals, may be termed as society"*. In brief, the study of society is the matter of concern of the sociologists.

On the other hand, education is a process as well as the product of the same process. It is the most important medium of all because of its potentiality to influence the human beings who in the aggregate, form the society. *'People and nations are as they are'*, as Professor *Nicholas Hans (1964)* perceives, *"... because of their educative process'*. Therefore, education and society are intertwined.

On the other hand, the system (and the process) of education acts as a subsystem of the gestalt social system, and is influenced by various social institutions – such as *religion, values, mores, norms, customs, family, state or polity, community, social and class stratification, technology, knowledge* and so on. A schematic diagram of the same is given below (Diagram-1):

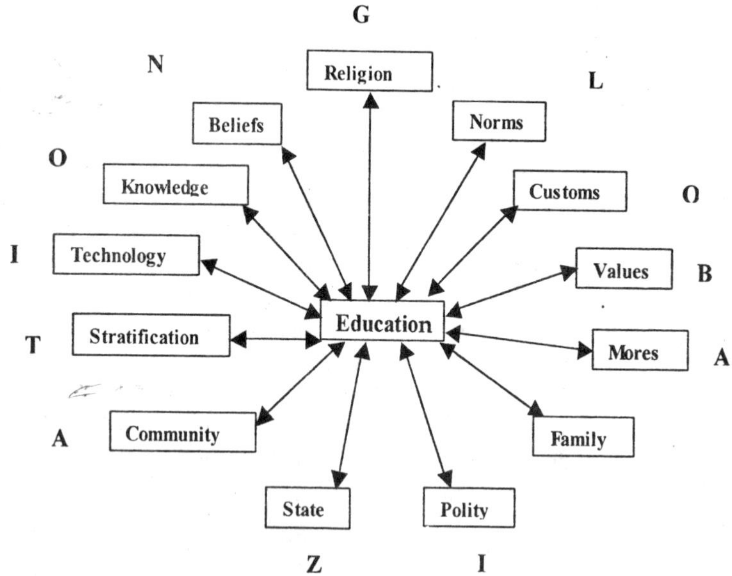

The *system* as well as the *process* of education constitutes a field of close interaction of all these variables (as depicted in the above diagram) as the components of society, which possess a synergic influence over the process of education, with global pressure.

In one hand, education as an area of research should possess its own functional aspects. Education acts as an agent of socio-cultural changes, which further enhances the techno-culture of society. The pedagogy of indigenous technology is rooted into the social process of education of any given society. Basically education performs three functions as follows:

- *Transmission of society-specific knowledge and its mode of transmission,*
- *Interpretation of facts in respect of any given society, and*
- *Innovation and creativity.*

On the other hand, all these three functions are inter-twisted with each other and form a composite function. Transmission of education and knowledge possesses it's own dimensions of socialization, enculturation and cultural cohesiveness. After transmission, interpretation plays its role on culture and personality development of the social atoms. It also furthers the method of interpretation of certain personality patterns, ethnography and cultural cohesiveness. Social mobility, integration, harmony, equality, fraternity, justice and such other social values follow the process of transmission and lead to social innovation. Innovation as a functional aspect of educational research serves for educational changes and, consequently cultural changes and acculturation. The researches in education, who deal with its sociological base, focus on all these aspects. However, the only sustainable model which has come up to this area of research, encompassing education and thereby contributing towards the formation of discipline, in the last five years, covers and explains the entire process in a nut shell. The researcher in the very model shows the interplay of the all bases (viz., philosophy, sociology, history and psychology) of education and explains the social process in a lucid way, contributing a model of social process in education, which he has denoted as ethno-pedagogic model of social process in education in relation to some specific status group. Before distinguishing the controversial concept of educational sociology and sociology of education, a glance perusal at the model will be better. (Refer to Diagram 2).

The distinction between educational sociology and sociology of education is one, which educationists have come to emphasis in contemporary period only. Though late than never, it reflects the growing interest, which both educationists and sociologists are

Diagram-2 The Approach Model

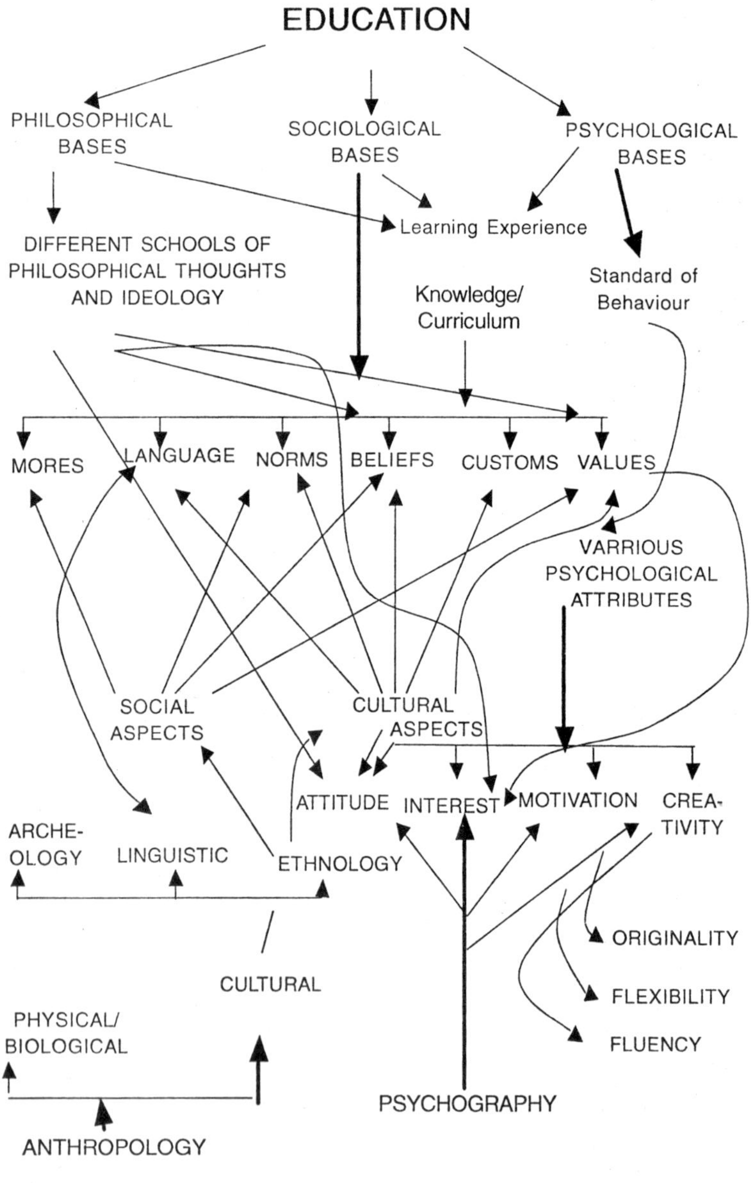

taking care of, at least in some aspects. Irrespective of huge differences of opinion in relation to the terminologies, since the last ten years (at least not less than that), majority of the educational researches has been carried out centering round this very 'base' of education – i.e., sociology.

'The differences between the two terminologies are more than a sterile argument between pedantic academies'. It suggests a divergence in perspective and method. *Brain J. Ashley et. al., (1969)* writes that "*... However, there is probably an element of gamesmanship involved.*" *Hansen, D.A. et. al., (1967)* writes in their book entitled *'On Education: Sociological perspectives"*, that, "*... at times the terms are used in a sort of academic one-upmanship, in which the sociologist may not be attempting to one up the educator so much so as to protect himself from one downery at the hands of his colleagues. All new field of research, as they forecasted, have to face the problem of obtaining recognition from those, which are already established.*"

The term educational sociology dates back to the early part of the last century when educational sociology was being offered in various colleges of the west, especially in United States (*Corwin, 1965*). In India the credit goes to the University of Calcutta, which started a postgraduate degree in Education and offered a paper on Educational Sociology during 1919. Unfortunately it had neither developed a sound theoretical framework, nor a rigorous methodology, but was more of an educational discipline than that of a sociological one. In the early phase, educational sociologist of the oriental and the occidental attempted to introduce a moral element into the discipline, based on a belief that social science could provide the appropriate guidelines for the *aims* and *values* of education. The use of the term *'Sociology of Education'* is a part of the attempt to throw off the tradition of moral commitment and to bring the discipline into the line with the rest of sociology. This involves the study of educational institutions using theoretical models and methodological techniques developed by sociologists. It is a sharp contrast with the view of educationists who are inclined to use sociology wherever it can help them, without paying much attention to rigorous theory and precise methodology. In educational sociology, where this was the practice, both the teacher and the student found this very approach inadequate as it lacks in unity.

In the Indian academic scenario, today one can find a multiple approach at the postgraduate level, and also in research orientation (i.e., M.Phil.) level, where the courses on 'educational sociology' and 'sociology of education' are taught, using the terms synonymously. The social process of education is dealt with in both the papers. ***Hansen et. al., (1967)*** has suggested long back "*...both these two terminologies are to be retained; - Educational Sociology* for the pursuit of a *normative theory of educational research;* and *sociology of education* for the pursuit of *empirical theory of research. This will retain the two separate usages and meanings, which have come up out of the development of the discipline of Education, with a stable base of sociology.*"

However, education itself is a value-loaded concept. Therefore, the idea of attempting to develop a value-free sociology of education, as proposed by *Hansen, (op. cit.)* is a hardly possible task. Again, Indian society, within which the Indian system of education functions, cannot be value free. Therefore, it is important to retain some of the moral concerns of the educational sociologists and not to limit the area of research in *'social process of education'* to study only empirical problems, although those are also needed. It is, therefore, advisable to concern ourselves sometimes with wider issues requiring value judgment so as to, say, the desirability of various ethnic education systems or various ideologies, running as social processes. It was expected that a sound modern sociology of education should emerge, which should include both the *empirical* and the *normative* elements.

Unfortunately, the research in this very domain of education, as a glance perusal over the trends reveals, mostly focuses on the empirical elements. It is also difficult to find out even a couple of studies, which actually enlighten the normative aspects.

In case of empirical studies, they have little significant contribution to offer in terms of methodologies to the discipline. Nor do these studies contribute theories to the discipline for its enrichment. This is one of the underlining reason that sociology, even with a comparatively recently introduced background, has already enriched it a lot and thereby in a position to claim itself as an independent discipline.

On the other hand, when Indian society is undergoing massive globalization, supplemented by a fast growing rate of urbanization, the findings of empirical research over varied social processes of education in our country are becoming less important in due course of time, if not obsolete.

The need of the day is to concentrate upon various aspects of social life, in terms of socialization as the primary process of learning within the wider social system. For this we must, first of all, examine the various subsystems of the society within which socialization, through the process of education, takes place. Therefore, attempts should be made to focus over the social process of education, as it takes place in various segments of the society. It is worthnoting in this context that majority of the researchers, who have already carried out empirical research-work in this very area, hold 'literacy' as the only indicator of education and thereby ignore the culture-specific indicators of education. This sort of misconception, in course of time, will lead to a wrong path of concluding and interpreting the 'system' and the 'process', which is most undesirable. Therefore, attempt should be made to plan the priority areas of research in the social process of education, which should direct the future researchers to pursue research, emphasizing the *normative aspects* apart from *empirical* research. Analysis of research in the social processes of education often reminds us of the most frequently cited dictum that *"Garbage in, Garbage out"*. Huge sample, with huge quantitave data, leading to quantitative interpretation does not necessarily lead to sound thesis. What we actually need is in-depth study, emphasizing both quantitative and qualitative data, which should further bear qualitative interpretations, supplemented by quantitative data, to interpret the social process of education in various segments of greater society by a non-ethnocentric and impartial interpretation. This will further help enhance the insight of the scholars initially, and obviously of the academicians, in general, in course of time.

Even after innumerable researches (almost tends to one hundred and fifty during the last five years, as pre the available information) in the domain of social aspects of education, the status of various segments, which are directly or indirectly related to imparting education and sustain the very process, is still unknown. This gap of knowledge requires immediate supplementation through appropriate research. Unfortunately, such studies are too scanty. Therefore, the output of research remains as a '(functional) heart-less body'. Such a situation is not conducive for opening up new avenues/areas of educational research.

The classification of research in social aspects of educational process as appears from the trend extended in the first survey, depicts mostly the broader sphere of educational sociology. In due course of time, and to somewhat a different classification is observed in the second survey of research in education. While well-known sociologist, Professor Suma Chitnis, proposed the classification in the first survey the second survey presents a classification by Professor Sneha Ben Joshi and B.V. Shah, of Maharaja Syajirao University of Baroda and Sardar Patel University, respectively.

A juxtaposition of these two classifications reveals that the second classification is comparatively more specific. However, such specific classification is not meant to categorize research studies, which have been carried out in the last five years, because the studies carried out are numerous in nature and consider so many dilatant factors and variables. Due to a wide range of factors and variables, a study may fall in various segments of categories and classes. It may create confusion for the researcher of the future in finding out the rationale of placing a study in a certain class and not in others. Therefore, it is felt that attempts of classifying research should be based on specific criteria, ignoring the other factors, if we really need to economies on the number of categories. Apart from that, some of the categories, in due course of time, emerge as separate domains of educational research, sometimes beyond the purview of social aspects. Though it is agreed that any research must contribute, either directly or indirectly, for social development, that does not justify that all such studies are to be considered under the same set of categories. For example, education and policy research, as it appears today, show more affinity towards planning and management aspect, than that of social aspect.

Keeping all these causal factors in mind, therefore the classification of research should be kept open to the future researchers. As it appears to the author, availability of huge number of research in education, with a much-accelerated rate of ongoing researches is establishing a trend, where ***'evolving taxonomy'*** of educational research will itself come up as an area for research in near future.

A survey of the research in education reveals that most of the studies are macro-surveys in nature, where the researches incorporate comparatively more number of factors and variables. As a consequence, most of the researches in the very area are surface

***A Classification of Research in Social Process of Education, as Depicted in the First Survey of Research in Education Research on Sociology of Education**

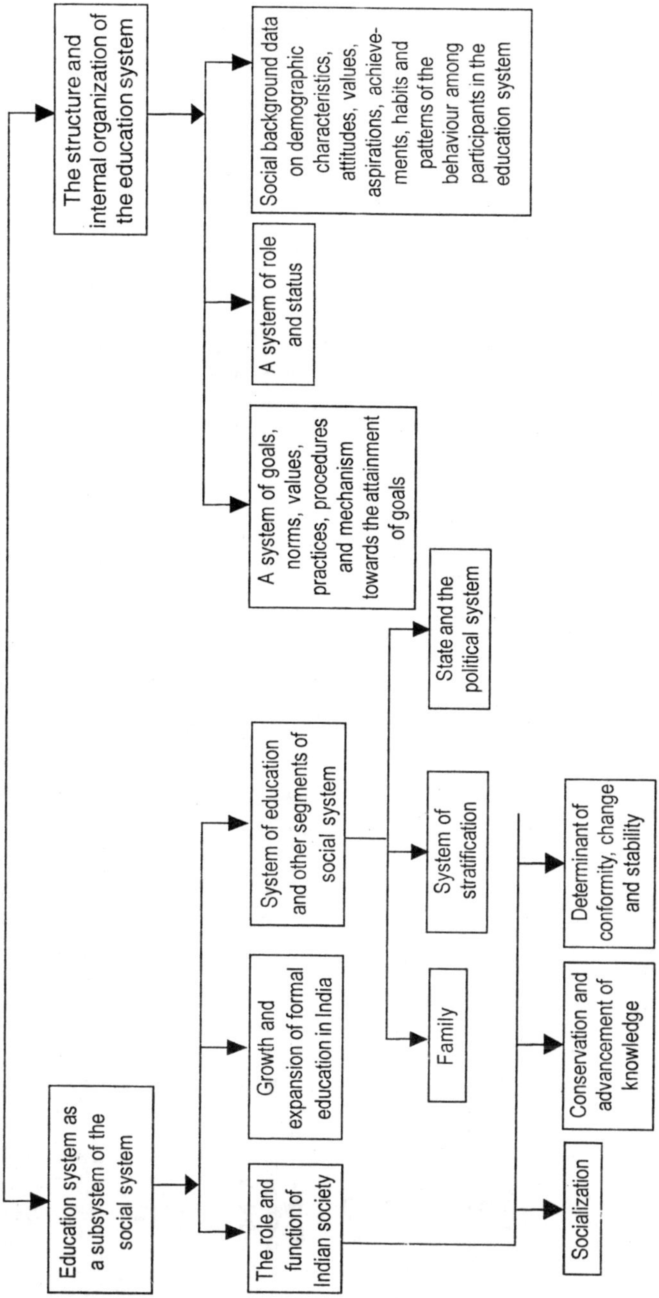

***A Classification of Research in Social Process of Education, as Depicted in the Second Survey of Research in Education**

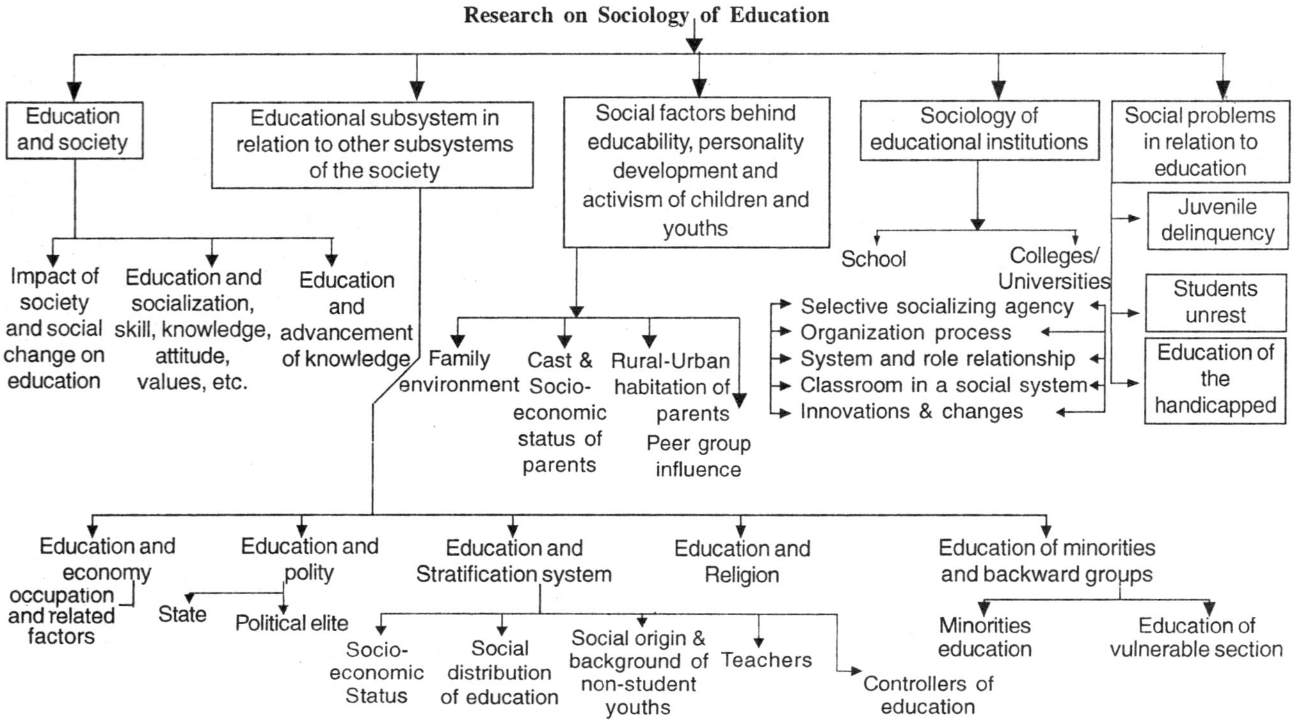

level studies. A change in this trend is also required so that in-depth studies can be emphasized. Due to earlier orientation towards sociology or allied disciplines, most of the researches in the area use to avoid experimental studies (i.e., the studies, which are carried out following an experimental design). They are more comfortable and biased towards survey type of research. Various organizations and institutions have already reported number of surveys. Keeping in view the findings of such earlier studies, researchers in future are to be encouraged to take-up studies, which should be in-depth studies about the social process. Use of experimental design should also be encouraged to explore the effect of various factors and variables, which influence social actions. Comparative studies of different social setup, and of the similar social setup in different time span, should also be encouraged. Such studies are supposed to follow a juxtaposition approach. Social science researchers have overall neglected this very area of research.

Another major problem with educational research is lack of communication among the scholars themselves. This is due to absence of adequate number of standard journals with International Standard Souvenir Number (abbreviated as ISSN), and is exclusively devoted for disseminating information about social research in Indian scenario. A very few journals which initiated the very task of disseminating information about educational research of the contemporary period, are either discontinued or become irregular due to unknown reasons. Therefore, attempts are expected from appropriate agencies to revive or to reintroduce such journals, which should be devoted for research in social aspects of educational process. If it is accepted that one of the basic purposes of research is to help in developing the society at large, the task cannot be set in motion until and unless the findings of such studies are disseminated among the academicians in general, and among the scholars in the area, in particular.

A bridge between the planners (in the area concerned) and the researchers is badly needed, as felt today. To solve the problems in a particular area, repetition of a task can be easily avoided if the bridge between the researchers and planners be established. Much human efforts, time, and money can be saved in this way. Good and standard journals can play this critical role.

The present trend is that a research report is hardly consulted by social planners, due to lack of information and ready availability of such reports. Therefore, immediate attempts should be made to establish an effective system for disseminating information about innovations. The task will remain with the researcher and scholars to extend the possible help to create a bridge of communication with the planners and administrators.

The Social Process within the Institution

The basic criteria, on which societies differ from each other is their system of education. The purpose of education, among the others, is to help in flowing the culture and heritage from generation to generation, and to help in developing acceptable social behaviour and also to refine it. Culture consists of patterns, explicate and implicit, of and for behaviour acquired and transmitted by symbols, constituting the distinctive achievements of human groups, including their embodiment in artifacts; the essential core of culture consists of traditional ideas and especially their attached values. Cultural system, may on one hand be considered as *products of action*, and on the other be considered as *conditioning elements of future action* (Kroeber & Kluckhohn, 1952). Institutions of formal types act as a melting ground to modify the behavioral pattern of the students and thereby their culture too. Physical, psychological and social development - are the basic three forms of modifications, take place within the institution. Among these forms, the social aspect is least understood. Topics falling in this very form of development cover a wide and ill-defined range of social process and concepts. The class treats the development, which results to the individual's progress through the various developmental stages in a successful manner. Such success in terms of individual's ability to negotiate the patterns, explicit or implicite of and for behaviour acquired and transmitted by symbols, constituting the distinctive achievement of human groups. The breadth of issues in the area is very extensive, covering such a variety of phenomena as *personality traits, aggressiveness, altruism, dependent and assertive behaviour, motivation, incentives, the assumption about rights and responsibilities, sex and ethnic differences in temperament, social responsiveness, social perception, value pattern and many more.* Therefore a wider variety of human behaviour should come under the preview of social process within the educational institutions, irrespective of their levels. Being citizen of a diversified country like India, it is more essential to enquire and thereby to understand the social process prevailing in educational institutions across the nation, their peculiarities and salient features. Such understanding is only possible through sincere research, centering round the varied social aspects of the educational process, prevailing in the educational organizations. It is to be agreed that the role of educational institutions in affecting the individual's development is complex. It is extra-ordinarily difficult to sort out the interrelationship among such factors as *economic condition, ethnicity, degree of urbanization, civic sense, polity and education*. The complexity is increased by the fact that educational organizations are not only the one of a wide range of cultural influences on development, but is also a major channel by which other cultural influences are distributed on the population. Because institutions are by nature, conservative. They use to pass on to the new generations the culture, which the political and social rulers of the present and the past generations prefer. The institutions are the combination of the caretaker, storehouse and communicator of cultural values. At the same time, the dominant variety of today also encourages characteristics of modernization and in this sense is a 'force' towards cultural change in traditional societies.

Interface between Social Aspects and Planning Aspects of Educational Process

The comment on 'Learning reforms as India Today (date15.05.1986, p. 9.) reads, *"...A society gets the kind of education system that it deserves; and change will come only if society at large is not just willing to but actively wants to make that change. The impulses that guide the conduct of schools and colleges emerge not from what the government decrees but from what society wants. People, who are simultaneously products of the education system and its users, must want changes and want it badly enough to actively participate in that change. Unless this realization goes home, all policy changes put together will result in little more than superficial, and a new education-culture will remain a distant dream."*

The comment quoted above is quite true in the scenario of research too. Not only the scholars but also the entire society enjoys the benefits of a plan. It should be accepted by almost each and every hand that the basic goal of social science research is to achieve social development. To make the entire process a more systematic one, proper planning is, therefore, quite indispensable. As like in other fields of academia, educational research also starts with the felt problem and that is why the process of research aims at finding the solutions for these problems. It has been experienced that the 'output' of research in 'social aspects of educational processes' are hardly utilized by the planners and executors in our country. The National Institute of Educational Planning and Administration (NIEPA), New Delhi, has been assigned with this task by the government since its inception. Even then it is observed that the country uses to follow a discouraging approach where change of governance in the nation often effects the implementation of plans, and in most of the cases, those are either half-done or undone, which result in a huge wastage to the national resources. Though many countries across the world have evolved an excellent planning system, India is still in the stage of infancy in this context. It is agreed that no administrative, political, cultural or social organization should enjoy monopoly of educational planning. It is neither desirable, nor practicable. The only alternative is to create a healthy coordination among such organizations to extend justice. Research in Education should be considered as a subsystem of such integrated planning process. The problems in the arena are quit well identified, supplemented by probable solutions, which came up as an output of studies of independent research scholars. It is high time to utilize the outcome of such research studies to solve the specific problems. The more expeditiously the problems are identified with possible solutions, it is easier to solve such problems, both in terms of economy and feasibility. Social problems invite a cascading effect if not solved at the right point in time. Therefore, it is essential to develop a proper plan to guide research in social aspects to find out the solutions to burning social problems, not in a haphazard manner, but in a systematic way. On the other hand, if educational research is to be more than a pious hope and is to become a reality, it must have its own budget. As educational research has a variety of aspects such as *adoption of manpower requirements, costs, content, methods* etc. it is obviously important that research work in each of these sectors should form part of an overall plan. A wider coordination among the university departments, action groups, government and research institutes is therefore, indispensable. However, this is far from the reality. Such organic and permanent liaison between the various educational projects during their implementation are responsible for efficiency of research in almost each and every stage, starting from identifying baseline information, up till reporting research findings. Therefore, apart from adding emphasis over 'the planning and management of the system and structure of education, emphasis should also be given to guiding the educational research, in general, and research on social aspects of educational process, in particular, to integrate them in a systematic way. This may be termed as the *process of planning research in education*, which will not only help to proceed in a systematic path, but also be helpful to carry in-depth studies and thereby to evolve empirical and normative theories of education. Methodology of educational research will also find a new vista to enrich and enhance the field.

Educational Sociology in Relation to Major Social Subsystems

Up till the end of last century economics of education was less within the purview of social aspect of educational process. The trend continues. However, question may be raised whether there can be any such specific and sharp distinction or not. Studies reveal that even now educators are essentially concerned with the educational and cultural ends and pay little attention to the social agencies such as economy, polity and so on.

The close link between educosociology in relation to economy could be well exemplified by the recent phenomenon of cuts in public educational expenditure. From experience, it may be said that each of the major educational reports published during the last decade may be considered neither too revolutionary, nor too impracticable. Yet, few of the recommendations of those reports have been put into in practice. And among those, which were practiced, a large number failed to succeed. The crunch of fund is not the only cause, and in some cases, it was not the cause at all. Take for example, *Sharva-Siksha Avhiyan,* which was well funded. The decentralized policy of handling the funds led to disappearance of fund in some of the eastern-regional states. So far planning of the *'Avhiyan'* was concerned it was done quite well. Then why hundreds of study centers were closed down? This underlines the other social factors and their influence over the interactive sub-systems of education, economics, and planning. Political intervention, as apprehended from the critical analysis of the situation, may become the adverse force for disruption of the programme. However, this is mere a hypothesis about a practical problem. Educational researchers need to explore the causes of such facts. In such studies, the emphasis is to be on the reciprocity of the relationship between education and economy, where the political (and may be other allied) factors will be explored as intervening factors in the disruption of an educational plan in its execution stage. Considering these studies as evaluative studies, it is to be said that such studies should set up the trend for educational research in coming days, which up till now failed to attract even a single research scholar in the last five years. The pattern of expenditure of scarce economic resources for socio-educational development needs to be considered as a priority area of educational research.

There is one more specific way in which the educational system is related with other major social subsystems. The function of a person in the society, as reflected by his/her occupation, political affiliation and the like are becoming much more important than traditional factors like religion, ethnicity or caste in placing him/her in social hierarchy. This is related to an increase in politicization, which entails the necessity to confirm to impersonal universalistic standards and then, in turn, generate a demand for efficiency or achievement. Therefore, as the volume of formal education has increased, so has the importance of formal educational qualifications. This is associated with the increase in occupational specialization in a highly toned consumerist society. Education is increasingly seen as the means by which consumerism can be translated into social mobility. Since education, as a grading agent for the system of social stratification, has become increasingly important, so has grown the concern to discover the extent to which the education is socially biased. The domain, which possesses the potentiality to become a gold-mine for the researchers interested in social aspects of educational process, is still neglected.

Less Emphasized Approaches of Educational Research

Hermeneutics, Multi Level Analysis of Data, Metacognition, Ethno-pedagogy and Oral History—all these methods possess high potential in the arena of educational research as various approaches of Research, however rarely used by the Indian scholars.

The *hermeneutic* approach to conduct research studies in Education and in the social sciences is not a new phenomenon in developed countries. Although this approach is less used in research on the social aspects of education in Indian academia. It involves the study of *meaning* and comprises the *theory* as well as *practice* of INTERPRETATION AND UNDERSTANDING in the varied social contexts, in which human beings live and work. The dictionary meaning of the term 'hermeneutics' is 'the study of methodological principles of interpretation'. Social hermeneutics deals with the interpretation of social facts and phenomena. As societies are not uniform, the process of interpretation of the subset of educational process needs varied forms of interpretation. The combination of the two approaches – qualitative as well as quantitative would result in better findings when the researcher would add the hermeneutics of a socio-educational phenomenon in connection with different social groups and thereby the observations would be more objective and appropriate for the varied cross-sections of Indian society.

Multi-Level Analysis of Data: Human beings act within specified contexts, which include both individual-level factors and group-level factors, which possess the following consequences:

(i) Known effect of aggregation bias.
(ii) Conceptual problems of de-segregation of data from the group level to the individual level.
(iii) Pedagogical fallacy associated with analysis undertaken at the group-level when in fact inferences at the individual level are required.
(iv) Lack of meaning and instability of estimates of contextual effects in individual-level analysis when using an aggregated variable.

Multilevel analysis of data is rare in Indian socio-educational research. It would have permitted individual-level effects to be disentangled from group level effects. Long-term strategic planning is urgently needed for research in social aspects of education to improve the quality of research and also for enhancing their applicability in Indian social context.

Meta Cognition: West, especially America claims to develop the concept of metacognition and is widely using it for enhancement of knowledge in relation to educational research. It deals with how the concepts and theories of social sciences influence and modify the personal-knowledge of individuals and isolated (small) groups, and how such personal knowledge influences the individual (and also the group)' s actions and, in turn, changes social concepts and theory. This would have been considered as a potential and appropriate field of inquiry in Indian scenario for enhancing national harmony and integration. It is unfortunate enough that Indian scholars, especially those who are engaged in educational research, up till now did not think of educational research in this perspective which promises an opportunity for knowledge generation, because of the reason that through the approach one can be assured that what one is thinking is clear. It helps in deducing uniform knowledge about a certain fact or phenomenon. It refers, among other things, to the active monitoring and consequent regulations and orchestration of these processes in relation to the cognitive objects or data, under consideration.

Oral History: History is nothing but 'past sociology'. It is also one of the major bases of education. Oral history, or to be more specific, the use of oral source in history was the first kind of historical inquiry. It has been rediscovered after being unjustly dismissed by several generations of professional historians. The recent growth in the use of oral history to explore ethnic societies in relation to educational research can be traced. Exploring the system and structure of education through oral history is having a wider application in studying the ethnic societies, number around 600 in India today. Educationists were using this approach for many years; however, this approach was not widely appreciated. As a result, contemporary researchers are ignoring the technique although the well-known social anthropologist like *R.K. Mukherjee studied the process of acculturation of specific communities* during the mid seventies of the last century using this very method. This is more applicable and acceptable method of pooling information, when the group lacks appropriate documents from which the required data can be pooled. Sometimes due to lack of understanding of the indigenous scripts, oral history approach becomes the only active device with the social scientists. As memory plays a vital role in the process of collecting data, crosscheck method may be followed to achieve objectivity irrespective of several hindrances. The approach remains an interesting device especially with the researchers who want to carry out research which are ethnographic and ethno-pedagogic in nature. It is wroth mentioning in this context that this approach is widely used by the social anthropologists for research purpose. The researchers pursuing research in social aspects of educational processes may also adopt the very method to explore various educational factors and forces, rooted into the system of education of Indian ethnic societies. Apart from studying ethnic population groups, socioeducational researchers may also opt for this method for studying students from other backgrounds, their intellectual growth and barriers to academic achievement. It is upon the efficiency of the researchers, how they want to utilize the method in their studies.

Post-Script

A glance perusal of the available studies carried out so far during last five years reveal that majority of these studies were carried over the samples taken from Various levels of educational institutions, starting from elementary schools up to university level. However major share of these studies come under ***school education*** and incorporates mostly students *[Dinesh (1997), Reddy (1998), Ali (1998) Sarangapani (1998), Sharma (1998), Singh (1998), Panda (1998), Singh (1998), Satyanatayana (1999), Tewary (1999), Bhatnagar (1999), Saxena (1999), Talniyzi (1999), etc.]* and occasionally teachers or both students and teachers *[Basu (1998), Moh'd (1998), Beware (1999), Roy (2001), Barman (2003) and others]*. In some cases sample has been deduced from outside the institution *[Sashikala (1999) and others]*. Handful number of studies hinge on varied psychosocial and socio-educational factors. Studies were carried out on ***management aspects of educational institutions*** by *Panda (1998), Roy (2001), (Bumar (2001), Das (2001), Ziauddin (2001) and by some other researchers*, where organizational pattern, Performance of teacher, interrelationship of management pattern with socioeducational factors, achievement level and school effectiveness were studied.

Studies also carried out to explore the ***impact of religion and religious institutions*** over social process and education. Such studies were carried out by *Goswami (2000), Mannath (2001) and Hrahsel (2002)*, where the role of religious organizations over the process of imparting mass education, and for improving the status of certain status-groups were focused. Notable fact between the last two studies is the impact of ***religious education over the tribe population group*** was explored following an ***ethnographic approach.*** Study was also carried out over the school dropouts, belonging to different religious groups by *Siddiqui (2001)*, which was basically a comparative study. In the study various cognitive and non-cognitive causal factors - such as *creativity, level of intelligence, socio-economic status* and *adjustment capacity* were taken into consideration. Some of the studies also bear the nature of ***comparative studies.*** Such studies were carried out by *Talniyzi (1998), Moh'd (1998), Roy (2001), Singh (2001), Sumita (2001), and Pandit (2004)*, where comparison was made among the students (and in some cases, among the teachers) in relation to numerous factors and variables, and where comparison is based on the factors like caste, tribe, state, and nation. While self-confidence, adjustment, attitude, modernization happened to be he factor on which comparison was made by *Talniyzi (1998)*, in *Moh'd (1998)*'s study, students' participation in school progprammes was compared in a ***cross cultural setting*** in two different countries – viz., Jordan and India. Socio-cultural environment of the schools in Uttar Pradesh and Manipur was compared by *Srivastava (2003)*, whereas method of teaching mathematics was compared between India and Nepal by *Pandit (2004)*.

In the domain of social process, studies were also carried out over the ***vulnerable sections.*** Such studies were initiated by *Talniyzi (1998), Sharma (2000), Singh (2000), Baharia (2000), Roy (2001) and Sumita (2001)*, where sample group represented by students from scheduled caste, tribe, and tea garden labourers. The studies observed, deficiency of socio-educational support hindering their social status and educational development even today.

School as a social institution acts the very role to impart education among the students. Instruction, as a social process, helps to educate the learners. With an aim to explore, and thereby to improve the ***instructional pattern***, handful studies were carried out by *Basu (1998), Chakraborty (2001), Kausalya (2001), Satya (2003) and Pandit (2004)*, who analyzed the process of instruction and also contributed over the methodology of teaching in various subjects in connection with numerous socioeducational factors.

In the era of massive value erosion, *Ali (1998), Singh (1998), Sashikala (1999), Singh (2002) and Islam (2002)'s* study incorporates the ***value pattern*** as a basic factor in relation to social process. While *Sashikala (1999)* assessed the value pattern and attitude of the society towards senior citizens, *Ali (1998), Singh (1998), Singh (2002) and Islam (2002)* considered value as a factor contributing towards the process of education and attempt was made to explore the relation of value with the other socioeducational factors.

Though quite marginal, however studies were carried out to develop and ***standardize the tools*** to measure socioeducational factors by *Singh (1998), Roy (2001)* and others.

Some studies were also carried out on ***gender issues***, where the impact of different psychosocial factors was examined over specific gender groups, mostly over females. *Tewary (1999), Sumita (2001), and Sagar (2003)* carried out such studies, taking into account psychological factors like ego-identity, emotional intelligence, rearing-up practices, locus of control, adjustment and academic achievement. In these causal effect studies, gender related activities and factors, having direct or indirect bearing with education are emphasized.

Knowledge base and its development was dealt by *Sarangapani (1998)*, using ethnographic methodology, which is a rare practice in educational research in India. Some other studies were also carried out. For example, *Chand (2003)* studied the *sociopolitical aspects* of students in University. *Singh (2003)* studied the *role stress, social support system and well being of dual-career-couple*, engaged in teaching. *Pariyar (2003)* studied the *vision of a better world* among the students.

So many studies considered *creativity* as an important factor within the social process and many scholars dealt its relationship with various other factors. Interesting factors and variables, which are thought out of by the scholars in the arena of research in social aspect of education includes- *academic climate, leadership behaviour, self-concept, cognitive style, nationalism, personality correlates, social support, role-stress, achievement, emotional-intelligence, sociofamilial factors, level of aspiration, temperament and memory determinants, future awareness and vocational interest, mental health, teacher effectiveness* and so on.

Finally it may be said without any hesitation that each and every study is unique in either broader or in restricted sense. The future researchers, having a detail understanding about those, can better assess their contribution towards the discipline.

Conclusion

In conclusion, it is to be noted that until and unless the scholar or the researcher is having a strong and positive interest towards the topic on which (she)he is working, the report of the research will become only a 'heap of papers' without making any significant contribution towards the area concerned, neither in terms of knowledge, nor in terms of methodology. Due to the existing policy of linking research degrees with career advancement at tertiary level of education, the 'candidates' need to acquire a research degree – Ph.D.; on the other hand, due to the havoc quantitative expansion of higher education, teaching at the higher level as well as research has become more a profession and usually not considered as mission. This results to a hike in the number of intending scholars coming for enrolling themselves for Ph.D. in different universities. Some of the departments are becoming like the factories to produce Ph.D., with an accelerated production rate.

Until and unless one is having an intrinsic motivation towards enquiry, the level as well as quality of inquiry suffers. This results to erosion of the quality of research. Social science and educational research is becoming a victim of these maladies, which is further supplemented by integrating 'guiding/supervising experience' for selection of senior faculty positions. This has resulted in a change in the scenario. Earlier, where intending scholars use to run behind supervisors, nowadays, it is not a rare phenomenon where supervisors are running behind the 'probable' scholar, to obtain 'guiding experience'.

Another important factor behind this deteriorating quality of research is that, in most of the cases, scholars hardly enjoy the freedom to pick up a research problem, on their own. Actually the 'topic' is thrust upon the scholar by the supervisor, ignoring the scholars' interest and motivation (towards the topic). In such a situation, the topic appears as a 'compulsion' to the scholar. Otherwise she/he is to waste time to find out another supervisor, with whom she/he can initiate research over a topic of his/ her choice. To improve the quality of research in social aspects of education, proper guideline is earnestly needed by the appropriate agency (i.e., University Grants Commission).

In view of improving the quality of research, what we actually need at the outset is a well-planned document indicating the thrust areas of research. A tracer study approach is quite inevitable to initiate 'depth studies'. Otherwise, the existing situation will prevail where the only purpose of socio- educational research will be just to obtain a Ph.D. degree.

Ethical consideration in social science research should be given due weightage. Simultaneously, authenticity of data and report should be assumed. The purpose of research is not just to make the authorities happy, but to offer the best possible solution to an adverse social phenomenon with a view of achieving 'development' and adding to the accumulation of knowledge. The author modestly wants to submit that an attempt is made here not to fix up the direction for social aspects of educational research in the coming days, but to generate a fresh and open thinking over the issues, which have been pointed out in the earlier pages.

SELECTED REFERENCES

1. **Anastasi, A. (1982):** Psychological Testing; Macmillan, New York.
2. **Ashley, B, J. *et. al.*, (1969):** An Introduction to the Sociology of Education; Macmillan, London.
3. **Bredo, E., & Feinberg, W. (Eds.) (1986):** Knowledge and Values in Social and Educational Research; Temple; Philadelphia; Pennsylvania.
4. **Carnoy, M. (1974):** Education as Cultural Imperialism, Mckey, New York.
5. **Crowin, R.G. (1965):** A Sociology of Education; Appleton, Washington.
6. **Durkheim, E. (1985):** The Evolution of Educational Thought; Routledge & Kegan Paul, Boston.
7. **Feinberg, W. (1983):** Understanding Education: Towards a Reconstruction of Educational Enquiry; Cambridge University Press, Cambridge.
8. **Gellner, E. (1973):** Cause and Meaning in the Social Sciences; Routledge and Kegan Paul; London.
9. **Giddens, A. (1984):** The Constitution of Society; Polity Press; Cambridge; Oxford.
10. **Hans, Nicholas (1964):** Comparative Education. Routledge and Kegan Paul Ltd. London.
11. **Hauser, R.M. (1973):** Sociological Background and Educational Performance; American Sociological Association; Washington D.C.
12. **Hansen, D.A. (1967):** On Education: Sociological Perspectives; Wiley.
13. **Hirsch, E.D. (1967):** Validity in Interpretation; Yale University Press, New Haven, Connecticut.
14. **John Dewey (1899):** School and Society: Social Aspects of Teaching and Learning, (NA).
15. **Keeves, J.P. (1986):** Theory, Politics and Experiments in Educational Research Methodology: A Response. Cit in *International Review in Education*, Vol. 32, No. 4.
16. **Kroeber, A.L. & Kluckhohn, C. (1952):** A critical review of concepts and definitions; Peabody Museum, Harvard University, Cambridge, Massachusetts.
17. **Myrdal, G. (1969):** Objectivity in Social Research; Pantheon, West ministry Maryland.
18. **Peters, R.S. (1983):** Educational Theory and it's Foundation Disciplines; Rout Ledge and Kegan Paul Ltd., London.
19. **Roy, R. (2001):** Status of Tribe Teachers in Assam and West Bengal: A Comparative Study; Unpublished Doctoral Dissertation, Assam University, Silchar.
20. **Tirtha, N.V. and Mukhyopadhyay, M. (1974):** 'Sociology of Education', Cit. in *'A Survey of Research in Education;* Center of Advanced studies in Education, Baroda.
21. **Trankell, A. (1972):** Reliability of Evidence: Methods for analyzing and assessing Witness Statements; Beckman, Stockholm.

22. **Weber, M. (1949):** Methodology in the Social Sciences; Free Press, New York.
23. **Whitehead, A.N. (1962):** The Aim of Education and other Essays; Ernest Benn, Limited; Great Britain.
24. **Williams, M. (1977):** Groundless Belief; Blackwell, Oxford.

The following studies has been directly referred in the trend analysis:

Agarwal (2002): Home-environment, in relation to values, like self-reliance, and modernization of secondary school students from Moradabad city.

Ali (1998): Interrelationship and relative contribution of personal value, career aspiration, academic achievement, and socio-economic status, as determinates of educational choice of students at senior secondary level.

Baharia (2000): Growth, distribution, density, demographic-characteristics, occupational pattern, and socio-cultural characteristics of tea garden laborers of undivided Dibrugarh district.

Bandopadhyay (2003): Self-concept and Cognitive-style of creative and non-creative students in secondary schools of Kolkata.

Basu (1998): Utility of Flanders Interaction Analysis Category System (FIACS) profile for teaching secondary school subjects in Kolkata metro.

Bawane (1999): Discrepancy between competencies expected and competence practiced among primary school teachers.

Bhatnagar (1999): Achievement of students in language, studying in government and public schools, in relation to certain non-cognitive attitudes.

Bumar (2001): Performance appraisal, job-satisfaction and work-efficiency of personals working in management institutions.

Chakraborty (2001): Developmental pattern of geometrical instruction of first-generation Learners and children of educated parents.

Chand (2003): Political orientations among the Kumayun University students in context of their personal, social and academic characteristics.

Dangwal (2003): Impact of NCC in terms of personality characteristics and sense of Nationalism.

Das (2001): Achievement levels of secondary school students in relation to organizational climate of the educational institutions with different pattern of managements in Mahabuba Nagar district.

Dinesh (1997): Interrelationship among scientific attitude, cognitive behaviour and school scientific activities of secondary school students and their combined effect.

Elizabeth Basant (2000): Parental belief about education and child's development and their relationship with school performance in cross-cultural setup.

Eric (2000): Giftedness and its relation to academic performance, socialization, stress- perception and adjustment among boys and girls.

Goswami (2000): Role of religious institutions with special reference to

Harimandira in imparting informal education among the people of Nalbari district of Assam.

Gupta (2001): Role of family-environment and counseling on the study habits of the students from intermediate colleges of Gorakhpur.

Gupta (2002): Future awareness, vocational interest and school adjustment of senior secondary students in relation to their economic status, habitation, and level of achievement.

Hrahsel (2002): Educational activities of various Christian denominations and their impact over the Mizo society.

Islam (2002): Value pattern of the college students, in relation to some selected socio-educational variables.

Joshi (2003): Career consciousness of female adolescent students in relation to their intellectual level and rearing practices.

Kausalya (2001): Socio-educational factors viz. cognitive ability, school environment, socio-economic status, teacher-effectiveness and performance in English among IXth grade students, and their interactive influence.

Kumar (2003): Test anxiety and academic achievement of students at junior and senior secondary schools.

Mannath (2001): Impact of Salesian education on the Santhals in the Murshidabad district of West Bengal.

Margaret (2001): Universalization of primary education in slum areas located in the twin cities of Andhra Pradesh i.e., Hydrabad and Secendrabad.

Mathur (2002): Mental health, creativity and academic achievement of adolescents in relation to their socio-economic status.

Mishra (2004): Organizational climate of different secondary schools and their relationship with leadership behaviour of principal and teachers' job satisfaction.

Moh'd (1998): Students' participation in school programme in cross-cultural setup.

Panda (1998): Relationship between socio-economic status and achievement of IXth grade students.

Pandey (2003): Emotional intelligence and attitude towards modernization of Kumaoni adolescents in relation to some socio-familial and educational factors.

Pandit (2004): Cross-cultural comparison of problems of mathematics-teacher-educators (MTE) of India and Nepal.

Pariyar (2003): Vision of a better world among the students of Arunachal Pradesh, studying in various colleges.

Pathak (2003): Family environment, locus of control and level of aspiration on predictors of achievement-motivations among undergraduate students.

Rahaman (2003): Achievement in mathematics of VIIIth grade students of different ethnic groups of Nepal.

Rastogi (2000): Self-acceptance in relation to peer acceptance and perceived per acceptance among junior high school students.

Reddy (1998): Impact of in-service training programmes organized at DIET for primary school teachers with emphasis on theme-specific programme of minimum level of learning (MLL's).

Roy (2001): Status of Tribe Teachers in Assam and West Bengal: A Comparative Study.

Sagar (2003): Ego-identity and emotional intelligence of female adolescents in relation to their rearing-up practice and parental age.

Sarangapani (1998): Social experience and the child's construction of knowledge

Sarma (1998): Gender-habitation correlates of cognitive and educational status of high-school students.

Sashikala (1999): Assess the potential and constraints faced by the senior citizens.

Satya (2003): Temperament and memory as determinant of Mathematics achievement of intermediate students and the role of temperament and memory variables in determining the mathematics-achievement of students.

Satyanatayana (1999): Student-support services in Indira Gandhi National Open University (IGNOU) to know the extent of learners' perception in relation to promptness of delivery, effectiveness achievement of instructional objectives and level of satisfaction.

Sawhney (1999): Achievement of Xth grade students in relation to personality traits, educational interest, anxiety and Level of achievement in relation to habitation and gender.

Saxena (1999): Parent-child relationship of junior high school pupils, in relation to psychosocial factors.

Sharma (2002): Vocational maturity and level of aspiration in relation to scholastic achievement.

Siddiqui (2000): Assessment of learning burden on the social behaviour and academic achievement of secondary school students.

Siddiqui (2001): Comparative study of cognitive and non-cognitive causal factors among secondary school-drop outs from Muslim and non-Muslim communities.

Sign (1998): Adjustment of students in the context of their attitude to educational authorities, their need, achievement and personality.

Singh (1998): Relationship between aesthetic sensitivity and aesthetic reasoning in relation to students' personality, gender and habitation.

Singh (2000): Caste as a factor in educational process and its outcomes at high school level.

Singh (2000): Comparative study of academic achievement and adjustment of scheduled caste and non-scheduled caste students in relation to self-adequacy.

Singh (2001): A comparative study of high school boys and girls with special reference to intelligence quotient, academic achievement and creativity.

Singh (2003): Role stress, social support and well-being among dual-career couples.

Singha (1999): Impact of modern education on sociocultural life of Meeteis (an ethnic community from Manipur) in Assam.

Srivastava (2003): A comparative study of socio-cultural environment of the Manipur and Uttar Pradesh and their relationship with some personality aspects of secondary level students.

Suguna (2001): Impact study of aksharankiranam programme (a literacy programme for rural adults) on women in Mahaboobnagar district of Andhra Pradesh in relation to their performance in 3 R's, affective and social aspects.

Sumita (2001): Achievement of male and female scheduled caste students in relation to their locus of control, adjustment and values.

Talniyzi (1998): A comparative study of self-confidence, adjustment, attitude towards modernization, and level of aspiration of scheduled caste and tribe children from Pithoragarh (rural and urban).

Teja (1998): Interpretation of Vedic scriptures as given by Swami Dayananda Saraswati.

Tewary (1999): 'Identity Status' and 'educational intelligence' of the female college students of Nainital, in relation to some socio-familial and educational factors.

Tewatia (2004): Academic-motivation in relation to socio-economic status and academic climate of schools under different type of management.

Tripathi (2000): Intelligence, achievement-motivation, academic achievement and dependence-proneness of new university entrants.

Verma (2001): Child rearing practices, personality and academic achievement of advantaged and disadvantaged students.

Ziauddin (2001): Organizational climate and school effectiveness (under various management pattern) in relation to certain selected personal variables.

21

Education for Development in Mauritius: Achievements and Challenges Ahead

Sareetah Devi Motee, Mauritius
Dr. Hemant B. Chittoo, Mauritius
B. Nowbutsing, Mauritius
M.P. Odit, Mauritius

Introduction

Following its Independence in 1968, Mauritius's economy was based primarily on sugar. In the late 1970's, the government established Export Processing Zones (EPZs) in an attempt to diversify the economy. By 1984, sugar's once nearly 100 per cent share had fallen to 15 per cent of GDP (World Bank Group, 2006). The government set up regulations and policies that were particularly nurturing to the EPZs, such as duty-free access for all imported inputs, tax incentives, and a separate labor market with different market conditions until the late 1980's. By 2002, EPZs made up 60 per cent of Mauritian total exports. Today, Mauritius faces several macroeconomic challenges. It has lost trade preferences in both textiles and sugar and, at the same time it faces rising global oil prices. In response, the government is committed to actively pursue diversification by transitioning from low-skilled agricultural and manufacturing sectors to the higher skilled sectors like financial services, tourism and Business Process Outsourcing requiring high-skilled workers.

The greatest challenge that the Mauritian government is facing to manage the unemployment level while undergoing this transition. Figure 1 summarizes the GDP growth, employment growth and unemployment rates from 1982 to 2002. Despite the rising unemployment rate, two paradoxical facts about the 1990s can be noted: (1) the EPZ was crippled by labor shortages, and was compelled to import foreign workers, mainly from China; and (2) the number of unfilled skilled-job vacancies, especially in the financial service sector, increased over the decade. These phenomena constitute a so-called Mauritian unemployment puzzle (Centre for Applied Social Research, 2002; Coe, T. *et al.*, 2001; IMF, 2003). There is little consensus in Mauritius as to the exact nature and causes of the unemployment problem. This paper makes a humble attempt to explain the unemployment puzzle from an educational perspective without diminishing the merits of possibly analyzing the problem from a multi-disciplinary perspective.

Figure 1: GDP Growth, Employment Growth and Unemployment Rate from 1982 to 2002 (Coe, D *et al.*, 2002)

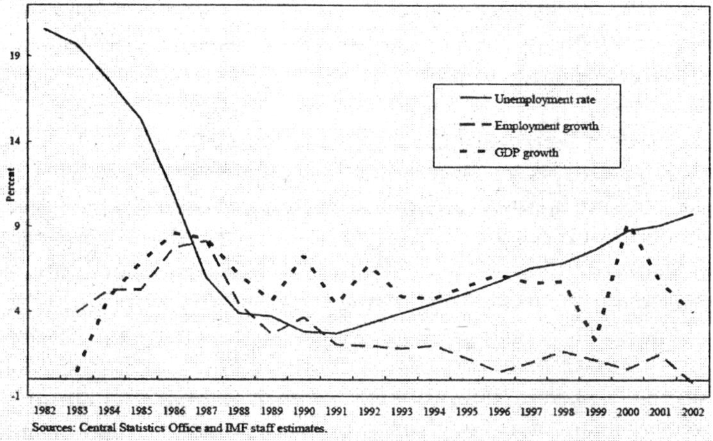

Section 2 of the paper, therefore, analyses existing policies, problems and recent developments in the education environment of Mauritius. Section 3 assesses their impacts on the labour market, to find possible explanations to the phenomenon of coexistence of labour shortage in some sectors along with relatively high unemployment rates over the recent years. Section 4 draws some relevant conclusions, recommendations and policy implications.

In Search of Explanations: Problems Recent Development and Impact Existing Education Policies and Labour Market

Education in Mauritius is largely free of charge and a right from primary through to tertiary level, while a system of grants exists for the pre-primary level. Structurally, the system operates according to the 6 + 5 + 2 principle. Nevertheless, various problems exist in the education system regarding access and equity, the qualitative dimension and management.

Problems Affecting the Education System in Mauritius

From a paper written by Dansingani, H., an informed educationist in Mauritius, the following problems affecting the education can be identified: While there is almost universal schooling from the age of 5 at the primary level, one out of every three pupils drops out by the end of the primary cycle, and only one out of twenty-nine pupils successfully reaches the end of the secondary system. Only 3 per cent of all students who pass the Higher School Certificate at the secondary level gain access to University education, thus jeopardizing the opportunity for the proper development of each person. Pre-service training is offered to primary teachers much more frequently than for secondary teachers because of a belief that primary schooling is the foundation for education. Some schools are ranked higher than others, although there is no official quality assurance or benchmarking system because of the absence of a well-structured inspectorate system. Some schools are poorly managed and there is a lack of motivation among teachers because of limited prospects for promotion. Another problem is that the system is highly centralized and schools are given very little financial autonomy. Curricula suffer from the following problems: *(i)* the inability schools to help learners adapt to and meet the socio-economic needs; *(ii)* over-emphasis on discipline-orientation at the expense of skills and competency orientation; and *(iii)* too much emphasis on summative assessment and not enough on formative assessment, since too much emphasis is placed on the outcomes of end-of-year and end-of-cycle examinations.

Recent Developments

The Mauritian Government has recently focused mainly on the structural change in the education system and curriculum renewal in the primary sector. The structural transformation aims at the achievement of universal, free and compulsory schooling lasting for eleven years and put more emphasis on construction of new secondary schools so that student in each region can be admitted to them. The best ('star') schools have become sixth-form colleges (i.e., upper secondary level). The new secondary curriculum, quality assurance and standard setting are projects that are still in the pipeline.

The major reform dates back to the 1980s with the introduction of the Certificate of Primary Education (CPE), which students had to sit after six years of primary education. It was an endeavour to move away from the previous curriculum geared towards producing clerks for the civil service. Transformations and reforms attempted to 'Mauritianize' the curriculum by making it more child-centred and interdisciplinary. The CPE used ranking as a basis for admission into secondary schools, thus the curricular goals ended up being more teacher-centred, favouring rote memorization and 'narrow thinking', since the objective seemed to be improving learner performance in the examinations. In 1993, a curriculum renewal project was embarked on at primary and lower secondary levels. At primary level, the Essential Learning Competencies (testing the minimal degree of learning competencies) and Desirable Learning Competencies (DLC) (testing higher order competencies) were introduced. One of the major problems experienced during the reform was that there was a massive failure rate (one out of every three pupils), which had a disastrous effect in terms of human resources, since learners were not able to continue with their studies. Current reforms in the form of regionalization at primary level aimed at eliminating the ranking exercise have not been thoroughly pursued so the trend is people leaving the education system without adequate literacy and numeracy competencies are likely to continue in the foreseeable future.

The new curriculum uses English as a medium of instruction in schools, with French being taught as a subject. It has been commonly felt that the education system must pursue dissemination of both French and English in order to meet the challenges of globalization and technical progress. The local Creole is used as a learning support, and is often resorted to in the classroom to facilitate the assimilation of difficult concepts. Furthermore, the current reform ensures that a pre-vocational stream and a suitable curriculum will be introduced in all State secondary and private schools so as to cater for those learners who have failed twice at the primary level because of the examination system (CPE). This pre-vocational curriculum will concentrate on six learning areas: Communication skills; functional mathematics; environment; science and technology; creative and performing arts; and self-development. Information and Technology (IT) has been introduced as a subject in all schools throughout the country. Teacher training in all of these areas is already in progress. The formulation of the new primary curriculum focuses on key survival skills that include problem-solving, group learning, creativity and flexibility. The reform project has involved the mobilization of large financial resources, a massive recruitment of IT and arts teachers, and a reorganization of the administration in order to ensure the sustainability of the reform. Some problems have been identified during the implementation process including the following: *(i)* Teacher resistance regarding the introduction of new subjects, such as citizenship education and the arts; *(ii)* an overloaded timetable through the addition of extra subjects (teachers have resisted the extension of working hours, even though they were offered extra pay); *(iii)* there is an ongoing debate as to whether IT should be used across the curriculum as a tool to reinforce teaching or whether it should be taught as a subject, as is currently the case; and *(iv)* a shortage of both physical and human resources for the production of quality teaching, learning materials and other aids. Most of the reform are still in the pipeline and yet to bear their fruits.

Synthesis of Impact of Education Policies

Inadvertently the education system plays a key role in supplying skilled labor. Although Mauritius has a comparatively high level of literacy, it is weak in secondary and technical education, especially in natural sciences, engineering, and vocational subjects. A large proportion of the young are unable to access secondary education because of the very competitive system for moving from primary to secondary schools, and thus cannot supply the needed skilled labor. Currently, almost 35 per cent of students fail to pass the completion-of-primary-education examination and drop out of the school system at the age of 12 or 13. This high failure rate is partly indicative of the inadequate availability of secondary educational facilities. The cost of acquiring secondary education is much higher than it would be with greater access.

Skills and Education of the Workforce

In a survey of 273 firms, it was found that the level of skills and education of the workforce was the fourth highest ranked constraint (Bank of Mauritius, 2002). 43 per cent of Mauritian firms believe that the skill level of their workforce pose a serious obstacle to their operations and growth. In fact, Mauritius has the highest percentage of firms with this perception of all its comparator countries (Centre for Applied Social Research, 2008). This problem will only become more severe as Mauritius makes its transition towards the service sector, which require a greater education level than manufacturing.

On average, only 10 per cent of workers attend university and/or graduate school and 25 per cent had no more than primary education. Nearly all of the rest finished only secondary school.

Since the majority of workers receive little education, on-the-job training is critical. 61 per cent of Mauritian firms provide training to their workers. This is similar to most comparator countries except for China, where 90 per cent of the firms provide training to their workers (IMF, 2003). However, despite the fairly high percentage of firms providing training, Mauritius ranks low in depth of training. Training has large effects on worker productivity and, therefore, wages; a worker who has received training will receive a 21 per cent higher wage than a similar worker who has not received training. Within the last decade unemployment levels have increased from 4 per cent to 10 per cent. This increase can certainly be attributed to the skills mismatch between the kind of labour firms want and the kind of labor that is available. In fact, according to a 2000 census, a majority of the unemployed were young, had never held a job, had failed primary or secondary school education, had no technical or vocational training, and were single and family supported (Bank of Mauritius, 2002).

The demand for high-skilled workers is expected to strengthen further in coming years as the government moves forward to actively promote the development of an Information Communications Technology sector and other modern sectors.

Conclusions, Recommendations and Policy Implications

The rapid structural changes during the 1990s in Mauritius have increased demand for skilled workers in the financial services, tourism, BPO sectors relative to the low-skilled textile and sugar sectors. Against this background of profound structural change and strong growth performance, the unemployment rate in Mauritius has been steadily rising. The consequence of the labour market institutions and the nature of the education system is that skilled-labour demand in the emerging sectors is largely unmet by the skilled-labour supply – a situation that has a dampening impact on labour demand growth. In summary, the high cost of access to secondary education leads to low-skilled labour supply thus limiting the growth in the emerging sector and less growth in economy-wide labour demand.

The Mauritian education system seems to have failed to impart to the low-skill-based labour force the higher skills that are needed by the emerging sectors, resulting in a skill mismatch problem. Both supply-side and demand-side reforms will engender increased labour market flexibility, reduce the unemployment rate, and help sustain growth at the relatively high levels that Mauritius has enjoyed during the past two decades. On the supply side, the government is already upgrading its education system. The government's education reforms aim to increase the years of compulsory schooling from nine to eleven years; improve and increase access to primary and secondary schools; introduce information communications technology in primary and secondary schools; review the quality and relevance of the curricula; and reform the examination system at the primary level. To accompany these reforms, the government has significantly increased capital spending in the sector. These reforms will need to be aggressively pursued to reduce the skill mismatch in the economy.

While there is no alternative to increase access to education and training in the short and medium terms, there is a need to simplify existing scheme/regulations on residency and work permits for foreign skilled workers to attract much-needed skilled labour and to establish new institutional and regulatory framework for private education and training to better meet the needs of the enterprises. The rising unemployment is largely structural in nature, spurred on, at least partially, by the skill-biased technological changes taking place in the economy. The Mauritian authorities' current educational reforms are important in increasing the labour supply of skilled workers and reducing the mismatch between labour demand and skill availability and help sustain growth at the relatively high levels Mauritius has enjoyed during the past two decades.

REFERENCES

1. Bank of Mauritius, (2002), "Annual Report," Port Louis, Mauritius.
2. Center for Applied Social Research, (2001), "Attitudes of the Unemployed Towards Accepting Employment in the Export Processing Zone in Mauritius," Port Louis, Mauritius.
3. Coe, David T., *et al.*, (2002), *Mauritius – Selected Issues and Statistical Appendix*, IMF Staff Country Report No. 02/144 (Washington: International Monetary Fund).
4. Dowrick, Steve, and Norman Gemmell, (1991)
5. Hirinand Dansingani, Mauritius, p. 54.
6. International Monetary Fund, (2003), *World Economic Outlook, April 2003: Growth and Institutions, World Economic and Financial Surveys (Washington)*.

22

A Comparative Study of Indian and Britain Educational System

Dr. Shobana Nelasco, India
Malaya Kumar Nayak, London

Introduction

Education is distinguished from other goods and services as it does not deplete and it is bound to produce multiple effects. Education engenders intergenerational and intra-generational effects. Education particularly female education is viewed as antidote to barging population.

Seeing the important of education John Kennoth Gaalbrainth in his book **"Economic Development"** oversees that education is neither consumption nor investment alone, but both the odor.

W. Schulty who is the first economist who conceptualized the word **"Human Resources"** emphasized the significance of education and human capabilities in the process of economic development.

A.K. Sam, a Nobal Laureate says that education opens up whole new vistas and a window of opportunity. And paves the way for enjoyment of choices and capabilities. The development planning, therefore, exposure the notion of equal opportunity for all in education.

Education produces satisfaction from new knowledge along with cultural opportunities for both parents. It helps increase the number of work options available to the individual. Education of human being can be viewed as human capital or embodied savings. Richard A. Musgrave says educational product not only includes the components of education usually distinguished as consumption (i.e., enjoyment of the fuller life permitted by education) and as direct investment (with the gains accruing internally and the form of increased earnings to the educated person) but also education as investment in the functioning of the economic and social system at large. These latter gains accrue externally, not only to those in whom the educational input is invested, but also to other members of the community. Temporal and regional dimensions of social yield of education also merit serious considerations.

Educational Reforms in India

The constitution of India and subsequent constitutional amendments have made **"education for all"** mandatory. The 11th Five Year Plan lays stress on inclusive economic growth for which education is one of the principal ingredients. The 10th Five Year Plan saw an expense of over Rs. 839 million.

Education and literacy attainments are one of the three components which determine the human development index and physical quality of life. The 11th Five Year Plan is basically a knowledge investment plan. The government's efforts are to create the next big way of investment in higher education. Education is declared as our **"mission"**. Since education, discipline and organisation are the primary factors of production, the governments is trying to universalize elementary education through the Sarva Shiksha Abhiyan, one of the flagship programmes of Government of India and to focus on a major expansion of secondary schooling. Each year million of people graduate from the Indian education system, many skilled in IT and engineering. This is the main reason for Indian economic advantages during the past few years, but even though these advancements are on the top level there are many problems that are deep routed in the Indian education system.

The Government of India and the states are ear marking substantial amount of funds for education and scaling up the resources during the successive plan periods. The resources allocated to the education sector have risen steadily as the government now realizes the importance of education. The efforts taken by the government in education sphere are reflected in terms of rising literacy rate. It was 18.33 per cent in 1951 at all over India. It went up to 64.84 per cent in 2001. In Tamil Nadu it was 20.9 and 73.5 per cent respectively. In Kerala the literacy rate was 47.18 and 90.86 per cent respectively. It shows that the literacy attainment in Kerala compares well to that of in developed countries. In other States the literacy rate has been improving over time. It may not be noted that in all States there are imbalances between male and female and urban and rural areas in literacy attainment. The literacy rate for SC and ST male and female was relatively and deplorably lower than that of other castes. At the tertiary level the number of technical institutions and medical institutions has increased. As a result, availability of technical manpower has increased. Since the nation is aiming at creation of a knowledge society these institutions should become centers of excellence like IIT. The gross enrolment rate in higher education is only a 10 per cent at present. The scheme for Universalisation of Access to Secondary Education aims at universal enrolment, universal retention and satisfactory quality of learning. The XI Five Year Plan aims at enhancing the gross enrolment it to 25 per cent.

On education front the Government makes primary education a compulsory one for attaining the goal of **"Education for All".** The Sarva Shiksha Abhiyan (SSA) is being implemented at the primary education stage.

Educational Reforms in the UK

Widely regarded as the single most important piece of education legislation were the Education Reforms Act 1988. It included main provisions like "No Child Left Behind." The Grant Maintained Schools were introduced whereby primary and secondary schools had the liberty to remove themselves fully from their respective Local Education Authorities and would get complete funding from the central government. Through the Local Management of Schools school were allowed to be taken out of direct financial control of the local authorities. The heads of the schools would have control over the finances. Key Stages which were most important for all stake holders were implemented as through this at different stages a number of educational objectives were to be achieved.

After these reforms more ambitious reforms took place in the UK's Education system in 1997. The Labour Government, headed by Mr. Tony Blair enacted a series of education reforms, which included, efforts to turn around failing schools, national strategies to improve student learning in math and literacy in elementary school, and teacher training and pay reforms. Impressive results have been produced by these reforms: The lowest performing school just within 3 years of the implementation of these reforms out did their past failing percentage with mark improvement.

Comparison between the Education Structure of the UK and India

The education structure of both the countries is vastly different from each other.

Structure in the UK

After the school stage in Britain Undergraduate stage which last for 3-4 years awarding the person a bachelors degree in art, science or other fields, here the students become more specialized and this degree is also known as the honours degree. Credit-unit or modular assessment has been adopted by some universities in others the students need to take foundation courses before being illegible for the bachelors degree. Foreign students are required to work a year in the country of their target language, so universities accelerate the speed of the procedure by adopting an accelerated policy where students study through the normal vacation period too. It is a rarity to see the degree class being judged purely on exam result bases. Majority of the courses also require research, thesis writing from the students.

After this comes the masters degree where the student is at the forefront of an academic discipline. Originality in application of knowledge is needed at this level. After 2 years of additional study, presentation of a thesis at the university the student is all set to receive his masters degree. After this if the students wishes to go further studies he may study beyond the master's degree, by presenting a theses for Doctorate of Philosophy. Another stage later the person may even move forward and get awarded with Higher Doctorate degree from a university of law, sciences, medical sciences, humanities, theology, music or mostly a senior university professor.

Apart from this teacher's are provided training, primary school teachers must hold a first degree and a postgraduate certificate of education from a university. Alternatively they should also have a qualified teacher's status which can be obtained after successful completion of Initial Teachers Training (ITT). For secondary school teachers the IIT degree should be either postgraduate certificate of education or bachelors of education course lasting 4 years. To become the higher secondary teacher the person must also have some higher degree than the bachelors degree fulfilling all other requirements as well.

Education Structure in India

In India based on an in-depth review of the whole gamut of educational situation and national consensus, a comprehensive framework for development of education was developed. Although the framework is still relevant the implementation over the past few years has brought to mind that certain modifications were to be made to the model. These modifications were introduced in May, 1992. Elementary school were universalized, educational opportunities were equalized, development and women education, secondary education was vocationalized, higher education was consolidated, technical education needed to be modernized, improvement of quality. In the field of education the main focus was the content and process of education. The biggest significant change that took place was that of being able to retain students from dropping out rather than get new ones to take their place. The revised Policy stated that "free and compulsory education of satisfactory quality is provided to all children up to 14 years of age before we enter the twenty-first century." The experience of the National Literacy Mission has proved that the more effective strategy is the mission mode in an attempt to achieve total literacy. Which would be the means of achieving adult literacy in the future. Generic vocational courses have been incorporated in the revised policy.

Organization and structure of education are largely the concern of the state and so within the policy framework, each State determines the structure which will be adopted, specially at the school age this is a problem as the education structure throughout the country will not be universal and so there will always be trouble when policies are to be implemented.

Although variations can be found in the educational structure at the school stage. Primary and middle stage joined together constitutes the elementary stage. It has been envisaged that there should be a common structure for the elementary stage consisting of 5 years of primary schooling followed by 3 years of upper primary/ middle school education. Where ever the system is any different to this the state will have to switch to this system as this will help universalize things. The secondary stage consists of 2 to 3 years of schooling which marks the completion of 10 years of general education program.

After 14 years of age the child can either join a secondary school for further education or a vocational school which would equip him or her with vocational skills so that he may be able to find a job. A person who has completed 10 years of general education has a similar choice of either taking up academic courses at the higher secondary level preparing to join collegiate education or go for the option of vocational streams within the higher secondary programme. Completion of higher secondary education qualifies the individual for entering first degree programmes. High competition is there when it comes to getting an admission in professional courses such as engineering and medicine. Demand for admissions in other programmes differ considerably each year the reason which is the deletion of art courses from the curriculum which has been discussed in detail later.

Common Problems in Education with Reference to the UK and India

Although both India and UK are far apart when it comes to physical distance but the Indian education system has been borrowed from the British. The time when India was ruled by the British the education was imposed on them back then but they still continue to follow the system. The only problem with the system is that even after over 50 years of independence the system is still the same, it has not been tailored to meet with the Indian needs. The British system on the other hand is much better organized, the education system is far better, keeping in mind the growth of the children the system is evaluated on regular bases and changes are made to it and items that are obsolete or not applicable anymore are removed from it on regular bases.

Realizing the importance of education the government of India has now started a scheme which aims at universalization of elementary education at the national level and attaining the goal of the Millennium Development. The 86 Constitutional Amendment, 2002 makes free and compulsory education for all children of 6-14 years of age. In addition to this scheme there are other schemes known as National Programme of Mid-Day-Meals in School and National Programme for Education for Girls at Elementary Education. The Government of Tamil Nadu has been extending schemes such as free bus passes, note books, etc. All the above schemes have yield desired results in primary education: Gross enrolment level has increased, drop-out rate has decreased and SC and ST girls and boys have been mainstreamed. The educational network and number of teachers have also increased simultaneously.

At secondary educational level also the net-work of schools, numbers of teachers and pupils has gone up. At this level the science education aims at creating scientific bent of mind among the students.

Though labour force is abundant in India, a larger part of it is either unskilled or semi-skilled we need brain as well as brawn to drive the economy to a higher plan of achievements. It calls for sound education system and effective delivery mechanisms. Inclusive economic growth can be achieved with the help of prime mover education. For this purpose the government is planning to set up vocational training for the students so that those who cannot or do not go to schools can at least learn some sort of a skill that will enable to earn bread and butter for their family. The only problem is creating a willingness among these people to enroll themselves in the vocational training programme.

The main reason for very high illiteracy in India is the fact that most women are not able to go to formal schools. These restrictions are there because of the conservativeness of families living mostly in the rural areas and also on the basic of caste, where the poorer children belonging to minority groups have no access to education. To meet with this challenge the government has started the Non-Formal Education System whereby children can go to some nearby home to gain education. This system favors the girl child as the teacher is a female from the community and parents show lesser reluctance sending their child to these schools. Although this is a good programme it is still to reach to a vast majority of Indian children living in India.

This isn't that big an issue in the UK, the only reason why a child remains illiterate is because they do not go to school, education is freely available to the children in the environment of a proper school, whether private if the parents can afford or government where the fee is very low or usually the education is given for free.

Both the Indian and the UK education system face the common problem of Standardized testing. Standardized tests are made to judge a child's intelligence in order to place them at certain levels in school. Experts claim that no single test has the validity and reliability to measure the skills and achievement of children coming from diverse backgrounds. Also standardized testing can have negative consequences especially on the child who is not able to achieve high, which can lead to morale problems among the children who out of frustration/disappointment give up their studies adding to the drop out percentage. The teachers should be allowed to judge the intelligence of children and not standardized testing, teachers supervise the children through out the year and can successfully identify each childs level of intelligence. Standardized testing restricts a child's creative ability and thinking out of the box is something which most children today lack. The main idea of teaching is grasping the concept. Even if standardized testing is used it should not be the only measure of judging a child's capabilities, other aspects of the personality should also be considered. Otherwise the system will not be able to recognize the persons real talent and thus he will end up doing a something in which he does not fit well. Due to standardized testing the students are under pressure for it are not able to pass this test they will not be allowed to progress to the next class so the real motive of learning which is grasping the concept is lost and the child forgets the concept once he passes the exam and moves on. Even if these tests are to be conducted they should be an evaluation method of the teachers, the teachers should be evaluated on how well they have been able to teach the children and how they can improve on their teaching skills. More emphasis is given to passing an exam rather than developing an understanding of the subject. We need to understand that test results is not education! The education system in the UK is properly developed and can easily adopt other methods of testing the students intelligence other than standardized testing, India where the educational standards are not well developed and still have a major influence from the time of the British rule the sudden implementation of other methods of testing than the one known to them for over 50 years will cause problems in digesting.

There are very few qualified teachers present in India and they too are looking for better job options so there is a difficulty in recruitment and retention of teachers all through out India, there is no guarantee that how long teacher will serve the school or how quickly they will quit on it and move out to some other better option than teaching, for this very reason no investment is made on the teachers because there is no surety that the investment made on them will ever be paid back to the schooling system or will it become human capital flight.

Also due to this fact there is variable quality, teachers hired leave and so this also create difficulty adjusting to the new teachers method of teaching. The demands of the Indian markets are not met through this education system as this system is not able to produce well educated human who can support different organizations in their operations.

In India there is little knowledge interaction which causes several problem as there is a problem with the study of the economic system, the kids are given facts and figures that are out dated and thus there is no progress, same is the case with the society standard which the books teach are far obsolete than what they are now. Also the schools have no interaction with any research institutions and so large majority of children are unaware of the researches that have been conducted and the advancements that have been made in the field of science.

The size of the classrooms today pose a major problem in the learning, the size of the class is usually too large and the teachers can only effectively teach only a small number of children at a time compared to the number of children that can benefit from their skills. The greater the number of students in the class the lesser will be the concentration. Also the teacher is not able to concentrate on all the children properly, plus most children in such a huge setting shy away from asking questions, thus there learning from a particular session is minimal and this is not the end of it because the lecture is in continuation so what ever the learning in one class it is carried forward to the next and so when a child is not able to learn much in the first session his learning in the remaining sessions will be even more restricted and he will not be able to grasp the who idea of the learning, he may even get disheartened and lose interest in the subject. The only possible way to deal with this is either to lessen the number of students in each class and encourage questioning. Once all the children freely ask questions they can be merged back together into a bigger class at a higher level. This problem once again is faced both by the Indian and the UK education system.

Although it would be far more easier to eradicate it in the UK then in India for in the UK there are more schools that can accommodate children, when dealing with this issue in India, there are two major hurdles, firstly, the education standard is such that there are not enough school to accommodate all the students and already there's a good percentage of students that do not go to school in India plus the rising population in India means if there are lesser children in one class they would need more schools and there are not enough schools available to accommodate all the children who are currently going to schools.

The education quality, access and literacy is also a major problem in India. There is severe regional, caste and gender disparities. The high drop out rates after the Tenth standard are another reason for low levels of learning and achievement. There is inadequate school infrastructure, poorly functioning schools, high teacher absenteeism, the large number of teacher vacancies, poor quality of education and inadequate funds. There is corruption of the highest level. Also no common school system exists instead channelization into private, government-aided and government schools take place specially for those who cannot afford going to private schools which have a proper curriculum approved for foreign systems they are affiliated with. The children coming to these government schools are also usually low on communication skills so it is hard for them to comprehend what the teacher is teaching, they are usually those who are poor or orphans, also those aren't even this fortunate end up getting no education at all. Those who cannot afford private schooling attend English-language government-aided schools, affiliated to state-level examination boards which are badly run and English language is only present in name. In the UK the system of these schools is a better than that in India, proper curriculum are made which are updated on a regular basis.

The Education System both in India and in the UK fails in teaching various arts also in particular common sense to the children. Budget cuts in the schools expenditure are a major problem for most schools, because when there is shortage of money something needs to be eliminated to remain cost effective, out of all the programmes in schools all around the world Fine Arts programmes are the first one to be slashed off these programmes are considered to be unnecessary on the contrary however such programmes are very important for a child's growth and development, these are the only programmes where the children can use their creative ability to the maximum without being stopped. The removal of fine arts is in a way taking away the childs right to express himself, subduing his right of self development. Also such slashing off is discouraging for children as they start to grow they start believing that these activities are of no use and so have been slashed off stopping the child from developing his creativity. A creative mind is as important as an analytical mind.

Another important issue which requires a lot of consideration is the degree of plagiarism there is at schools specially in India when the students are assigned some research work they do not put in a lot of research into it in fact they just copy some already done research, this is a problem which prevalent in India for there is almost no method of counter checking the work, the person gets appreciation for work which is not really his, this acts as a major problem when such students go abroad for their education where such practices are forbidden. They go to culturally diverse regions and there plagiarism becomes a problem. When they go abroad to countries like the UK they find it a major problem as it has something that they have been doing for a long-time and they are unaware that it is a crime, only when they are caught doing so in countries like the UK that they find out that this is a crime and there are stringent laws in the UK about it. The line between illegal copying and innocent repeating is lost between the cultural difference. Plagarism is something that have been doing for a long-time and they are unaware of its consequences so they take time to adjust to the new environment, mostly aren't able to adjust and so drop out easily. There is no claim on intellectual right in India, that is one of the main reason why piracy still prevails in Indian.

Having followed it for so long the student usually even copy idea they have no information about so rather than conceptualizing they copy paste the idea. Most of the students usually make use of highly easily accessible material over the internet and then use it in their writing as it is, rather than conceptualizing it. The Indian student going abroad for higher education will take a lot of time to realize that this is a crime, values like these need to be taught to them at the grass root level like it is done in the UK but unfortunately due to the poor level of education in India it is not possible. The main problem for this backwardness is the lack of research and technology in the Asian countries, as there is very little research the countries bank on foreign research journals which are easily available on the internet to be copied off. Although research and development is there in India but it is progressing at a very slow rate and it mostly take help from foreign researches.

Recently the UK job market is not finding any good prospects from those who graduate and a great part of those getting into the job market aren't local graduate but ironically they come from Asian countries. A large population of these turns out to be Indians. Because of non-availability of well trained and well educated children from inside the UK the, the businesses are forced to hire individuals from the foreign markets, like India. Results over the year have improved there has been a decline in the number of drop outs. But in the UK there is a clear gap between the demanded skills and those provided by the education standards in the UK. When it comes to hiring locals the companies usually are reluctant cause most of them lack skills the business require instead they prefer hiring indigenous people coming from different parts of the world mostly Asia.

The governments performance on education and skill development is considered unsatisfactory which has caused the standard of education to fall. Due to the nature of the exam system in the UK there is little willingness to learn in the children which is something that is needed greatly by companies from their employees today. The kids from these Asian countries grow up in an environment where they have to learn to survive thus willingness to learn in them is cultivated from the very early stages of school. Foreign students that come to study to the UK from these Asian countries that is why end up achieving good grades and finding the system to be a lot easier than what they are used to while studying in India and else where. These problems have been recognized in India also due to the lack of job opportunities in India the student are encouraged in taking electives from disciplines outside their stream to gain additional job related skills. In the UK there are problems in the vocational training education for it is a system that is little understood by the employers. Employers in the UK bank more on the academic qualifications of the person and so the vocational qualification of the person mean little to them, as they feel that it will make little difference to the organization, this is something that keeps away students from acquiring any sort of vocational training as it will not bring to them any advantage or fruitful results.

With the advancement of technology new sciences are being developed and for countries like India which do not have proper technical knowledge to teach those sciences there also arises a problem of capital flight, where by individual who are bright want to learn these new sciences but due to the unavailability in India they are forced to go abroad, once they gain the experience and knowledge they see that there is no future scope for the learning in India and so they decide to stay back and work in the UK where there learning has some worth, thus these is important capital flight taking place due to the backwardness of technology.

In India there is very little support from the public sector and thus there is system inefficiency, the number of schools that were to be opened were only done on paper, there exists a large number of ghost schools that in reality do not exist and so the children in these areas remain illiterate.

The government to help improve the condition of the schools should support the Education Commission of India in way in which they are given full responsibility but with all this they should be accountable to the Government of India on all levels be it financial, managerial, academic or administrative.

As the country has limited resources efforts should be made where there is collaboration between schools, where there is sharing of resources, the school libraries should be shared so that the information from one library is available to all the students that way there will be knowledge sharing.

India is facing almost the same problems that were faced by the United Kingdom, but it has now recovered as is better able to provide education to the masses than India. Although there is lack of knowledge that has to do with critical thinking in the UK which is the main reason for the decline in the standard and the children not being able to meet up with the challenges they face in the corporate sector. The British Government too would like to see this changing and for achieving this purpose they are changing the curriculum often as they see fit. The lack of Research and Development in India is what is hindering it from developing further as most of the bright students usually like to travel abroad to be able to work on and groom themselves further in the field. Britain has an edge over India when it comes to infrastructure, education infrastructure in the UK is well developed while India needs to improve on its basic infrastructure to improve the reach of the education and to remove illiteracy.

Conclusion

The schooling system of India is quite different, whereas in Britain the main emphasis is on getting education, the emphasis in India is on getting vocational training. The former aims that the individual is able to compete in the corporate world while the later focuses skills which may be able to help him in future when there is shortage of job opportunities. Jobs in India are a highly competitive area where by jobs aren't that easy to come that is also one of the reasons why most Indian try to move and settle abroad because for them it is easier to get a job abroad rather than staying back looking for a job in their own country. In Britain jobs are easier to find but the required competency for the jobs is also difficult that is why foreign students get more preference over the locals.

All in all these two countries are totally opposite of each other when it comes to the educational standards, one emphasizes more on getting knowledge while the other focuses more on gaining skills training.

REFERENCES

Haynes, Nigel. *Bullying: An evil at the Heart of our Schools* 29 February, 2008, Accessed on October 9, 2008.

The Time, 2008 *Safety in Old Knowledge* 29 April, 2008, Accessed on 9 October 2008.

The Times, *There is no Systematic Approach to Providing Expert Help for Children with the Most Severe Problems* 15 July, 2008, Accessed on October 9 2008.

Sunday Times, *Attack on UK Skills* 17 August, 2008, Accessed on October, 9 2008.

The Times, *You just can't get the staff* 8 July, 2008, Accessed on October 9 2008.

Government of India, *Economic Survey, 2006-07,* Accessed on October 9 2008.

Tamil Nadu, *An Economic Survey, 2005-06,* Accessed on October 9 2008.

Government of India, *11th Five Year Plan Document,* Accessed on October 9 2008.

Government of Tamil Nadu, *11th Five Year Plan document,* Accessed on October 9 2008.

Rich and A. Murgrave and Peggy B. Musgrave. *Public Finance,* Accessed on October 9, 2008.

Standby Fisher and Rudigar Dorubush (1983) *Economic.*

23

Examination Malpractices: Implication for Educational Quality in Nigeria

Dr. Tola Olujuwon, Nigeria

Introduction

Education has long been recognized as a central element in development. With the advent of formal educational in the country, more than four decades ago, education was perceived as a means of not only of raising political and social consciousness, but also of increasing the number of skilled works and raising the level of trained manpower in the country.

The populace view education as a means of achievement and a "must do" in life. The various benefits together with the visible gains for individual from education stimulated an unprecedented growth in enrollment of students from primary to tertiary level in every year and the huge budgets allocated to the educational sector by the government.

With the unprecedented increase in enrolment and desire to be educated, there must be a process of selections, admission and the like to achieve this, that is when examination comes in. That is why Oyerinde (1996) cited in Olujuwon (2001) sees examination as an assessment of standards to ascertain to what extent, they have benefited from the teachings of their teachers in a given subjected, while Liman (1996) noted that examination in a broad perspective is an instrument for testing, assessment, evaluation and accreditation.

That is why Eckstein (2003) sums it that "examinations have become a major and universal means to access achievement, to select qualified individuals possessing relevant and advanced knowledge and to distribute limited opportunities for study and employment on the grounds that it can serve as instruments for making objective and neutral judgments. To buttress the above, Curson (1980), Gartside (1970) and Ausubel (1968) opined that examination have more salutary effects on the learner, the teacher and the curriculum, in that examination is used to diagnose learners difficulties, help them to work steadily and productivity over a measured period of time and provides the learner with the knowledge of his achievement in relation to desired objectives and the like.

In spite of the salutary effects of examination Iyewarun (1979) believes that examinations have diverted teaching from its main course of achieving the purpose of education and that the very purpose of schooling is undermined by in-ordinate desire to pass prescribed examination. This view was upheld by Ufot (1980) who adds that the school system is so examination conscious that it is hardly conscious of the individual students except in so far as he can contribute to impressive statistics of performance in examinations.

To Denga (1993) the pervading emphasis on good grades and the overwhelming importance attached to certificates in Nigeria have contributed significantly to corruption and corrupt practices among youth in Nigeria.

The examination fever syndrome according to Obanya (2007) is a common psychosis in Nigeria, which affect both learners and parents, as parents exert enormous pressures on students to pass at all cost. The society passes judgment on schools, individual teachers and students based on their examination performance. It would be recalled that performance in examination in specified subjects was one of the criteria used to give grants in aid to assisted school by the colonial government in the 1882 Education Ordinance, Lawal (2002).

That is why Obanya (2007) summed it that examinations distorts the process of teaching and learning, since teaching is excepted to be exploratory, interactive and activity oriented, if this is absent, examinations will produce misfits into the 21st century knowledge economy, since key competencies required by the knowledge economy of the current century may not be examinable. These competences are skills, values, knowledge and attitudes, which are considered valuable in today's world of work. This chapter will attempt definition of examination malpractice, its origin in Nigeria, the probable causes of examination malpractices, its effects on the stakeholders in the educational enterprises and efforts to curb this malaise and above all provide sustainable suggestions to remedy the situation.

What is Examination Malpractice?

Corruption and corrupt practices in the educational enterprises is on the increase world over and Nigeria is not an exception. Examination malpractice cast doubt over reliability, integrity and certification and the students produced.

The varieties of corrupt practices prevalent in schools are sorting, plagiarism, certificate and admission racketeering, impersonation in examinations, bribery and cultism, but the one that poses extreme concern to all and sundry in Nigeria is the examination malpractice which has been defined variously by excepts like Arinze (1993), Imogie (1993), Bunza (1996). Oluyeba and Daramola (1993) sees examination malpractice as an irregular behaviour exhibited by candidates or anybody charged with the conduct of examination in or outside the examination hall before, during or after such examination. While to Shonekan (1993) it is irregularity, which are premeditated and perpetuated by the candidates or their agents with the intention of gaining undue advantage in the examination. This was supported by Olayinka (1993) when he considers that examination malpractice as misconduct or improper practices in any examination with a view of obtaining good results through fraudulent action.

The Origin of Examination Malpractice

The genesis of examination malpractice according to Afigbo (1993) could be traced to the colonial period in Nigeria. This is so when people saw Western Education as a kind of "magic" that could be acquired through magical means. This enormous belief made the colonial period the age of "abracadabra" in the life led by many Nigerians.

The belief in the use of Indian or American ring, magic or invincible ink, magic blotting paper, magic candle and brain pills (Ogun Isoye in Yoruba Parlance, which means retentive dose) holder sway then up till the 80s, because it was a topic discussed regularly in the secondary school the author attended.

It is believed that a candidate wearing the appropriate ring can manifest correct answers to any question in any examination by waving his hand over a blank sheet of his answer script, also with the magic or invincible ink, the candidates was expected to answer leaked examinations questions in the comfort of his study at home in synonym writing and the hall would manifest the answer by mumbling some magic words over the otherwise plain answer sheets.

It is also believed that magic candle at midnight makes reading and comprehension easy. There is no statistical record to show how many pupils were helped or ruined by the belief in and the use of these occultic practices.

The first major incidence of examination malpractice occurred in Nigeria in 1914, when the Senior Cambridge Local Examination leaked as reported by the *Nigeria Chronicle* of 9th January, 1914 and cited in Afigbo (1993) the examining authorities wondered, "how the questions got leaked before being made public". This act was described as one that stinks like an ointment with a "dead fly in it" and the populace asks the authority to take positive steps to stem it (Omotosho, 1990).

This scenario took an unprecedented surge in 1963, when there were leakages of two public examinations namely, the First School Leaving Certificate and the School Certificate. Also in 1967, two major occurrence of examination malpractice were also recorded, one is the leakages of the School Certificate Examination question papers, which has traced to the printing press and the second examination leaked, due to wrong packaging of question papers.

This incidence becomes more sophisticated, pervasive and assumes more dimensions in the 70s and 80s as a result of the depreciation of the naira and harsh economic realities of Nigerians. The poor remuneration of teachers who are the bedrock of invigilation and supervision in public examinations made teachers to be vulnerable likewise, security agencies to monetary and materials inducements during examination.

Incidence of Examination Malpractices in Nigeria

As Nigerians saw the need for education and that placement and selection can only be done through public examination, the desire to pass, no matter the cost become the order of the day. In 1973, almost all secondary schools in the Eastern, Western states and some schools in Lagos, did not have the result of their West African Examination

Council released because students "became custodians" of examination papers' before the actual dates of the examination (Afigbo, 1993).

Also in 1974, the examination malpractice perpetrated by students was attributed to supervisors of various examinations. The printing of examination papers caused the widespread (Expo 77) in 1977. The 1981 leakage was however the most widespread and worst in the history of Nigeria and West African Examination Council as a result of wrong packaging of question papers and this led to the leakage of all question papers of the examination that year.

In 1982, examination leakage's led to the postponement of the affected papers in order to reset another questions written at rescheduled dates. In the 1981 and 1987 leakages, examination bodies or persons were indicted for their involvement in this ugly incidence.

The various leakages in the WAEC Examinations made the Federal Government to set up the Alexander Sogbetan and Ojo tribunals to investigate the extent of the leakages. (Olujuwon, 2001).

In recent times in public examinations in Nigeria like WAEC and Joint Admission and Matriculation Examinations students had their results cancelled. Examples are: JAMB Exam of 1991, 30,982 students were involved in examination malpractice, while in 1992, 35,479 cases of examination malpractices were recorded in the same examination (Olujuwon, 2001).

In 1997, the National Examination Council (NECO) cancelled 51, 381 result affecting some 25 examination subjects. (Obanya, 2003).

In addition, in 2007, JAMB examination, 15,763 candidates were involved in examination malpractices. In 2003, 116,900 students results were withheld due to examination malpractices, while in 2006, 108,769 results were also cancelled just like the 3,735 results that were cancelled in the Monotechnic, Polytechnic Colleges of Education examination (MPCE) in 2006. In 2005, 23,146 results were cancelled.

(Retrieved from http://ndn.nigeriadailynews.com/templates/?a=7823&z=12 on the 18th June, 2008)

In the November/December 2007, West African Senior School Certificate Examination in Nigerian 37,000 candidates had irregularity and their results were withheld based on their allege involvement in Examination Malpractice.

In the May/June 2008 WASSCE, it was reported that armed robbers waylaid the bus conveying WAEC questions papers, which led to the cancellation of English paper 1 (Essay). (Retrieved from: http://news.dailytrust.com/content/view/3290/27/ on June 18th 2008)

Causes of Examination Malpractice

Examination malpractice could be seen as a by-product of existing societal ills. The major identifiable causes of examination malpractices are:

1. The over emphasis on certificates.
2. Incessant closure of schools either by the government, school management staff or students.
3. Immorality and corrupt practices in the wider society.
4. Inadequate coverage of the syllabus by teachers in their various classes.
5. Parental pressure on pupils to pass at all cost.
6. The absence of severe punishment for those caught cheating.
7. Inadequate teaching and learning facilities.
8. Poor living conditions of Nigerians.
9. Absence of guidance and counseling services in schools. Limited numbers of invigilation for crowded examination halls.
10. Inadequate motivation for teachers etc.
11. Inadequate instructional facilities. (Gbenedio (1993), Bunza (1993), Shonekan, (1996), Denga (1993).

Forms of Examination Malpractice

Researches have shown that examination malpractices take different forms. The following list is not exhaustive but the major ones being identified by Ogunu (1992), Ivowi (1993), Imogie (1993), Denga and Denga (1998) and these are;

Collusion, Impersonation, Smuggling of answer scripts, Examination Leakage's, Mass Cheating. Insult/Assault on any Examination Officials, Irregular Activities Inside and Outside the Examination Hall, Expo, Examination Contractor. ECOWAS or AU, Dubbing: Super print, Bullets or Missiles, Microchips, Hi-Tech Micro Computer, Networking, Giraffing, Certificate Forgery or

Racketeering, Submission of more than one Answer Script, Sitting for the Examination at Wrong Centres, Refusal to Submit Answer Script at the end of an Examination: The voice of Esau but the hand of Jacob, Substitution of Names, Swapping of answer booklet and many more.

Agents of Examination Malpractice

According to researches carried out by Aina (1993), and Bunza (1993), the following have been identified as the perpetrators of examination malpractices.

- *(a)* Parents/Guardians who buy 'live' papers or bribe examiners or invigilators.
- *(b)* Teachers/Head Teachers: Those who collect money and turn a blind eye at examination malpractice.
- *(c)* Lazy students who do not take their studies seriously and still want to get the best score.
- *(d)* The examiner who set and mark the paper.
- *(e)* The printer of the question papers.
- *(f)* Officials of the examining body, who process question papers, supervise printing arrangements or transport printed questions.
- *(g)* Supervisors/Invigilators at the centers.
- *(h)* Government by establishing schools without adequate equipment and staffing.
- *(i)* Law enforcement agents.
- *(j)* Society due to its quest for materialism.
- *(k)* Government officials.
- *(l)* Institutions—use of our crowded hall and inadequate incentives for invigilators.

Factors that Militate Against Effective Supervision of Examinations

In spite of efforts being made by government and examining bodies, to stem the tide of examination malpractice, the following still tends to perpetuate the occurrence of examination malpractice.

1. Inadequate personnel for invigilation.
2. Shortage of facilities for example, Chairs, tables and large halls for examinations.
3. Immorality and lack of dedication by some teachers.
4. Teachers' lack of supervisory skills. It is assumed that an invigilator should pace up and down like policemen,

whereas it is more than that. Courtesy and good human relations is also entailed.

5. Inadequate time between the completions of one paper before the commencement of another.
6. Inadequate provision of essential services for example, No first aid for indisposed candidates or invigilators or refreshment or electricity or water.

The Effects of Examination Malpractice on Educational Standard

Examination malpractice according to Shonekan (1993) affects educational standard in the following ways:

1. It destroys the moral integrity of the culprits, giving them false sense of values and wrong impression of their capabilities.
2. It distorts the psychometric properties of any tests with respect to validity and reliability.
3. It increases the cost of administering examination as new methods are usually tried to combat examination irregularities.
4. It deprives the assessor and the candidates alike, the opportunity of determining how much knowledge the learner has actually acquired.

To Aina (1996) it has both social and economic implications.

Economic

(a) It may lead to cancellation of examinations resulting in wastage of examination materials, time, money and energy.

(b) Certification of incompetent and semi-literate individuals who do not possess the skills for the development of the country.

(c) Low productivity on the part of those awarded certificates for which they are not qualified.

Social

1. Lack of confidence in the youth.
2. Threat to the validity and reliability of examinations conducted.
3. Moral decadence and indiscipline as people are bound to erroneously believe that engaging in examination malpractice is the only way to make it academically.

Oluyeba and Daramola (1993) supported the above view that the above will ultimately affect the quality and standard of education in Nigeria. In the same vein, Itotoh (1992) cited in Olujuwon (2001) believes that examination malpractice will make nonsense to educational qualifications and discredit institutions of learning and the nation as a whole. Also, that the destiny of the nation will be placed in the hands of half baked elements with low mental abilities, men and women without good or pure conscience; if this trend is not checked, it will affect the few honest learners, who may feel cheated and aggrieved.

The Exam Ethics, a non-government organization in its own contribution to the eradication of examination malpractice believes that the implication is too high. It is believed that cancellation of results of entire schools and communities by exam bodies are sources of great agony and injustice to innocent students. It is also a waste of resources to society, parents who laboured hard to pay school fees. The individuals or institutions marked for examination malpractices have their image badly damaged and individuals in this regard becomes bad role models for youth.

The implication of examination malpractice above all will lead to loss of job and dignity when the truth on examination malpractice is covered. The psychological and traumatic effects on parents who deny themselves all comforts to see their children through school, the existence of anti-social acts, which can become serious sociological problems if not curb on time. The stress on the examining bodies and time wasted to conduct leaked papers. It could lead to unacceptability of results by the public within and outside the country and lastly. The financial and manpower loss by the examining bodies in an attempt to curtail and counter the examination malpractice activities of the candidates.

Efforts Towards Eradication of Examination Malpractice

The Government in its bid to stop this ugly incidence promulgated decree 27 of 1973, which succeeded the 1952 WAEC (Nigerian Status) ordinance, which stipulates procedures and punishment for examination malpractices. In a similar vein, the miscellaneous decree 20 of 1984, stipulates a jail term of 21 years for offenders and reports shows that culprits have been jailed but this has not deterred would be offenders. There is another examination malpractice Act 33 of 1999, which list the following as punishable offences and these are:

Cheating at examination, stealing of (examination materials) impersonation, disorderliness and disturbance at examination, forgery of result slips, breach of duty (by examination officials) and conspiracy (to commit any of these offences). Cancellation and withholding of examination result, prohibiting specific schools from serving as examination centres.

Also, examining bodies have put in place rules, regulations and mechanism to ensure free, smooth and fair examinations. Notable one is the option A4 by Jambs in which centre A and E questions will be different from centre B and D. Also in an effort to eliminate impersonation, WAEC acquired state of the art Microplex Solid 90E Continuous Laser Printer embossing candidates' photographs on certificates (retrieved from. http://www.waecnigeria.org/exams_1.htm 18th June, 2008).

Also concerned organization like the Nigerian Union of Teacher has adopted the "Study Circle" strategy to curb examination malpractice (Guardian 26th December, 1998), while a Non-Government Organization, the Exam Ethics Project has devised means to monitor public examinations in a bid to curb examination malpractice (Punch, 1st June 1999).

In addition, section 16(d) of the miscellaneous offences decree of 1990, prescribes a jail term not exceeding ten years for those convicted of complicity in examination malpractice.

The Cost of Examination Malpractice

The Exam Ethics Project (a non-government organization) that has campaigned against examination malpractices in its 2007 Annual Exam Ethics report has reported that the total amount of money lost by parents and government to results cancellation by examination bodies in Nigeria on the account of Examination malpractice has risen to 107 billion naira in the last five years, while the street value of revenue from examination fraud rose to 25 billion naira in 2006.

The report went further to indicate that 410,000 results were cancelled in the post-primary public examination of candidates by WAEC, NECO, National Business and Technical Education Board (NABTEB) and Jamb in 2006.

It was noted in the report that examination malpractice has evolved into organized crime over the years such that syndicates control it with links in the Ministry of Education, Examination Bodies and Educational Institutions (for more stories see www.sunnewsonline.com/webpages/feature/education2007/oct/23/education -10 23-2007.htm)

Suggested Remedies to Examination Malpractice

With such on array of negative effect of examination malpractice on educational systems and students performance in public examinations, it becomes logical that remedies be sought to curb this malaise that affects everyone in the society, one way or the other.

1. There should be provision of adequate facilities and literature for the students on the examination, notifying students ahead of rules and regulations and motivating examination staff/invigilators adequately.
2. The setting up of Anti - Examination Malpractice brigades in schools, to report any unhealthy academic behaviours to the authorities.
3. The mounting of public enlightenment campaigns through seminars, workshops, jingles in media organizations coupled with IEC materials, with the support of CBOs / FBOs/CSOs on the effects of examination malpractice.
4. The need for stakeholders to have a better grasp of conditions that makes for improved learning and test performance.
5. The educational planners putting in place a mechanism for a virile educational system that emphasizes skill, life long learning and not an examination system as being practiced now. The quest for certification, which is the bane of our educational system, should be discouraged.
6. Guidance and counseling programmes should be introduced in schools for students to know the effects of their choice and the effects of examination malpractice on themselves, parents and the society.
7. There should be stiff penalties for examination malpractice offenders, be it security agencies, officials of examining bodies and various decrees or acts on examination must be reviewed, while provision must be made to reward honest, committed and dedicated students/staff.
8. Examination malpractice should be seen from the perspective of culprits, so that educational planners would know how to solve the problem.

Conclusion

The major causes and factors of examination malpractice are dimensional and the various perpetration need to be checked.

Our educational system should not lay too much emphasis on certificates but on life long learning, hard work, integrity. This will reduce the incidence of examination malpractice.

REFERENCES

Afigbo, A.E. (1993) Examination Malpractice in Historical Perspectives in Onyechere, I. (ed.) *Promoting Examination Ethics the Challenge of a Collective Responsibility*, Lagos, Exam Ethics Project Publication, pp. 13-22.

Aina, O. (1996) "Promoting the Ethics and Integrity of Business and Technical Examinations" in Onychere, I. (ed.). *Promoting Examination Ethics the Challenge of a Collective Responsibility*, Lagos, Exam Ethics Project Publication, pp. 121-135.

Ausubel, D. (1968) *Educational Psychology: A Cognitive View*: Holt, Rinechart and Winston, U.S.A., p. 11.

Azinge, E. (1993) "Legal Aspects of Examination Malpractice in Nigeria" In Maduka C. (Ed.). *Examination Malpractice: Causes, Implication and Remedies* University of Benin publications, pp. 77-76.

Bunza, M.M. (1996) "The Role of Teachers in Promoting Examination Ethics" in Onyechere, I. (ed.). *Promoting Examination Ethics the Challenge of a Collective Responsibility*, Lagos, Exam Ethics Project Publication, pp. 187-204.

Curson, L.B. (1980) *Principles and Practice of Technical Education*, Cassel Publishers London, pp. 206-210.

Daramola, S.O. and Oluyeba, N.F. (1993)" Incidence and Detection of Examination Malpractices in Nigerian Public Examinations in Maduka, C. (Ed.) *Examination Malpractice: Causes, Implications and Remedies* University of Benin Publication, pp. 17-30.

Denga, D. and Denga, H. (1989) *Educational Malpractice and Cultism in Nigeria* Calabar Rapid Educational Publishers Ltd., pp. 1-20.

Denga, D.I. (1993) "Examination Cheating Behaviour Among Nigerian Secondary School Youth; Implications for counseling, "*Journal of Education and Development*, Vol. 3 (2) July, pp. 204-209.

Eckstein, M.A. (2003) *Combating Academic Fraud Towards a Culture of Integrity*, Paris, IIEP UNESCO Publication.

Gartside, L. (1970) *Teaching Business Subjects: The Modern Approach* London Macdonald and Evans Ltd., pp. 1-10.

Gbenedio, U.B. (1993) "Examination malpractice as communication problem" in Madukla, C. (Ed.), *Examination Malpractice: Causes, Implications and Remedies* University of Benin Publication, pp. 50-56.

Imogie, A.I. (1993) "Implications of Examination Malpractice for Instructional Accountability in Nigeria Secondary School" in Maduka, C. (ed.),

Examination Malpractice: Causes, Implications and Remedies University of Benin Publication, pp. 57-63.

Iyewarun S.A. (1979) "Traditional Systems in Nigeria the need for its revision", *Journal of Science Teachers Association of Nigeria* Vol. 17, (3) August 1979, pp. 146-7.

Ivowi, U.M.O. (1996) "Examination Malpractice; Profile, Causes, Warning Signs, Case Studies Prevention and Detection Strategies" in Onyechere, I. (ed.) *Promoting Examination Ethics the Challenge of a Collective Responsibility*, Lagos, Exam Ethics Project P. Publication, pp. 76-96.

Lawal, M.B. (2002) Nigeria *Education: Past, Present* and *Future*, Lagos, Ibadan, Joytal Printing Press.

Liman, M.T. (1996) Opening address at the First Phase of Exam Ethics Conference in Ota Ogun State 27th May, 1996 in Onychere, I. (ed.). *Promoting Examination Ethics the Challenge of a Collective Responsibility*, Lagos, Exam Ethics, Project Publication, p. xiv.

Obanya, P. (2007) Examination: Thou Shall Die in *Journal of Contemporary Educational Issues* Vol. 3, (1) February, 1-28.

Obanya P. (2003) Secondary Education in Nigeria:Contemporary Challenges and Future Demands – A World Bank Research Project.

Ogunu, M.A. (1993) "Strategies for Effective Supervision of Examination to Curb Examination Malpractice in Tertiary Institutions in Nigeria in Maduka, C. *(ed), Examination Malpractice: Causes, Implications and Remedies* University of Benin Publication, pp. 113-125.

Olayinka M.S. (1993) "Guidance Counselling as a Method for Mitigating Examination Malpractice "in Maduka, C. (Ed.). *Examination Malpractice: Causes, Implications and Remedies* University of Benin Publication, pp. 126-133.

Olujuwon, O.T. (2001) Examination Malpractie and the Academic Performance of Secondary Students in Public Examination, an unpublished M.Ed. thesis of the Department of Educational Management of the Lagos State University, Ojo.

Omotosho, H.M. (1990) "Examination Malpractices in Nigeria; Causes, Implications" *WAEC News*, Vol. 4, No. 3 September-December, 1990.

Ufot, O.A. (1980) "The Conduct and Place of Examinations in Nigeria Schools", *The Nigeria Principal*, Journal of ANCOPSS, 1967-1980, pp. 88-92.

The *Punch Newspapers*, June 1st 1999.

The Guardian Newspaper, October 15th 1998.

24

Education System and Labour Market in Vietnam: Economy and Education in Transition

Dr. Ulas Basar Gezgin, Vietnam

Vietnam shows a steady improvement in life standards as there exists an increasing trend in Human Development Index (HDI) rankings which involve a composite calculation of economic performance, education and health indices for Vietnam since 1975 (UNDP, 2007). Despite the improvements, Vietnam is still on 105th ranking in HDI, consecutively worse than Algeria and consecutively better than Palestine (UNDP, 2007). Population under poverty line is 28.9 per cent (UNDP, 2007). Nevertheless, the average annual growth rate in GDP per capita for Vietnam is 5.2 per cent between 1975-2005 and 5.9 per cent between 1990-2000 (UNDP, 2007).

115 over 1000 people in Vietnam were mobile subscribers in 2005 and 129 over 1000 people in Vietnam were internet users in 2005 (UNDP, 2007) but these figures have increased in a short-time. By September 2007, Vietnam's information profile is the following: 38.8 million telephone subscribers; 28.87 million mobile phone subscribers; 9.93 million land liners; 16.2 million internet users, 753.000 ADSL internet subscribers (Viet Nam News 2007a). On the other hand, 13.2 Vietnamese people were still without electricity (most of them live at mountainous highlar d areas) in 2005. The Gini index measuring inequality is 34.4 in Vietnam, which means high inequality (UNDP, 2007).

Vietnam is a Young Country

29.6 per cent of the population (85 million in total) is under age 15, and 65 per cent of the population is under age 35. Since Vietnam's annual population growth rate between 1975-2005 is one of the highest (1.9%, UNDP, 2007) and since Vietnam is a young country, education is vital for the country. Contrary to the low level of GDP per capita which is US$ 3,071, Vietnam holds a high literacy rate (90.3%) (UNDP, 2007).

Education was a cultural value in Vietnam due to the past Confucian tradition. Though the illiteracy rate was 95 per cent in 1945, that's the year of independence, the rate was quickly decreased to around 10 per cent (Vo and Trinh, 2005) which is mostly concentrated in highlands ethnic minorities. Vo and Trinh (2005) point out that Vietnam's literacy index is higher compared to the countries with the same level of GDP per capita, as the figures provided above show.

Primary school enrolment rate is 88 per cent and secondary school enrolment rate is 69 per cent (UNDP, 2007). Primary education is compulsory, while secondary education is not (Henaff, Lange and Tran, 2007). 544,000 children (ages: 6-15) are out of school, most of which are girls (Seel, 2007). Poverty is the main factor behind dropouts from the educational system at all levels of education, as some students need to contribute to their family subsistence –leaving aside the extra costs of education such as uniforms and textbooks. Secondly, poor families have higher number of children and this fact decreases the probability of having a proper education for each children (Henaff, Lange and Tran, 2007).

As a solution to poor students' financial difficulties, VND 2.5 trillion (US$ 156.6 million) study credit has been distributed to university students which are due after graduation (Viet Nam News 2008a). However, since most of the graduates are unemployed they cannot pay back the loans they had for their university education. To solve this problem, adding a line indicating that the student has "debt overdue" on their diploma is proposed and immediately protested by various academicians due to the fact that diploma is the document of educational proficiency and it is not a financial sheet and that it is quite humiliating to have that indication on the diploma (Nguyen *et al.*, 2008).

Van (2007) criticizes the proposal for increasing tuition fees since he points out that tuition fees constitute a smaller share of budget for education. According to him the real problem is lack of transparency in intra-budget allocation and planning failures.

Vietnam's total budget for education in 2008 is VND 76.2 trillion (US$ 4.8 billion) and the share of budget for education constantly increasing by years (World Bank 2006). 2008's total budget for education shows an increase over the last year by 14 per cent (Viet Nam News 2007b). However, most of budget is allocated for teachers' salaries and thus increase in budget does not directly translate into more investments in education (Henaff, Lange and Tran, 2007; Vo and Trinh, 2005). Hoang (2007) rejects the proposed relationship between inadequate funding and low quality education. According to Hoang, the problem is the insistence on outdated teaching methods. If it were to be inadequate funding, the quality of education would have been improved by the increases in budget allocations for education in the last decade. But this is not true (Hoang, 2007). Van (2007) suggests that disadvantaged regions should be the government's priority in educational budget allocation. They have to be funded more. However at more developed regions, Van (2007) adds, the opening of private schools should be encouraged. On the other hand, Vo Nguyen Giap (2007) considers these and similar proposals as violations of the constitution that favours equality among citizens.

In 2005, 1,537,252 students had sit for higher education entrance test and only 15 per cent has been able to enrol to a higher education programme (Ngo, 2006). Both the number of students applied and enrolled are increasing by years due to population boom and new private universities. However, the universities are quite far from being highly qualified as 7 main Vietnamese universities' ranking in South East Asia and world below shows:

Table-1
Main Vietnamese Universities, SEA and World Rankings

Universities	*SEA Ranking*	*World Ranking*
HCM City University of Natural Sciences	28	1,920
HCM Technology University	36	2,190
Can Tho University	47	2,532
National University Ha Noi	54	2,850
Ha Noi University of Technology	62	3,156
University of Technology	90	4,217
National University- HCM City	96	4,462

Reprinted from Viet Nam News 2008b, p. 3.

Around 22,500 lecturers are teaching at Vietnamese universities (164 universities in total) with 15 per cent holding Ph.D. degree; 10 per cent holding only Master's degree and the remaining 75 per cent holding undergraduate degree (Viet Nam News, 2007c). Ngo (2006) attribute the low quality of education in Vietnam especially in technical areas to the fact that only a small minority of researchers can get education abroad. From an employee (i.e., lecturers') point of view, lack of incentive and promotion for academic success and improvement is one of the main reasons for obsoleteness of lecturers' skills and knowledge (Viet Nam News 2007d). Furthermore, private universities in Vietnam are still not developed due to the following reasons: University entrance scores of students enrolling to private universities are low, thus the student quality is far from expected; the physical resources are more limited due to small budgets and most of the faculty members are recent graduates along with minority of retired professors (Ngo, 2006). In this vein, Vo and Trinh (2005) state that there are mainly two sets of factors affecting the quality of education in Vietnam: The first set involves student learning such as curriculum programmes and physical facilities which are old and outdated, while the second pertains to teachers' quality. Do (2007) in that respect is one of those who complain of prevalent use of multiple choice testing in Vietnam which is most of the time the most unsuitable way of measuring students' proficiency.

Vietnamese Government's 2020 education targets are: 450 students per 10,000 citizen, one Vietnamese university ranked in world top 200 and some others in top 500; 30 per cent of university staff and 15 per cent of college staff to hold Ph.D. (Viet Nam News 2008c).[1] We will see whether the country will attain these targets and whether this would be the solution to the social problems.

Vietnam, as a developing country, is an exporter of unskilled labour and an importer of skilled labour (Gezgin 2007). According to UNDP (2007), the country has a workforce of 42,316,000 (58% agriculture sector, 17% industry sector, 25% service sector) by 2005. Table 2 and 3 witness the economic development: The agriculture and forestry sector still constitutes nearly half of the employment. This is no surprise along with the fact that 73.6 per cent of the Vietnamese population, i.e., 60 million people are still living in rural

---

In Vietnamese education system, College corresponds to 2 or 3 year vocational school for higher education attended after high school (Ngo, 2006).

Table-2
Structure of Employed Population as of Annual 1 July by Ownership and by Kind of Economic Activity

	%						
	2000	*2001*	*2002*	*2003*	*2004*	*2005*	*2006*
Total	100.0	100.0	100.0	100.0	100.0	100.0	100.0
By ownership							
State	9.3	9.3	9.5	9.9	9.9	9.5	9.2
Non-state	90.1	89.7	89.4	88.8	88.6	88.9	89.2
Foreign investment sector	0.6	0.9	1.1	1.3	1.5	1.6	1.6
By kind of economic activity							
Agriculture and forestry	62.5	60.6	58.7	57.0	55.4	53.8	52.1
Fishing	2.6	2.8	3.2	3.3	3.4	3.5	3.6
Industry	10.3	11.0	11.5	12.3	12.7	13.5	14.3
Construction	2.8	3.3	3.9	4.2	4.6	4.7	4.6
Trade	10.4	10.5	10.8	11.2	11.5	11.6	11.7
Hotels, restaurant	1.8	1.8	1.8	1.8	1.8	1.8	1.8
Transport, storage and communications	3.1	3.1	3.0	2.9	2.9	2.7	2.6
Culture, health, education	3.6	3.7	3.8	3.9	4.0	4.1	4.2
Other services	2.9	3.1	3.3	3.5	3.7	4.4	5.2

Source: Government Statistics Office.

areas (World Bank 2006). Only 18.8 per cent of the population was living at cities in 1975; but this rose to 26.4 per cent in 2005 (UNDP, 2007). Thus, the declining number of rural population goes in tandem with the fading of agriculture and forestry sector from 62.5 per cent of the employment in 2000 to 52.1 per cent in 2006. This transformation underlies the increasing urban unemployment in Vietnam. Fishing sector is developing and this may be attributed to increasing seafood exports, especially catfish. Industry has increased by years unsurprisingly as it is the engine of development. In contrast to the relatively constant trade sector and hotels and restaurants sector that are expected to grow by economic development, construction sector is growing. It is the main sector for non-qualified

Table–3
Employed Population as of Annual 1 July by Ownership and by Kind of Economic Activity

Thous. pers.

	2000	2001	2002	2003	2004	2005	2006
Total	37609.6	38562.7	39507.7	40573.8	41586.3	42526.9	43347.2
By ownership							
State	3501.0	3603.6	3750.5	4035.4	4108.2	4038.8	4007.8
Non-state	33881.8	34597.0	35317.6	36018.5	36847.2	37814.7	38639.0
Foreign investment sector	226.8	362.1	439.6	519.9	630.9	673.4	700.4
By kind of economic activity							
Agriculture and forestry	23492.1	23385.5	23173.7	23117.1	23026.1	22860.0	22567.0
Fishing	988.9	1082.9	1282.1	1326.3	1404.6	1482.4	1555.8
Industry	3889.3	4260.2	4558.4	4982.4	5293.6	5741.1	6198.7
Construction	1040.4	1291.7	1526.3	1688.1	1922.9	1998.8	1994.0
Trade	3896.9	4062.5	4281.0	4532.0	4767.0	4933.1	5071.6
Hotels, restaurant	685.4	700.0	715.4	739.8	755.3	767.5	783.4
Transport, storage and communications	1174.3	1179.7	1183.0	1194.4	1202.2	1148.2	1127.0
Culture, health, education	1352.7	1416.0	1497.3	1584.1	1657.4	1726.1	1806.0
Other services	1089.6	1184.2	1290.5	1409.6	1557.2	1869.6	2243.7

Source: Government Statistics Office.

rural immigrants. Each year 1.2 million people participate to the labour force (Viet Nam News 2007e) while 1,785,000 Vietnamese (% 2.1) are unemployed.

However, the skills taught before graduation do not match with those necessary after graduation (Banh *et al.*, 2007). In other words, "Vietnamese universities and research institutes are still largely irrelevant to Viet Nam's industrialization" (Cheshier and Penrose, 2007 p. 28). Thus, although shortage of skilled labour is the biting problem of many of the sectors, 63 per cent of the university graduates are unemployed and 37 per cent of those who are employed have a job irrelevant to their university degree (Viet Nam News 2007e). In that sense, Vietnam's problem is not an African problem: Employment opportunities are not limited, but the graduates are not skilled enough to get those positions. This picture is also different compared to unemployment in Central and Eastern Europe: In the latter, unemployment is due to a significant shrinkage in workforce because of the accession to EU rather than lack of skills in general (Viet Nam News 2007f). As an ex-command economy just like the East European counterparts, Vietnam sends many workers abroad, but the number of Vietnamese workers abroad constitute a negligible number compared to the Vietnamese workforce in total.

What happens in Vietnam is the contrast between unemployed graduates and the shortage of skills at the same time as the Minister of Education and Training Nguyen Thien Nhan puts it (Viet Nam News 2007g). This problem naturally goes in tandem with the economic growth that is based on FDI, as the former formula for Vietnamese economy was cheap unskilled labour. As the foreign enterprises diversify their production and new foreign companies with different profiles enter Vietnam and as Vietnam tries to connect with the rest of the world economy, the formula is rendered obsolete. Economy as infrastructure exerts enormous pressure on education in this transformation process. With this obsolete educational infrastructure, shortage of 10,000 skilled IT workers is expected on 2010 for Vietnam (Viet Nam News, 2007h).

To encourage skills updating, Ministry of Education and Training declared that tax cuts are due for the companies who hold in-service training activities (Nguyen, 2007). On the other hand, surprisingly enough, in-service-training may be detrimental to the firm as the workers with upgraded skills switch to higher paying jobs in Vietnam and elsewhere (Cheshier and Penrose, 2007).

Conclusion

In this chapter, a brief overview of social indicators of Vietnam is followed by a specific overview of Vietnamese education and the presentation of the problems in education. It is pointed out that whether the problems stem from inadequate funding or inefficient planning with obsolete pedagogy is a moot issue. Besides, upgrading of the levels of university lecturers stands to be as the one of the most significant issues among others.

REFERENCES

Banh, T.L., Le, V.A., Nguyen, T.D., Nguyen, D.N., Ha, T.M. 2007, 'Enterprises, Universities Must Unite to Make Education Work', *Viet Nam News*, 24 December, p. 6.

Cheshier, S. & Penrose, J 2007, *Top 200: Industrial Strategies of Viet Nam's Largest Firms*, United Nations Development Programme, Viet Nam.

Do, L.D. 2007, 'To Improve Education, Students' Needs Must be Addressed First', *Vietnam News*, 10 December, p. 6.

Gezgin, U.B. 2007, 'Social and Economic Development of Vietnam: Governmental and Management Challenges', paper presented to International Colloquium on Business and Management, Bangkok 2007, 19-22nd November, 2007.

Government Statistics Office 2007, *Employment Statistics*, Government Statistics Office, Vietnam, viewed 23rd February, 2008, <http://www.gso.gov.vn>

Henaff, N., Lange, M.F., & Tran, T.K.T. 2007, *Viet Nam country case study*, UNESCO, viewed 23rd February, 2008, <http://unesdoc.unesco.org/images/0015/001555/155533e.pdf>

Ngo, D.D. 2006 'Viet Nam', in S. Shaeffer & S. Yavaprabhas (eds.), *Higher Education in South-East Asia*, UNESCO, Bangkok, pp. 219-250.

Nguyen, T.N. 2007 'Businesses see Incentives for Getting Involved with Vocational Training', *Viet Nam News*, 22 November, p. 6.

Nguyen, T.N., Dao, T.T., Hoang T., Van, N.C. & Pham, P. 2007, 'Increase in education fees could affect long-term social equality', *Viet Nam News*, 13 October, p. 6.

Nguyen, T.N., Vo, V.Q., Mai, N.L., Vo, T.X., Vu, H.S., Pham, D.P., Nguyen, M.H. 2008, 'Education leaders weigh in on the debate over diplomas and debts', *Viet Nam News*, 3 January, p. 6.

Seel, A 2007, *China, Vietnam, Cambodia, Philippines and Indonesia: Country case Studies*, Commissioned paper for 2008 EFA Global Monitoring Report, UNESCO, viewed 23rd February, 2008, <http://unesdoc.unesco.org/images/0015/001555/155579e.pdf>

UNDP 2007, *Human Development Report 2007-2008*, United Nations Development Programme.

Van, N.C. 2007 'Higher Education Fees not the Answer; education needs better planning', *Viet Nam News*, 4 December, p. 6.

Viet Nam News 2008a 'Student loans make the grade: Disadvantaged students set to get half a billion dollars in loans this year', *Viet Nam News*, 29 January, p. 1.

Viet Nam News 2008b '7 schools appear on SEA's top 100', *Viet Nam News*, 11 January, p. 3.

Viet Nam News 2008c 'Education gets dissected: Tertiary education levels in Viet Nam continue to sag', *Viet Nam News*, 7 January, p. 1.

Viet Nam News 2007a 'Viet Nam seeks improved IT cooperation with US', *Viet Nam News*, 19 September, p. 6.

Viet Nam News 2007b 'Government sets education spending', *Viet Nam News*, 9 October, p. 6.

Viet Nam News 2007c 'Vietnamese Universities face shortage of qualified teachers', *Viet Nam News*, 4 October, p. 4.

Viet Nam News 2007d 'Educational institutes lack qualified lecturers', *Viet Nam News*, 17 September, p. 5.

Viet Nam News 2007e 'Too many university grads, not enough skilled workers: Study', *Viet Nam News*, 5 November, p. 2.

Viet Nam News 2007f 'Labour shortages hit Central, East Europe', *Viet Nam News*, 1 October, p. 11.

Viet Nam News 2007g 'Education to be drastically overhauled, says Deputy PM', *Viet Nam News*, 11 September, p. 3.

Viet Nam News 2007h 'Aptech targets dearth of IT workers', Viet Nam News, 1 September, p. 6.

Vo, N.G. 2007 '6-step programme steers education', *Viet Nam News*, 12 September, p. 6.

Vo, T.T. & Trinh, Q.L. 2005, *Can Vietnam Achieve one of its Millenium Development Goals? An Analysis of Schooling Dropouts of Children*, William Davidson Institute Working Paper Number 776. viewed 23rd February, 2008, <http://www.wdi.umich.edu/files/Publications/WorkingPapers/wp776.pdf >

World Bank 2006, *Vietnam Development Report 2007: Aiming High Joint Donor Report to the Vietnam Consultative Group Meeting*, World Bank, Hanoi, Vietnam.

Contributors

Shobana Nelasco, is a reader in Economics of Fatima College, Maryland, Madurai, India, working for twenty years, is a recipient of *Best Teacher in Economics Award* from Malcolm Adiseshiah Trust, *Young Economist Award* form Association of Economist of Tamil Nadu and *Lion's International Award.* She has done researches in the area of 'External debt of Asian Developing Countries', 'Women Empowerment' and in issues of developing countries. Her academic background includes M.A., M.B.A., M.Phil. with distinction, Diploma in Computer Application and Doctorate in Economics. At present pursuing Post-Doctoral work and guiding doctoral scholars in Management and Economics. As the Head of U.G. Economics Department, Fatima College (2005-06), she introduced drastic changes in teaching, learning and evaluation practices. She has conducted 11 workshops and training programmes. She has published many papers in International Journals and in National Journals. She has presented papers in 18 International Conferences and in 30 National Conferences. (www.shobananelasco.wetpaint.com)

Peter Stewart is a Professor in Development Studies at Unisa, South Africa. He is the research coordinator for Development Studies. He is currently supervising three doctoral candidates and three masters students. Professor Stewart has published widely and is the author of a book entitled *Segregation and Singularity. Politics and its context among white middle class English-speakers in late apartheid Johannesburg.* He was also the editor of two other books. He was the Editor (with Sybert Liebenberg) of *Participatory Development Management and the RDP* and Editor (with Marylyn Aitken) of *Relocation: The Churches' report on forced removals in South Africa.* Professor Stewart has received a number of awards and written a number of articles. He has participated strongly in University affairs, with involvement in the staff association UDUSA for two years, and participation as an elected member in the Institutional Forum for two years. He currently serves on Senate, on the College of Humanities Higher Degrees Committee and the University Equity Committee. Formerly he has been a visiting Scholar of Cambridge University.

Tola Olujuvan, the Executive Director of Central Educational Service, an organization which is working towards education and empowerment based in Lagos. He has BA. Ed. in English and Masters in Educational Management from the Lagos State University, Ojo, Nigeria. He has published articles in Learned Journals both locally and internationally in different areas of interest especially in Teacher Education, Values and the Rights to education. He is an academic staff at the Department of Educational Foundations and Administration, Adeniran Ogunsanya College of Education, Otto/Ijanikin, Lagos, Nigeria.

Dr. Adenuga, R. Alaba received his PhD. in Personal Psychology from University of Ibadan, Nigeria in 2004. He was the deputy dean for undergraduate faculty of education, Olabisi Onabanjo University between April 30, 2004 and April 30, 2008. He is presently a senior lecturer and head, department of education foundation and counselling, Olabisi Onabanjo University Nigeria. He has attended Conferences in Nigeria, America, Germany, Spain, Belgium and other Europeans countries. Dr. Alaba Adenuga has over 45 publications to his credit.

Adenuga, F. Titilola received her M.Ed. in language education from Olabisi Onabanjo University, Nigeria, 2002. She is currently a lecturer and the coordinator center for external degree Programme College of humanities, Tai Solaria University of Education, Nigeria. She is currently on her Ph.D. Programme at Olabisi Onabanjo University, Nigeria. Titilayo Adenuga has a sizeable number of publications to her credit and has also attended conference in America and European countries.

Dr. Adeyemi completed his PhD in educational management from Olabisi Onabanjo University Nigeria in 2007. He is presently a lecturer in the department of educational management and business education in the same university. Muyiwa Adeyemi is a member of many professional associations in Nigeria. He has sizeable number of publications in local and international journals. He is currently the postgraduate coordinator in the department of education management and business education, Olabisi Onabanjo University Nigeria.

Kemi Adekola received her M.Ed. in Language Education from Olabisi Onabanjo University, Ago-Iwoye, Nigeria in 1998. Presently, she is at the same University as a Lecturer in Language Education in the Department of Curriculum Studies and Instructional Technology, Faculty of Education. Her main interests are in Reading and Language Teacher education. She is about completing her research work for the award of her Ph.D. in Language Education.

Ahmad Azman Mokhtar is an English language lecturer at University Teknologi, Mara Perlis, Malaysia. A holder of a Bachelor of Education (TESL) degree and Master of Science (TESL) from University Putra Malaysia. He has over 14 years of ELT experience at secondary school and tertiary level. His research interest revolves around vocabulary learning.

Rafizah Mohd. Rawian is an English Language lecturer at University Teknologi MARA Perlis. A holder of a Bachelor of Education (TESL) degree and Master of Science (Pedagogy). She has over 13 years of ELT experience at secondary school and tertiary level. Her research interest revolves around reading skills.

Andreas Becker received his 1st and 2nd State Exam. in Education, Geography, Music and Technology from Ph Ludwigsburg/ Germany in 1992 and in Mediation with emphasis on Family, School and Victim—Offender Mediations from University Hagen, Germany in 2003. Presently he is writing on his Masters Thesis in Mediation and working as a CEO/CIO Consultant for LisAndi Co. Ltd. Phuket, Thailand. He is Innovator and Visionaire and likes to solve Problems others have already given up. Nothing is impossible! As Educator and Teacher developing new individual learning methods and learning materials for all age groups from Baby to Seniors is his favourite task. He is also creator of T3Pack Packages (t3pack.com) based on TYPO3 and other Open Source Solutions like to webempower people and institutions with an easy way to get their businesses and activities presented online. International Conferences like to listen to his unconventional talks about Global Classroom, Homeschooling, eLearning and education for all beside TYPO3 which is his major technical interest. As TYPO3 web developer he is setting up UNESCO Bangkok Website.

Dr. Anne Fabiyi, specialist in Educational Planning and Administration, has passion for teaching, research, supervises doctoral projects, consultant and administrator. Papers are presented in conferences including 2nd International Special Education Conference, University of Winneba, Ghana (2005); British Education Leadership, Management and Administration Society Conference on Innovation in Educational Leadership Management Practice and Research, England (2007) etc. Publications include Fostering Inclusive Education in Nigeria: A Study of Teacher's Receptivity of Locally Biased Integration Strategies (Journal Publications). Area of interest includes institution governance, policy, leadership and gender issues. Awardee of the best researcher in the Faculty of Education (2005) and presently, SubDean, Faculty of Education.

Dr. Simeon A. Oladipo, holds a B.Ed., M.Ed., and Ph.D in Educational Management. He specializes in Educational policy analysis. He lectures in the Department of Educational Administration, University of Lagos, Nigeria. He has previously taught at the Primary, Secondary and College levels. While in the College, he held the positions of Head, Department of Curriculum and Instruction, Acting Dean of Education, member of Academic Board and Deputy Director Centre for Higher Programme. He is a member of Governing Council, Adeniran Ogunsanya College of Education, Lagos; member of the British Educational Leadership, Management and Administration Society (BELMAS); Nigeria Institute of Management (NIM); Nigerian Association for Educational Administration and Planning (NAEAP); and Educational Research Network for West and Central Africa (ERNWACA).

Dr. Austin Njiribeako Nosike is a leading scholar, editor and Senior Research Fellow at The Granada Management Institute. Since 1996, Dr. Nosike has been President of Development Africa Consortium (DAC) and Editor of African Journal of

Development Studies. He is also a Visiting Fellow at Centre for Applied Development and Public Policy and maintains consulting status with the United Nations Economic Commission for Africa, Afro-Euro Centre for Development Studies and many other institutions. Dr. Nosike has been a Consultant on human capacity building to the African Union Commission, Addis Ababa-Ethiopia. He has over 100 publications to his credit and received several awards, honours, grants as well as contributed to many research projects.

Nkasiobi S. Oguzor is Chief Lecturer(Associate Professor) and Provost, Federal College of Education(Technical), Omoku-Rivers State, Nigeria.

Prof. M.O.N. Obagah is Professor of Measurement and Evaluation and Director, Institute of Education, Rivers State University of Science and Technology, Port Harcourt, Nigeria.

Dr. R. Dayanandan is an Associate Professor in Economics, Mekelle University. He is a prospective researcher and his major research interest as well as publications are in the field of Applied Economics and Rural Development. He has written few books and has contributed a number of papers in national and international journals. He is a life member of several professional and academic bodies as well as board of examiner for adjudication of Ph.D thesis. He is also one of the resource persons for different capacity building training programmes for the officials of government and non-government organizations. He has also been involved in different international projects as an active member.

Emylou C. Visaya obtained M.A. degree in English from the University of the Philippines. She took up postgraduate studies in Philosophy and Humanities in Rome, Italy. At present, she is the Associate Director for Academic Formation of PAREF Woodrose School. Her work focuses mainly on curriculum development, faculty training, and assessment of learning. She is also actively involved as a consultant and mentor in non-government organizations focusing on youth development and women empowerment.

Greg Tabios Pawilen received his M.A.Ed. degree in Curriculum Studies from the University of the Philippines in Diliman, in

2004, and in 2006 his M.Ed. in Science Education from Ehime University in Matsuyama City, Japan as a Mombukagakusho Scholar. Currently, he is an Assistant Professor of Curriculum Studies at the College of Education of the University of the Philippines in Diliman. As a scholar, he published papers and researches on Curriculum, Indigenous Education, and Early Childhood Education in local and international journals.

Dr. Manabu Sumida is associate professor of science education and chief of international academic and student exchange division, faculty of education at Ehime University in Japan. He earned his PhD in science education from Hiroshima University. His research area is culture studies in science education. He was a committee member of TIMSS (Third International Mathematics and Science Study) 2003, TIMSS 1999 Video Study, PISA 2006. He published over 50 papers in and out of Japan and received Young Scholars' Award from Japan Society for Science Education in 1996, Young Scholars' Award from Society of Japan Science Teaching in 1999, Best Paper Presentation Award from Japan Society for Science Education in 2007 and 2008.

Javier Bilbao obtained the degree in Electrical Engineering from University of the Basque Country, Spain, in 1991. At present he is Ph.D. in Applied Mathematics and professor at the department of Applied Mathematics of that university. He has been General Chairman of some conferences of WSEAS organization. Current and previous research interests are: Distribution overhead electrical lines compensation, Optimization of series capacitor batteries in electrical lines, Modelization of a leakage flux transformer, Losses in the electric distribution Networks, Artificial Neural Networks, Modelization of fishing trawls, E-learning, Noise of electrical aerogenerators, Light pollution, Health risk of radiofrequencies. Prof. Bilbao is the General Chairman of the International Conferences on Engineering and Mathematics (ENMA) and member of the committees of the Technical and Physical Problems of Power Engineering (TPE) International Conferences.

Eugenio Bravo obtained the degree in Electrical Engineering from University of the Basque Country, Spain, in 1991. At present he is Ph.D. in Applied Mathematics and professor at the department of Applied Mathematics of that university.

Olatz García obtained the degree in Mathematics from University of the Basque Country, Spain, in 1989. At present she is Ph.D. in Applied Mathematics and professor at the department of Applied Mathematics of that university.

Concepción Varela obtained the degree in Mathematics from UNED, Spain, in 1986. At present she is Ph.D. in Economics and Statistics and professor at the Department of Applied Mathematics of the University of the Basque Country.

Miguel Rodríguez obtained the degree in Physics from University of Navarra, Spain, in 1978. At present he is Ph.D. in Electronic Engineering and professor at the Department of Applied Mathematics of the University of the Basque Country.

Purificación González obtained the degree in Energetics Engineering from University of the Basque Country, Spain, in 1979. At present she is Ph.D. in Applied Mathematics and professor at the department of Applied Mathematics of that university. She is now the Head of the Applied Mathematics Department of that university.

M.E. Uranga obtained the degree in Sciences from University of Zaragoza, Spain, in 1969. At present she is Ph.D. in Sciences and professor at the department of Applied Mathematics of the University of the Basque Country. She was Academic Secretary of the Engineering School of Bilbao (1985-1987) and Head of the Applied Mathematics Department (1990-1997) both of them of the University of the Basque Country.

Ki-Seok Kwon obtained a BSc in Physics from Korea Advanced Institute of Science and Technology and a MA in Public Administration from Seoul National University, Korea in 2002. Currently, he is a doctoral researcher in Science and Technology Policy Studies at SPRU in Sussex University, UK. His main research interest is a university-industry linkage in catch-up countries. Before joining SPRU, he worked as a policy analyst at Korea Astronomy and Space Science Institute and Seoul Development Institute.

Ogunleye S.B., is a faculty of Education in Olabisi Onabanjo University, Ago-Iwoye.

Onanuga P. Abayomi is a faculty in the Department of Curriculum Studies and Instructional Technology (CSTI), Faculty of Education, Olabisi Onabanjo University, Ago-Iwoye, Ogun State, Nigeria.

Dr. Paul TJ James is a Senior Lecturer/Reader in the Graduate School, Bangkok University, Thailand. He holds a Ph.D. in Quality Management (Education) from Lincoln University, UK, and has four Masters degrees (M.Phil., MBA, M.Sc. and an M.Eng./B.Eng.) from various universities including Cambridge University. He has written 9 books on quality management and ICT in Education and also 3 children's books; and produced a variety of academic articles. His current research interests involve e-learning in universities in Thailand, ICT in Asian Schools and quality management in Asia.

Prof. V.F. Peretomode is a Professor of Educational Administration, Faculty of Education, Delta State University, Abraka, Nigeria.

Dr. R.A. Chukwuma is a Lecturer in Educational Administration, School of Education, College of Education, Agbor-Nigeria.

Dr. Raihani is currently working at Universitas Islam Negeri (UIN) of Sultan Syarif Kasim, Riau–Indonesia. He completed his M.Ed. and Ph.D. at Faculty of Education, The University of Melbourne, Australia under the AusAID scholarships. He has produced scholarly works including a book on Successful School Leadership in Indonesia published by SUSKA Press 2006, another on Pesantren Curriculum Development by SUSKA Press 2008, several journal articles both local and international. He presented several international and local seminars and conferences such as International Symposium on Religious Education in Muslim World in 2007 in Istanbul, Turkey. He is also one of World Bank Jakarta Office's researchers on education matters.

Rajarshi Roy is Assistant Professor of Education of National Institute of Technical Teachers' Training & Research [NITTTR], Kolkata. He has completed Ph.D.(Education); M.A.(Sociology); M.Ed. His areas of interest zoomed over Pedagogy for development, Environmental education and indigenous technology for the life improvement of the population at crisis; apart, he offers courses on teachers' burnout and stress management. He has visited countries like Bangladesh, Myanmar, Republic of China, Hong Kong [Special Administrative Region(SAR)], Thailand, Singapore and Republic of Korea in connection with academic assignments.

Sareetah Devi Motee is a research assistant working with Dr. H.B. Chittoo. She has completed her bachelor degree in Information Technology Enabled Services (ITES) and is now pursuing her postgraduate degree in Banking & Finance at the University of Technology Mauritius. She has written a paper "Training Needs Analysis in the BPO Sector in Mauritius" which was presented at the 6th IIDS Conference 2008.

Dr. Hemant B. Chittoo is Associate Professor in Development Management in the School of Public Sector Policy and Management. He has more than 15 years experience of lecturing, research and consultancy. He is member of several boards nationally. Dr. Chittoo has advised governments internationally on Development issues and public sector reforms and has provided consultancy services to several international organizations. He is presently Head of School for the School of Public Sector Policy and Management in the University of Technology Mauritius.

B. Nowbutsing is an academic at the University of Technology Mauritius since January 2005. He has previously served as Economist at the Ministry of Finance and Economic Development (Mauritius). Mr. Nowbutsing is registered for a Ph.D. jointly supervised by Prof. Oliver Morrissey (University of Nottingham) and Dr. H.B. Chittoo, the title of his Ph.D. is "FDI Impacts and FDI Incentives." His research interest includes: Public Policy, Poverty and poverty alleviation, development financing (i.e. foreign aid, FDI).

M.P. Odit is a lecturer at the University of Technology, Mauritius. His research interests are in Financial Leverage, Corporate Investment, and Earnings Management. He finished his bachelor degree of commerce in 1998 at the University of Pune, India. Furthermore he holds an MBA. Mr Odit is member of several boards, for instance, he is a member on the accreditation programs by the Tertiary Education Commission in Mauritius. At the University of Technology he acts as Programme Director for B.Sc. in Public Sector Financial Management, Master in

Banking and Finance and also he is a Member of the School Board (SOPSPAM, UTM).

Malaya Kumar Nayak is an IT Manager at Optimity Ltd., London and Director of U-Com Software (P) Ltd., Orissa, India. He has over 12 years of IT management and IT infrastructure design experience, with a focus on networking and security systems. He has received his B.Sc. degree from Utkal University, Orissa and M.Sc. degree in Information and Communication Technology from Assumption University of Thailand. He has also a Professional Diploma in Network-Centered Computing. He is currently a Senior Member of the IEEE & IEEE Computer Society, USA and Senior Member of Computer Society of India. He is also a Chartered Member (CITP) of the British Computer Society, UK. He got awarded Chartered Engineer (CEng) from Engineering Council, UK and Certified IT Project Manager (CITPM) from IDA & Singapore Computer Society. He has published papers at several National and International IT/ Management Conferences. His current research interests include project management and risk management.

Dr. Ulas Basar Gezgin (Ph.D., Cognitive Science, 2006; M.A., Social Psychology, 2002; B.A., Educational Sciences, 2000) is a lecturer of economics at RMIT International University, Vietnam. He holds a regular column about Asia-Pacific Region at a Turkish newspaper and among his 13 literary and academic books published mainly in Turkish is *Asian Essays* (Izmir, Turkey: Ara-lik, 2007) which is a compilation of his ideas about Asian Development. He had offered courses in psychology, anthropology, linguistics and cognitive sciences before, and by his move to Vietnam, he focuses on East Asian economic cooperation and the Vietnamese economy in particular.

Index

Accidental factors, 73
Addis Ababa University (AAU), 97
Addis Ababa, 95, 97, 100
Adopt-a-Public school, 75
Agricultural education, 208
Agriculture education, 209-210, 214
  curriculum, 210
Agriculture science, 206, 208
Ahmadu Bello University (ABU), 92
American missionaries, 160
Animal husbandry, 95
Animal production, 208-210
Applied sciences, 148-149
Arbaminch Water Technology Institute (AWTI), 97
Auditory encoding, 44, 51-53
Autonomy, 25-26, 29, 143, 146, 151, 153

Basic education programme, 20
Bergen declaration, 144-145
Berlin declaration, 144-145
Bologna
  declaration, 142, 146-149
  process, 144
Bottom-up revolution, 186
Brain
  drain, 99
  gain, 166
Brain Korea, 21, 174
Budget Monitoring, 12
Budget Office of the Federation, 12
Buhari/Idiagbon's War against Indiscipline, 208
Bulletin board displays, 36, 56
Bullets or Missiles, 330

Capitalism, 1
Caring children, 112-113
Catholic Youth Organisation, 203
Centre for Applied Social Research, 305, 308
Certificate of Primary Education (CPE), 306
Changing Role of Secondary School, 72, 74, 76, 78, 80, 82
Choson dynasties, 159-160
Code of conduct, 30
Code of ethical behaviour, 26
Code of ethics, 25-26, 30, 200
Collaborative culture, 253-255, 260
College of Agriculture and Mechanical Arts, 97
Commonwealth of Learning, 18
Communication, 13, 36, 65, 70, 90-92, 114, 129, 216, 287-288, 342
  skills, 264, 266, 307, 320
Community Accountability and Transparency Initiative, 75
Community Based Organizations (CBOs), 17
Community folks, 124-125, 137
Comparative Study of Indian and Britain, 311-312, 314, 316, 318, 320, 322

Comparator countries, 308-309
Competency-Based Curriculum (CBC), 256, 264
Components of agriculture education curriculum, 210
Comprehend graphic codes, 221
Compulsory education, 315-316
Compulsory Universal Basic Education Act, 11
Computer revolution, era of, 105
Concept integration, 208, 210
Confucianism, 159, 169
Consolidated revenue fund, 11
Contextual encoding, 44, 51-53
Controlled Active Vocabulary Test, 39, 41, 45, 52, 55
Convergence process, 145, 150-151
Correlation, 51-53, 241, 244
Corrupt practices, 326-327, 330
Corruption, 105, 160, 320, 326-327
C-programme, 156
Crash programmes for teacher training, 28
Critical social science, 272
Crop production, 208-210
Cultivation, 89, 117
Cultural
  anthropology, 272
  cohesiveness, 279
  communities, 122-124, 127
  diversity, 119, 122
  heritage, 127, 130, 132
  scripts, 120

Darker World Education Forum, 9
Decent livelihood, 212
Declaration of Bologna, 147
Delta State of Nigeria, 238-239
Delta State University, 240
Desirable Learning Competencies (DLC), 307
Dewan pendidikan, 256
Dewey, John, 275
DFID, 18
Dictionary strategies, 39, 43, 51-53
Drop-out, 316
Dual-career-couple, 297
Dubbing, 330

Early childhood education, 125, 138
Education Commission, 323
Education for all, 1, 12-13, 20, 312-313
Education Reforms Act, 313
Education Trust Fund, 77
Education
  policies, 96-97, 99, 104, 160, 166, 171, 308
  reform, 72, 74, 310
  technical, 308, 315
  tertiary, 75, 83, 167, 170, 179
  university, 42, 95, 306, 339
  vocational, 144, 165
  western, 122, 327
Educational aid, 106, 162
Educational context, 43, 69
Educational planners, 33, 335
Educational reforms, 28-29, 171, 310, 313
Educational revolution, 207
Educational theory, knowledge of, 26
Educational value, 4, 219
Effective citizenship, 6, 33, 206, 212, 214
Egalitarian society, 6
Elementary education, 312, 316
Emotional stability, 201-202, 204
Empirical research, 277, 282-283
Encoder and decoder, 216
Engineering Research Center (ERC), 174
English proficiency, 61, 63, 65-66
English vocabulary learning questionnaire, 39
Erasmus-Socrates Programme, 141, 145
Essential learning competencies, 307

Ethnography, 272, 279
Ethno-pedagogic model of social process, 279
European Commission, 144
European Higher Education Area (EHEA), 144
European University Association, 151
Evolving taxonomy, 284
Exam Ethics Project, 334
Examination malpractice Act, 333
Expert-knowledge, 272
Export Processing Zones (EPZs), 304

Fachhochschule, 146, 148
Family
  day, 112
  outreach, 112
  visioning, 112
Father-daughter activities, 112
FDI, 344
Female lecturers, 239, 243, 246
Field trip, 128-130
Filipinos, 122, 133
Fine Arts programmes, 320
Five Year Plan
  10th, 312
  11th, 312-313
Flip chart, 98
Foreign education, era of, 104
Foreign scholars, 168
Formal education, 25, 31, 122, 218, 237, 262, 292
Forum, 68, 112
Free active
  vocabulary knowledge, 37, 51-52, 54-56
  vocabulary test, 39, 42, 53
Free-distribution compiler, 156

G9 Group of Universities, 141-142, 152, 157
G9 Virtual Campus, 152, 154
General English Proficiency Test, 64
General Service List, 39
Giraffing, 330
Girl child, 317
Gonder Public Health College, 97
Goryeo, 159
Graz Declaration, 143
Guessing strategies, 39, 43, 51-53
Guidance and counseling programmes, 335
Gwangju Institute of Science and Technology (GIST), 172

Hermeneutics, 292-293
Higher education programme, 340
Historical materialism, 272
Hi-Tech Micro Computer, 330
Home values and school values, conflicts between, 112
Honours degree, 314
Human Development Index (HDI), 1, 338
Human Resources Development, 1, 180, 262
Humanities, 27, 166-169, 172, 239, 243, 247, 314

IMF, 3, 305, 309
Impersonation, 327, 330, 334
Inclusive education, 2
Indian Council of Social Science Research (ICSSR), 273
Indigenous knowledge, 119-121, 127, 130, 133, 137-138
Indigenous Peoples Rights Act, 134
Industrial education, 166, 175
Information and Communication Technology (ICT), 59-60, 62-63, 65-66, 71, 83, 144, 154, 172, 264
Information and Communications University, 172
Initial Teachers Training (ITT), 314
Institute of Building Technology, 97

Institutional authorities, 85-86, 90-91, 92
Instructional pattern, 296
Intellectual Property Rights (IPR), 175
Inter-African cooperation, 8
Intergenerational continuity, 271
International Development Association, 167
International Development Partners, 18
International Labour Organization, 32
International Successful School Principalship Project (ISSPP), 251

JICA, 18
Joint Admission and Matriculation Examinations, 329
Jomtien declaration of Education for All, 8

Kindergarten
  children, 122, 124, 128-129
  teachers, 130-132
Knowledge-based society, 143
Knowledge Management (KM), 2
Korea Institute for Advanced Study (KIAS), 172
Korea Institute of Machinery and Materials (KIMM), 166
Korea Institute of Science and Technology (KIST), 165, 170
Korea Institute of Technology (KIT), 170
Korea Ocean Research and Development Institute (KORDI), 166
Korea Polytechnic University, 173
Korea Science and Engineering Foundation (KOSEF), 169, 173
Korea University of Technology and Education, 173
Korean academic revolution, 159, 163, 173-174
Korean academic system, 158, 178, 185, 187
Korean Association of Colleges and Universities, 162
Korean education system, 159, 162
Korean higher education system, 158-161, 163, 166
Korean universities, mission of, 183-184
Kotebe College of Teacher Education, 97
Kyungsung imperial college, 161-162

Lecture presentation, 98
Less Emphasized Approaches of Educational Research, 292
Lexical Frequency Profile (LFP), 41, 45, 54-55
Lifelong learning, 143-145
Literacy
  programme, 17
  rate, 133, 312-313
Loans, 339

Management Committee and School Board, 116
Manpower Development and lecturers' Productivity Questionnaire (MDLPQ), 240
Mass media, 88-89, 225
Massive value erosion, era of, 296
Mauritian unemployment puzzle, 305
Memory strategies-encoding, 51-52
Metacognition, 194-195, 292-293
Microchips, 330
Millennium Development Goal, 1, 95
Minority group, 317
Modern organizational systems, 83
Mother-daughter activities, 112
Mover education, 2, 317

Multilingual proficiency, 59-60
Musyawarah Guru Mata Pelajaran (MGMP), 261

National Business and Technical Education Board (NABTEB), 334
National Commission for Colleges of Education, 13
National Commission for Mass Literacy Adult and Non-formal Education, 13
National Commission for Nomadic Education, 13
National consciousness, 6, 206
National Examination Council (NECO), 329
National Institute of Educational Planning and Administration (NIEPA), 290
National Literacy Mission, 315
National Parents/Teachers Association, 13
National Policy on Education, 5, 23, 28, 32, 73, 75, 207
National Programme for Education for Girls, 316
National Programme of Mid-Day-Meals, 316
National Teachers Institute, 13
National Universities Commission (NUC), 248
Networking, 330
Nigeria Association for Comparative Physical Education and Sports (NACPES), 200
Nigerian English Studies Association, 31, 34
Nigerian professional teaching organizations, 33
Nigerian Union of Teacher, 25, 29, 31, 34, 334
Non-formal education, 10, 13, 317
Non-Governmental Organizations (NGOs), 17, 20

OECD, 179
On-line universities, 165, 172
Operation of KIST, 166
Operation Reach All Secondary Schools (ORASS), 75
Oral
  history, 292, 294
  repetition, 44, 51-53
Organization into Professional Group, 27
Overhead projector, 98

Pan-African declaration on the education of girls and women, 8
PAREF Mentoring Programme, 114
PAREF schools, 111-115
Parenting
  education, 112
  literacy courses, 112-113
Parents-Teachers Association, 18, 20, 77
Participatory research, 272
Passive vocabulary test, 39, 41, 44-45, 51, 54-55
Pearson product, 241, 244
Pedagogic programmes, 227
Personal conflicts, 114
Pohang Institute of Science and Technology (POSTECH), 170
Pohang Steel Company, 170
Political authorities, 143
Polytechnic Institute at Bahir Dar, 97
Positioning and re-positioning, 230
Practical Attachment Reports, 105
Prague declaration, 143
Preschool
  classes, 127-128
  education, 128
Presidential Advisory Council on

Science and Technology (PACST), 173
Professional
association, 27, 30-31
code of ethics, 32
Programme brand management, 228, 232
Promotion of
invention act, 175
technology transfer act, 175
Public–Private-Partnership (PPP) model, 72, 74-76, 79, 81-82

Qualitative education, 16, 73
Qualitative methodology, 252
Quality of education, 2-3, 104, 277, 320, 340-341

Radical group, 86
Recognition of problems, 200, 202
Regional Research Center (RRC), 174
Regional research center, 174
Research and entrepreneurial activities, emergence of, 158, 160, 162, 164, 166, 168, 170, 172, 174, 176, 178, 180, 182, 184, 186
Research invigoration, 171, 173
Reverse brain drain, 166
Royalties, 184

Safe potable water, 95
Sarva Shiksha Abhiyan (SSA), 312-313
Scheme Teachers Association of Nigeria, 31
School alumni, 77
School-based management, 256
School management organisations, 77-78, 80
Science Citation Index, 180-181
Science-related activities, 129
Science Research Center (SRC), 174
Science Teachers Association in Nigeria, 34
Scientific
education, 148
knowledge, 121-122, 125-126, 131
Second order changes, 266
Secondary education reform questionnaire, perception of, 76
Self-reported
strategies, 56
vocabulary learning strategies, 39
Sequential implementation plan, 16-17
Situational analysis, 123, 125-126, 135
Small and Medium Business Administration, 184
Social phenomenology, 272
Socialist revolution, 97
Socio-cultural background, 134-135
Socio-educational
factors, 295-296
research, 293
Sorbonne declaration, 141-142
Structural Adjustment Programme (SAP), 87
Suma Chitnis, 284
Sung-kyun-kwan, 159
Super
learning, 59, 68
print, 330

Tae-hak, 159
Tax incentives, 304
Teachers salary structure, 33
Teachers' Registration Council of Nigeria, establishment of, 25
Teaching-learning activities, 22-23
Teaching-training programmes, 218
Technological revolution, 96
Technology
licensing office, 176
transfer, 184

Theology College of Holy Trinity, 97
Top Industrial Managers for Europe (TIME), 142
Tracking assets for progress, 75
Training centre, 150
Transformational functions, 266
Transmission of
  education, 279
  society-specific knowledge, 279

UNESCO, 8, 18, 32, 68, 119
UNICEF, 8, 18
Unified Silla, 159
Unity Schools, 75-77, 80, 83
Universal Basic Education, 5, 8-10, 12-14, 18, 20, 28, 75
Universal Basic Education Commission, 8, 10, 12-14
Universal Primary Education, 7, 28
University Grants Commission (UGC), 273, 298
University-industry
  cooperation act, 175
  cooperation strategy, 177
  government cooperation; 177
University management, 232-234
University of Applied Sciences (UAS), 148
University Word List, 42, 44-45, 50, 54-55
US Bayh-Dole Act, 175
USAID, 18,

Vietnamese economy, formula for, 344
Visual encoding, 44, 51-53
Visual repetition, 44, 51-53, 57
VocabProfile, 41-42
Vocabulary knowledge, 37, 40, 43, 55
  controlled active, 51, 54-56
  depth of, 56
Vocabulary learning, 35
Vocabulary size, 55-57
Vocational agriculture, 207, 211, 214
  education, 206, 208, 210, 212, 214
Vocational training programme, 317

West African Examination Council, 329
Western Missionaries, 159
Western type of education, 31
White board, 98
World Bank, 3, 7-8, 18, 170, 304, 340, 342
WTO, 3

Young countries, 338
Youth organizations, 115-116, 210, 214

Zonal Offices of Universal Basic Education Commission, 14